Up the Republic!

Towards a New Ireland

Edited by

FINTAN O'TOOLE

faber and faber

First published in 2012
by Faber and Faber Ltd
Bloomsbury House
74–77 Great Russell Street
London WC1B 3DA

Typeset by Faber and Faber Ltd
Printed and bound by CPI Group (UK) Ltd, Croydon, CRO 4YY
All rights reserved
Selection © Fintan O'Toole, 2012
Individual essays © individual authors, 2012

The right of Fintan O'Toole to be identified as editor
of this work and author of '"Do you know what a republic is?":
The Adventure and Misadventures of an Idea'
has been asserted in accordance with Section 77
of the Copyright, Designs and Patents Act 1988.

A CIP record for this book
is available from the British Library

ISBN 978–0–571–28900–4

2 4 6 8 10 9 7 5 3 1

In memoriam
Mary Raftery 1957–2012

Contents

Contributors

ELAINE BYRNE is adjunct lecturer in the Department of Political Science at Trinity College Dublin. She initiated the *We the Citizens* project with three academic colleagues. She is the author of *Political Corruption in Ireland 1922–2010, A Crooked Harp?* www.elaine.ie

THEO DORGAN is one of Ireland's leading poets. His most recent volumes are *Greek* and *What This Earth Cost Us*. His prose works include *Time on the Ocean* and *Sailing for Home*.

TOM HICKEY is University Fellow at the School of Law in the National University of Ireland, Galway. He was a visiting research scholar at Princeton University (at the University Centre for Human Values) in 2009.

ISEULT HONOHAN is senior lecturer at the School of Politics and International Relations, University College Dublin. Her books include *Civic Republicanism* (2002) and (as editor) *Republicanism in Ireland* (2008).

DEARBHAIL MCDONALD is the Legal Editor of the *Irish Independent* and an Eisenhower Fellow. She is the author of *Bust: How the Courts Have Exposed the Rotten Heart of the Irish Economy* (2010).

FINTAN O'TOOLE is assistant editor of the *Irish Times* and Leonard L. Milberg lecturer in Irish Letters at Princeton. His most recent books are *Enough is Enough* and *Ship of Fools*.

PHILIP PETTIT is Laurance S. Rockefeller University Professor of Politics and Human Values at Princeton. He is from Ballygar in County Galway. He was invited by then Spanish Prime Minister José Luis Zapatero to assess the performance of his government in the light of Pettit's 1997 *Republicanism*. His most recent books are *On the People's Terms* and *Just Freedom*.

FRED POWELL has been Professor of Social Policy and Head of the School of Applied Social Studies at University College Cork, since 1990. In 2008 he was appointed Dean of Social Science at UCC. His books include *The Politics of Civil Society: Neoliberalism or Social Left?*

Government ought to be as much open to improvement as anything which appertains to man; instead of which it has been monopolised, from age to age, by the most ignorant and vicious of the human race. Need we any other proof of their wretched management, than the excess of debts and taxes with which every nation groans, and the quarrels into which they have precipitated the world?

Thomas Paine

'Do you know what a republic is?': The Adventure and Misadventures of an Idea

FINTAN O'TOOLE

Either we shall find a way to reinforce republican politics
and culture, or we shall have to resign ourselves to living
in nations whose governments are controlled by the
cunning and the arrogant.

Maurizio Viroli

The Twentieth Century Never Happened

In November 2011, the finance committee of parliament discussed Ireland's forthcoming budget in considerable detail. It
pored over figures such as a 2 per cent rise in value added tax,
a household tax of €100 and changes to capital gains tax.
This was an excellent example of a republican democracy at
work, with important policies being tested in public rather
than merely handed down by a minister for finance like Moses
bringing the tablets from the mountain top. Practices that are
central to the notion of a republic – openness, accountability,
the power of the executive being challenged by the elected
representatives of the people – could be seen in action. It was
exemplary stuff.

Meanwhile, far away, in another, less enlightened European
country the finance committee of another parliament was also
in session. It knew nothing of these budgetary decisions. And

why should it? Except that the parliament that was scrutinising the Irish budget was the Bundestag in Berlin and the one that was ignorant of it was the Dáil in Dublin. In relation to one of the most basic functions of an independent government, its annual budget, the German parliament was in the know and the Irish parliament was in the dark.

And not just the Irish parliament – it was clear that even the cabinet in Dublin had not yet discussed, let alone decided on, the tax rises that were being scrutinised in the Bundestag. The Taoiseach Enda Kenny put it plainly: 'Let me confirm something to you, the cabinet has made no decision in regard to the budget which is on December 6th.' Yet somebody had decided what was in the budget. When it became public that the Bundestag had all of these details, the official line in Dublin was that the relevant document was only a draft. But this was obviously not so. A letter from the Irish finance minister Michael Noonan to the European Commission, accompanying the document (it was the Commission in turn that had sent it to the Bundestag), uses the phrase 'we have decided' before listing the measures. And in fact the details as set out in the document were exactly those later unveiled when the budget was presented to the Dáil.

This meant, in effect, that the Irish constitution had been quietly suspended.

Article 28 defines the cabinet directly as 'the Government'. It then states, with the same absolute simplicity, that 'The executive power of the State shall, subject to the provisions of this Constitution, be exercised by or on the authority of the Government.' This power, moreover, must be exercised collectively: 'The Government shall meet and act as a collective authority . . .' The standard work on the constitution, by John Kelly, glosses this as meaning that, in relation to the statutory functions of government, 'the valid exercise of these functions must presuppose a formal consideration and decision at a Government meeting'. There is no doubt that in relation to the 2012 budget, executive decisions were made and communicated to the EU before they were brought to the cabinet table, let alone presented to the Dáil. 'This', an unapologetic German government official told the *Irish Times*, 'is the shape of things to come.'[1]

As indeed it was. Something similar happened in late February 2012, when the Bundestag again discussed a European Commission document on the Irish economy, suggesting that further 'fiscal tightening' might be necessary. The document had not been given to the Dáil. The Taoiseach shrugged off the significance of the event in a way that suggested that this kind of thing was no longer a big deal: 'These things are unhelpful but sometimes they're overplayed.'

The German finance ministry was again patiently unapologetic, explaining that the only problem was that the document had been leaked from the parliamentary committee to which it had been given:

> German law requires parliament to be involved and informed before any EFSF [European Financial Stability Facility, i.e. bailout] moneys can be disbursed. In order to fulfil this legal obligation, members of parliament require full documentation and information. The government, which has a duty to provide MPs with the information they require, very much deplores it whenever confidential information finds its way into the public domain.[2]

In fact, at around the same time, the German supreme court ruled that it was not enough that such information should be given to a small select panel of Bundestag members. Either the entire parliament or at least the 41-member budget committee would have to be convened every time a decision was to be made in relation to the use of European bailout funds. The court cited the need for 'as much parliamentary legitimisation as possible' as a reason for upholding a complaint by two opposition MPs that the panel infringed the basic right of lawmakers to decide on budgetary matters. The strong message to Ireland and to the other heavily indebted nations of the eurozone was: get used to it. The right of public, democratic scrutiny of your affairs now lies within our German democracy.

The ironies would have been too heavy-handed for good fiction. The German courts and the Bundestag were acting as such institutions ought to do in a republican democracy: insisting on openness, transparency, scrutiny and 'parliamentary legitimisation' of decisions that might affect German citizens. But they were doing so in relation to a supposed republican democracy where none of these things actually function. There could be in Ireland no openness, no advance scrutiny, no insistence on 'full documentation and information', no legitimisation of policies by elected representatives of the people. At a stroke, these parliamentary episodes demonstrated two things: (a) what republican democracies are, and (b) the fact that Ireland emphatically cannot be listed among them.

The three institutional pillars of democracy are the government, the parliament (Oireachtas) and the constitution (and hence the courts). The presentation of the budget to the Bundestag did Irish people the favour of making a nonsense of all three at once. It clarified what had been murky: that the government is no longer the executive authority, that the parliament is largely irrelevant and that the constitution has been silently suspended. It marked the death of an illusion: that Ireland is, in any meaningful sense, a republic. And it raised a poignant question: what was all that fuss and bother of the Irish twentieth century, all the thrill and trauma of a struggle for independence, actually about? It was as if the twentieth century had not happened, or rather as if a different twentieth century had unfolded in its place.

In the approach to the First World War, and in the early stages of that conflict, militant Irish nationalists asked themselves a sensible question: what if Germany wins? In 1913, in the *Fortnightly Review*, the Scots-Irish writer Sir Arthur Conan Doyle posed this three-pipe problem for Ireland, suggesting that, if Irish nationalists thought British rule was bad, they should think what the future would be like under the German Reich:

> I would venture to say one word here to my Irish fellow-countrymen of all political persuasions. If they imagine that they can stand politically or economically while Britain falls they are woefully mistaken. The British Fleet is their one shield. If it be broken, Ireland will go down. They may well throw themselves heartily into the common defence, for no sword can transfix England without the point reaching Ireland behind her.

In the *Irish Review*, a publication closely associated with two of the later signatories of the 1916 proclamation of an Irish republic, Thomas MacDonagh and Joseph Mary Plunkett, the pseudonymous 'Sean Van Vocht' replied to Doyle. He or she considered in some detail the idea that an Ireland administered, say, by Prussians would soon bitterly regret the milder manners of the Anglo-Saxon and pine for the good old days of 'doles' from Westminster. I know many Irishmen who admit that as between England and Germany they would prefer to remain in the hands of the former – on the principle that it is better to keep the devil you know than fall into the hands of a new devil. German rule, we are asked to believe, would be so bad, so stern, that under it Ireland, however much she might have suffered from England in the past, would soon yearn to be restored to the arms of her sorrowing sister.[3]

But 'Sean Van Vocht' believed that this was nonsense. What, after all, would be so bad about being ruled by Germany?

An Ireland annexed to the German Empire . . . as one of the fruits of a German victory over Great Britain, would clearly be administered as a common possession of the German people, and not as a Prussian province . . . What, then, would be the paramount object of Germany in her administration of an overseas Reichsland of such extra-ordinary geographical importance to her future as Ireland would be? Clearly not to impoverish and depress that new-won possession, but to enhance its exceeding strategic importance by vigorous and wise administration, so as to make it the main counterpoise to any possible recovery of British maritime supremacy . . . A prosperous and flour-ishing Ireland, recognising that her own interests lay with those of the new administration, would assuredly be the first and chief aim of German statesmanship. The very geographical situation of Ireland would alone ensure wise and able administration by her new rulers had Germany no other and special interest in advancing Irish well-being; for to rule from Hamburg and Berlin a remote island and a discontented people, with a highly discontented and separated Britain intervening, by methods of exploitation and centralisation, would be a task beyond the capacity of German statecraft. German effort, then, would be plainly directed to creating an Ireland satisfied with the change, and fully determined to maintain it. And it might be remembered that Germany is possibly better equipped, intellectually and educationally, for the task of developing Ireland than even 20th-century England.

Ireland, the writer imagined, would be at first like Alsace-Lorraine, annexed from France by Germany forty years earlier. The nation would feel 'alien in sentiment to her new masters to a degree that Ireland could not but be to any changes of authority imposed on her from without'. But it would learn to enjoy the benefits of wise German administration, just as Alsace-Lorraine had 'doubled in prosperity and greatly increased in population, despite . . . a rule denounced from the first as hateful. However hateful, the Prussian has proved himself an able administrator and an honest and most capable instructor. In his strong hands, Strassburg [sic] has expanded from being an ill-kept, pent-in French garrison town to a great and beautiful city.' Ireland, likewise, would benefit from 'the ablest brains in Germany, scientific, commercial and financial, no less than military and strategic' who 'would be devoted to the great task of making sure the conquest not only of an island but of the intelligence of a not unintelligent people, and by wisely developing so priceless a possession to reconcile its inhabitants, through growing prosperity and an excellent administration, to so great a change in their political environment'.

Even James Connolly, who in 1916 strung up a banner on Liberty Hall proclaiming that 'We serve neither King nor Kaiser but Ireland' was not unhappy at the thought of Ireland as 'an overseas Reichsland', a little bit of Prussia in the Atlantic. He felt that 'the German people are a highly civilised people, responsive to every progressive influence, and rapidly forging weapons of their own emancipation from native tyranny'. But even that 'tyranny' of empire seemed reasonably pleasant to his usually sceptical mind, despite the appalling realities of German colonialism in Namibia:

> The German Empire is a homogeneous Empire of self-governing peoples; the British Empire is a heterogeneous collection in which a very small number of self-governing communities connive at the subjugation, by force, of a vast number of despotically ruled subject populations. We do not wish to be ruled by either empire, but we certainly believe that the first named contains in germ more of the possibilities of freedom and civilisation than the latter.[4]

By 1916, of course, the Germans had become, in the words of the proclamation read out by Patrick Pearse in the same year, 'our gallant allies in Europe' – the Irish republic would implicitly be born under the wing of the German imperial eagle.

There is, now, no German empire. Germany did not win the war, nor the next one. And it would be hysterical to suggest, as some English eurosceptics do, that the European Union is now effectively a German Reich under another guise. Germany is a fine and admirable democracy, not a militaristic Prussian autocracy. Ireland has not been annexed to anybody's empire – it used its independence to destroy its own sovereignty. But there is none the less an inescapable reality that the centre of governance that was moved from London to Dublin in 1922 has now moved again to Berlin and to Frankfurt, home of the European Central Bank, which is unquestionably the single most powerful institution in Irish public life.

This happened because, in the banking crisis that erupted in 2008, the Irish government did exactly as it was told by the ECB. Brian Cowen, who was Taoiseach at the time, has since made it plain that he was only following orders when he made the catastrophic decision to guarantee all of the debts of the Irish banks, including the extravagantly delinquent Anglo Irish Bank:

> At no stage during the crisis would the European authorities, especially the European Central Bank, have countenanced the dishonouring of senior bank bonds. The euro-area policy of 'No bank failures and no burning of senior bank creditors' has been a constant during the crisis. And as a member of the euro area, Ireland must play by the rules.[5]

There were in fact no such 'rules' – at no point did the Irish parliament ever debate, let alone accede to, the idea of a legal requirement to nationalise private debt at the cost of destroying its own public finances, losing its capacity to borrow on international markets and being forced to give up its sovereignty in return for a so-called bailout by the same people who had pushed the country into beggary.

This, indeed, is a perfect example of what writers in the classical tradition of republicanism defined as tyranny: the imposition on a people of laws it had not itself made or consented to. In this sense, Irish sovereignty was not lost in the dramatic moment when officials from the European Commission, the ECB and the International Monetary Fund arrived in Dublin to impose conditions in return for money. It was lost when an Irish government was bullied or persuaded to follow 'rules' that had no basis in law or democracy, even when doing so had dire long-term consequences for its own citizens.

Ireland's current status, resulting from those decisions, is not unlike the kind of Home Rule that was supposed to come into force in 1914: local autonomy without fiscal or budgetary control. Except that such control does not reside in England but in Germany. This was, for the revolutionaries of 1916, not their desired outcome, but an acceptable second best. And it is now, in a highly qualified but none the less grotesque sense, the terminus of the journey they initiated. The country is now actually rather like the 'self-governing' entity under German hegemony that Connolly thought it might be if the outcome of the First World War had been different. In a strange and unexpected way, the alternative future that radical Irish nationalists imagined at that time has become the one in which their political descendants actually live.

Forgetting the Republic

There is, in the approach to the centenary of the 1916 Rising, a concern with how the declaration of the republic is to be remembered and commemorated. But in fact what characterises the Irish republic is much more the act of forgetting it. At least three times, the republic has been declared and then allowed to slip from the national consciousness.

Amnesia, as the French thinker Ernest Renan suggested in 1882, is essential to the foundation of nations. 'Forgetfulness, and I shall even say historical error, form an essential factor in the creation of a nation.' What must be forgotten? The 'deeds of violence that have taken place at the commencement of all political formations . . . Unity is ever achieved by brutality.' A nation is also based on a common forgetting of its inevitably mixed ethnic origins. 'But the essence of a nation is that all its individual members should have many things in common; and also that all of them should hold many things in oblivion . . . It is good for all to know how to forget.'[6]

The Irish republic, though, is not quite like this. It is steeped in forgetting but in a most peculiar way. Renan's amnesia is a creative act – nations found themselves on acts of forgetting. But the Irish republic goes much further – it forgets its own foundation, time and again. And what it shoves to the back of its mind is not the circumstance of its creation but its own existence.

There is something decidedly odd about the 1916 proclamation. Its signatories 'hereby proclaim the Irish Republic as a Sovereign Independent State, and we pledge our lives and the lives of our comrades in arms to the cause of its freedom, of its welfare, and of its exaltation among the nations'. The authors seem to forget that the organisation to which they belong, the Irish Republican Brotherhood, had long since declared this Irish republic as an existing entity. Logically, the 1916 proclamation should have been a restatement or a rededication, not a founding act at all.

For, almost half a century earlier, in 1867, the IRB issued an apparently definitive declaration: 'Herewith we proclaim the Irish Republic.' That this first proclamation is remembered only by historians and never referred to in public discourse is in itself unremarkable. What is remarkable is that the IRB seems to have wilfully dis-remembered it. Perhaps it was felt to be more dramatically potent to begin again, to mark the Easter Rising as a self-conscious point of origin. Perhaps a grand proclamation is easier to kill and die for than an act of memory and recapitulation.

Or perhaps the first declaration of the Irish republic was a little uncomfortable in its social radicalism and open secularism. The 1867 proclamation has none of the religious and mystical language of the 1916 proclamation. God, invoked twice in 1916, was not imagined as an honorary citizen of the 1867 republic – he or she is entirely absent. Ireland is not invoked as an abstract entity, summoning 'her children to her flag'. The 1867 references to the country are concrete: 'the soil of Ireland'; 'the Irish people'. On the other hand, the 1867 proclamation does mention certain things absent in 1916: a republican form of government (as against both 'oligarchy' and 'the curse of Monarchical Government'); economic injustice ('the oppression of labour'); and economic equality ('we aim at founding a Republic based on universal suffrage, which shall secure to all the intrinsic value of their labour').

Even more uncomfortably, the 1867 proclamation resists ideas of either religious or ethnic solidarity as the basis for the Irish republic. It is explicitly secular: 'We declare, also, in favour of absolute liberty of conscience, and complete separation of Church and State.' And it does not create a simple opposition of 'Irish' to 'English'. It declares war on 'aristocratic locusts, whether English or Irish, who have eaten the verdure of our fields'. On the other hand, it imagines, however fancifully, a common cause with the English working class: 'As for you, workmen of England, it is not only your hearts we wish, but your arms.'

This putative Irish republic had to be forgotten in 1916, even though the leaders of the Rising had in fact sworn oaths of allegiance to it. Strikingly, though, this is not the only act of wilful amnesia in the 1916 proclamation. It explicitly calls to mind the idea of oblivion, declaring the new republic to be 'oblivious of the differences carefully fostered by an alien Government, which have divided a minority from the majority in the past'. The desired import is that 'differences' – the profound division between largely Catholic nationalism and largely Protestant unionism that had just brought the island to the brink of civil war – *should* be forgotten. But the effect is, rather, that they *have* been forgotten. The proclamation is in this sense too an act of forgetting – its whole gesture of declaring a republic relies on the throwing of a mental cordon sanitaire around Unionism. It is delicately and euphemistically broached, but only in order to be immediately dismissed from consciousness. 'Oblivious' here is a well-chosen word.

In any event, the 1916 republic was itself quickly forgotten. It was, in part, overtaken by partition. But it was also treated with little respect by its own heirs – the politicians who came to power in the southern Free State. In 1919, the first Dáil attempted to formulate in concrete terms what the republic might actually mean. That meaning, it agreed, would have to centre on the idea of social equality – the republic would have to belong equally to all its citizens. In introducing the Democratic Programme which the Dáil adopted, Richard Mulcahy said, 'A nation cannot be fully free in which even a small section of its people have not freedom. A nation cannot be said fully to live in spirit, or materially, while there is denied to any section of its people a share of the wealth and the riches that God bestowed around them.' Accordingly, the Democratic Programme explicitly announced that the 1916 proclamation meant that 'all right to private property must be subordinated to the public right and welfare'. It defined the republic as one whose first duty would be to the welfare of children, which would create 'a sympathetic native scheme for the care of the Nation's aged and infirm, who shall not be regarded as a burden, but rather entitled to the Nation's gratitude and consideration'; and which would create an effective public healthcare system.[7]

All of this was adopted unanimously and without debate – a sign not that it represented the serious commitment of the Dáil but in fact that it did not. In Irish political culture, it is a safe bet that anything that is unanimous is a mere gesture. The first Dáil actually did something extraordinary: it teased out what the real meaning of the republic declared in 1916 would be and then promptly forgot all about it. Within four months, by April 1919, Eamon de Valera announced that the implementation of the Democratic Programme would have to be postponed. Kevin O'Higgins, one of the most influential figures in the early years of the Free State, later dismissed the Democratic Programme as 'mostly poetry'. It was, in the event, not merely consigned to oblivion but actively traduced: child welfare, for example, was monumentally abused.

But did the 1916 republic ever exist in any corporeal form? In 1935, the senior surviving leader of the Rising, Eamon de Valera, declared that 'they were not going to declare a republic during this period of office'.[8] Yet, by 1937, he was declaring that his new constitution gave Ireland 'all the symbols and institutions of a Republic except the title'. But yet again in 1937, he declared that 'the unity of Ireland under a new Constitution is far more desirable for him than any declaration of a republic for the truncated country'.[9] Even the arch-republican could not say whether Ireland was a republic or not.

And so the republic, twice forgotten, was declared all over again. The Irish republic was inaugurated, this time by an

Irish government, on Easter Monday, 18 April 1949, with a ceremony at the General Post Office in Dublin. The day and place were chosen to resonate with the declaration of the republic at the same spot thirty-three years earlier. But the irony of the gesture seems to have escaped the government: it was proclaiming again the republic that had been proclaimed in 1916 by those who believed it had already been proclaimed in 1867. This was a republic so good they proclaimed it thrice. Or, perhaps, one so nebulous that, however often it was declared, it remained always intangible and out of reach.

And this third declaration of the republic was itself effectively being forgotten even as it was being declared. It generated little public excitement: 'It was noted that the ceremonies chiefly involved politicians and the military. The inauguration of a republic and the ceremonies associated with it failed to engage the enthusiastic support of the population in general.[10] This is unsurprising. The declaration had been made suddenly and without prior discussion in the Dáil or in public: the citizens of this new republic learned of it in news from Canada, where it was announced by the Taoiseach, John A. Costello.

In fact, the great day of the third inauguration of the republic had elements of high comedy. It provided an Irish twist on Karl Marx: the republic was declared the second time (in 1916) as tragedy and the third (in 1949) as farce. De Valera refused to attend, ostentatiously spending the day at Arbour Hill 'praying for the men of 1916'. (Considering the men of 1916 had long since been canonised, it is not clear why they needed his prayers.) A barman – that source of infallible popular wisdom – commented, 'Sure, it's all politics. Costello and his crowd have wiped Dev's eye and now Dev is trying to get his own back on them.'[11] The Irish Grand National at Fairyhouse drew larger crowds than the birth of the republic.

Brian Inglis in the *Irish Times* reported:

There was very little real warmth in the cheering, very
little real gaiety in the atmosphere. There were loud
cheers, but they were the cheers of people just tired of
standing there, waiting for something to happen. There
were gay crowds, but they were the usual, idle, bank
holiday crowds, prepared to watch any free show until
such time as the cinemas opened their doors, and they
could settle down in earnest to the business of enjoying
the holiday.

There was even trouble getting the new republic's tricolour
of green, white and orange right:

There appears to be some doubt in the public mind, or
in the minds of the manufacturers of flags, as to what
exactly constitutes the national flag of the Republic.
Apart from the normal variations in the hue – primrose
yellow to blood orange – quite a number of the small
hand flags had the orange instead of the green next to
the staff, and I saw one small girl waving a tricolour on
which the green, white and orange stripes had been
arranged horizontally instead of vertically.

Souvenir sellers were having a hard time. They shouted 'get
your Republican colours . . . get your colours for the Republic' in the same tone, Inglis noted, as they usually roared 'get
your colours for the match'. But to little avail. The price of
souvenirs – small Irish flags with gold tassels and pictures of
Wolfe Tone or the GPO – started at sixpence. By the time
the military parade got under way, the price was down to

twopence, and even before it ended they were being knocked down for a penny.[12]

Souvenirs, after all, are meant to stir memories. The crowd may have sensed that this republic, too, would be forgotten. In reality, the declaration of a republic in 1949 changed nothing much. Ireland left the British Commonwealth and this negative act was the only meaning the new republic ever had. Asked by the London editor of the *Irish Times* whether the Republic of Ireland Act marked a step forward in Ireland's development, a sceptical George Bernard Shaw replied, 'Ask me five years hence. If the terrible vital statistics improve to a civilised level, then our steps will have been steps forward. If not, there will be nothing for us but the ancient prescription of the submergence of the island for ten minutes in the Irish Sea.'

Shaw's scepticism was entirely justified. The new republic changed little – not even the name of the state, which remained simply Ireland. The term 'Republic of Ireland' was declared to be 'the description of the State' – not its name. The Republic of Ireland Act is in fact a desultory piece of legislation, containing five sentences totalling 96 words. It could be so short because it had nothing to say, nothing to bring into effect. Everything carried on exactly as before. The vital statistics of the population – life expectancy, health status, poverty, levels of education – did not improve, unless, of course, people left for other countries, as they did in their droves in the decade after the new republic was inaugurated.

This, in itself, surely says something about the idea of an Irish republic. If you can declare it in 96 words that have no consequence, it is only because you have become used to forgetting it. It is an airy, insubstantial thing.

The Republic of Vague

One of the things that makes 'the republic' a slippery concept is the existence of two quite separate traditions of republicanism. Philip Pettit has drawn a sharp distinction between them. The first tradition is the one that emerged from classical Roman thought ('what affects all must be decided by all'), by way of the Italian Renaissance. It took shape in Florence, Venice and the other city states, and went on to underpin the overthrow of monarchs in Poland, Holland and England in the seventeenth and eighteenth centuries. It enormously influenced the American Revolution and partly (but only partly) shaped the French.

This stream of thought had three basic elements. First, freedom should be understood as the condition, in Pettit's formulation, of 'not having to live under the potentially harmful power of another' person: in other words, 'non-domination'. The state's job is not merely to uphold this freedom but – crucially – to uphold it equally for all citizens.

This makes the idea of republican freedom very different from liberal and neoliberal definitions of 'freedom', which include the freedom to exploit and control others. 'Non-domination' is not the same thing as 'non-interference'. Non-domination actually requires radical state interference at times: to uphold the equal rights of women, for example, or to prevent employers from exploiting their dominance over their workers, or to stop banks from engaging in behaviour that will impose crushing debts on citizens. It may even require at times a degree of compulsion: paying taxes, for example, is a duty because the state has to have the resources to provide those things that are necessary for everyone to live with dignity. 'The continual whine of lamenting the burden of

taxes . . .', says the great republican Thomas Paine, 'is inconsistent with the sense and spirit of a republic.'[13]

Classical republicanism is concerned, in a way that liberalism is not, with the cost to human dignity of being in a state
of dependence on the whims of others. As Maurizio Viroli
puts it:

> Liberal liberty aims to protect individuals only from inter-
> ferences, from actions interfering with their freedom of
> choice; republican liberty aims to emancipate them from
> the conditions of dependence. What worries a liberal is
> having anyone's freedom of action dominated or con-
> trolled; a republican worries about this but worries
> even more about the dispiritedness that affects men and
> women who live dependent lives.[14]

In this sense, republicanism is very much at odds with the
currently dominant idea that good societies can be shaped by
governments whose main concern is simply not to interfere
with the functioning of markets. It is an ideal of freedom –
but freedom defined much more richly than the liberty that
right-wing orthodoxy proclaims as its central principle.

Republicanism requires a strong state, therefore, but it also
seeks to limit and contest the power of the state. Hence the
second and third elements of classical republican thinking.
The second principle holds that government should be
'mixed', its various powers and functions broken up among
different and independent bodies to ensure that no one could
exercise unaccountable power. Third, it is up to citizens,
individually and collectively, to keep the republic on its toes,
in Pettit's phrase to 'track and contest public policies and
initiatives'. Crudely, in a republic, nobody gets to dominate

anybody else, nobody gets unaccountable power and citizens have a duty to be obstreperous. The aim of all of this is to strike a balance: the state should be strong enough to stop one citizen from bullying another, but not so strong that it itself becomes the bully.

These ideals were, historically, limited in their application. The citizens who made up the early republican states were male property owners. Slaves, women, the poor and colonial subjects were generally beyond its pale. Other groups – non-whites, indigenous peoples, Jews, Catholics and so on – might or might not be allowed into the republic. Republics often acted in practice as guarantors of non-domination for their members but as instruments of domination towards others. But this does not mean that the principles themselves are to be despised. On the contrary, the very fact that privileged groups have hoarded them for themselves and kept them from others suggests that they are well worth possessing. Their point, after all, is human dignity, the ideal, in Pettit's words, of 'being sufficiently empowered to stand on equal terms with others, as a citizen among citizens . . . [to] be able to walk tall, live without shame or indignity, and look one another in the eye without any reason for fear or deference'.

There is, though, another, radically different, tradition of republicanism. It is the tradition of Rousseau, crucially influential on the French Revolution and on much Continental European thinking since. It accepts and indeed insists on the first principle of the other tradition: that citizens should be free of domination by others. But it rejects the other two: the ideas of mixed government and of the obstreperous citizenry. Instead of the idea that power should be deliberately divided, the Rousseau tradition argues for the notion of a single, sovereign popular will: 'the People' effectively taking the place of the king in a monarchy. A popular assembly should decide the 'general will', which then becomes absolute law. There is no room in the general will for different parts of government holding each other in check. This would 'turn the Sovereign into a being that is fantastical and formed of disparate parts'. And it follows also that there is no room for obstreperous citizens. Once the 'general will' has been expressed by the assembly, it must be accepted and obeyed – otherwise it would not be general. As Pettit characterises this position:

> Far from every law being a fair target for civic critique and challenge, each comes draped in an authority and majesty that brooks no individual opposition. Having been party to the creation of the popular sovereign no one as an individual retains the right of contesting the decisions of the collectivity, even if those decisions were ones that the person argued against in assembly.

In this view, a republic is essentially the right to participate in decision-making. Once decisions have been made, the entire force of the state and of the citizens collectively is assumed to be behind them.

The immediate question that faces us here is not which of these republican traditions is best but which of them Ireland has followed. Is the republic, as it has taken shape in nine-teenth- and twentieth-century politics, of the first (let's call it Renaissance) kind? Or is it of the Rousseau variety? The answer, as with so much in Irish culture, is both and neither. The Irish republic has strong elements of both traditions but has never functioned as a coherent expression of either. There are good historical reasons for this – Irish republicanism being halfway between the American and French Revolutions

– but the result is a blurry, and therefore largely impotent, concept.

In some ways, the Irish republic has been expressed in terms that Rousseau would recognise. In the way Rousseau's ideas are developed through European nationalism, 'the people or community gets to be sacralized, as it assumes the role of the popular, incontestable sovereign, incapable of doing wrong to its own members'. There is a very strong tradition of imagining Ireland in this way, as a sacred, incontestable and sovereign entity who commands the allegiance of her children. In the opening paragraph of the 1916 proclamation: 'Ireland, through us, summons her children . . .' 'Ireland' is imagined as a single, sacred and sovereign force, the embodiment of the popular or general will.

But there is a refinement. At least in Rousseau, the general will is decided by a deliberative assembly of the people before it becomes sacred and commanding. But the conditions of Ireland – first British rule, then partition – mean that this great democratic assembly has never happened, except, perhaps, as a result of the 1918 general election when the whole island voted at the same time. So who is to decide the general will in the meantime? A vanguard or elite that has distinguished itself by the absolute nature of its commitment to Ireland. It will act, often violently, in the certain knowledge that it is expressing the general will and that the great assembly, whenever it becomes possible, will retrospectively endorse those actions. This is an extreme version of Rousseau – sacred, unified and implacable sovereignty but without the initial act of democratic deliberation.

This is what those who are habitually referred to, even now, as 'republicans' – members of the IRA or one of its many offshoots – believe. But the idea has also had a milder expression in the less fanatical politics of the real Irish state. The idea of Ireland as a single, sovereign entity that is sacred and therefore not to be argued with lies behind an authoritarian streak in Irish politics. Here, the 'general will' becomes the 'national interest' – a concept that always happens to coincide with the specific interests of a ruling party and/or of a powerful section of society. (It was in the 'national interest' that all private banking debts be rendered public, therefore public discussion or scrutiny was deemed irrelevant at best, impertinent at worst.) In vulgar terms, the appeal is made to 'pull on the green jersey' – to obey the summons of 'Ireland' without further discussion. The idea of accountability implicit in mixed government is ditched. And the citizenry's duty to be obstreperous is annulled. On the contrary, its duty is to be stoical, taciturn and 'resilient'.

This strain of republicanism has been expressed in Irish politics chiefly through the historic dominance of an organisation that saw itself, quite explicitly, as the expression of the 'general will'. Fianna Fáil, The Republican Party (to give it its full official title) refused to see itself as one political party among others and therefore as a group of citizens engaged in the open contest of democracy. Its self-image is, rather, that of a 'national movement'. This is the primary idea in its constitution which begins 'Fianna Fáil is a National Movement' and then dictates that 'the Movement shall be organised and known as Fianna Fáil, The Republican Party'.

The suggestion here is that of a relationship similar to that of God the Father to God the Son. On earth, God the Son takes a physical, corporeal, human form: Fianna Fáil. But this physical and temporal form is just a manifestation of something entirely beyond our human ken, the national movement. And, of course, inherent in this mystical politics is the notion that the national movement really is the nation and that disloyalty to the party is really a form of treachery. Even after its humiliation in the 2011 general election, the party's self-description continues to state baldly, 'Fianna Fáil represents the mainstream of Irish life.' To be outside a party that 80 per cent of Irish people do not support is thus to be outside the Irish mainstream, to be marginal and inauthentic.

But this idea could be, and was, pushed even further. The party connected itself rhetorically to the French Revolution, defining its republicanism as a mixture of nationalism and internationalism. 'Republican', it says, 'stands both for the unity of the island and a commitment to the historic principles of European republican philosophy, namely liberty, equality and fraternity.' But just as the 'general will' in the French Revolution found its ultimate expression in Napoleonic triumphalism, Fianna Fáil inevitably produced its own mini-Napoleon, Charles Haughey. Haughey (who was privately obsessed with Napoleon) gave his grandiose collection of speeches the Rousseauesque title 'The Spirit of the Nation'. The logic was impeccable: if the party was really the mere physical manifestation of the nation, its leader must represent in himself the embodiment of the general will, the nation's abiding spirit. (And bribes to the leader were not bribes but votive offerings, sacrifices to the nation itself.)

Ludicrous as all of this was and is, it is well to remember that the claim that Fianna Fáil represented 'the mainstream of Irish life' was perfectly tenable for seventy-five years. It had – and may still have – a powerful hold. There are, therefore, strong elements of the Rousseau tradition of republicanism in Irish political culture.

But only elements. For at the same time, Irish republicanism, in the institutional form it has taken in the southern state, draws heavily on the other, Renaissance, tradition. It accepts, at least in theory, the two principles that Rousseau rejects. It has a classic mixed government, with power divided among the executive, the judiciary and the parliament. It is a society of laws: courts can and do overrule the actions of the government when they impinge on the rights of citizens. And it does acknowledge at least the basic foundations of active, vigilant citizenship – rights to freedom of expression and assembly, for example.

In practice, however, the Irish state has been very far from the conception of a classical republic. It can be tested against the three basic components of that tradition and found starkly wanting:

Non-domination

For most of its history, the state failed miserably in the basic task of ensuring that citizens were free from subjection to the arbitrary will of others. It allowed the institutional Catholic Church (as opposed to Catholics themselves) to exercise unaccountable and secretive power in key areas of the public and private lives of citizens, from access to contraception to basic public services such as healthcare and education. The state also actively colluded in grotesque systems of arbitrary power, such as industrial schools, Magdalene Homes and mental hospitals – incarcerating without trial a higher proportion of its citizens than the Soviet Union did.

More recently, the state itself has been dominated by private interests. Corruption allowed wealthy citizens to purchase public policy, to the detriment of the majority of their fellow citizens. The skewing of the planning process for the capital city over two decades is just one example. And even when corruption was not at play, specific interest groups – the banks being an obvious example – acquired a position of complete (and in the event, disastrous) dominance over key areas of public policy.

Mixed Government

In principle, the Irish state was structured around a classic division of power, with the idea that the government, the courts and the parliament would each keep the others in check. In practice, the division of power has been at best partial. It is broadly true that courts have acted as a check on government, though even this has to be qualified by three important factors. One is that access to the courts has been unequal, with some citizens having no practical way to vindicate their rights. The second is that the law itself has been unequally applied, with some categories of intensely destructive crime (corruption, fraud, tax evasion) enjoying large-scale impunity and others (generally those committed by the denizens of the underclass) being harshly punished. Thirdly, the independence of the judiciary from the government it is supposed to check is severely limited: judges depend on government for appointment and there is a strong connection between judicial appointments and membership of the party in power.

But if the judicial and legal side of the exercise of power has been imperfect, the parliamentary side has been virtually non-existent. Parliament, in general, does not initiate legislation; it passes it. Scrutiny of legislation is often extremely minimal. The accountability of ministers is barely existent, and that of senior civil servants (who in effect make many key decisions) is virtually non-existent. This key aspect of republican tradition amounts, in the Irish case, to little more than a constitutional fiction.

Obstreperous Citizens

The third plank of the Renaissance republican tradition is the idea that citizens, individually and collectively, have both the right and the duty to be critically engaged with everything the state is doing on their behalf. It is somewhat ironic that the most famous formulation of this idea is Irish: John Philpot Curran, on his election as Lord Mayor of Dublin in 1790 said that the 'condition upon which God hath given liberty to man is eternal vigilance' (subsequently quoted as 'the price of liberty is eternal vigilance' and widely misattributed to Thomas Jefferson). It would be an exaggeration to say that this vigilant citizenry has been absent from the Irish republic. But its presence has been limited and ineffective.

The limitations are fourfold. First, the political system (and the wider political culture) has encouraged Irish people to think of themselves not as citizens but as clients. Voting is a deal: I get you a state or local-government service and you pay me with your vote. The model is closer to the logic of the marketplace than to that of an active democracy. Second, the arena in which it should be easiest for citizens to acquire the habit of exercising their right to a voice and their responsibility to make good choices – local democracy – is extraordinarily weak by international standards.

Third, the basic precondition for an engaged citizenship is information. Citizens need to know what it is they're supposed to be vigilant about. The Irish republic has an extremely poor record of transparency and openness. For much of the history of the state, free discussion was heavily discouraged by the power of the institutional Church, its 'moral monopoly' on opinions on a range of issues, and by active censorship. More recently, experiments with freedom of state information in the 1990s were actively and deliberately rolled back. The capacity of citizens to know what the state is doing remains extremely limited. The blanket guarantee given to Irish banks in 2008 is a prime example – at no point was the public ever given the most basic information about its cost until it was far too late.

Lastly and more nebulously, Ireland has a very strong cultural orientation towards the acceptance of orthodoxies and the marginalisation or co-option of dissent. The very weak role of ideology in the political culture (with the two main parties being effectively identical in almost every area of policy) has discouraged the notion that a clash of ideas is healthy. The intimate nature of the society has encouraged an ideal of consensus. The heavy concentration of ownership, especially in the print media, has limited the scope for genuine debate. Those in power have been very adept at buying off useful dissidents when they can and closing them down when they must. And Irish culture is heavily shaped by fatalism and a sense of powerlessness. Its instinct is to adapt to circumstances rather than to change them. All of these factors have greatly weakened the idea of a powerful, engaged citizenry that is so central to classical republicanism.

Ireland has thus had elements of both the competing traditions of republicanism, without fully engaging with either of them. It has been, at best, a blurry republic, in which the two traditions have tended to cancel each other out. The vagueness has not been entirely disadvantageous. It is a reasonable guess that if one of the traditions were to have clarified itself sufficiently to have become entirely dominant, it would not have been the more open, sceptical and engaged Renaissance one. That tradition might have been relatively weak, but it was strong enough to act as a barrier to the complete triumph of the 'general will'. It was able to resist the pull of an ethnic, mystical, authoritarian republicanism which the Provisional IRA tried to mobilise between the 1960s and the 1990s. And though it failed to stop Haughey from doing immense harm to the body politic, it did at least put limits on the extent of his power.

A blurry republicanism with some saving graces is, however, still too slippery and uncertain to achieve what a republican ethic is supposed to: to create and sustain a political community that belongs equally to all its members and has their common good as its purpose. And arguably one of the reasons that never happened is that there has never been a time when Irish people have been offered the hard bargain that a republic implies: an offer of freedom and dignity that demands in return a collective commitment to the maintenance of the conditions that make those things available to all.

Terms and Conditions Apply

During the French Revolution of 1848, an angry crowd stormed the Hôtel de Ville in Paris where the provisional government was sitting. They demanded to see its head, the poet Alphonse de Lamartine.

'We have upset the monarchy, let Lamartine tell us do they mean to give us the republic?'

'Who said republic?' asked Lamartine.

'All!'

'Do you know what you are asking? Do you know what a republic means?'

'Tell us.'

'The republic, do you know that it is the government of the

reason of all men? Do you think you are prepared to be rulers of yourselves, and to have no other masters than your own reason?'

'Yes!'

'The republic, do you know that it is the government of justice? Are you just enough to do right even to your enemies?'

'Yes!'

'Are you virtuous enough to forbear vengeance, proscriptions, and blood, which dishonoured the former republic?'

'Yes, yes!'

'You will? You are? You swear it? You call Heaven to witness it?'

A thunder of affirmation followed.

'Well, then,' said Lamartine, 'you shall be a republic, if you are as worthy to keep it as you have been to conquer it. But understand, we must not begin the republic by injustice: we have no business to steal a republic, we can only declare our wish in the name of the people of Paris. It is a glorious initiative; but the thirty millions of men who compose the French people are not here: they have a right to be consulted. The forms of our institutions shall be decided by the universal suffrage of the French people: it is the only basis of a national republic.'

'Yes,' cried the crowd. 'It is just. Paris is the head, but it is not France. The head has no right to oppress the members. Vive la République!'[15]

The story has obviously been shaped as a heroic epic, but it is suggestive none the less. It is striking that Lamartine says, not 'you shall *have* a republic', but 'you shall *be* a republic'. A republic is not something people are given but something they choose to become. The choice is conscious, deliberate and difficult. And it is tested. There is this moment in French history when the demand for a republic is met with three key questions. Do you know what it is? Are you ready to take on the responsibilities of self-rule? And do you accept that terms and conditions apply, that your own anger and passion are not enough but must be qualified by reason, justice and democratic consent? At least in this epic myth, the French crowd is given the opportunity to answer 'yes' or 'no'.

These questions have never actually been asked of the Irish people, even in a romantic myth. The Irish have no narrative of republican call and response; they have only the call, the 'summons' of the 1916 proclamation. Republics have been declared for them: in 1867 and 1916 by secretive revolutionary vanguards and in 1948 by a Taoiseach on a trip to Canada. Each time, the republic has come as a surprise to its putative citizens. It has been easily forgotten because it was easily invented. Lamartine's hard question – Do you think you are prepared to be rulers of yourselves? – has never been truly probed.

That question is about one of the basic ideas that has always been present in republican thinking: civic virtue, defined as the 'willingness and capacity [of citizens] to serve the common good'. Citizens have to be 'as worthy to keep' a republic as they are to get it in the first place. A republic demands constant care. In 1944, just before he was executed at the age of nineteen by a fascist firing squad, the Italian resistance fighter Giacomo Ulivi wrote of the republic he was willing to die for that 'we need to take direct, personal care of it'.[16]

It is obvious that the Irish people as a whole have taken spectacularly bad care of their republic. If it was a child, the social workers would have come for it long ago, for it has shown terrible signs of abuse and neglect. They have not demanded accountability of their leaders. They have continued to elect politicians they know to have abused power. They voted in large numbers for Haughey, who openly flaunted extreme wealth after a lifetime in public office. They chose to suspend their disbelief in the ridiculous lies spun by Haughey's protégé Bertie Ahern to explain large sums of cash for which he could not account. They displayed what the report of the Mahon Tribunal into the perversion of the planning process calls 'general apathy' towards the existence of 'systemic and endemic' corruption.

To return to Ernest Renan, he argued that a nation is made up of two things: the past and the present. A nation 'implies a past; but it is summed up in the present by a tangible fact – consent, the clearly expressed desire to live a common life'. The same might more accurately be said of republics. Ireland is very strong on the first aspect, the past. But is very weak on the present. It has never manifested 'the clearly expressed desire to live a common life'. But then the citizens have never really been asked to express clearly their commitment to a republic.

Talk of civic virtue conjures up unfortunate images of idealised Romans dressed in togas or of fanatical Robespierres sharpening their own incorruptibility to such a keen edge that it can cut off the heads of the unworthy. In fact, it is a much simpler and less po-faced idea: 'Civic virtue is not a martial, heroic and austere virtue, but a civilised, ordinary tolerant one.'[17] It is not even at odds with the idea that is often counterpoised against it: self-interest. It simply asks that self-interest be enlightened. It suggests that the 'self' in which we are interested is not an isolated, robotic machine for calculating immediate advantage, but a nexus of connections to family, to place and nature, to community, to society, to the imaginary but potent entity we call a nation. It entails a belief that human beings take personal pleasure in trust and decency and collective achievement. It imagines the self to include both a moral sense that finds satisfaction in justice and an aesthetic sense that is repelled by the chaos, disorder and obscenity of a society that pits all against all and is gratified by balance and decency.

It would be ridiculous to suggest that Irish people lack these qualities. There is no genetic flaw that makes the Irish less inclined to public virtue than other people. On the contrary, it is the very strong sense of collective identity, the obvious hunger for a sense of common purpose and the evidence of altruistic commitment at both the local and international levels that make the inability of these qualities to manifest themselves at the level of a national republic so extraordinary.

There are many factors at work and the biggest ones are obvious. Machine politics with a clientilistic ethic were already well established, both at home and in the wider culture of the Irish diaspora, before the foundation of the state. The strongest moral and philosophical influence on society – institutional Catholicism – was overwhelmingly concerned with ideas of private virtue (the control of sexuality in particular), largely to the exclusion of civic virtue. Cities – the arenas in which classical republicanism was incubated – were few and small. Conversely, an intense sense of and attachment to the local, which developed in response to the remoteness of power when Ireland was ruled from London, worked against identification with national politics: given a choice between a politician who would bring short-term benefits to the locality but harm the national body politic and one who would promise little for the locality but benefit the country as a whole, Irish voters would almost always choose the former.

Mass emigration continually undermined the idea of a 'we' on which a republican culture is based. The 'desire to live a common life' might have been present, but it was literally diffused. The 'common life' that binds together a culture shaped by mass emigration is a life of the imagination – memory, nostalgia, the myths of identity – but not of daily reality. It is, in Renan's terms, a life of the past but not of the present.

Those who stayed at home, meanwhile, were caught in a largely static economy in which the idea of mutual benefit – an idea essential to republicanism – was not at all obvious. In a static world, everything is a zero-sum game. There is only so much of everything – money, land, prestige, education – so everything you get is something I'm not getting. Thus the inbred ethic of begrudgery so well caught by Joe Lee:

> The Irish carry from their mother's womb not so much a
> fanatic heart as a begrudger one. The begrudger mentality
> did derive fairly rationally from a mercantilist concept of
> the size of the status cake. The size of that cake was more
> or less fixed in more or less static communities and in
> small institutions. In a stunted society, one man's gain
> did tend to be another man's loss. Winners could flourish
> only at the expense of losers. Status depended not only
> on rising oneself but on preventing others from rising. For
> many, keeping the other fellow down presented the surest
> defence of their own position.[18]

One of the preconditions of a republic – that one's status depends on one's willingness to help others to rise – was not merely absent but turned on its head.

Another aspect of this culture was fatalism. Generations of suffering and poverty bred a habit of being grateful for small mercies. The German novelist Heinrich Böll, who lived much of the time on Achill island, wrote in 1957:

When something happens to you in Germany, when you miss a train, break a leg, go bankrupt, we say: It couldn't have been any worse; whatever happens is always the worst. With the Irish it is almost the opposite: if you break a leg, miss a train, go bankrupt, they say: it could be worse; instead of a leg you might have broken your neck, instead of a train you might have missed Heaven . . . Whatever happens is never the worst; on the contrary, what's worst never happens: if your revered and beloved grandmother dies, your revered and beloved grandfather might have died too . . . 'It could be worse' is one of the most common turns of speech, probably because only too often things are pretty bad and what's worse offers the consolation of being relative.[19]

There is an element of stereotype in this, of course, but also a large element of truth: even in the years of prosperity, 'Could be worse' remained a standard response to the question 'How are you?'

Beyond these obvious forces, there is the role of nationalism. There is no necessary contradiction between republicanism and nationalism. An ethnic or sectarian nationalism that insists on a homogeneous identity as the condition of full citizenship is certainly incompatible with classical republicanism. Ireland has obvious experience of that brand of identity. But there are other kinds of civic, pluralist nationalism that can sit perfectly well with the existence of a republic. In principle at least, Irish nationalism and a genuine Irish republicanism might have made comfortable bedfellows. But two aspects of nationalism – one general and one highly specific – made this marriage impossible.

The general question relates to the notion at the heart of civic virtue – that a republic can't just be declared, it has to be maintained as a daily concern of all of its citizens: 'We need to take direct, personal care of it.' A republic can be gained, but it can also be lost: it can be hijacked by oligarchies or interest groups or it can slowly corrode through neglect or corruption. But this is absolutely not true of a nation in the way nationalism imagines it. In nationalist thinking, the nation is always there. It was created by god or nature or history. It is entirely independent of any particular set of laws and institutions. If Ireland was a monarchy or an anarcho-syndicalist commune, it would still be Ireland.

This sense of the permanence and robustness of the nation is especially strong in Irish culture. Its experience is precisely that of the survival of an Irish nation even under the rule and domination of another culture. The whole narrative of Irish nationality is one of indestructibility: it survived everything from invasion and colonisation to famine and mass emigration.

Because of the vagueness of Irish republicanism, there is a strong tendency to confuse the nation and the republic, to imagine that they are the same thing. In this confusion, there is a habit of thinking of the collective entity both as something given and natural and as something durable and indefatigable. It doesn't need to be taken care of because it has shown through the centuries that it can take care of itself. But a republic is completely the reverse. It is not given or natural; it is a collective invention, a choice, a deal that people make with themselves and with each other. And it is not indestructible or indefatigable. It has to be watched over with the vigilance of civic virtue. It has to be recreated again and again. Membership of a nation is accidental and passive; citizenship in a republic has to be conscious and active.

It is perfectly understandable that the newly independent Irish state should be drawn towards the national, rather than the republican, side of this dichotomy. The achievement of national independence, however fraught and problematic, was both a triumph and relief. It might have changed little socially or economically but it provided a deep psychological satisfaction. Something long desired had been attained. It would have been hard to turn the mindset of relief and pride on its head and to say that actually the task of creating a republic had scarcely even begun. And that, even if a republic were built, it would always be in danger of being lost again.

The other, more specific aspect of nationalism that was problematic for republicanism actually came from the opposite direction – a sense not of permanence but of transience. Its focus was on partition and the quest for a United Ireland. This sustained the idea that the Irish state was radically incomplete and therefore temporary. The state was a limbo in which the spirit of the nation had to reside while waiting for admittance to the heaven of a United Ireland. It existed only provisionally, 'pending', in the words of the constitution, 'the reintegration of the national territory'. (It is not accidental that this phrase has overtones of the Catholic imagining of souls waiting for their ultimate appointment with God. It was personally crafted by the Archbishop of Dublin, John Charles McQuaid.[20])

The underlying psychology of this belief was deeply inimical to the task of creating and sustaining a republic. 'The Republic' was by definition something that did not and could not exist within the territory of the state. As with so much else, mainstream southern politics actually hovered continually between this belief and the idea that, for all practical purposes, the existing state was a republic – hence de Valera's inability to say whether or not the state he had created by the 1937 constitution was actually a republic. But in the half of the official brain that still saw the state as a temporary thing, the republic must always be 'pending'. To create a working republic in the south would be like pouring your savings into repairing and beautifying a house rented on a short lease. It could even be seen as a betrayal of the ideal of a United Ireland: if a fulfilled and fulfilling democracy were built in the twenty-six counties, what would happen to the notion that they need the missing six to make them whole?

All of these factors help to explain the weakness of civic virtue for most of the history of the state. What they do not explain, however, is why this culture did not change when the country was apparently transformed in its boom years between 1995 and 2008. Three huge things happened, after all. Ireland became a 'modern' economy of urbanised, industrial or service production. The power of the institutional Catholic Church was broken. And nationalism, in the shape of the quest for a United Ireland, the sense that the southern state was just a temporary contingency, was literally and intellectually disarmed by the peace process and the Belfast Agreement of 1998. If localism, the Church's obsession with sexual morality and the effects of nationalism were major contributors to the weakness of classic republicanism, how come these shifts didn't create the opportunity for it to flourish? Especially since the changes were happening in a context of economic buoyancy, optimism and collective confidence.

Rationally, the effects should have been more favourable to the creation of a republic because one of their most striking manifestations was the breaking of the links between ethnicity, religion and a sense of Irish belonging. On every front, there was a push towards pluralism. The Belfast Agreement enshrined the idea of a plural, complex Irish identity. Internal religious change created much larger faith minorities, both of believers and of non-believers. And the huge influx of migrants from central Europe, Africa and elsewhere added a sudden and profound element of ethnic and cultural diversity. Classical republicanism should have been enormously attractive in this context. On the one hand, it already had a powerful, if contradictory and unfulfilled, existence in Irish culture, so it could not be seen as an alien imposition. On the other, it is the one political ethic that offers a sense of common belonging without appealing to a specific religious or ethnic identity. Yet not only did its time not come, but whatever elements of a republican culture actually existed were in fact further eroded. The republic wasn't remade, it moved steadily towards its present state of complete collapse.

Some of the reasons for this could be seen as accidental, the poor quality of political leadership being the most obvious. But there were deeper reasons, more large-scale forces that operated, not separately, but in association. Each of three positive changes – 'modernity', the breaking of institutional Catholicism and the disarming of mystical nationalism – had, from the point of view of classical republicanism, a dark side.

It is tempting – because largely accurate – to see the failure of Irish public culture to adapt successfully to the opportunities of boom-time prosperity as a result of a resurgence of essentially nineteenth-century habits of mind: an obsession with land and property as the primary source of wealth, the machine politics pioneered by Daniel O'Connell, and a lack of interest in the very technologies that were driving the economy.[21] But international 'modernity', in the form it came in the 1990s, didn't offer an alternative that was especially hospitable to classical republicanism.

Ireland can be said, indeed, to have been unlucky in that it acquired its version of international 'modernity' at a time when the heroic age of that concept was well past. The classic period of the 'modern' state in the West was in the decades between 1945 and 1980. It was not a utopia by any means, but it did have certain key characteristics: a faith in the power of government to create better societies, a consequent prestige for the idea of public service as an admirable ethic, a commitment to the belief that societies should become more equal over time, and an optimistic view of human nature in which altruism, trust, self-sacrifice and mutual benefit were given at least as big a place as the potential for violence, hatred and self-destructive selfishness.

The problem for Ireland was that, just as it was reaching a point where it had its best opportunity to construct a republic, all of these ideas were being systematically dismantled. Beginning with a specific strain in mathematical economics in the United States, the idea took hold that human beings are actually isolated, coldly rational creatures who are programmed to seek only their own advantage. These instincts and desires could best be served and kept in equilibrium by understanding people as both competitors and consumers. They get resources by ruthlessly competing with each other and they express their individuality by using those resources to make consumer choices. Everything else – altruism, 'the public interest', 'public service' – is an illusion. Those who believe in such notions are either idiots or – in this mentality, more admirably – hypocrites, using rhetoric to mask their real pursuit of their own personal advantage.

This notion is literally paranoid: it was formulated in mathematics by John Nash while he was a paranoid schizophrenic who believed that everyone was plotting against him. But it became mainstream economic and political wisdom. Everything of value must be measurable by numbers: hence the ubiquity of numerical 'targets' in all forms of public life. (For example, the time that a home help can spend with an elderly person is now broken down into a series of timed tasks: 10 minutes to get up and dressed, 15 minutes for a shower and so on. Things that cannot be reduced to numbers – holding someone's hand, having a chat – are not measurable and are therefore of no value.) And all public servants, including those in areas such as healthcare and higher education, must be encouraged to think of themselves as competitive individuals pursuing personal interests: hence the ubiquity of 'incentives' to reach 'targets'. The implication of the bonus culture that became the norm is that no one really does anything except for money. The idea that worked well enough for thirty-five years – that people might acquire pleasure, satisfaction and self-worth from doing something that could benefit the community as a whole – was scrapped. That 'modernity' came in this cynical and pessimistic form limited its power to act as a catalyst for a new republican ethic in the boom years.

The changes in the nature of both Irish Catholicism and nationalism also proved to be much less useful to a republican project than they ought to have been. In part, this has to do with the way the changes happened. It would be nice to imagine, in a heroic republican narrative, that they happened on a wave of optimism, when empowered citizens cut off their chains and overthrew oppressive structures of thought. Some of that did happen – aspects of Irish public discourse, especially the rise of movements such as feminism and gay liberation, or in the searing testimonies of survivors of institutional abuse – have had their heady, exhilarating moments. There has been heroic courage. There have been moments when an individual insistence on personal honesty and witness has transformed the way the community has understood itself. If, in the future, a healthy republican democracy wants to erect monuments to its founders and exemplars, it will find plenty of them in the decades after 1960.

But the emotion that destroyed the power of both institutional Catholicism and of warped 'republicanism' was not heroic or triumphal. It was disgust. Violent 'republicanism' ended up disgusting even itself. As its logic became ever more nihilistic in acts such as the Enniskillen and Shankill bombings, it pushed itself to the edge of a moral abyss and realised that it had no choice but to step back. It had to defuse its own intellectual and psychological bombs. The credit it deserved for doing so did not occlude the reality that what was happening was about as heroic as an alcoholic's moment of self-revulsion when the only remaining options are absolute abasement or a reconnection with the everyday world. It didn't help, either, that the act of abstaining from hideous violence was accompanied by the equivalent of the reformed alcoholic's self-satisfaction, the demand to be continually applauded for not being a destructive wreck.

With the institutional Church, disgust had the same centrality. (Again, I emphasise *institutional*. What is at issue is not Catholicism itself but the quasi-monarchical power structure that was built on top of sincere faith.) It is certainly the case that the political power of the Church would have declined gradually in any case. It was ebbing away because of urbanisation, education, the liberation of women, the emergence of new forms of authority through the mass media, the general resistance to obeying diktats in a plugged-in culture. But this process was dramatically short-circuited – by utter disgust. It was the revelation, especially through the extraordinary work of a single journalist, Mary Raftery, of the sheer horror of physical and sexual abuse of children by

42

priests, nuns and religious orders, and the breathtaking cynicism of bishops in covering it up, that transformed the gradual erosion of a system of power into a catastrophic implosion.

Disgust can be a cleansing emotion and in these instances it was both rational and healthy. It was a visceral reaction against two forms of depravity: a nihilistic murder campaign and the enabling – by supposed moral arbiters – of the enslavement and exploitation of the country's most vulnerable children. But if disgust is hygienic, it is also caustic. It is not keyhole surgery; it is radical chemotherapy – it sickens even as it heals. For an Irish person of a Catholic background to look squarely at some of the atrocities committed by 'republicans' in his or her name, or to read the Ryan or Murphy reports on child abuse by religious orders and priests, was to look into the vilest, darkest, most abysmally nightmarish aspects of one's own culture. This was not the Goddess of Liberty storming the barricades of repression. It was the experience of looking into the hideous face of a distinctively Irish and Catholic Medusa and being turned to stone. Objectively, what was happening might have been a liberation, but subjectively it was petrifyingly awful.

Republics are not made up of petrified people. They are created at moments when people feel powerful, when they can sense in every sinew the pulse of civic dignity. Ireland, even in the years of the boom, did not feel like that. It felt betrayed and traumatised. The founding of republics requires a certain concrete illusion, a utopian spirit in which everything seems possible. Republics will settle down into something more sober and qualified, but they need that initial energy of heady hope. This simply wasn't the way Ireland was in those years of glorious opportunity. It was, rather, bombarded with contradictory energies: on the one hand the great buzz of consumerism and a surging, apparently endless property bonanza and on the other the terrible, heartstopping thud of revelations that everything you believed in – the holiness of clerics, the decency of nationalism, the idea of public service – was a lie. It was much easier to drown out the insistent whisper of the second of these realities with the triumphant roar of the first than to take on the hard task of making a republic.

Being a Republic

How to begin again? By recognising, in the first place, that something is over. The vague, incomplete half-republic that existed between 1922 and 2008 is gone for good. It survives, vestigially, as a puppet show. The institutional forms carry on as if nothing much had happened. Ministers strut around as if they were rulers of a sovereign state – except when they have to explain some especially nasty cutback and plead utter powerlessness, at which point they insist that the troika (the European Central Bank, the International Monetary Fund and the European Commission) made them do it. The Dáil continues to sit in all solemnity as if it did not know that the Bundestag has vastly more power of scrutiny over Irish economic and budgetary affairs than it does. The legal system continues to ponder the constitution, as if it had not been quietly set aside. The citizens even continue to vote in referendums, as if they were a sovereign people whose 'general will' is sacred. Everybody keeps a straight face: deadpan humour is the quintessential Irish mode.

Perhaps this show is necessary to preserve some semblance of collective dignity. There is, after all, a certain kindness in allowing people to save face, to go along with the story of the genteel beggar who tells you he's lost his wallet when you and he know very well that he is merely destitute. Keeping up appearances is not an ignoble or despicable enterprise. Irish culture even has its very own, rather touching phrase for it: 'the relics of old decency': 'When a man goes down in the world, he often preserves some memorials of his former rank, a ring, silver buckles in his shoes &c – the "relics of old decency".'[22]

But we also have to detach ourselves from this theatre of the absurd – to recognise that it is a show, even if, for appearances' sake, we have to carry on with it. This means facing an unpleasant truth: that the relics of old decency is exactly what Irish republicanism currently amounts to. It is the silver buckle in our scuff-heeled, toeless shoes. It still shines with idealism and self-sacrifice and the light of a desire for national dignity. It can bring back powerful memories. But in any form that is real and concrete and current, it is just a reminder of something that we do not now own.

And, in reality, never did. In the run-up to 2016, it is easy to lapse into mourning for the lost republic declared in 1916. But the point, surely, is that it was always lost. Ireland's relationship to its republic is that of a lothario to a conquest – feverish declarations of undying love, a moment of more or less satisfactory coupling and then a long, deep amnesia.

Owning up to this reality does not have to induce cynicism or fatalism – on the contrary. If we had something and lost it, the proper response would be to mourn the death of something precious. There is, on the other hand, a certain sober optimism in facing up to the truth that what we've lost is something that was always vague, half formed, contradictory and ultimately disabling. The Irish republic didn't collapse by accident – it imploded because it was gerry-built. It was philo-sophically incoherent, wide open to corruption and riven by contradictions. It lacked the mortar that holds republics together: the active, conscious consent and commitment of its citizens. The Irish people as a whole never accepted the res-ponsibility of making and minding a republic. But, in their defence, they were never clearly and openly offered that choice.

They do, however, know at least one thing about republics: that there's no point in declaring them. We've done it at least three times and much good it's done us. The gesture may be beautiful (as in 1916) or ridiculous (1949). But a republic is not a gesture. It is a long-term, open-ended contract. It asks hard questions and makes importunate demands: to be awake, to be alive, to be vigilant, to consider one's life as being lived not just in the family home and the immediate locality, not just in the workplace and the shopping mall – valid as all those arenas may be – but in that tough and potentially wonderful place called 'the public realm'.

So, the first task is to be simultaneously hard and easy on ourselves: hard on the illusions about what we have been and what we are now, and easy in the knowledge that realism creates the freedom to begin from scratch. If freedom really is a word for nothing left to lose, the Irish public realm is free. There is nothing to be saved, nothing to be salvaged – and therefore everything to be gained.

The second task is to decide. Lamartine's questions have to be asked and answered: Do you know what you are asking? Do you know what a republic means? Do you think you are prepared to be rulers of yourselves? And perhaps the answer is 'No, thanks.' People such as the present writer wish to imagine that there is no alternative to a radical reinvention of the Irish public realm as a real republic. But this is not true.

There is an alternative to a republic, one that is undoubtedly viable. Irish society and culture, in truth, have a rich bank of experience to draw on: experience of how to survive humiliation, domination, mass unemployment, mass emigration, psychological oppression, abuse and enforced servility. The culture, in many ways, has been shaped precisely by its reaction to these conditions. It adapts brilliantly to circumstances that other societies would find intolerable, not least by deciding that 'it could be worse'. Böll, astutely, noted that this ingrained cultural mechanism isn't merely passive. It is creative, even poetic: 'To persuade someone who has broken his leg, is lying in pain, or hobbling around in a plaster cast that it might have been worse, is not only comforting, it is an occupation requiring poetic talents.' Relativistic fatalism is a superb defence mechanism, drawing on Irish culture's immense resources of imaginative evasion and inventive denial. And, in fairness, this is not an entirely unrealistic impulse. When your history is as grim as Ireland's history is, it is quite logical to look at well-educated emigrants Skyping from Australia and think that it's not as bad as it was when we had an American wake for emigrants because they were effectively dead to their communities in which they were born. It is perfectly reasonable to buckle down to a decade of stumping up extra taxes to pay off the gambling debts of Sean FitzPatrick of Anglo Irish Bank and Michael 'Fingers' Fingleton of Irish Nationwide and think, 'Ah sure, it could be worse. We could be peasants in a thatched cottage having our rent raised because the master gambled us away on the faro table in his London club.'

So there is an option and it is one that is deeply embedded in Irish culture: making the best of a bad job. Arguably no nation on earth is more adept at this task. Irish culture has, quite literally, raised it to a fine art. It is the entire aesthetic of one of the great Irish geniuses, Samuel Beckett. As Beckett showed, it is a war we can fight with black humour, a sophisticated sense of irony, even a wistful, lyrical, poetry. The real Irish national anthem is not 'Amhrán na bhFiann', it is Gloria Gaynor's 'I Will Survive'. There is, as we also know very well, a price to be paid for this survival, a psychic distortion that manifests itself in secret horrors of abuse and depravity. But there is plenty of sanction from Irish history for the idea that this is a price worth paying.

There is a decision to be made. Ireland can hunker down for a long stretch of dependency and domination, and it is perfectly capable of doing so. Or it can confront the terrifying and exhilarating task of making a republic from scratch. But before that decision can be made, Lamartine's questions must be answered: Do you know what you are asking? Do you know what a republic means? If the first task is to acknowledge and the second to decide, the third is to know.

It is, in these days, rather unfashionable to suggest that people have a duty to educate themselves. But there's no way round this embarrassing truth. The basic precondition for a republic is that the people know what they're doing. That they should 'know what a republic means'. At the risk of obnoxious arrogance, it has to be admitted that, in general, the Irish people do not know what a republic means. This is not because they are ignorant. It is because 'republican' has become, in their public culture, a word that deserves either revulsion or contempt. It calls to the mind either the kleptocracy of Fianna Fáil The Republican Party or the viciousness of a self-appointed ethnic militia. Put the word 'republican' into the search engine of an archive such as that of the *Irish Times* and 99 per cent of the results will refer either to that embodied oxymoron, the US Republican Party, currently at war with every single principle of classical republican democracy, or to some deranged zealot who continues to believe that the only problem with the Irish republic is that not enough people have yet been killed in its name.

This bizarre reality means that Irish people don't just have to learn, they have to unlearn. The very word 'republican' is so debased that there is a very good case for simply abandoning it, at least in the Irish context, to the dustbin of history. What is the point of trying to give meaning to a word that has been so thoroughly corrupted?

The point, in fact, is twofold. There is, as this essay has attempted to sketch, a deep and resonant republican tradition that stretches back over thousands of years and that represents a strain of tolerance, decency and respect for genuine freedom that is remarkably resistant to the pressures of power, cruelty and imperious arrogance. Irish people are, after all, human, and humanity is not so overburdened with sources of hope that it can lightly give up on the few that it has. Republicanism is a form of sober, difficult but genuine optimism in which people make the choice to value the better aspects of their natures.

The second response to the question is itself a question: What is the alternative to this tough hope? Nothing but a surrender to the bleak belief that human beings are isolated, atomised, paranoid machines, programmed by their genes to kick each other in the face. It is society as a system of organised begrudgery. In the short term, such a system is perfectly viable, and the Irish, as a result of their history, are brilliantly adapted to survive within it. But is such a life worth living?

If it is not, then there is a duty to know, to be able to answer the Lamartine question: Do you know what a republic means? There is no avoiding the reality that this involves at least some engagement with the history of an idea. Classical republicanism isn't abstract; it has been formed and forged, tested and tempered, by people trying their best both to imagine and to create a sphere in which, in Philip Pettit's formulation, everyone could hold his or her head high and look everyone else in the eye. But it does demand, especially in the Irish context, the effort of firstly 'unknowing' a tradition of abusive or confused notions of republicanism and secondly engaging with a rich but essentially simple intellectual tradition. That engagement, in turn, has two aspects: the willingness of intellectuals to move out of their comfort zones and set out both to speak and to listen to a much wider public; and the willingness of that public to recognise that the deficit of ideas in Irish public discourse is not rooted in a deep respect for 'popular wisdom'. It is in fact a way of excluding people from power by leaving all important matters to experts, consultants, technocrats and a 'common sense' consensus that is usually a cover for the pursuit of very specific sectional interests.

Is it naive to think that people are willing to make the effort to 'know what a republic means'? Perhaps. But it has happened before. The quarter-century between roughly 1890 and 1916 was a time when hundreds of thousands of Irish people, women and men, engaged themselves in the hard task of trying to understand what a free Ireland would really mean. They went out after long days at work to study hard things: Irish grammar or lace-making or the economics of agricultural co-operation. It is true that they were not, in the end, rewarded with the creation of the republic that their efforts deserved. But they did create that substratum of civic dignity on which a republic could have been built. It is worth something, though, that they deserved better than they got and that the current generation of Irish people has a much softer task. It is already highly literate and sophisticated. The basics of republican philosophy are easy to grasp. But they do come with a condition attached: once grasped, they create civic obligations that are as imposing as they are compelling.

After acknowledgement, decision and knowledge, there is a fourth task: to fight. Republics don't 'come dropping slow,/ Dropping from the veils of the morning to where the cricket sings'. They are born at breaking points. There comes a point at which an existing order becomes intolerable, but that point is itself unpredictable. Who knows precisely which of a billion straws breaks the back of the over-burdened beast that is a citizenry loaded with private debt? The task of republicanism is to identify the right straw.

It is a matter of certainty that Ireland's circumstances of so-called austerity dictated from Berlin and Frankfurt will generate resistance. But, in the absence of a coherent public ethic and a self-respecting citizenry, there is every chance that the breaking point will be one that has no possibility of being a catalyst for something bigger than itself. If the breaking point is septic tanks or a €100 property tax, it will have no purchase on a possible future. It will function merely as a pressure valve, a release of steam after which some meaningless but ostentatious concessions will be made and the general view will be that 'things could be worse'.

Of the many possible final straws, there are, in truth, only two that might spark a real republic in the resulting friction. They are clearly labelled. One is called 'justice' and the other 'equality'. Both, as it happens, are central to the republican project. And this is the fifth task that any ambition to create a republic must face. After acknowledgement, decision, knowing and fighting, come the interlinked struggles for justice and equality. Both are animating principles of the classical republic. And neither, in Ireland's immediate and pressing crisis, have the slightest chance of being addressed in the absence of a real republic. Justice and equality are the forces that make the Irish republic an urgent necessity. Without them, Ireland will be, for the foreseeable future, a Home Rule outpost of a well-meaning but distant Reich. But if they are to mean anything at all, a dignified republic is the only viable possibility.

They sound, of course, like empty pomposities: justice, equality. But concepts cease to be empty and abstract when you experience their precise opposites: flagrant injustice and shameless inequality. And Ireland knows with great clarity what injustice means: the imposition of monumental levels of private gambling debt on the citizenry as a whole. Ireland has been plunged into an existential crisis, not by the stupidities of public policy whose name is legion, but by an utterly incomprehensible and obviously demented decision to assume all private banking debt as a public responsibility. This is a grotesque example of the way injustice results from the absence of a functioning republic. In a republic, the instinctive common sense of citizens would have bridled at the notion that each one of them should work part of his or her day for every day of the foreseeable future to pay off the liabilities of, for example, a German bank that lent money to a private Irish bank that lent it on to an English investor to speculate on an office block in Manhattan.

Basic civic virtue would have prevented this disaster. If the citizenry as a whole had the power it should have in a real republic, the proposition that this same citizenry should be punished collectively for the greed and idiocy of private individuals would not have merited a moment's debate. A republic based on the freedom of its citizens could not possibly allow those citizens to be shackled to obligations they did not, at any point, consent to. Equally, that same citizenry would have a sufficiently strong sense of dignity that it would refuse to accept the injustice of the proposition that an autistic child should be deprived of basic services so that a speculative investor who took a stupid risk on a corrupt bank should have every dollar of his failed gambling stake 'honoured'. A republic would see that its own honour was considerably more at stake in its treatment of a desperately vulnerable child than in its obsequiousness towards a spiv who bought in to a bubble economy at the height of its fantasy. The assumption of a republic is that so-called ordinary citizens understand the idea of justice more clearly than their supposed betters do. The Irish crisis proves the point.

Equality makes the same demand for the necessity of a republic. Even if we accept that so-called 'austerity' is the inevitable response to the crisis that has overtaken Ireland, any basic idea of public morality would impose one condition: share the pain fairly. But the reality is that a non-republican, Home Rule system will not meet even this minimal standard. In the crudest, most minimal idea of austerity, those who have most would make the largest sacrifices. But Home Rule under Berlin and Frankfurt has had exactly the opposite effect: the poor have borne more of the burden than the rich. Austerity, in its classic meaning in societies such as post-war Britain, cut deeply into the excesses of privilege and narrowed the gap between the top and the bottom. But Ireland's austerity has had precisely the opposite effect. The gap between the lowest earners and highest has actually increased dramatically. In 2009, the top 20 per cent earned 4.3 times what the lowest 20 per cent got. In 2010, the multiple was 5.5 per cent. The overwhelming likelihood is that this trend has been embedded within an 'austerity' project that shows an austere visage towards the weak while smiling warmly on the strong. Which means that, if the project continues for another decade, the result will be a society so divided that it can no longer be imagined as a political community. Ireland will have been repartitioned – this time along the lines not of ethnicity or religion but of class.

Injustice and inequality are now starkly visible. They are the governing principles of the new polity. The choice is either to learn to live with them by forgetting the republic again – this time for good – or to cease to have either to remember or to forget the republic because it has become a reality.

2

The Republic as a Tradition and an Ideal in Ireland Today

ISEULT HONOHAN

Introduction

In Ireland, 'the republic' is an ideal that is readily invoked but its meaning is not entirely clear and unambiguous. There has been a trend in recent times to reclaim it from its identification with the pursuit of national independence through military means, and to use it to represent a broader and more intangible ideal of the kind of society that Ireland could become, with the implication that this has either not yet been fully realised, or that the country has drifted away from it in various ways. Thus recent invocations speak of 'realising', 'reclaiming', or 'renewing' the republic.

The ideal to which we are being recalled is usually seen as specifically Irish, but within a broader European or Atlantic frame. Here I address what republicanism means in the broader tradition, and the way in which Irish republicanism has fitted into this tradition. I suggest that republicanism has something to offer in our current predicament, and conclude by identifying some challenges that arise, and pitfalls that should be avoided.

Republican Ideals

The broad republican tradition originated in Greece and Rome, and was developed in Italian Renaissance city states (especially Florence), seventeenth-century England and in the American and French Revolutions. Republican ideas were articulated in these contexts by thinkers from Cicero through Machiavelli and Rousseau. There have been many different kinds of republics, and republican ideals have been interpreted in many different ways. But we can identify three principal themes that distinguish republicanism from mainstream liberalism, nationalism and other political traditions.

I

It expresses a commitment to realising *freedom in the context of interdependence* among those who are subject to a common power or government.

This is freedom understood in contrast to slavery, or 'non-domination', defined as not being subject to the arbitrary will of others. This is also in contrast to simple 'non-interference' – not being interfered with at any one point in time. The danger of domination arises within society from individuals and groups, as well as from the state. To reduce domination by increasing security from the threat of interference – rather than simply providing recourse to law after the event – is quite demanding. It is achieved firstly through political structures that institutionalise the rule of law; a republic, in James Harrington's term, is 'the empire of *law* and not of men'.[1] The law must give all citizens a significant and secure equal status that allows each to look the other in the eye.[2] In addition, reducing the threat of arbitrary power also requires limiting the concentration of executive power, which can itself be dominating. Thus the rule of law is combined with an emphasis on the dispersal of power – through formal separation of powers, constitutional limits and balances, and measures providing for accountability.

Freedom, on this long-standing and recently rearticulated view, is something that has to be achieved, and it is fragile. It needs more than the legal structures and limits on central-government power that mainstream liberals have tended to emphasise.

2

The second feature of the republican tradition is an emphasis on *self-government*. A republic is a polity of self-governing citizens. It is this, rather than either national independence or the absence of a monarch per se that is implied in the republican idea of the sovereignty of the people. As citizens are interdependent, however, their freedom is not so much a matter of individual autonomy or independence, but of participating in determining, to the extent that this is possible, their joint future. As Hannah Arendt put it, 'the ideal of uncompromising self-sufficiency and mastership is contradictory to the very condition of plurality'.[3] To use the metaphor of authorship that is sometimes invoked in this context, it is not so much a matter of being the sole author of one's life, but being a joint author of the collective life of the polity. It involves the possibility that citizens can be to a greater or lesser extent active in their own self-rule. This may include some degree of representation rather than extensive direct participation, and may be a matter of being enabled and prepared to contest unjust laws and policies rather than continuous involvement in politics; but republicans see politics as a matter of self-government rather than simply representation of interests.

This constitutes one dimension of the 'active citizenship' associated with the republican tradition.

It should be noted that in this tradition, citizens are regarded as people who become interdependent, through a common history, and by virtue of being subject to, and potentially dominated by, the same government – a much broader conception than the nationalist idea of citizenship being defined simply by membership of the same national group.

3

The third feature of republicanism is the idea that a primary goal of politics is *the common good* shared among citizens. The Latin from which the term 'republic' comes, *res publica*, 'the public thing', conveys just this – that the aim of the republic is to provide for the common good, rather than sectional or purely individual interests. This does not mean overriding all individual interests (which would itself constitute domination), but recognising the importance of common interests. Unlike individual interests, common interests are not secured by markets, which even tend to erode them. The rule of law and formal institutions cannot themselves sustain them. This depends also on the attitude of citizens, who internalise the common good, recognise the importance of their common interests, or develop *civic virtue*, which essentially means an inclination to put public shared interests before their private interests where necessary. Because there is a natural tension between individual private and common public interests, this too is a fragile achievement; it does not come naturally. The inherent tendency for individuals to put private interests first is one aspect of corruption. Countering it requires education in awareness of the common nature of common interests, and willingness to consider shared interests and the opinions of others. Hence the importance of education in the republican tradition. (See the discussion in Tom Hickey's essay in this book.) Yet, for republicans personal corruption is part of a wider feature of the fragility of republican self-government, such that institutions tend to decay away from their initial purpose and to need renewal.

This commitment and taking of responsibility constitutes the second dimension of active citizenship.

What Republicanism Is Not

Interpretations of and priorities among these core elements have varied; so have the institutional forms intended to realise them – from unitary to federal, more or less aristocratic to more or less democratic systems. The republic thus cannot be easily identified with any one political form.

The ideal of citizen self-government in the republican tradition is not to be identified simply with 'pure democracy' or majoritarian rule; the aim is not so much to rule others as not to be ruled by them. As Machiavelli wrote, the people in a republic 'neither arrogantly dominate nor humbly serve'.[4]

In addition, although the equal status of citizens implies that there should be certain limits of inequality among citizens, republicanism does not provide a specific economic and social model; it is not socialism. For early modern republicans dependence could be avoided by citizens only if they were property owners; since then, there has been right- and left-wing republicanism, and it has been combined with egalitarian, socialist, conservative, and other positions, some inherently more compatible with it than others. In Marx's work reflecting on the rise of Napoleon III from the revolution in France in 1848, *The Eighteenth Brumaire of Louis*

Napoleon, he dismissed as 'republicans in yellow gloves' the more socially conservative participants among the divided revolutionaries.

What Republicanism Can Offer Today

Even if it does not provide a blueprint for society or support a particular economic strategy, republican ideas have something to offer in this period of crisis and change. They point at least to some important areas we need to reconsider. It should be borne in mind that republican theory in the past has been developed, not by armchair theorists, but by those in the midst of political crisis from Cicero in the dying days of the Roman republic to Machiavelli in Florence threatened by the domination of the Medici, and James Madison in the early United States, attempting to create new institutions to suit a large modern republic.

The ideals of non-domination, participation in self-government, and the dispersal of power are essential to political reform. This requires not just constructing more efficient institutions, but also re-empowering citizens, and finding ways to regulate domination by agents other than the state, whether economic or social.

Such reform, and any politics that might emerge from it, needs to maintain a focus on the common good. But one argument for greater democracy, formalised by the French revolutionary and mathematician Nicolas de Condorcet, and once more now the focus of attention in democratic theory, is that the more people are consulted and the greater the number of different points of view that are brought to bear, the better may be the answers reached to the questions society faces, and that therefore we should not leave these questions to experts. This depends, however, on citizens, in making decisions, being willing to take into account other positions and common interests. Responsible citizenship requires a deliberative approach to political participation. This is the 'jury' model of democracy, as distinct from the 'marketplace' model of democracy, where citizens are thought of as expressing or defending their own interests, and producing a result that represents the best resolution of individual interests.

♦ Finally, economic globalisation and engagement in supranational institutions and international treaties and agreements mean that interdependence (and the threat of domination) extends more intensively beyond state boundaries than ever before. It follows for republican theory that institutional provision for non-domination needs to think beyond national boundaries, and the idea of the republican state, based on interdependence, may be better able to adapt to this than the idea of the national state, based on ethnic affinity or similarity.

Irish Republicanism

In Ireland, republicanism has – at least since the early nineteenth century – been conflated with nationalism, with revolutionary austerity, an authoritarian political style, and especially with separatism from Britain. Thus there has often been a narrow focus on national independence and the means by which it can be secured rather than on freedom and non-domination. (Hence W. B. Yeats's couplet, 'Parnell came down the road and said to the cheering man: "Ireland will get her freedom and you still break stone."')

The range of positions of those who styled themselves republican has led some writers to see it more or less as an inconsistent, empty term.[5] In Ireland, too, as in the broader tradition, it has included positions as divergent as those of James Connolly, Eamon de Valera, Sean O Faoláin and, more recently, Gerry Adams and Michael McDowell. There was a more systematic and coherent tradition of republican thought, articulated most notably by the United Irishmen, that carried right through the nineteenth century.[6] But it has never become the official ideology of the Irish state, as it is in France.

When not confused with nationalism, republicanism has featured in Irish discourse as a call to return to the origins of what is seen as positive in the country. It is especially used to invoke a tradition of non-sectarianism that stretches back to 1798. Indeed, reflecting on the three key ideals of freedom, self-government and the common good, we can see how they can be brought to bear on some of the frequently criticised features of Irish politics: its clientilism represents a form of dependence on representatives rather than on active delibera-tion by concerned citizens; its centralised government institu-tions represent the distancing of government from the people; and its traditional localism and more recent tendency towards hedonistic individualism can run counter to the common good. Republicanism in this sense has also been associated in the discourse of both the former President, Mary MacAleese, and her successor, Michael D. Higgins, with the need to focus on the common good and equality of citizens, to move away from individualist consumerism, and for citizens to address political, social and economic issues in terms of constructing their common future as well as amending the practices that brought about the economic and political crisis in the first place.

In this light, more than merely institutional political reform, such as the reduction of the number of TDs, or the abolition of the Senate, needs to be considered. It is not as important that the republic should be mentioned in the constitution, as it is that there should be both greater accountability and a sense of responsibility in the exercise of power. Citizens also need to be able to reclaim some power. This would be more extensive than in the experiment involved in the *We the Citizens* project. (See Elaine Byrne's essay in this book.) But that project at least provided an insight into some of the possibilities and difficulties of a deliberative politics that aims to engage citizens more substantially than current electoral politics in Ireland.

Challenges

Attempting to realise the ideals of the republic in the present very difficult climate involves substantial challenges. These are not all economic. Here I will focus on just two.

First there is the question of how to deal with the increasing diversity of Irish society since the 1990s, and how to integrate immigrants as full members of society or citizens.

From a republican perspective the state is the body of those who are interdependent in their subjection to a common government, and who have developed a common history, rather than some essential pre-political national identity. In so far as immigrants are subject to the power of government, they are at risk of domination. In fact, in contemporary liberal democratic constitutional states immigrants and non-citizens are perhaps those most likely to be subject to the arbitrary and discretionary power of government, whether at their point of entry to the country, in their applications for work or residence status, or in their attempts at family reunification.

They too have a claim to participation in self-government, but they lack full political rights – even though Ireland is more inclusive than many other countries in granting local voting and standing rights to all residents. While the general requirements for acquiring citizenship through naturalisation are not particularly onerous compared with other European countries, the fact that the process is still ultimately subject to ministerial discretion needs to be addressed.

There is also the question of how much accommodation should be made to both indigenous and immigrant cultural and religious practices. Here again, we should think twice before assuming that the French model of the republic, which is strictly neutralist and secularist (in, for example, banning women from covering their faces in public), is the only or necessarily best way to go. Rather than a neutralist (or hands-off) approach to cultural and religious diversity, which allows people to carry on cultural and religious practices in private but insists on a neutral public realm, an even-handed approach may be more compatible with the republican principle of non-domination. Such an approach would acknowledge the particularity of citizens, and aim to accommodate different practices to which they are committed, where there are no serious reasons based in justice that do not outweigh them.[7] The increasing diversity of Irish society requires us also to rethink what it means to be Irish. This is a process that has hardly begun, though the extensive reflection on Irish identity over the last forty years and the attempt to create a more generous definition that could include the Protestant and Unionist population in Northern Ireland, offers an encouraging precedent.

The second challenge is what it means to be a republic in a world of global interdependence. It is no longer (if it ever was) appropriate to conceive of the world as a set of wholly autonomous or self-sufficient states, each sovereign in at least four dimensions – internally with respect to their populations, externally with respect to other states and also to individuals seeking admission to the territory and to membership in the state, and internationally as having the capacity to engage in international agreements. The fact of international inter-dependence and the potential for domination across borders requires a rethinking of republican theory itself – and a more nuanced account of sovereignty, in terms not of the state but of the people, and in terms not of mastery, but of non-domi-nation. In such an approach, sovereignty would not imply complete independence of international political institutions, but rather security from arbitrary external interference through, for example, greater accountability of international institu-tions, and more democratic engagement in their decision-making.[8] This, as we have seen, is a challenge for republican theory itself, but one it might have the resources to meet.

Pitfalls to Be Avoided

There are a number of pitfalls that can arise in connection with the invocation of republican ideas. These are not neces-sarily inherent in republicanism, though they may result from its misinterpretation. I shall mention four.

The first pitfall, which is associated with popular sover-eignty, is *populism*. This represents the body of citizens, 'the people', as an abstract, homogeneous entity. Perhaps it would help to understand the ideal of popular sovereignty as entail-ing that 'people' are self-ruling, rather than that there is some-thing called 'the' people, which is self-ruling. There is a truth that underlies populism: that it is people and not the state or its appointed or elected officials that are sovereign, and that contemporary liberal democratic government has distanced itself from its citizens and tended to monopolise power. But populist approaches, in reaction to this, tend to draw an exaggerated contrast between the people and an internal or external enemy, whether this be identified as elites, political parties, corrupt politicians, strident minorities, or the media and others.[9] They may offer simplistic solutions, which reject the complex procedures and compromises that politics entails. Furthermore, those who call on the authority of the people may be self-appointed spokesmen, closer to AstroTurf than grass roots. If such movements are authoritarian and exclusionary in their definition of the people, and oppose all established institutional power, they may undermine the possibility of citizens actually becoming empowered and involved in decisions about their future.

While excessive individualism or self-interest, and the way that this fed into unthinking support for many neoliberal positions, may have been the besetting vice of the Celtic Tiger period, it may be that populism is a comparable danger now.

A second pitfall, associated with active citizenship, is an *overemphasis on service* or the responsibility of citizens at the expense of empowering them. This focus on service is a widespread tendency, which can be seen in the direction taken by the Taskforce on Citizenship, set up by Bertie Ahern when Taoiseach, and in the 'Big Society' programme of David Cameron's government, and has long been a tendency in formal citizenship education. Where responsibility and commitment is expected, divorced from extending the resources or capacity of people to act, and independent of participation in political decision-making, citizens can end up being subject to increased domination.

Thirdly, as already noted, it is a mistake to take other models, for example the USA or France, as a blueprint or essential realisation of a republic. This is quite common among commentators in Ireland. France is indeed the state most self-conscious of its republicanism, but it is a very specific realisation, developed in the context of France's unique history. Moreover, in facing the challenges of dealing with diversity and globalisation, it has not necessarily adopted the laws and policies most appropriate for a republicanism that wishes to deal justly with cultural diversity.[10] In any case, to determine what kind of republic is possible in Ireland, it is necessary to examine what follows from basic republican principles, given our particular history and where we find ourselves now.

Finally, in response to the pressures and constraints from Europe and beyond that have been a result of the economic crisis, there is a risk of invoking republicanism to support a form of isolationism. While it is beyond question that our loss of sovereignty needs to be addressed, there is also a need to work out what sovereignty might mean in an interdependent world – and whatever this will be, it will not be self-sufficiency or withdrawal from international institutions. 'Sinn féin', the historic slogan, might be better translated as 'we ourselves'– taking initiatives and assuming responsibility – rather than 'ourselves alone' – cutting off connections – as it has often been understood in the past.

Republicanism cannot simply be taken ready-made off the rack. For those who see the republic as an ideal yet to be realised, there is a task ahead in reimagining it as a polity that protects its citizens from domination from other agents and groups in society and from state power, both within the state and externally. And there is a job to be done in thinking about what institutions best promote non-domination and the common good, and what it means for both indigenous residents and newcomers to be a citizen of a republic.

The Democracy of a Republic

ELAINE BYRNE

Democracy means rule by the people for the people but that does not mean that democracy is actually democratic. Democratic reform in the ninetieth and twentieth centuries meant the extension of the franchise irrespective of gender, property rights and age. The democratic reformers of the twenty-first century are less concerned about the quantity of opportunities to participate – that battle has largely been won – but rather on the quality of that participation. The focus instead will be on the capacity to impact meaningfully on decision-making rather than the paltry endorsement of a fait-accompli policy agenda.

The principles of liberty, equality and autonomy are not always best served through the collective expression of voting. If they were, parliaments around the world would not be dominated by well-educated, middle-class, middle-aged men but would reflect the age, gender, ethnicity and socio-economic background of the society they seek to represent. Democracy is, by its very nature, flawed. Majority rule often disappoints because it produces decisions that are determined by what is popular, as opposed to what is 'best'. The popular good and the public good compete with one another in a system that rewards short-term decision-making while encouraging the illusion of immediate and positive outcomes for the majority.

Participation is ultimately determined by individual self-interest disguised as collective action.

The global economic crisis exposed the fundamental weakness of this limited conception of democracy. The genesis of Ireland's current structural deficit was conceived by the 2002 and 2007 election contests. This was a period defined by auction politics for the purpose of achieving power. The manifestos of political parties were contradictory: they simultaneously promised low taxes and high public spending. The faculty for informed long-term decision-making is limited when there is an absence of knowledge and independent sources of truth. Democracy does not guarantee that the best decisions are made because the public have an insatiable demand for uncomplicated expediency.

This is the very antithesis of a republic. Well, at least the notion of what we in Ireland consider a republic to be. The violent struggle to fulfil the audacious demands of the 1916 proclamation of independence cost almost five thousand lives in the War of Independence and the Civil War. A further 3,722 died during the thirty-year conflict in Northern Ireland known colloquially as 'The Troubles'.

This human sacrifice for an Irish republic has been offered again and again in the absence of any proper definition or acknowledgement of what a republic is. Here lies Ireland's deepest contradiction. The Irish constitution does not contain the word republic. Although the 96 words of John A. Costello's 1948 Republic of Ireland Act state that Ireland is officially a republic, it never goes beyond this legal statement. Thousands may have died for the principle of republicanism but they did so without any formal expression of it since the 1916 proclamation.

If anything, the notion of a republic is an abstract political philosophy that was inherited by accident. Ireland's greatest revolutionaries were ambiguous about their ambitions for a republic. 'The British form of government was monarchical. In order to express clearly our desire to depart from all British forms, we declared a Republic.' Michael Collins went on to explain in his only published work, the *Path to Freedom*, that Ireland 'repudiated the British form of government, not because it was monarchical but because it was British. We would have repudiated the claim of a British Republic to rule over us as definitely as we repudiated the claim of the British monarchy.'

So, what can be done? What is the optimal means of ensuring that individual citizens decide what the 'best' possible collective decision should be? How can this be achieved within the context of a republic? Is it possible to marry the different ideals of democracy and republicanism? This essay seeks to explore how the quality of participation in the Irish polity can be improved. In doing so, it considers the contemporary challenges to democratic action.

Trilateral Commission 1975: Too Much Democracy

An influential book published in 1975, *The Crisis of Democracy: Report on the Governability of Democracies to the Trilateral Commission*, argued that the revolutionary decade of the 1960s had produced an 'excess of democracy'. Founded by David Rockefeller in 1973, the Trilateral Commission sought to 'bring together experienced leaders within the private sector to discuss issues of global concern', particularly between Europe, the United States and Japan. Only 'apathy and non-involvement' by citizens would ensure that order could be maintained. The expectations of citizens had to be lessened. Demands for greater democratic participation were dismissed. The political roadmap advocated by the Trilateral Commission, called for a pronounced reduction in the role of government through deregulation and privatisation and a confined public space. A crisis of democracy existed because there was simply too much democracy.

The Trilateral Commission demanded duty-based conformism, where participation in the bargaining process of democracy was narrowly confined to those who vote in each electoral cycle. Concepts of citizenship have traditionally stressed the responsibilities of citizenship and reinforced the existing political order and authority patterns. This elitist, top-down, model of democracy envisages a limited role for the citizen. This was especially evident in the intellectual assumptions underlying neoliberal thought in the 1970s, and so strikingly expressed in the Trilateral Commision's report.

People now, after three decades of unregulated free-market economics, wish to engage more in democracy, rather than merely voting for a political party once every few years. The definition of political participation has expanded into new forms of action such as signing petitions, joining citizen interest groups and engaging in unconventional forms of political action. Many people prefer to join public interest groups, social movements and NGOs rather than political parties. Political action is now characterised by direct forms of communication through the internet and mobile phones, by the emergence of generalised anti-establishment sentiment, the demand for democratic innovation and for the devolution of decision-making. This sea-change in citizens' expectations has occurred because attitudes to authority have simultaneously undergone a radical transformation.

This was especially evident in Richard Stengel's explanation for making Facebook's Mark Zuckerberg *Time Magazine*'s

2010 Person of the Year. 'There is an erosion of trust in authority, a decentralizing of power and at the same time, perhaps, a greater faith in one another.' The managing editor of *Time* also noted that Facebook 'has wired together a twelfth of humanity into a single network thereby creating a social entity almost twice as large as the US'. The boundaries of public and private, of openness and secrecy, will never be the same again.

Internet-based organisations such as Anonymous and WikiLeaks share Facebook's ethos of self-actualisation and autonomy but have taken it one step further by directly confronting influential gatekeepers who control the political and communications agenda. Anonymous, a decentralised online community, acts in a co-ordinated manner to attack the technological abilities of organisations through what is known as a distributed denial of service (DDoS). Such acts of civil disobedience have included attacks on the government websites of Tunisia, Egypt, Iran, Australia, Brazil, France, the United States and Ireland. Julian Assange's WikiLeaks imposed transparency on the world's only remaining super power with the release of 251,287 diplomatic cables that have proved embarrassing to the United States.

Anonymous and WikiLeaks have sought to defy the modus operandi of highly secretive elite institutions and redistribute information back into the hands of citizens. These republican-minded actions are the very antithesis of the traditional notions of authority espoused by the Trilateral Commission, which emphasised the values of obedience, unwavering loyalty and deference to centralised hierarchical structures.

The same is true of the global protest movements of the Arab spring, the Indignants movement in Spain and the global Occupy movement, which are woven together with the same underlying motivation to challenge unaccountable centres of economic and political power. Disproportionately well educated and young, these citizen-led initiatives are formed without encouragement from or endorsement by existing political forces. 'The power of the people is greater than the people in power' became the Egyptian pro-democracy slogan. All of these movements share in the belief that their countries' political systems and economies are dysfunctional and corrupt. All demand more accountable democratic structures with more meaningful prospects for people to participate in their own destinies. No surprise then that *Time* described 'The Protester' as 'fervent small-d democrats' in their conferral of the 2011 Person of the Year.

At the outset, it appeared that by virtue of their critical mass – rule by the people – the internet phenomena of Facebook, Anonymous, WikiLeaks and the global protest groups were redefining the social contract. The extent to which they changed the rules of the game remains to be seen. By mid-2012, the Occupy movement had dissipated, Islamism and military power had strangled the Arab spring and Assange's credibility was undermined by allegations of sexual crimes. None the less, by virtue of their existence and their underlying demands for greater democratic freedoms, these phenomena have punctured previous narratives of how participation was defined.

Deliberative Democracy

The existing challenges to democracy offer the possibility for the democratisation of democracy – the fulfilment, in a way, of the aspirations of the 1960s generation, which were denied by the Trilateral-style mindsets of the 1970s and 1980s governments, symbolised by the authoritarian populism of Thatcher and Reagan.

There is a crisis of trust in Irish public life. In the 2009 Eurobarometer poll, Ireland recorded virtually the lowest level of public trust in its political institutions across the twenty-seven European countries surveyed, with only Hungary, Latvia, Lithuania and Greece registering lower degrees of trust. This is not unique to Ireland. The Organisation for Economic Co-operation and Development (OECD) also observed in the same year, 'The financial crisis revealed failures of governance.' The OECD warned, 'For the sake of keeping the trust of voters, governments also need to be able to reassure citizens that their affairs are in safe hands.'

There is no magic-bullet solution to restore this trust. Governments and civil society in Iceland, Brazil, Canada and elsewhere have increasingly resorted to deliberative democracy as a mechanism to improve the process of decision-making. The fall in confidence and the perceived weakening of participation in formal politics has corresponded with the perception that a democratic deficit exists. Does this collapse in trust therefore demand a departure from the traditional institutional architecture of politics?

This renewal can be accomplished through deliberative democracy. This process emphasises the broad participation of citizens in the operation of political systems. It is an alternative means of reaching collectively binding decisions through reasoned agreement. Citizens have the opportunity to express their views and preferences and justify their decisions within this auxiliary institution, which serves to complement existing parliamentary structures. Above all, it improves the quality of participation. The renewed expectations of civil society, in terms of enhanced good governance and citizen empowerment, can deepen democracy by introducing 'lay' perspectives into policy areas where there has been limited involvement of citizens in decisions that profoundly affect their lives.

The pooling of knowledge and the sharing of life experiences widens the breadth of public understanding on complex issues. It can serve to educate the wider population. Deliberative democracy also has the potential to inject popular legitimacy into any proposed reform because it introduces transparency and accountability into policy-making by encouraging citizens to scrutinise the decisions of their representatives. Moreover, it promotes greater popular engagement with democratic institutions because it gives citizens the power to take ownership of decisions.

Political decisions are ultimately about making trade-offs between competing interests. The scarcity of goods in a democracy forces elected representatives to determine how best to distribute limited resources. The decisions about and delivery of these goods have tended to operate within a closed and secretive system. Irish politics, for instance, has in the past been captured by vested interests. The 'bricks and beef' cabals of developers and cattle barons have unduly influenced the formulation of public policies, laws and regulations for their private benefit.

Open scrutiny of the criteria and justifications used for the allocation of public commodities therefore helps to expose inequalities within the system. It also gives expression to the very definition of a republic where the supreme power rests in the body of citizens and not the vested interests of a few. The 'best' possible collective decision can be made only when the citizen body actively contributes to choices made on its behalf.

The definition of a republic also entails that the supreme power that rests within the citizen body is ultimately exercised by representatives chosen directly or indirectly by them. The necessity to engage in trade-offs, and the difficult decisions that this demands, is often not fully appreciated by a public that has to bear the costs of such decisions. The capacity of politicians to justify their decisions to the public is quite low in a climate that is distinguished by a fervent distrust of politics. Anti-politics has to be replaced by more realistic democratic mechanisms.

Deliberative Democracy in Ireland: *We the Citizens*

Deliberative democracy was tested throughout Ireland in 2011 in a civil-society initiative, generously funded by Atlantic Philanthropies. Elaine Byrne, David Farrell, Eoin O'Malley and Jane Suiter were members of the academic team.

We the Citizens had two distinct stages, at regional and national level. Seven open-door, open-agenda events were organised in Blanchardstown, Tallaght, Letterkenny, Athlone, Kilkenny, Cork and Galway. The regional events partially informed the agenda of a subsequent national Citizens' Assembly in Dublin. The formula was simple. The process of deliberation was the same for both the regional and national events. Members of the public participated in a round-table facilitated meeting, which encouraged a constructive rather than negative dialogue. Each table had a facilitator who fostered discussion by ensuring that everyone had the opportunity to speak and that no single person dominated the conversation. The deliberative format was designed to give everyone the opportunity to raise their own viewpoints and to allow for disagreement. This consensus-building technique – through argument and justification – facilitated greater engagement and mutual respect. The tone of the debates was noticeably non-aggressive and allowed for issues to be discussed freely and openly. The participants at both the regional and national events welcomed the depoliticised nature of the deliberation. 'Eoin', for instance, contrasted this experience with the confrontational and adversarial tenor of parliamentary debates: 'The Dáil is all about verbally defeating your opponent's argument. People don't really listen to one another. If someone has a 180-degree u-turn on something, it's regarded as a sign of weakness rather than a response to logic.'

A series of polls was carried out by in a professional polling company before the national Citizens' Assembly met. Ipsos MRBI asked a representative sample of the Irish population a number of survey questions. Some of these questions were framed as a consequence of the issues that emerged from the regional events. Ipsos MRBI recruited 100 people from this original sample of 1,242 people to attend the Citizens' Assembly. In the weeks following the Assembly, Ipsos MRBI carried out a second series of surveys, to see if participants' opinions had shifted because of their involvement in the deliberative experiment and to what extent.

Participants represented a cross-section of Irish society in terms of age, gender, ethnicity, religion and socio-economic background. In other words, they were a better mirror image of the Irish population than those elected to the parliamentary legislature. As 'Áine' said, 'The people here looked like me. When I watch Oireachtas reports, the politicians are usually male, middle-class teachers, farmers and barristers.'

The Evidence

The polls showed statistically significant changes as a consequence of participation in the deliberative experiment. Not only did people's opinions shift on policy issues, but citizens felt more empowered because of their involvement in the Citizens' Assembly. This is borne out in the evidence presented in Table 1. On a scale of 1 to 7, where 1 is strongly disagree and 7 is strongly agree, participants had a greater interest in politics, a greater willingness to discuss politics and a decline in the belief that ordinary people have no influence.

Table 1

	Interest in Politics	Willingness to discuss politics	More willing to get involved in politics	Ordinary people have no influence?
Before Citizens' Assembly	5.22	5.2	4.51	4.42
After Citizens' Assembly	5.7	5.65	5.74	4.0

The biggest change observed was a willingness to become more involved in politics. The *We the Citizens* experiment conferred a belief among participants that they had the ability to influence outcomes. This was very noticeable over the course of the weekend. People developed confidence as the two days progressed. This was especially evident among women and young men. Participants said that they had never taken part in lengthy political discussions because they did not think their opinions mattered. When they were given the chance to voice their views, they did so with growing self-assurance.

This was particularly pronounced among women. Before the process, 35 per cent of female participants believed that they could have no influence on politics, and this feeling of impotence diminished by 14 points to 21 per cent after the process. This suggests that the deliberative method not only encourages a greater parity of participation but supports the evidence that women are turned off by the adversarial nature of formal politics. A sentiment shared by a female participant, 'Roisin': 'What I got out of this was that it took the discussion on politics away from the politicians. I got to participate about the questions that affect my daily life. For one evening at least, that made a change.'

Aside from the evidence demonstrating increased trust in political action, *We the Citizens* also proved that participants' opinions shifted on policy issues when they had the opportunity to become better informed and to debate the trade-offs associated with them.

Expert witnesses provided testimony on a range of topics such as economic issues and political reform. To that end, the Citizens' Assembly members heard from two fiscal specialists who represented very different sides of the argument on tax increases and spending cuts. Fergal O'Brien of the Irish Business and Employers Confederation (IBEC), told the participants that 'it would be impossible to achieve a balanced budget without reducing public expenditure'. He acknowledged that 'some tax increases' might be necessary though the Irish industry spokesperson believed that 'the bulk of the adjustment must be on the expenditure side'. In contrast, Dr Nat O'Connor of the left-leaning TASC (Think Tank for Action on Social Change), outlined why he was 'generally opposed to cuts' and instead advocated for 'increased taxation to pay for quality public services'.

This access to balanced information facilitated reflective judgements by participants and the time to develop preferences.

'John' stated the obvious about his experiences in the Assembly: 'When we shared the information among ourselves it turned out that what we were actually doing was pooling our knowledge and our life experiences. It was like being on a jury.'

The survey results found that there were considerable effects on the attitudes of the participants when it came to economic beliefs. The fiscal position of the attendees at the *We the Citizens* initiative moved significantly on every economic question they were asked. As Table 2 shows, 48 per cent of participants were in favour of the sale of state assets before the Citizens' Assembly met but this had fallen to 10 per cent when the same individuals were polled after the event. As a consequence of increased information and the space they were given for deliberation, over a third of participants reversed their views on the sale of state assets. On the question of property tax, just 40 per cent of participants were in favour before the weekend, but this jumped to 56 per cent by the end of the weekend. A similar shift took place on the question of water charges with a 25 per cent change in attitudes before and after, adjusting from 60 per cent in favour to 85 per cent.

Table 2

	In favour of property tax	In favour of water charges	In favour of the sale of state assets
Before the Citizens' Assembly	40%	60%	48%
After the Citizens' Assembly	56%	85%	10%

Lessons from Ireland

The Citizens' Assembly model offers three possible alternatives for democratic engagement:

1   The Citizens' Assembly produces a specific proposal for change that may be directly acted upon by the government in the form of a legislative act.

2   In a case where a matter has constitutional significance, the Citizens' Assembly produces the wording for the referendum question. This may go to a parliamentary committee for consideration or be put to the people in a referendum.

3   In the case where the matter in question relates to local budgetary issues, the decision of the Citizens' Assembly should have a direct impact on a portion of budgetary expenditure in the local area.

The evidence proves that participants are more disposed to accept tax increases as a consequence of expert testimony and deliberation. However the methodological framework in which this data was collected must also be considered. The time allocated for the IBEC and TASC evidence was fifteen minutes, or seven and half minutes each. The time spent on deliberation of the three policy areas, relating to property taxes, water charges and the sale of state assets, was one hour in total or twenty minutes each. These debates were fractured and the feedback by participants noted that they had insufficient time for discussion.

None the less, a shift in opinions did occur. 'Aoife', for example, was adamant about her opinions before her participation: 'I wasn't sure what the point of me coming to the Citizens' Assembly was. I have very fixed opinions on lots of things. My mind was made up a long time ago on a range of issues.' Aoife was 'surprised because my opinion changed on some things when I got new information from the expert witnesses who made me think differently about some of the topics'. Changes of mind were also observed on the questions of political reform that were discussed. For instance, deliberation on the role of Dáil deputies prompted participants to assert that TDs should concentrate more on national legislative and policy work and less on local services.

The reason why people's views and attitudes changed varied. The facilitators who moderated the deliberations were aware the extent to which the tone and ethos of the debate ensured that participants genuinely listened to one another. This was evident in the case of two participants who had distinctly diverse life experiences. 'John' was very pro-environment while 'Shauna' was very pro-business and entrepreneurial and rarely gave much thought to the environment. However, after hearing the thoughts of John, Shauna said she had never considered how the environment can be part of economic growth rather than the two being mutually exclusive. Michael Courtney, the facilitator of that discussion, believed that Shauna's 'way of thinking had been significantly affected by someone who she would otherwise never have met'.

Public debate often becomes polarised into black or white positions. 'Playing the man, not the ball' becomes the de facto approach for an anti-intellectual public discourse that feeds on straw men. The space for pluralist discussion narrows when the opportunity to engage with those from different socio-economic, generational, ethnic, gender or even professional backgrounds is limited. The randomness of the selection was crucial. This cross-cutting participation exposed individuals to dissimilar views from that of their normal life experience. A willingness to accept unfamiliar points of view of course depends on how open people are to alternative stances.

We the Citizens prioritised deliberation on political reform issues such as gender quotas, the role of TDs, reform of the Seanad (the upper house of the Irish parliament) and the electoral system rather than matters relating to Ireland's relationship with the European Union, membership of the euro, the possibility of default on the national debt, the deficit and the conditions imposed on the Irish population by the EU–IMF–ECB bailout. Although they were a feature of the discussions at the regional events, the original Ipsos MRBI survey did not focus on these questions. These issues were regarded as too contentious and politically unsound for the Assembly process, a view not shared by this author, who served as a member of the academic team on the project.

If the objective of a Citizens' Assembly is to include citizens more directly in decision-making, then the agenda of any such deliberation is best informed by the issues that citizens themselves wish to discuss. The public legitimacy of a truly deliberative process is dependent on the avoidance of what political theorists call 'salience transfer'. According to agenda-setting theory, salience transfer refers to the ability of particular stakeholders to transfer their agendas or issues onto the public agenda. It is only when citizens feel that they own the agenda from the outset that the process itself can capture public imagination. The Fine Gael–Labour government established the Irish Constitutional Convention in 2012. There was no consultation with the public regarding the topics for discussion. A third of the Convention's seats were reserved for political representatives which defeats the very notion of deliberative democracy.

A depoliticised process may be politically expedient because it deprioritises certain issues. As 'Eadaoin' observed during the Citizens' Assembly weekend, 'I'm concerned that if a Citizens' Assembly is introduced by the government for some decisions, it will be used by politicians to give the perception of legitimacy but will actually diffuse momentum for change.' A clear policy implementation process is therefore necessary to ensure that decisions are followed through with political action.

Is it realistic though for deliberative democracy to act as a fourth popular branch of government? Can decisions made through this process claim greater legitimacy than those in a representative democracy? The establishment of a fourth branch of government is not without its difficulties. It would necessitate a clear relationship and power structure in its relations with the judiciary, the executive and the legislature. An institutionalised system of checks and balances is necessary. A fourth branch would necessitate the redefining of roles. If the legislature represents the representative branch of democracy, the executive is popularly elected and the judiciary is appointed, which branch of government would have the legitimacy to curb this new fourth branch?

The Corruption of Democracy

Deliberative democracy offers the possibility of embracing republican ideals at a time when the democratic deficit has widened very sharply. The lack of trust in Irish institutions, as identified earlier, can only have multiplied with the deepening of the global economic crisis. The public's expectations about its democracy have been undermined. Irish citizens are no longer remote from decision-making; they are completely removed from it because the representative function of democracy has been made redundant.

The intervention of the IMF, the ECB and the EU into Irish domestic policy-making has warranted the introduction of conditionality into every aspect of internal decision-making. The IMF defines conditionality as an agreement by a government to 'adjust its economic policies to overcome the problems that led it to seek financial aid from the international community'. This reliance on international organisations is diluting democracy. Rule by the people for the people is emasculated when the policy straitjacket of conditionality is worn. When governments sign up to loan agreements, their decision-making capacity is limited because of the conditional nature of such arrangements. This loss of economic sovereignty was nowhere more apparent than the German Bundestag's review of confidential details of the Irish budget in November 2011, three weeks before the Irish parliament debated the measures and again in March 2012. The Tánaiste (deputy prime minister) Eamon Gilmore said he was 'unhappy' about these incidents.

The real effect of external participation in a country's domestic affairs is ultimately the decline of democratic practices. The forces that drive IMF policies – heavily influenced by the major Western powers – have in the past been accused of being insensitive to their social impact. When the burden of structural readjustment falls disproportionately on those who depend on social and public services, the upshot is civil unrest. As happened in Greece in 2011, the government feels that it has no other option but to limit civil liberties in the attempt to subdue the social upheaval that results from the stark structural readjustment prescribed by the IMF and others. The deep sense of public contempt for the political class can then potentially cannibalise the very belief in the possibility of political action. The overwhelming perception that a country's institutions are weak, incompetent and illegitimate feeds into the destructive notion that politics is futile.

This belief in the ineffectual nature of politics gained support among some unlikely bedfellows on the left and the right in Ireland. Both argued that non-elected parliamentarians should become ministers. Fianna Fáil's 2011 pre-election manifesto contained many of the same reform proposals that appeared in a document circulated to leading public figures by one of Ireland's wealthiest and most controversial businessmen, Dermot Desmond. Peter Sutherland, chair of Goldman Sachs International and European honorary chair of the Trilateral Commission, assisted with the document.

Authored by two Irish political scientists, *Ireland First: Political Reform – Effective and Efficient Government* called for the appointment of external Ministers. It did however include the polite concession to democracy that 'in order to maintain the link with voters . . . a majority of the cabinet should have been elected as TDs'. Democratic legitimacy is now considered an unnecessary extravagance or an optional extra. The indignity of asking the public for their trust through the democratic apparatus of voting is routinely dismissed and steadily eroded.

The response to economic crisis throughout Europe has been to reject the principle of democracy: rule by the people, for the people. The instinct of power is to preserve and amplify itself. The Irish government's 'radical' political reform agenda is defined by initiatives, such as abolishing the Seanad, that seek to reinforce a centralisation of power through the camouflage of popular support. This trend is very pronounced within the newer democracies of Eastern Europe. Prime Minister Viktor Orban, for example, deliberately undermined the independence of key parts of the Hungarian state in December 2011. His constitutional reforms included the removal of traditional democratic checks and balances on the government such as the autonomy of the central bank and the judiciary.

Trilateral Commission 2009 and Too Much Democracy (Again)

In a 2009 keynote speech, entitled 'The Intellectual Underpinnings of the Trilateral Partnership in the 21st Century', Henry Kissinger sought to redefine the role of the Trilateral Commission. In 1975, it was the 'excess of democracy' that was perceived as the cause of political stability. Now, 'the fundamental flaw of the globalized economic system . . . was that the economic model and the political model' are, Kissinger believes, 'out of sync with each other'. Noting that the 'political world is in a period of fundamental change' and that 'governments are so preoccupied with immediate issues', the Trilateral Commission, he contended, could 'indicate direction' on how sovereignty is defined in the multipolar international system.

Enter the technocratic, unelected leaders of Greece and Italy, Lucas Papademos and Mario Monti, who became prime ministers in 2011. Papademos is a former vice president of the European Central Bank, governor of the IMF for Greece and member of the Trilateral Commission. Monti is a former European Commissioner, adviser to Goldman Sachs and European chairman of the Trilateral Commission. The Italian was sworn in as a senator for life in November 2011 and appointed as both Prime Minister and Minister of Economy and Finance a week later. Papademos and Monti were tasked with the implementation of harsh austerity budgets in their domestic economies, measures conceived by the international organisations that had previously employed both of them. The Fine Gael–Labour 2011 programme for government proudly proclaimed that with 'the stroke of a pen, in thousands of polling stations' a 'democratic revolution' had taken place. The coalition had secured the largest parliamentary majority in the history of the state 'with an absolute resolve to bring the change the people so clearly demand'. Yet the ECB and the IMF maintained that Ireland's economic programme had been negotiated on behalf of the state rather than on behalf of a particular government. Olli Rehn, EU Economic Commissioner, wryly remarked, 'The EU has signed the Memorandum of Understanding with the State, with the Republic of Ireland, and we expect continuity and respect of the memorandum.' He made these comments just a week before the general election and tellingly said, 'If there will be any changes . . . it will take place for the overall European reasons not specifically because of electoral statements in Ireland.'

Voters can change governments but they cannot change the policies of international organisations, bondholders and external lenders. Ireland's 'democratic revolution' has been replaced by unaccountable technocracy, just as it has in Italy and other established democracies. Antonis Samaras's election as the Greek Prime Minister in June 2012 merely represented a continuation of Papademos's measures. Like Papademos, Samaras has vowed to reduce Greece's total debt to 120 per cent of GDP by 2020 under the terms of its international loan agreement with the troika.

Since the economic crisis began in 2008, some €25 billion, almost 15 per cent of current gross domestic product, has been removed from the Irish economy. Yet the terms of the IMF–ECB–EU troika programme dictate that Ireland is only halfway through its recovery plan.

It was Marcus Tullius Cicero who introduced the teachings of Greek philosophy to his native Rome. He railed against those in power who had corrupted political action through power struggles and dictatorship. 'A nation can survive its fools, and even the ambitious,' Cicero wrote in 45 BC.

> But it cannot survive treason from within. An enemy at the gates is less formidable, for he is known and carries his banner openly. But the traitor moves amongst those within the gate freely, his sly whispers rustling through all the alleys, heard in the very halls of government itself.
>
> For the traitor appears not a traitor; he speaks in accents familiar to his victims, and he wears their face and their arguments, he appeals to the baseness that lies deep in the hearts of all men. He rots the soul of a nation, he works secretly and unknown in the night to undermine the pillars of the city, he infects the body politic so that it can no longer resist.

For Cicero, the republic was *res publica*, the Latin term that translates as 'public affairs'. The republic is the foundation of order and political stability because of its emphasis on civic virtue. Only the knowledgeable citizen can become the competent citizen.

Deliberative democracy is one means by which the quality of participation in a democracy can be enhanced. That assumes we still have a democracy in the first place.

4

Civic Virtue, Autonomy and Religious Schools: What Would Machiavelli Do?

TOM HICKEY

A republic, fundamentally, is a political community that protects the liberty of its citizens. Republicans have a distinct understanding of liberty: to enjoy liberty is to enjoy equal protection from 'domination', where domination is defined as arbitrary or unchecked power.[1] If I enjoy that status, I can be confident that no individual or group of individuals, whether in the public or in the private sphere, has the capacity to interfere at will in my choices. There will be interference in my choices, of course. That much is unavoidable in the context of a shared social and political community. But, in the ideal republic, no one – not any employer, not the police, not any political figure or administrative official, not any religious or community power-wielder, not any family member or work colleague – will enjoy the *unchecked* capacity to interfere in my choices.

Inevitably, in any real-world community, there will be domination to one degree or another, across every sphere. The republican state seeks to *maximise* non-domination. It strives for ever greater levels of non-domination across all aspects of the lives of all of its citizens. It seeks to empower the citizen to the point, in the ideal scenario, where she can look other citizens in the eye, and confidently assert that she enjoys resilient protection from arbitrary power. She need not 'bow and scrape' in the manner of the slave of a 'kindly master'. She can walk unafraid as an equal citizen.

So what must be in place if citizens are to enjoy this kind of liberty? There are certain familiar requirements. There must be an appropriate set of political institutions, for instance. These institutions must be designed such that power is dispersed through the polity, rather than concentrated in one individual, or in one institution. Typically, this will require a separation of powers between different arms of government: the legislature, the executive and the judiciary. In a republic worthy of the name, the executive will be accountable to the legislature in a meaningful way; in a way that ensures that people's representatives in parliament can contribute to the laws that emerge through deliberation, and can hold government to account, every day and every week, as the monotonous process of politics unfolds. Similarly, there is a need for a constitution that protects fundamental rights in the face of populist pressure. For republicans, domination by a majority group is as objectionable as domination by an individual despot.

These ingredients are well understood. They are necessary conditions for liberty, but they are by no means sufficient. Political institutions and constitutional provisions are lifeless instruments. They cannot be relied upon, on their own, to protect liberty. The political institutions cannot survive, for instance, without at least some general participation by the citizenry. There must be some kind of commitment to the democratic institutions, and at least minimal civic patriotism. Moreover, citizens must have some regard for one another, and indeed for their own status and responsibilities as citizens. There must be a general distaste for the arrogation of arbitrary power. And so on.

The point is that in order for the republican state to promote equal liberty as non-domination, it can legitimately develop virtue amongst its citizens. Indeed it *must* do so.

Civic Virtue: Do Republicans Insist on Too Thick an Account?

This presents a challenge that is of capital importance for contemporary proponents of republicanism.[2] The idea of civic virtue occupies an important place in the history of republican idealism.[3] Indeed 'civic republicanism' has often been dismissed by liberal philosophers on the ground that it sets too much store by civic virtue.[4] It is argued that republicans adopt too robust an account of virtue bearing in mind the fact that individuals living in free societies hold different reasonable world views, often radically so. Or to use John Rawls's vernacular, free societies necessarily feature a diversity of 'comprehensive doctrines': a diversity of moral, religious or philosophical 'conceptions of the good'.[5]

The argument is that republican civic virtue includes values that are 'comprehensive', and that are accordingly rejected by at least some reasonable people. Imposing a particular conception of the good on all citizens, in the form of a thick account of civic virtue, undermines the liberty of citizens who subscribe to values that differ from that account. The question might therefore be: how can republicans argue for a robust account of civic virtue, in the interests of promoting liberty as non-domination, while not going so far as to end up dominating some individuals or groups whose values clash with the account promoted?

Too many 'republics' and 'republicans' have ventured into dominating territory in this way in the past. The 2004 French law prohibiting the wearing of conspicuous religious symbols in schools, for instance, is *arguably* a dominating intervention of this kind. One justification for the prohibition, among others, was that the wearing of conspicuous religious symbols (the Islamic headscarf, effectively) in the public sphere communicated a prior loyalty to a particular religious identity, thereby intolerably undermining civic loyalty.[6] And yet the Stasi Commission (named after its chairman Bernard Stasi) deliberations that brought about the prohibition excluded the voice of Islamic women. The idea that a Muslim woman might independently choose to wear a headscarf, and that she might be simultaneously committed to the French Republic, was treated as more or less implausible. The Commission members declared themselves simply 'not sensitive to their arguments'.[7]

Another example of a dominating account of virtue – again arguably – is the attempt, orchestrated by an alliance of Eamon de Valera's Fianna Fáil and the Catholic hierarchy, to promote a particular Catholic and Gaelic, chaste and 'spurning-of-luxury' image of the ideal Irish citizen from the 1930s through much of the twentieth century.[8] This is illustrated by, for example, some provisions and the general ethos of the 1937 constitution, the official policy of conflation of civic education with Catholic social thought, and the staunch support for the control by the Catholic hierarchy over the schooling system.

There is another related argument concerning republicanism and civic virtue. This suggests that some republicans, historically, have insisted on intense political participation as the one truly 'flourishing' life.[9] They argued that human beings cannot enjoy true liberty unless they actively engage in the politics of their community, and impact directly on political deliberation and lawmaking.[10] This similarly suggests that republicanism is an inappropriate guiding philosophy for modern, ethically diverse, political communities. The citizenry of Ancient Greek city states may have had the time and means to engage in the politics of their *polis*, and, of course, citizenship was the preserve of the propertied and male elite. But many citizens of modern polities have neither the time nor the inclination. Many prefer – quite reasonably – to spend their time reading great literature, catching up on the latest celebrity gossip, or doing their best to make ends meet. Indeed, even if it were desirable, it would be simply unfeasible for all of the citizens in today's vast political communities to have a direct impact on lawmaking.

The challenge for neo-republicans, then, is to come up with an account of civic virtue that is sufficiently robust to protect equal liberty as non-domination, while not becoming so robust that it amounts to an imposition of a particular conception of the good on all citizens in circumstances where there is a deep diversity of reasonable conceptions of the good. This is quite a challenge, as the line between the un-dominating virtue and dominating imposition is a very fine one. It asks very deep questions of those seeking to defend republicanism.

The remainder of this essay is in three parts. The first part provides a broad sketch of the skills and dispositions that the state can and must develop in its young citizens. It considers the appropriate 'civic mission' of education and schooling in the modern republic, although briefly, as it is intended mainly to set up the arguments that follow. The second part is devoted to a particularly difficult challenge within the broader challenge already set out. It considers the comprehensive value of autonomy, and assesses to what extent the republican state can legitimately educate children to be independent from the ethical commitments (religious or non-religious) of their parents? These arguments then carry into the third part, which assesses the relative merits of 'common' schools and religious denominational schools in the light of this civic mission, with a particular eye on the situation in Ireland.

A Sketch of the Civic Skills and Dispositions

The legitimate civic mission of education and schooling in the modern, ethnically diverse, republic might be considered in four, closely related, categories. First, the state can promote a minimal *civic patriotism*. This should not be an overly robust or unthinking patriotism. Plainly, the temptation to present young citizens with a romantic and simplistic image of a country's history, for instance, is to be resisted. There must be a genuine effort to capture the complexity of a nation's history – and the disputes within it and about it – rather than the simplistic 'us versus them' or 'good versus evil' narrative that can all too easily prevail. Similarly, young citizens must become aware of the role and importance of the democratic institutions of the state. They must develop some commitment to these institutions, and a sense of the importance of at least minimal civic participation.

Second, young citizens must develop strong *skills of contestation*. Domination, by definition, is incontestable power. Therefore, young citizens must first be equipped with the necessary skills to identify when others enjoy arbitrary control over them (think here of the psychological impact that oppression can have over time, or the idea of 'Stockholm Syndrome'). This suggests at least rudimentary critical reasoning and autonomy-related skills. Beyond that, it suggests that they become capable of actually contesting decisions, in an appropriate and an effective way, where those decisions conflict with their interests.

Quite obviously, young citizens must develop the skills to challenge government decisions, and to contribute to the development of public policy. But dominating control can be exercised across various spheres: the political, the civic, and the private. Therefore – perhaps less obviously – young citizens must be capable of voicing their concerns and interests in the school environment, or within the clubs and associations in which they may participate. In the case of insular religious or cultural groups, for example, young members must be equipped with the skills to contest the influence of group leaders over such matters as the interpretation of religious texts or cultural traditions, and to contribute to the evolution of such interpretations. In the same vein, young people must become capable of critically assessing their own inherited religious or non-religious commitments, so that they are not permanently in thrall to those of their parents. These ideas are taken up further in the next section.

Third, the state must educate young citizens towards an appreciation of the common good of the republic as a whole, and towards an awareness of how their own private good – and the good of their families and localities – is intimately connected with that common good. Iseult Honohan argues along these lines that citizens in contemporary states must be educated towards an awareness of their 'shared common predicament and common fate' which implies that they must learn to exercise 'civic self-restraint'.[11] As Honohan suggests, rather than requiring citizens to engage in any form of political self-denial, this will require citizens to develop a deeper understanding about the ways in which their own interests are profoundly bound up in the interests of their fellow citizens. Reaching such understanding will make citizens more likely to accept, for example, redistributive economic measures to promote equality and to engage in good environmental practices.[12] In an Irish context, it would also likely counter the wretched clientelism and localism that continues to bedevil the political system.

Related to this, the state must inculcate a general distaste among young citizens for domination such that they will not seek to achieve arbitrary control over others, in the form, for instance, of excessive economic, financial or political clout, at least not for the sake of having that clout. The deeply misunderstood republican scholar Niccolò Machiavelli was particularly exercised on this point. Machiavelli lamented what he deemed the rotten factionalism among the political classes in late Middle Ages/early Renaissance Florence. The different factions sought dominating control of the levers of political power, but were motivated by their own interests, and the interests of their supporters.[13] In the Roman republic of over a millennium earlier, on Machiavelli's reckoning, different groups understood the political institutions as institutions of their own shared liberty, rather than as levers to be manipulated for personal gain.[14] The threat of being dominated by a given faction that might win power for a particular cycle led each group to secure equal liberty through good, un-dominating, non-factional laws and institutions. The idea is that citizens ought to be capable of abstracting away from their immediate whims and short-term interests, and to see the ways in which they share more valuable long-term interests in common with all citizens.

It is worth reflecting, in this context, on the extent to which the woes of post-Celtic Tiger Ireland can be attributed in great part to the excesses and the factionalism of the Celtic Tiger era. For some citizens, power-wielders and political representatives, it was about pilfering as much of the wedding cake as possible for one's own table. 'Pigs-with-their-snouts-in-the-trough' is as illuminating as any other metaphor as an illustration of Machiavelli's old argument.

Finally – and this is related to the previous point – young citizens in modern political communities must be educated towards an understanding of the 'fact of reasonable pluralism' (in John Rawls's phrase). This is the idea that an inevitable feature of any free political community is that citizens hold different moral, religious and philosophical world views, or different 'comprehensive doctrines'. More to the point, young citizens must be able to respond appropriately to the fact that they share a political community with others, many of whom hold different reasonable comprehensive doctrines. One important implication is that they must develop skills of 'public reason'.[15] For political engagement to be truly non-factional, participants in that engagement must be willing and able to offer one another non-factional (or avowable) reasons in support of their arguments in political deliberation. They must be capable of realising the unreasonableness of making arguments in political debate that are grounded only in their own deepest ethical or religious commitments.

This means that citizens must not only seek political power for more noble reasons than naked self-interest but, even more burdensomely perhaps, they must engage in the common deliberative process of politics by means of argument that they can reasonably expect their fellow citizens to accept. They cannot expect other citizens to be moved in political debate by arguments based in factional perspectives that others necessarily do not share, or by virtue of sheer political power.

Rather citizens owe one another reciprocal reasons: reasons that they can reasonably expect others not merely to understand, but to accept as legitimate.[16]

To illustrate the point, take an Irish citizen who holds Islamic beliefs, and a debate that begins (as it well might in the coming years) around the wearing of conspicuous religious insignia in public, in schools or hospitals for example. That citizen can choose between two different modes of argumentation in such a debate, along the following lines:

1. I am Islamic. Wearing the headscarf is important to me. Personally, I would fare badly if a prohibition were to be introduced. Accordingly, Ireland should not introduce a prohibition on conspicuous religious symbols.

2. All people value the norm of religious liberty. Indeed, when that norm is interpreted in a coherent way, it is as valuable to the non-religious, and to the unconventionally religious, as it is to conventional religious citizens such as myself. The right to manifest one's religious beliefs flows from that deeper norm. When the manifestation of religious belief does not undermine the equal right of others to religious liberty, it should not be restricted. Accordingly, Ireland should not introduce a prohibition on the conspicuous religious symbols.

The latter mode observes the strictures of public reason, and citizens arguing such a point might reasonably be expected to opt for it rather than for the former mode. The same kind of expectation falls on citizens from a majority ethnic or ethical group, in different debates. Catholic parents cannot argue, therefore, for a public schooling system that is run by the Catholic hierarchy, even if there is majority support for such a system (would they be happy if the atheists applied the same standards should they gain the upper hand?). Virtuous citizens living in a republic that resiliently protects them from arbitrary power can reasonably be expected to be capable of more sophisticated argumentation than the 'because-this-is-what-suits-me' kind.

This capacity for undominating democratic deliberation requires, at the very least, that young citizens be exposed to and be acquainted with other ethical perspectives, and must learn to appreciate that those other perspectives express conceptions of value that are sincerely held by other reasonable people. The beginnings of the argument concerning the relative merits of 'common' as against religious denominational schooling, which is taken up in the final section, emerge from this idea.

Educating Children Away from Inherited Beliefs: Too Much or Not Enough?

The idea that domination can be enjoyed by individuals or groups within the private sphere has already been emphasised. This section considers a particular form of domination: domination of children's ethical commitments by their parents. This quandary brings out the kernel of the dilemma: how far must a state committed to the promotion of non-domination go in educating young citizens towards virtue, and when does it go too far? When does the state begin to oppress individuals and families, in the sense of imposing an alien conception of the good on them? The starting point for any argument of this kind must be that the ethical lives of young children are the concern, first and foremost, of their parents.

While the quandary applies to all kinds of ethical commitments – religious or otherwise – it might none the less be useful to consider it in the context of a fundamentalist religious group that more or less rejects the value of autonomous ethical reflection. A helpful illustration of this dilemma is provided by a famous case that came before the US Sixth Circuit Federal Appeals Court in 1987: *Mozert v. Hawkins Co. Board of Education.*[17] The case emerged in the early 1980s from Hawkins County, Tennessee.[18] It concerned a group of Protestant religious fundamentalist parents who objected to a compulsory reading programme being taught at the public school at which their children were students. The reading programme was aimed at advancing reading skills beyond mere word and sound recognition 'to develop higher cognitive skills that [would] enable students to evaluate the material they read, to contrast the ideas presented, and to understand the complex characters that appear in the reading material'.

The parents' argument ultimately was that the reading programme exposed their children to a diverse range of ethical perspectives and encouraged 'critical reasoning', rendering it more difficult for them to pass on their particular religious beliefs to their children. They believed that it was an 'occult practice' to use the imagination beyond the limitations of scriptural authority and that exposure to secular ideas – and to religious ideas other than their own – would encourage their children to think independently about the merits of alternative ethical perspectives.

In rejecting the parents' claim, the court emphasised the civic aims of the programme. Judge Lively argued that the purpose of the public school was to teach fundamental values 'essential to a democratic society', including 'tolerance of divergent political and religious views' and the ability to 'consider . . . the sensibilities of others'. He rejected the claim that there was a violation of religious liberty on the ground that 'exposure to something does not constitute teaching, indoctrination, opposition or promotion to the things exposed'.[19]

We may agree that the *Mozert* parents are hardly representative of parents in post-Celtic Tiger Ireland, and that their objection is much more dramatic than any that is likely to emerge in that context. But their case is still illustrative. First, the same quandary applies to various degrees across the full spectrum of ethical commitments. Every parent has a particular set of ethical commitments, even if most will be much less doctrinaire than the set subscribed to by the *Mozert* parents. The set of commitments subscribed to by every parent is likely to deviate to at least some extent from whatever scheme of civic education might be promoted in a particular state. In this way, *Mozert* simply provides a particularly stark illustration of a difficulty that will be quite general across all liberal democracies. Second, while the scheme of civic education promoted in a modern republic is not likely to deviate too sharply from the ethical commitments of the majority of citizens, it might deviate quite sharply for minority groups. Hence, this quandary is all the more pressing in the light of deeper ethical heterogeneity in modern political communities.

The disputed critical reading programme in *Mozert* would seem to have pursued legitimate civic aims when judged according to republican standards. It sought to equip students with the skills and dispositions required of citizens in culturally and religiously diverse political communities. The parents objected to the manner in which the programme encouraged skills of critical reasoning, and the questioning of authority. Yet these skills are fundamental to republican citizenship, given that their absence will bring about near absolute deference to authority, and a chronic inability to identify and contest arbitrary power. Similarly, the lack of exposure to alternative ethical perspectives not only tends to trap children within their groups of origin (especially in the case of 'insular' groups, where members tend not to mix with non-members), but also fails to develop any sense of empathy for other perspectives. It undermines the development of any understanding of a shared political predicament and of the myriad ways in which citizens, even in cases where ethical or religious ends are radically different, share common interests and goods. It seems also to conflict dramatically with the development of even rudimentary skills of public reasoning.

And yet the scheme of civic education in *Mozert* – or the scheme envisaged for the modern republic – seems to promote quite forthrightly the value of autonomy. Indeed it seems bluntly to encourage children to engage actively in critical reflection concerning inherited ethical commitments. Rawls argues that the value of autonomy (at least in the sense of the active or regular scrutinising of one's ethical commitments) is very much a 'comprehensive' one. That is, it is a value that many individuals may embrace but, equally, that some may reasonably reject on the basis of a preference for a life lived in devoted and unquestioned commitment to God, for instance. For the state to use its coercive power to promote that value, then, is to impose a particular comprehensive doctrine on all individuals. It is oppressive.

Rawls himself was plainly troubled by this matter. He deals briefly with it in *Political Liberalism*, but seems conscious that it reveals a certain incoherence at the heart of his theory of liberalism. He suggests that there might be some unfortunate overspill from comprehensive into political liberalism, in the sense that children educated in the way required by political liberalism might unavoidably pick up comprehensive liberal values such as that of autonomy. He concludes, somewhat perfunctorily, that 'the unavoidable consequences of reasonable requirements for children's education may have to be accepted, often with regret'.[20]

The same concern applies in the case of republicanism. If republican liberty requires a 'mission of enlightenment' of this kind, does it not veer into dominating territory? Does it breach the moral rights of parents, and lose the claim that it is an account of 'liberty'? Through the lens of the argument over civic education, a grave issue emerges for those who wish to defend republicanism as a compelling public philosophy.

Rescuing Republicanism: Distinguishing 'Ethical Independence' and 'Outright Autonomy'

So how, then, does the republican state approach these kinds of dilemmas in civic education? How does it seek to develop what appear to be crucial skills and dispositions in young citizens without being vulnerable to the charge that it is venturing into oppressive territory? Where de Valera promoted the Gaelic and God-fearing republican citizen at the cost of the liberty of those who were not so minded, contemporary republicans may make the same error in promoting the autonomous and secular citizen. This contemporary citizen is wired to engage endlessly in critical reflection on her ethical commitments. She regularly discards commitments that she no longer deems worthy, and takes them up again at a later stage when she changes her mind.

In seeking a way out of this web, it is worth recalling the essence of republicanism: it is about independence from the will of others. Indeed, republicans famously use the image of the 'kindly master' to illustrate the superiority of their conception of liberty (as non-domination) over the conception of liberty (as mere non-interference) associated with the likes of Hobbes, Mill and others.[21] The kindly master may not interfere, or be likely ever to do so, but he enjoys the *capacity* to interfere, and this brings with it the bowing and scraping, the dehumanising ingratiation of someone seeking to protect herself from interference.

This seems to shed light on Rawls's problem, and on the broader quandary in contemporary liberal democracies over civic education programmes that insist on exposure to diversity, critical reasoning skills and so on. Rather than autonomy being the issue, as such, it seems that it is independence from the will of others that is fundamntally at stake.

The image of the 'Ethically Servile' child, presented by the philosopher of education Eamonn Callan, illustrates the argument.[22] Callan does not use the language of domination, but his imagery seems to fit neatly within the republican frame. He first asks his audience to consider the example of a father of a 'Deferential Child'. The Deferential Child has been reared to believe that her duty to her father is paramount, and that her own happiness and fulfilment is contingent on her making choices that are fully at one with her father's will. The father may be totally devoted to his child's happiness and well-being – he may be the most caring father imaginable – but ultimately he is convinced that his daughter's well-being requires that she defer to him on all matters of ethical significance and so he rears her to believe that to be the case.

Callan then suggests a comparison with the 'Ethically Servile Child'.[23] This child is reared with the same goal in mind – to ensure permanent control of the child's ethical life for his understanding of her own good and happiness – but this time a different strategy is employed. Rather than rearing the child to be deferential, the father rears the child in such a way that that child will maintain an 'ignorant antipathy' towards ethical perspectives other than her inherited ethical perspectives. This notion of 'ignorant antipathy' means more than a lack of information about alternative ethical perspectives: it means a 'settled affective disposition to refuse to register whatever reason might commend in the objects of one's antipathy, even if, at some later date, one might acquire knowledge about them'.[24] The child reared towards 'ignorant antipathy' of alternative ethical perspectives is the 'Ethically Servile' child:

> Unlike the Deferential Child, my Ethically Servile Child does not think of herself as under any duty to defer to me [her parent]. She may enumerate her rights correctly, talk eloquently about their meaning, and prize them as highly as anyone reasonably could. Yet in a deep sense she remains subordinate to my will because the choices I make in moulding her character effectively pre-empt serious thought at any future date about the alternatives to my judgement. Ignorant antipathy regarding those alternatives secures her ongoing subordination in much the same way that the Deferential Child's belief that she has a duty to defer to her parents guarantees her subordination. In each case the field of deliberation in which the agent operates as an adult has been constrained through childhood experience so as to ensure ongoing compliance with another's will.[25]

Most parents, of course, would not seek to instil this kind of 'ignorant antipathy' towards other ethical perspectives in their children as a direct and self-conscious strategy. But it may be instilled, in varying degrees, subconsciously and gradually over the course of a child's upbringing. Parents, however well intentioned, cannot seek to deny their children the opportunity to become independent of their will. This is the essence of domination, with the parents as the quintessential 'kindly masters'.

By moving the analysis away from autonomy towards questions of servility, subordination and subservience to another's will, it becomes clear that any reticence among republicans in cases such as *Mozert*, or indeed about a scheme of civic education that forthrightly promotes this kind of independence for young citizens, is unjustified. The republican state cannot legitimately seek to inculcate full-blown autonomy in its young citizens, of the kind Rawls had in mind when he refers to autonomy as a comprehensive doctrine. It may not seek to instil the propensity to engage actively in intense ethical reflection such that all citizens will regularly consider which ethical commitments to continue to pursue and which to abandon. This would amount to domination by the state. But independence from the will of others is quite a different notion, and it is fundamental to republican citizenship. Republicans can forthrightly promote this good, and can legitimately call on the coercive power of the state to do so.

The point, in the end, is that the better understanding of republicanism is that which positions civic virtue appropriately, and which avoids the error of many republicans historically. If republicanism is to be compelling in the modern world, it must be a philosophy that is capable of accommodating difference and diversity. On the other side, not all 'diversity' is to be accommodated. Fundamentalist groups that reject the value of minimal autonomy, for instance, or that reject the idea of independence from the will of others, are not to be accommodated in the form of exemptions from civic education programmes that promote reasonable civic goals.[26]

The Debate Concerning Religious Denominational Schools

Finally, there is the vexed question of the relative merits of religious denominational as distinct from 'common' schooling. The question is quite urgent in Ireland, as the extent to which the Catholic Church wields control over the primary schooling system has been the subject of widespread concern in recent years. The Minister for Education, Ruairi Quinn, established the *Forum for Patronage and Pluralism in the Primary Sector* in 2011 to assess reform of the system, although the reforms proposed in the Forum's 'Advisory Report' are underwhelming.[27] Much attention has been focused on the topic over recent years, and the most striking statistic is quite familiar: more than nine out of every ten schools in the primary system are run by Catholic patrons.[28] This level of dominance straightforwardly violates the religious liberty of non-Catholics with children of school-going age all across the Irish state.[29] This section focuses on a different question: the more abstract question of whether religious denominational schools are appropriate in the light of the legitimate civic mission of education and schooling already (briefly and roughly) sketched in this essay.

Many parents want their children to be educated in schools dedicated to a particular religious ethos. These are 'sectarian' schools in the strict sense, inasmuch as they consciously promote a set of 'comprehensive' ideals. They tend to be made up of staff and students holding the same broad set of religious beliefs, and to infuse those religious beliefs into the school day and year. The 'common school', by contrast, is not defined by reference to the religious or non-religious commitments of the staff or students, nor is it dedicated to the promotion of any particular 'comprehensive' doctrine in terms of its educational ethos or mission. The common school is usually composed of teaching staff and students of different ethical perspectives, holding different religious and non-religious beliefs.

This seems to suggest, when taken at face value, that the common school is preferable in light of the civic mission of education in the modern republic. That is, it seems more likely that young students will develop attitudes of respect and empathy for citizens holding different ethical perspectives if they are educated in an environment that includes such citizens. They are more likely to develop the rudimentary skills of non-factional reasoning, and so on. This argument emerges from a simple version of the Aristotelian thesis of habituation: that 'a state of character arises from the repetition of similar activities'.[30] That is, moral character can be acquired only through active practice of the virtues; it cannot be acquired merely by abstract teaching of those virtues. If children are to be effectively segregated in their education along religious lines (or indeed along any other 'comprehensive' lines), the prospect of developing the republican skills and dispositions is undermined.

The common school, by implication, is a 'virtual republic' within which children from different cultural and religious perspectives engage with one another in a critical formative environment. They are better placed to gain an appreciation of the fact that they share a common political fate with such citizens and with all citizens in the diverse modern polity. This seems to place the onus on those arguing for religious or otherwise sectarian schools to offer strong reasons as to why they might be permitted.

Is There a Case to be Made for Religious Schools?

The first response by those wishing to defend the legitimacy (and, perhaps beyond that, the value) of religious schools to the argument as presented is that it is presented in a gravely simplistic way. It treats all 'religious' schools as if there were no important differences between institutions that fall into that broad category. Not all religious schools are 'totalistic' institutions, in which every aspect of the education they provide is determined by religious prescription. In the Irish context, although there is ample evidence of exclusion of non-Catholics in Catholic schools across the state – particularly in cases of over-subscription – it is clear that most such schools have non-Catholic staff and students, and indeed in many cases draw a considerable proportion of their member-ship from non-Catholics. There are deep concerns around religious liberty in these schools and in the schooling system generally, but as regards exposure to diversity and their general suitability for promoting skills and dispositions of republican citizenship, advocates of such schools are on firmer ground.

Correspondingly, the common school has often been pre-sented in highly idealised terms, as if it necessarily features the perfect spectrum of ethical perspectives among its students and staff. The reality, of course, is that the composition of schools is more typically determined by local demographic factors and residential arrangements, and is accordingly usu-ally much more homogenous than the ideal suggests. This would be especially true even if the common school formed the backbone of the Irish schooling system, as, despite shifts towards religious and ethical diversity over recent times, the vast majority of the population still claims to subscribe to one particular belief system.[31] (It is worth pointing out in this context that the ills of residential segregation and ghettoisation along ethnic and socio-economic lines are at least as destructive, if not drastically more destructive, to the civic mission of republican education as religious or any other kinds of sectarian schooling.)

In any case, what is clear is that the permissibility of religious schools – or indeed of any schooling environment – hinges on the question of whether such schools are willing *and able* to develop the skills and dispositions of republican citizenship. If they are, common schooling is permissible, as is home schooling, as is schooling in a school linked with a professional football club, as is schooling in a school linked with a particular religious denomination. It would seem reasonable to suggest that the common school has a significant advantage over other schooling environments, but to argue that those other environments are necessarily illegitimate is quite a jump, and probably an unreasonable one. It seems also reasonable to suggest that 'totalistic' religious schools should not be permissible.

It is critical, of course, that the republican state carefully regulates all aspects of the education and schooling environment, across all its aspects: from teacher training and pedagogy, curriculum, institutional arrangements, admissions and employment policy and so on. The difficulty of that task is clear, considering that the skills and dispositions in question are not readily amenable to quantitative assessment. Whether children are adequately protected from ethical servility, for instance, or are equipped with skills of non-factional reasoning – and whether a particular environment is or is not adequately conducive to the development of these skills – will never be straightforward.

It should also be clear that there are certain restrictions which the republican state can legitimately place on religious schools.[32] These restrictions are presented here only in abstract form. First, such schools must expose students to religious and non-religious perspectives other than the set of beliefs underpinning the school's ethos. This goal must be pursued in a genuine and comprehensive way. It must be pursued in such a way as not only to engender respect, empathy and understanding for those holding different ethical commitments, but in such a way as to present them as potentially attractive ethical lives. This will mean, at the minimum, that religious schools must be open to staff and students from outside of the endorsed faith community. Not only that, but such staff and students must enjoy their positions within those schools on an equal footing. It cannot be that they are simply tolerated, or presented as guinea pigs upon which to practise good republican virtues. On this point, the exemptions enshrined in Irish equality legislation that allow religious schools to discriminate against non-coreligionists are simply intolerable in a republic.[33]

Second, religious schools cannot incorporate religious doctrine into each and every subject in the curriculum. Although it may be permissible to teach the biblical account of creation in Religion class, for instance, it would be intolerable that that account should be taught in Biology. Similarly, there seems no good reason to incorporate religious doctrine into other classes such as History, English and so on, although it would go too far to argue that reference to religious doctrine would be impermissible.

Third, there must be a meaningful commitment across all aspects of the school to non-religious reasoning. That is, teachers must give – and insist on receiving – reasons for academic claims and rules or policies that are entirely independent of religious doctrine.[34] This will often require reasoning that conflicts with religious doctrine. Take the example of a Catholic school and questions concerning divorce, contraception or homosexuality in a class such as Social, Personal and Health Education. Although it may be permissible for students and teachers to engage in specifically Catholic argumentation on these questions, this cannot be to the exclusion of conflicting non-Catholic argumentation. Even in Religion class, the tensions within Catholicism on these questions must be thoroughly considered, as must conflicting religious and non-religious views.

In light of these arguments, it is clear that the objections to religious schooling are easily overstated. The concept of religious schooling is not necessarily in conflict with the civic mission, and so cannot be perfunctorily dismissed by republicans.

We shall never know what Machiavelli's views might have been on the question of the legitimacy of religious schooling. This essay – although drawing broadly on the tradition to which Machiavelli contributed perhaps more than anyone – has had the more modest aim of sketching a rough republican approach to civic virtue in the modern, ethically diverse, political community. Republicans need not be shy in insisting on programmes and strategies that develop independence from the will of others, including independence from the will of kindly and well-meaning parents in respect of something as sacred as their children's ethical commitments. Needless to say, the moral rights of parents to develop their children's ethical commitments must always be respected by any state committed to liberty. It is just that such rights are not absolute. And the burden is on proponents of religious schools to demonstrate that such schools are capable of educating citizens towards virtue.

5

The Law and the Republic

DEARBHAIL MCDONALD

Any debate about the law and the republic, at a time when we are asking if we still have one, invites the question as to whether the law has served or continues to serve our republic well. The surrender, in all but name, of fiscal sovereignty to the European institutions and the Sisyphean demands of 'the troika' have undermined Ireland's credentials as a republic in the hearts and minds of many of its citizens.

We are not alone among our European peers in grappling with the reality that we are no longer a self-determined state. That is if we ever truly can be a self-determined state following the gradual (then sudden) loss of sovereignty that has accompanied our largely positive membership of the European Union. Apart from the sovereignty predicament, the dawn and demise of the Celtic Tiger has led many to question the efficacy of our home-grown democratic and legal order. The extraordinary journey from boom to bust raises the question as to whether the law, in whole or in part, is somehow not fit for purpose. The purported demand for a new republic assumes that the law is not.

The fundamental design flaw at the heart of the European project (a common currency without a proper fiscal union) as well as factors such as cheap credit and regulatory failures in the financial sector, led to the near collapse of the Irish economy. And those failures, facilitated by weak and ineffectual political oversight, continue to pose a threat to our social cohesion through mass unemployment and emigration, a burgeoning mortgage and credit crisis and an ever-widening gulf between the haves and have-nots.

The dramatic bailout of many European banking systems, including Ireland's, exposed the need to develop stronger democratic institutions and a much more nuanced understanding of sovereignty and what constitutes a threat to society and the rule of law.

We know now that wrongdoing in the banking sector as well as other forms of corruption (whether negligent or malignant) in politics and business can pose as serious a threat to national security as 'ordinary' street crime and organised crime, including terrorism. The scale of disruption that followed the 2008 global economic crisis led to the introduction in Ireland of a range of emergency financial measures. These included the creation of the National Assets Management Agency (NAMA), the toxic bank that removed soured property loans from participating Irish banks, but which notably failed to offset an EU–ECB–IMF bailout in November 2010.

It also includes a series of Credit Institutions Acts, aimed, among other things, at protecting the stability of the banking system, restoring confidence in the financial sector and allowing for the orderly resolution of distressed lenders.

These laws granted extraordinary, wartime-like controls of regulation and intervention to the state, through the aegis of the Minister for Finance and the Central Bank of Ireland, over the financial system. These measures and others that followed together heralded the introduction of a special-powers regime with far-reaching consequences not seen since the time of the Troubles.

If the republic faltered in part because of a wholesale lack of regulation – a failure of the law in the broadest sense – would the birth of a new republic demand a new legal order or constitutional document? The economic crisis has understandably forced us to take stock of our mores and values, but are we at risk of overstating what went wrong in Ireland when other countries across the globe are facing similar problems? Can this crippling malaise sow the seeds for genuine constitutional and legal reform that will revive our republic or will it give birth to an entirely new one? Or are these questions themselves moot if the Irish constitution and Irish democracy are becoming mere footnotes to big country power politics?

Irish people have (historically at any rate) had an innate sense of justice, a national trait we like to think was fashioned long before the 1916 Easter Rising, the foundation of the Irish Free State in 1922 or the drafting of the 1937 Irish constitution. The writer Michael Ragan has observed that one of the reasons for the 'astounding durability' of Ireland's ancient Brehon law was the great respect that Irish natives held for justice and the law. And Sir John Davies, the British Attorney General in Ireland tasked with suppressing Brehon law, also observed that there was no nation of people under the sun that loved equal and indifferent justice better than the Irish. I wonder, given the huge socio-economic disparities in our society at present, what Sir John would make of contemporary Irish attitudes towards injustice and inequality.

Republics and the constitutions that underpin their legitimacy are typically born or recast in the wake of crises, revolutions or when, to borrow the words of T. S. Eliot, we are no longer at ease in the old dispensation. The Irish republic was itself born out of the sorry, bloody depths of the Anglo-Irish struggle. And, despite the desire for a symbolic as well as a de facto break from the British Empire, the fledgling Irish state relied heavily on that tradition for its politico-legal DNA, incorporating and maintaining much of the British parliamentary and common-law customs into the new republic. It has often been said that the Irish simply replaced the crown with a harp – once banned by the British Crown to stifle Irish rebellion – when it broke free from its former political masters. This is, in my view, a trite observation, because it ignores the dynamism inherent in Bunreacht na hÉireann, the bedrock of our republic that in 1937 replaced the 1922 constitution of the Irish Free State.

For all its faults, including a heavy reliance on Papal encyclicals and Roman Catholic teaching that has cast a long shadow on Irish politics, religion and social policy – including family, education and health – the 1937 constitution has, for the most part, proved to be a robust and innovative charter. The 1937 constitution inaugurated not just a new era of parliamentary sovereignty and representative democracy. Irish citizens also gifted to themselves a bill of fundamental rights capable of being litigated in the courts, a concept that Britain is still struggling with to this day, as its testy relationship with the incorporation and interpretation of the European Convention on Human Rights (ECHR) confirms.

The drafters also embedded the separation of powers and an express power of judicial review of legislation into the constitutional framework. The constitution itself could be changed only by way of referendum. This architecture facilitated the creation of an enduring if imperfect system of checks and balances on executive excess and granted power to judges to strike down laws deemed invalid with the provisions of the constitution. The Irish judiciary did little in the early years of the republic to heighten the fears of some of the drafters that the new constitutional contract would pave the way for un-trammelled judicial activism. But no one could have imagined that the combined phenomena of judicial review and funda-mental rights capable of being articulated and protected in court actions would lead, in time, to the creation of a host of unenumerated personal rights identified by an emboldened, liberal judiciary in landmark challenges such as *Ryan*, the famous water-fluoridation case.

Unenumerated rights are personal rights that are not expressly mentioned in legal texts such as a written constitu-tion, but are inferred, divined or carved out from existing protections or the spirit of a given document.

In an Irish constitutional context, they are unspecified rights that judges have deemed, much to the chagrin of strict opponents of judicial activism, that are implicitly guaranteed in the constitution.

In *Ryan v. Attorney General* (1965), the Supreme Court held that a water-fluoridation scheme did not infringe the plaintiff's right to bodily integrity. Critically, however, the Supreme Court found that a right to bodily integrity did exist, despite the fact that it was not explicitly mentioned in the constitution.

The landmark case established the doctrine of unenumerated rights in Irish constitutional law – that rights guaranteed by the constitution are not confined to those expressly recognised in it.

The *Ryan* case and the jurisprudence it subsequently spawned have been dogged by controversy. Not least because Mr Justice Kenny in the High Court leg of the *Ryan* case opined that this new potential tranche of unspecified personal rights – which judges would ultimately interpret – flowed from 'the Christian and democratic nature of the State'.

Cases such as *Ryan* and *McGee* (1974) which recognised a right to marital privacy – which in turn encompassed the right to use contraceptives whose importation was banned at that time – paved the way for recognition of a series of unenumerated personal rights.

Other unenumerated rights including the right of the citizen to sue the state and the right to justice and fair procedures, were subsequently divined from the constitution by judges.

These judges themselves were, it seems, inspired by their fellow jurists in the United States whose activism was attracting international acclaim. After a slow start, pioneers such as Supreme Court judge Mr Justice Brian Walsh – arguably the single most influential judge in modern Irish constitutional jurisprudence – construed the 1937 constitution as a living, breathing document where no interpretation, in Judge Walsh's own words, was 'intended to be final for all time'. And it fell to this new generation of judges, and to litigants and their lawyers who saw the potential within the constitution, to haul Irish society further into modernity than prevailing social, moral and political norms permitted.

The appetite for the kind of liberal judicial lawmaking that thrived in Ireland from the 1960s onwards did not suit all tastes. Nor did that dynamic first wave of judicial activism last. Citizens have continually tried, and failed, to persuade the courts to recognise a host of social and economic rights inherent in the constitution or to reinterpret existing personal rights in the light of new social and technological advances. Perhaps the judiciary did, on occasion, cross the constitutional line with innovative interpretations and sporadic diktats from their unelected perches, but has the pendulum swung back too far?

It seems to me that we have, in recent years, entered into a period of entrenched, judicial conservatism where the courts –

with some notable exceptions – are loath to compel government to take any positive steps to protect citizens' rights, to
identify new ones or to carve out fresh interpretations from
existing rights. This may stem from a genuine and understandable fear that the separation of powers will be breached
if, for example, judges are accused of directing social or economic policy from the bench or instructing the state on when
and how to use its limited resources. Equally, however, the
public interest is not served if the constitutional process grinds
to a halt because of excessive judicial conservatism that plays
into the hands of politicians unwilling to breathe life into the
law and uphold their duty to legislate. It also leads to the perception that judges, more than a third of whom have direct
party political or family links to legislators, are afraid to
offend the political masters who appointed them.

The development of express and implied constitutional
rights is not the exclusive preserve of elected representatives,
who have failed abysmally to legislate in areas such as repro-
ductive and abortion rights and family law in order to adapt
to the needs of modern society. And so, some two decades
after the 1992 X case that convulsed the country, we have no
legal clarity on the status of the unborn or the circumstances
in which women can avail of legal abortion in Ireland.
Abortion has been (and remains) a criminal offence in Ireland
since 1861.

But in 1983, in a pre-emptive strike against the possibility
of Ireland's strict abortion regime being liberalised by judicial
activism, the eighth amendment was passed to the Irish constitution. The amendment, comfortably passed, granted
constutitional protection to the unborn, acknowledging as it
does the equal right to life of the unborn, with 'due regard' to
the equal right to life of the mother.

The fear that Ireland's criminal ban could be reviewed or liberalised by judges in part stemmed from the 1974 *McGee* decision (above) where the Supreme Court interpreted Article 40.3 of the Irish constitution as including an uneneumerated right to marital privacy and, by extension, to use contraceptives.

The eighth amendment was also motivated by factors such as the perennially controversial US Supreme Court *Roe v. Wade* ruling which recognised, on the basis of privacy law, a right to abortion in the United States of America.

In *Roe v. Wade* (1973) the US Supreme Court ruled that a right for a woman to terminate her pregnancy flowed from the right to privacy that had been established in a previous US ruling (*Griswold*, 1965), subject to the need to balance the right to life of the unborn foetus.

It was feared by some groups in Ireland that the domestic criminal ban on abortion might also be circumvented, on the grounds of privacy, by an activist Supreme Court here. Or that abortion might be liberalised courtesy of rights that might accrue to women under [then] EC law.

Designed ostensibly to placate those opposed to any relaxation of Ireland's strict abortion law, the 1983 amendment in fact laid the groundwork for an inevitable series of legal conflicts and, ultimately, the X case.

The X case, the Achilles heel of successive governments, involved a fourteen-year-old girl who became pregnant as the result of a rape. In December 1991 the girl revealed the abuse and her pregnant state to her parents and, after discussion, it was agreed that she should travel to England for an abortion.

When the distressed teenager's parents contacted the Gardaí (Irish police) to inquire if DNA evidence extracted from the aborted foetus could be used as evidence against her abuser, Gardaí contacted the Office of the Director of Public Prosecutions. The DPP, in turn, contacted the then Attorney General Harry Whelehan SC who obtained a High Court injunction preventing X from travelling abroad to terminate her pregnancy.

The resulting publicity about the injunction and X's plight proved extremely divisive and placed the courts in the unenviable if impossible role of balancing the equal right to life of the mother and her unborn foetus.

The High Court upheld the injunction, but the Supreme Court discharged it, mindful as members of the court were of the contention that there was a real and imminent risk that X would commit suicide if forced to proceed with her pregnancy.

In its ruling, the Supreme Court inisted that it was not for the courts to programme society and the late Supreme Court judge Mr Justice Niall McCarthy berated the government for its 'inexcusable' failure to introduce appropriate laws with regard to abortion.

In the end, the Supreme Court came up with a formula that allowed X to travel, although tragically she later had a miscarriage. The formula led to the recognition of legal abortion in Ireland, albeit in highly limited circumstances. As a result of X, abortion is permissible in Ireland if it is established as a matter of probability that there is a real and substantial risk to the life – as distinct from the health – of the mother which can be avoided only by the termination of the pregnancy.

This risk to maternal health includes the risk of suicide. But the formula angered many, not least because some questioned what evidence would be required to establish a threat to a mother's life (including a risk of suicide) and also because the court's formula did not place any time limits on when a termination could take place.

Since X, there have been numerous abortion-related referendums and a heartbreaking alphabet soup of cases brought in Ireland and before the European Court of Human Rights (ECtHR) by women seeking – among other things – for the law, post-X, to be clarified.

It has yet to be clarified and I often wonder what X, born in the same year as I was, must think of that landmark case now.

For Irish society, the abortion issue seems intractable: for elected representatives, it is political suicide. But that difficulty does not, as Judge McCarthy highlighted all those years ago, excuse our politicians from failing to legislate.

The X vacuum has had significant consequences for related areas such as IVF treatment, surrogacy and embryo research where medical advances alone, not to mention changes in attitudes over time, have demanded fresh legal and moral responses. This political dereliction of duty, coupled with a kind of judicial cowardice, has forced citizens, increasingly, to look outside the state, to bodies such as the ECtHR to safeguard civil and political rights that should find a domestic remedy within the body and spirit of our constitution and national body of laws.

Most citizens' lives are far removed from the often elitist debates about Irish constitutional jurisprudence, and the law is much more than a single document or set of rules. I spend much of my working life in the Four Courts and the Criminal Courts of Justice, less frequently at the Circuit and District Courts, even though this is where the vast majority of citizens interact with the legal system. From that vantage point you get to see the very best in Irish legal practice, including world-class advocacy and lawyers willing to take on unpopular or hopeless cases, often for no fee. You see the work of judges who are fair, fearless and independent, compassionate too in their rulings and the exercise of their wide-ranging discretion. On occasion you see glimpses of the worst in human behaviour and I have been genuinely shocked and saddened at the manner in which a small number of judges address citizens and non-nationals alike, who are treated in a summary and dismissive manner. Citizens have little or no recourse if they are unhappy with the way in which they have been treated in court, as distinct from appealing a decision on a point of law or the merits of a case. It is at times like this that I think of our forefather Brehon judges, whose traditional badge of office was a torque worn around their necks, which reputedly tightened if they lied or delivered an unfair or biased ruling. Their cheeks would blotch out of fear that they would be made personally liable for damages – or lose their jobs.

What about judicial ethics and conduct in this republic? More than ten years have passed since the Sheedy affair, which led to the resignation of two senior judges.

In 1999, Supreme Court Judge Hugh O'Flaherty and his High Court colleague Judge Cyril Kelly resigned after a Dublin man, Philip Sheedy, had the remainder of a four-year jail sentence suspended after serving one year. Mr Sheedy, an architect, had been convicted of dangerous driving causing death and the circumstances surrounding his early release prompted calls for a mechanism to allow judges' conduct to be subject to review.

The Judge Brian Curtin controversy also still sticks in the craw. In 2004 Circuit Court judge Brian Curtin was acquitted on on alleged child-pornography charges. The jury was directed to acquit Judge Curtin when it was revealed that

Gardaí had seized his computer illegally on an out-of-date search warrant. The judge later resigned after the government moved to impeach him.

In the wake of the Sheedy affair, the former Chief Justice Mr Justice Ronan Keane compiled a report that recommended the establishment of a judicial council with specific powers to conduct inquiries into allegations concerning the conduct of judges. The government is finally moving in this direction. So too is the judiciary, which – in what some viewed as a pre-emptive strike – has set up its own representative council, the Association of Judges of Ireland (AJI).

The relationship between the executive and the judiciary has, like many relationships, been strained by the economic crisis. The failed Oireachtas Inquiries Referendum, which planned to grant powers to politicians hold inquiries – but left doubt as to whether those being inquired into could access the courts if they believed their rights were being infringed – led to concerns that politicians were trying to take power back from judges. The flawed wording itself reflected the frustration of many politicians who resort to grandstanding because of a weak parliamentary edifice, copper-fastened by the whip system that emasculates them. It reflected a system that allows the Seanad, our upper house, to function as a nursery cum retirement home for party apparatchiks instead of a vital check on the executive and parliament. It is a system that lacks a strong independent committee system, as in Britain or the United States, to facilitate the formulation of policy in an inclusive and considered manner instead of allowing laws to be executed by guillotine.

In short, it is a system that – to our shame – has reduced our politicians to sheep, rather than the statesmen many aspire to be. Those weaknesses, and the overarching dominance of the executive, need to be addressed as part of any discussion about a new republic. But not, I would suggest, at the expense of an independent judiciary, without which there is no democracy.

The referendum to overturn the constitutional ban on reducing judges' pay while in office provided another source of antagonism between the executive and the judiciary. The seed for the success of the referendum to reduce judges' pay was sown by judges themselves. The bench scored a spectacular own goal when judges failed to sign up as a group to a voluntary scheme with the Revenue Commissioners in lieu of a mandatory pension levy for all public servants. Most, in time, did so, but the gesture was not sufficient to appease the citizenry's wrath. The referendum to reduce judges' pay was an easy one to pass, tapping as it did into the populist urge to force well-paid judges with lucrative pensions to take a pay cut. But the *raison d'être* for the former constitutional ban, to ensure politicians would not target judicial earnings at a whim – and that judges would not feel pressurised to placate their political paymasters – was largely lost in the debate.

Now we have a situation where judges, unelected and virtually unimpeachable, are dealing directly with government – with no independent body to intervene – on issues of pay, pensions and other matters that the public may never become aware of. This is the potentially dangerous scenario the original constitutional ban sought to ensure would never happen.

Added to this mix is our outdated and unsatisfactory system of appointing judges. Notwithstanding the introduction, in 1995, of the Judicial Appointments Advisory Board – a body established to depoliticise the judicial appointments process – judges are still political appointees, and this carries a risk, however small, of undue influence by the executive.

More damning than the risk, however small, of undue influence by the executive is the public perception that politicians are packing the courts with political appointees.

Any assessment of whether the law is serving the republic requires an examination of some or all of the fundamentals that are said to define a republic. One of the grounding principles is access to justice. At present, vast numbers of citizens are denied access to justice owing to a range of factors, including inexcusable delays in court procedures that could be diminished by simple structural reforms and targeted investment. The creation of the Commercial Court, which was set up to fast-track big-business disputes and make Ireland an attractive place for corporations, is one excellent example of how the state can facilitate access to justice when it needs to.

The prohibitive legal cost of going to court is arguably the biggest barrier to seeking justice. It seems that only the very rich or the very poor, with everything to gain or nothing to lose, can have their day in court or afford the independent legal advice they need to assert and protect their rights. Access to civil legal aid is woefully insufficient and is a major barrier to ordinary members of the public getting access to the courts and legal representation. And for those living on the bread line deemed lucky enough to qualify for the scheme, they have to endure a chronically long waiting time, which only adds to the injustice. A key role is now being played by a host of non-governmental organisations such as the Free Legal Advice Centres (FLAC) and the Northside Community Law Centre (NCLC) who are stepping into the breach to provide access to justice for those on the margins of society and the new 'working poor' struggling to deal with mortgages and personal debts.

The surge in demand for these services and recourse to state agencies such as the Legal Aid Board and the Money Advice and Budgeting Service (MABS) – notwithstanding the excellent services under difficult circumstances these bodies provide – is not a cause for celebration: it is a damning indictment of the state's failure to provide access to justice for the bulk of its citizens.

The issue of legal costs has been shamefully kicked into touch by both the legal profession and the government, which – as the largest single buyer of legal services – bears a huge responsibility for allowing costs to spiral and maintaining them at artificially high levels. Separately, a somewhat disturbing campaign has been mounted against the criminal legal-aid scheme, arguably the one part of the criminal-justice system that works quite well. Successive governments have introduced a range of legislative measures encroaching on the custodial and pre-trial rights of accused persons who are almost exclusively drawn from Ireland's lowest socio-economic ranks.

Efficiencies can always be improved and the criminal legal-aid scheme is not immune from abuse. But it seems obscene and disproportionate to be attacking underclasses that need the financial assistance of the state in order to fight the extensive resources of the state – especially at a time when more than €260m a year is being paid to legal panels hired by NAMA to carry out due diligence on loans that should have been carried out by lawyers and the banks they worked for in the first place. It is worth dwelling on the fact that some €2.6bn or more has been earmarked to cover legal and related fees in connection with the various transactions that will take place over the projected ten-year lifespan of the Kafkaesque agency whose inner workings are shielded in secrecy. This is money that will be spent on lawyers and others to clean up the failure to regulate our banks. In comparison, the criminal legal-aid scheme costs less than €60m a year – and this amount is in steep decline. The cost of running the Office of the Director of Public Prosecutions is still less at some €40m a year.

It is not the fault of the legal profession that the banks almost collapsed, although the legal sector and other professions certainly had a role to play. But if the €85bn price that current and future generations must pay has its roots in a wholesale lack of regulation, at heart a catastrophic failure of the law, then the law did not serve the republic well: it almost destroyed it. What is even more galling, and without prejudice to the many investigations that are under way into the activity of individuals at certain financial institutions and elsewhere, is the fact few people have been charged, let alone convicted, in relation to the near collapse of the economy. And yet we continue to send thousands of people to jail every year over their failure to pay civil debts such as credit cards, credit-union arrears, dog and television licences, while leaving high-flying tax evaders – including elected representatives – at large and free from prosecution.

This two-tier justice system is deeply corrosive. It undermines society's faith in the prosecution of white-collar crime and is an affront to social solidarity and the republican ideal of equality. And despite the need to reform radically the legal profession and the system it serves, I doubt whether the proposed Legal Services Regulation Bill (LSRB) will address many of the critical issues facing ordinary members of the public seeking access to justice.

There are many ways in which citizens can be denied access to justice. The destruction of much of our human-rights infrastructure, including the Irish Human Rights Commission and the Equality Authority, is one such example. The filleting of the Freedom of Information regime is another. One of my own personal bugbears is the operation of the In Camera rule that cloaks all family law and almost all childcare proceedings in privacy. The case for a considered relaxation of the In Camera rule in family law proceedings and proceedings involving children is overwhelming. It has been for some time. The blanket ban enshrined in the Courts (Supplemental Provisions) Act 1961 and reiterated across several statutes including our divorce, domestic violence and childcare laws, is designed to protect the privacy of families and children embroiled in family and child law cases. But the blanket nature of the ban is a disproportionate measure, an insult to the constitutional principle of open justice and is unfair to families seeking justice in the courts. No one expects the veil of secrecy to be lifted entirely in family and child law cases, but it should be pierced sufficiently to enhance public confidence in the family law courts to promote the type of public debate that, in turn, will lead to better-informed social and legal policies in this area. The bar is raised even further in childcare proceedings. The treatment of children in care is a matter of public law in the broadest sense and, all too often, the need to protect the identity of troubled children coincides with the need to protect the system that is failing them. Given the competing constitutional rights at stake, any reform of the In Camera rule must be measured, but it must be done.

Another issue to be addressed in this period of post-crisis reflection is how far threats such as terrorism or financial emergency can be used to justify encroachments on our civil liberties and personal rights. This is the cry of emergency, which Supreme Court judge Mr Justice Adrian Hardiman described in the constitutional challenge against NAMA by property investor Paddy McKillen as an 'intoxicating one, producing an exhilarating freedom from the need to consider the rights of others and productive of a desire to repeat it again and again'.

There are legitimate situations in which the rule of law must be suspended or subdued to meet a crisis. The present constitution identifies these situations as a state of armed war or rebellion. The rule of law can also be set aside in times of natural disaster or in an acute public-health crisis. And it is accepted, in a country that introduced special powers to stand down subversive activity during the Troubles, that terrorism and gang-related crime could test the rule of law to its limits and require legitimate responses.

One of the reasons, I suspect, why there have been calls in some quarters to reimagine a new republic stems in part from the abuse of the cry of emergency by the executive in recent years, including crucial decisions such as the now discredited banking guarantee issued in 2008 without any democratic discussion of its consequences.

The night of the bank guarantee, involving as it did the convening of an 'incorporeal' cabinet meeting in the wee small hours as Gardaí were sent to the home of a sleeping government minister, continues – in the absence of transparency surrounding the circumstances leading up to the all-encompassing guarantee – to cause huge offence and suspicion. This at a time when public confidence in the political system, debased by lasting images of politicians and developers frolicking in the tent at the Galway Races, has been decimated.

The public's reaction to the present crisis and its origins resembles, at times, much of the caustic rage expressed during the notorious Dublin Lockout by the Irish poet William Butler Yeats in his seminal poem 'September, 1913', in which Yeats castigates those in power who do not do right by the citizens of Ireland.

Almost a hundred years after Yeats's searing attack on the political and merchant classes, Irish citizens are suffering from what might be described as a lockout syndrome. Many look with contempt on the political as well as the banking, corporate and legal classes. They hold those classes, with their light-touch regulation, responsible for 'fumbling in a greasy till' during the good times and drying marrow from the bones of the poor and new working poor during the current recession.

This is not to say that the politicians and civil servants tasked with dealing with the economic crisis have not faced tough choices and many, no doubt, hold a sincere belief that they acted in the public interest. But the executive has failed to justify to the public many of the emergency measures and the unreviewable powers it granted to itself and to external agencies such as the European Central Bank. All too often, the emergency measure becomes normalised and, when that happens, democracy and the rule of law are the real losers. That is one of the reasons why, I imagine, so many citizens feel powerless.

This loss of sovereignty, more real than imagined, is fuelling demand for a new republic, a reordering of our democracy. And that leads us to the big white elephant in the room: Europe. It is simply not possible to contemplate a new republic or constitution without considering the future of Europe, that still unfolding drama. There are so many tough questions we must ask as we harbour hopes of a new republic.

How far are we prepared to go to alter our society radically? Can the constitutional supremacy of the family based on marriage be maintained in light of the changing nature of Irish families? Should we extend full marital rights to gay and lesbian couples as part of a true equality agenda? Should a new constitution incorporate meaningful social and economic rights such as the right to housing and healthcare? Is a new constitution enough to renew our democracy and do we have the guts to back our aspirations up with radical institutional reform to give life to our ideals?

But these questions, and many like them, seem redundant when compared with Ireland's awesome loss of sovereignty engendered by the financial crisis, as well as the debate about the future of Europe and Ireland's role within it. The fiscal treaty referendum, and the Lisbon Treaty before it, was passed out of fear, voters ticking yes from the confines of their fiscal straitjackets. Other countries have experienced social unrest as a consequence of the imposed austerity programme, but the Irish population it seems has been cowed into submission.

The big questions, such as under what law was the transfer of resources from current and future generations of Irish citizens to French and German bondholders mandated, are not being asked. Questions such as which European constitution or rule requires the ECB to account to Irish citizens are not being raised because of a fear of jeopardising the chance of future bailouts. Few are asking how the Irish state and other small democracies at the periphery of Europe can truly protect their citizens when their authority and the constitutions from which they derive their power are incidental to the main European drama. The silence that follows these questions speaks volumes about the health of our republic and the difficulties of imagining a new one.

The Herculean debate we need to have around sovereignty, the core of any republic, also makes a mockery of the government's planned Constitutional Convention. The 'comprehensive constitutional reform' to be discussed, including lowering the voting age by a year and reducing the presidential term by two years, is wholly inconsequential compared to the fundamental debates around sovereignty and electoral reform we badly need.

The task of reimagining a new republic, therefore, will not be an easy one, but the role of the law will be critical to that task. The law, like life, is relentless and must move forward. And the law will be one of the most important components of any reordered republic as it will hold up – as it does now – a mirror to our heritage and values. Any new republic will necessarily have to incorporate a new legal order, but how much of the old republic would we discard? I imagine that if we did imagine a new republic, if we rewrote the Irish constitution, much of the spirit and substance of the 1937 document would survive the transition to a new sovereign order. In doing so, we can find inspiration in our rich legal ancestry and the community-based ethos much loved by the ancient Irish. Yeats summonsed the ghosts of John O'Leary, Edward Fitzgerald, Robert Emmet and Wolfe Tone, patriots who sacrificed themselves so that Ireland could be a great nation. Is Romantic Ireland truly dead and gone; can we prove Yeats wrong? A new republic will require brave revolutionaries of the kind who are willing to stand up for Ireland's best interests and honour the plight of our new 'wild geese' disenchanted or exiled by the economic crisis.

6

Citizens or Subjects? Civil Society and the Republic

FRED POWELL

Saturday 3 December 2011 saw a hugely successful pre-budget 'Parade of Defiance' against the IMF-imposed cuts throughout the streets of Cork. This was a creative protest organised by *Occupy Cork* to show the city's opposition to austerity measures and to raise our voices together against the undemocratic forcing of these cuts on the people of this country. Between 1,000 and 1,200 people marched behind banners with messages such as 'Not my Debt' and 'This is not a Recession, this is a Robbery'.

Occupy Cork, issue 3, 2011

The Little People came suddenly. I don't know who they are. I don't know what it means. I was a prisoner of the story [*IQ84*]. I had no choice. They came, and I described it. That is my work.

Haruki Murakami,
New York Review of Books, 8 December 2011

Two recent events captured the essence of our times. First, the Occupy movement which began in Wall Street, New York City, on 17 September 2011, and spread across the world. The message of the Occupy movement is a simple one. It opposes the austerity measures imposed on ordinary people around the world, the 99 per cent who it argues have been expropriated by the wealthiest 1 per cent of the population. Second, the much anticipated Haruki Murakami novel was published in 2011, entitled *IQ84*. Clearly inspired by George Orwell's *1984* parable about Stalinist tyranny, *IQ84* takes the reader into a counterworld of unreality. Surveillance is all-pervasive and the innocent 'Little People' hide from a weirdly unsettling Lewis Carroll wonderland of horrors and the horrifying exercise of power over the mesmerised. Both the Occupy movement and Murakami's *IQ84* illuminate aspects of the world we currently inhabit: the dominance of unaccountable and largely invisible systems of power but also the willingness of citizens to struggle against these dark forces. The 'Little People' have become the 'unsignified signifiers' probing behind the mirror of power.[1]

This essay is about the meaning of civil society and its relevance to the idea of 'The Republic' in the conditions of economic and political crisis that define twenty-first-century Ireland. It is also about the relationship between fiction and reality in our contemporary political narrative. It offers, finally, ten principles for critical citizenship.

Civil Society, Rights and Democracy

In the debate about civil society the key terms – civil/civic, society, virtue, community – all originate in the ancient world. For our purposes however, the debate in the modern world is traceable to the Enlightenment. Key early influences were Thomas Hobbes (1588–1679), John Locke (1632–1704) and Benedict de Spinoza (1632–1677). Hobbes and Locke constructed civil society 'as a contractually produced and politically guaranteed instrument of individuals who came together to attain some conscious purpose'.[2] Spinoza rejects Hobbes's conservative contractarianism as too negative in terms of constraining human freedom, most prominently in the latter's book *Leviathan* (1651). He similarly rejects Locke's more liberal reformulation of Hobbes. Instead Spinoza presents liberty 'as a positive good or inalienable potential', in which political freedom can flourish and where reason and virtue are connected in a benevolent relationship between the citizen and the state.[3] The logic of Spinoza's argument is fundamentally radical. Russ Leo asserts 'it is Spinoza and Spinozism which promotes the adoption of secular reason and government, universal toleration and shared equity among all men, personal liberty, freedom of expression and democratic republicanism'.[4] Conservatives rejected 'Spinozist claims as anarchic and atheistic innovations that quickly breach the limit of what is necessary to maintain order, and morality in a civil (and religious) society'.[5] Despite censorship and police surveillance 'by the mid-1670s Spinoza stood at the head of an underground radical philosophical movement rooted in the Netherlands but decidedly European in scope'.[6]

After Spinoza's death in 1677 a 'forbidden movement' inspired by his ideas spread across Europe despite the constraints of censorship, suppression and hostility.[7] Liberal thinkers of more moderate persuasion also began to explore the importance of civil society – notably in Scotland. The Scottish Enlightenment sought to resolve the relationship between faith and reason through Scottish Common Sense, which put it at odds with the Radical Enlightenment of Spinozism.[8] *The Theory of Moral Sentiments* (1759) by Adam Smith (1723–1790) 'offered a powerful conjecture about the way in which some citizens acquire that sense of fitness and ethical beauty which makes it possible for them to aspire to a life of virtue'.[9] John Ehrenberg concludes 'it was Adam Smith who first articulated a specifically bourgeois conception of civil society. His effort to integrate economic activity and market processes in a more general understanding of the anatomy of civilized life is a milestone in the development of modern thought.'[10] The explicit use of the term is first evident in a treatise by the Scottish Enlightenment thinker, Adam Ferguson, who first published *An Essay on the History of Civil Society* in 1773. In this work Ferguson explores the tensions and paradoxes inherent in the concept of civil society, which persist to the present day.

Similarly the German philosopher, Georg Wilhelm Friedrich Hegel (1770–1831), explored the concept of civil society in the definitive version of his monumental system of political and social philosophy, as it appeared in the 1821 edition of *Philosophy of Right*. For Hegel, civil society incorporates the spheres of economic relations and class formation as well as the judicial and administrative structure of the state. He does not include pre-state relations, such as the family and community, which essentially define the term 'civil society' in its most common usage today.

The debate about civil society in modern social and political thought started in the Old World, but quickly crossed the Atlantic to the New World of the American Colonies. Essential to the widening of the debate was Thomas Paine (1737–1809), raconteur, polemicist and republican, who dominated progressive political thought in Britain, France, America and Ireland during the age of revolutionary struggle against absolutist tyranny in the last quarter of the eighteenth century. In his highly influential pamphlet, *Common Sense*, published in 1776, Paine introduced the term 'civilised society' as a natural and potentially self-regulating form of association, counterpoised to 'Government', which was in his view, at best, a necessary and artificial evil. However, Paine was vague about what precisely he meant by civil society.[11] Paine's radical republicanism spread to Ireland and proved a formative influence on the United Irishmen.[12] His pamphlet *Rights of Man* sold 40,000 copies in Ireland.[13]

The French aristocrat Alexis de Tocqueville (1805–1859), who visited the United States in the 1830s, was a great deal more cautious. Liberal by political persuasion, de Tocqueville is sometimes regarded as having depoliticised the term 'civil society', celebrating any form of associational activity for its own sake in his study *Democracy in America*, first published in 1835. In fact, de Tocqueville laid considerable stress on participation in local democracy as the best method for ensuring that civil association reinforced and protected democratic politics against tyranny. However, the core of his conception of civil society devolved on the health of intermediate institutions, usually the family, the community and churches. As de Tocqueville put it:

> Amongst the laws which rule human societies, there is one which seems to be more precise and clear than all others. If men are to remain civilised, or to become so, the art of associating together must grow and improve in the same ration in which equality of conditions is increased.[14]

Howard Zinn[15] in his classic study *A People's History of the United States* has cast doubt on de Tocqueville's positive vision of American civil society, arguing that it was in reality profoundly divided between rich and poor. De Tocqueville's cautious liberalism was to prove highly influential on the Young Ireland movement during the 1840s.[16]

While de Tocqueville was commenting from the perspective of liberal individualism other contemporary thinkers addressed the concept of civil society from a very different ideological standpoint. Utopian Socialists, including Henri de Saint-Simon (1760–1825), Charles Fourier (1772–1837) and Etienne Cabet (1788–1856), saw the great sources of evil in society as cut-throat competition, deceit, greed and inhumanity, and the great remedy as association and co-operation to restore harmony to human life. Fourierist communities, based on the ideals of association and co-operation, were established in New Jersey, Wisconsin and Massachusetts. In Ireland Robert Owen (1771–1858) and William Thompson (1775–1833) advocated similar ideals. Thompson's co-operativist ideals led to the establishment of the Ralahine community in early nineteenth-century Ireland.

On the other hand, Karl Marx (1818–1883), who along with a group of fellow German refugees in Paris in 1832 established the League of the Just (later the Communist League) as a bulwark against capitalism, rejected civil society. Marx regarded 'civil society as an illusion that needs to be unmasked'.[17] Later Marxists, notably Antonio Gramsci (1891–1937), who struggled against fascist tyranny in twentieth-century Italy, reworked the Marxist position. In his *Prison Notebook*, commenced in 1929 at the beginning of a twenty-year prison sentence, Gramsci wrote:

> What we can do, for the moment, is to fix two major superstructural 'levels': that one can be called 'civil society', and that of 'political society' or the 'State'. These two levels correspond on the one hand to the

function of 'hegemony' which the dominant group exercises throughout society, and on the other hand to that of 'direct domination' or rule exercised through the State and the judicial Government.[18]

For Gramsci, social inequality and class domination were exercised by a variety of cultural institutions that enabled the dominant group to impose its sense of reality on the rest of society. It was only through addressing the labyrinthine cultural complexity that the oppressed could liberate themselves and wrest control of civil society from the bourgeoisie, which had traditionally opposed popular participation. In Gramscian terms civil society was conceived as the site of alternative hegemonies.

From Gramsci's perspective the revolutionary task was not about the Jacobin–Leninist seizure of power, its inevitable violence and totalitarian outcome, with 'the Party becoming the Prince'. Political rupture in Gramsci's theory of action was about a struggle to liberate human consciousness from hegemonic domination. There is a direct link between Spinoza and Gramsci in their emphasis on a 'revolution of the mind', as a prelude to and condition of human freedom. Both sought to address existing hegemonies of power.

Gramsci had fundamentally changed Marx's economic determinism by adding culture to the cause of revolutionary change. In doing so he opened the way for a radical civil society, based on gender, ethnicity, sexuality, disability and environment to flourish during the second half of the twentieth century. New social movements have created a democratic force 'from below' that has revived the Ancient Greek tradition of civic republicanism based upon the *agora* – as a gathering place or citizen's assembly.

However, as Chris Hann and Elizabeth Dunn observe, 'it is the liberal strand that has become almost hegemonic in most recent debates'[19] about civil society. This is most obviously due to the transformation of Eastern Europe during the 1980s that brought about the overthrow of Stalinist tyranny. A more profound and subtle influence has been the universalisation of Western notions of freely associating individuals in a pluralistic democratic society, which have become the dominant political paradigm in postmodern society. Postmodernity represents the replacement of standardisation, nation states and uniformity that characterised the modern era by fragmentation, globalisation and the affirmation of individual difference.

While the struggles of Eastern European dissidents, most famously the Czech playwright Vaclav Havel, highlighted the threat to civil society in state-dominated regimes, there is a growing sense of the complexity of issues in postmodern society. Havel, later installed as the President of the Czech Republic following the Velvet Revolution, argued for 'anti-political politics'. Subsequently, a more sober analysis has emerged of the tide of change sweeping Eastern Europe since 1989. Hann and Dunn have observed that:

> The recent revolutions in Eastern Europe were the first in human history not to be concerned with establishing some form of rational Utopia. These societies (post-communist) are seen as characterised by unfettered egoism and consumerism. Only individuals exist, and they are allegedly devoid of significant human relationships.[20]

Vladimir Putin's Russia is manifestly democratically compromised and challenged by its internal critics. His suppression of civil society is also undemocratic.[23]

The equation of civil society with a generic Euro-American state is clearly an ideological position that has more to do with post-Cold War politics than serious social analysis. There are, manifestly, various definitions of civil society in the history of social and political thought, as outlined above. But the core distinction is probably a lexical conflict of meanings inherent in the term 'civil society', between 'citizen society' and 'market society'. This ambiguity is apparent in the German term for civil society, *burgerliche Gesellschaft*, translatable as both 'citizen society' and 'bourgeoisie society'.

Jean L. Cohen and Andrew Arato[24] have demonstrated how these two counterpoised meanings might be harmoniously reconciled without either becoming dominant over the other. They advocate a three-part model of social structure differentiating between (1) the activities of commerce, (2) the administrative powers of the state and (3) civil society that fosters a vibrant lifeworld of symbols and solidarities. Cohen and Arato consequently define civil society as 'a sphere of social interaction between economy and State, composed above all of the intimate sphere (especially the family), the sphere of associations (especially voluntary associations), social movements, and forms of public communications . . . institutionalised and generalised through laws'.[25]

The definition offered by Cohen and Arato creatively avoids conceptual ambiguity. But deeper, longer-term historical issues are also at stake. While much of the current social condition is novel, there is clearly an ongoing debate about the nature of society and the role of the individual. The debate about civil society is emblematic of this more fundamental debate in an age when the grand historical narrative (Christianity, Marxism, and so on) has lost its persuasive force, at least in Western society. The replacement of the modern project of the nation state, latterly the welfare state, by 'post-modernity' raises larger questions about the idea of civil society to which we must now turn.

Political Language, Truth and Power

Civil society is politically about humanity's desire to nurture a public sphere for the common good. But there political contestation begins. Truth is shaped by ideology. Because we live in an era when conservatism is once again in the ascendant, we should not be blinded by its truths. The 2005 Nobel Laureate for Literature, Harold Pinter, reminded the world in his acceptance speech that 'there are many truths', adding that 'these truths challenge each other, recoil from each other, reflect from each other, tease each other'. He observed in relation to power and truth:

> Political language, as used by politicians, does not venture into any of this territory since the majority of politicians, on the evidence available to us, are interested not in truth but in power and in the maintenance of that power. To maintain that power it is essential that people remain in ignorance of the truth, even the truth of their own lives. What surrounds us therefore is a vast tapestry of lies, upon which we feed.[26]

Pinter concluded: 'Sometimes you feel you have the truth of the moment in your hand then it slips through your fingers and is lost.'[27] These wise observations on the many-sided nature of truth underline the complexity of the task of understanding civil society in political terms. That a great seer of Pinter's stature should find the truth so challenging underlines the task for us lesser mortals. He has posed profound questions about the quality and reality of our democratic experience. Civil society has a key role in monitoring democracy.[28]

Strong Democracy: Beyond Political Zoology

Benjamin Barber in his book *Strong Democracy*, published in 1984, laments the erosion of democracy from within, through the triumph of thin (representative) democracy – which in his view marginalises citizens from the decision-making process. He likens this process to 'politics as zookeeping', in which 'democracy is undone by a hundred kinds of activity more profitable than citizenship; by a thousand seductive acquisitions cheaper than liberty'.[29] Thin democracy shifts power to distant representative institutions, far from communities where citizens live. Instead of participation in decision-making, citizens are reduced to a passive state like animals in a zoo waiting for their keepers to decide their lives for them. Strong democracy envisages the participation of all the citizenry in at least some aspects of governance at least some of the time. Civil society opens up the public realm to the possibility of participative democracy. As Barber puts it:

> From the perspective of this political zoology, civil society is an alternative to the 'jungle' – to war of all against all that defines the state of nature. In that poor and brutish war, the beasts howl in voices made articulate by reason – for zoos, for cages and trainers, for rules and regulations, for regular feeding times and prudent custodians. Like captured leopards, men are to be admired for their unshackled freedom, but they must be caged for their untrustworthiness and anti-social orneriness all the same.

Indeed, if the individual is dangerous, the species is deadly. Liberal democracy's sturdiest cages are reserved for the People.[30]

Strong democracy offers society the choice of taking responsibility for the democratic restoration that has the potential to give substance to the somewhat hackneyed slogan 'power to the people'.

Thomas Prugh et al. assert:

Strong democracy offers several immediate advantages over current systems:

- It would make communities stronger and more reflective of their residents' visions for their common lives. Strong democracy builds community by engaging people with each other as they struggle to address common issues. It strengthens the 'us' without sacrificing the 'me'.
- Strong democracy disperses power, redistributing it downward so that governance is less susceptible to dominance by specific interests.
- Strong democracy acts as a reality check by bringing citizens more directly into contact with the problems of governance.[31]

They add: 'We need a politics of engagement, not a politics of consignment, in other words participative rather than representative democracy.'[32]

We live in a world where many active citizens are concerned to address the democratic deficits that have arisen in the period of globalisation. Participation has become a pivotal concern.

Iris Marion Young asserts that 'beyond membership and voting rights, inclusive democracy enables participation and voice
for all those affected by problems and their proposed solutions'.[33] In essence, this is a statement of strong democracy. It
promotes participation and inclusion. In contrast, thin democracy leaves it to political elites to speak for us and represent
our interests. There is a fundamental issue of political equality
and republican respect at issue here. Moreover, there is an issue
of trust and toleration that defines pluralistic democracy. The
reality is that not everybody is given equal voice in liberal democratic societies. Monarchy survives in its exalted role as a
wholly undemocratic institution based on the most extreme
form of exclusion – blood lineage. But perhaps more troubling
is the role of the oligarchies of power and wealth in manufac-
turing consensus, through their capacity to monopolise the
media and purchase political influence. In this hierarchal world
of power, exclusion is rife. As Young puts it, 'perhaps the most
pervasive and insidious form of external exclusion in modern
democracies is what I referred to as the ability for economically or socially powerful actors also to exercise political domination'.[34] She asserts that 'one task of democratic civil society
is to explore and criticise exclusions such as these, and doing
so sometimes effectively challenge the legitimacy of institutional rules and their decisions'.[35] The above critique of the
limits of democratic inclusion invites the question, 'Is there any
point in participation?' Bill Cooke and Uma Kothari (2002)
suggest that there might not be any value in participation and
add that it is unreasonable to push people in that direction.[36]
They view the postmodern political landscape as barren and
civil society as a meaningless concept.

In reality politics often rests on the cultivation of fictions
upon which narratives are constructed. The history of the

modern Irish state is based on a series of political fictions. Within these political fictions politicians have wrestled with Ferdinand Tonnies's classic distinction between *Gemeinschaft* (community) and *Gesellschaft* (society). The first fiction of 'an Irish republic' was distinctly communitarian and traditional, and not in conformity with republican values as generally understood.

The Communitarian Republic and Militant Democracy

The nation-builders of the new Ireland sought to put the concept of 'local community' at the centre of their political vision. Paddy O'Carroll has observed in this regard:

> The small community was, therefore, not only the reality of the lives of most; it was also the key basis of their vision. As a cultural symbol central to most Irish identities of the time, community was an obvious rhetorical device to be used in the building of the nationalist state. It implied unity, wholeness and belonging; it imparted a strong sense of place and a hierarchy of entitlements. All of this reinforced in a commonsense way by Catholicism in general, by the experience of the Catholic parish locally and by the irrefragable unity of the image of the island.[37]

With the collapse of traditional community in Europe, Ireland fell back on a religious concept of the nation – based on traditional community. The idea was to find (or invent) a shared idea of national community, rather than social transformation. It was a collective political fiction contesting modernity that eschewed class politics in favour of a traditionalist vision of the past as the future. This was based on a morally centred ideal of community. The sustainable rural community came to embody the ideal of Ireland, spared from the pernicious influence of modern urban society. The parish became synonymous with the ideal of community. Priests became shamans of social Ireland totally dominating local civil society and exercising a hegemonic grip on the public sphere.

These kinds of cultural and political impulses have been characterised by Clifford Geertz as 'essentialism'.[38] He viewed them as characteristic of newly formed nation states. The vision of the 'community' as opposed to 'society' as a locus of the new nation state also evokes Tonnies's distinction between *Gemeinschaft* (community) and *Gesellschaft* (society).[39] Tonnies's social vision was shared by Ireland's nation-builders, most notably Eamon de Valera, arguably the nation's founding father. It was a traditionalist vision deeply rooted in cultural pessimism that feared modernity. Terence Brown observes that this pessimism was warranted, noting the 'spectacle of an Irish rural world without cultural hope or energy'.[40] Contemporaries shared this cultural pessimism. George Russell (Æ) (1867–1935) records, in his first journal the *Irish Statesman* (the voice of Fabianism in Ireland and alternate to the *New Statesman* in Britain), that in the immediate aftermath of independence there was social disintegration.

Faced with a series of challenges to the fledgling state, Eamon de Valera responded in a repressive manner to combat threats from militant republicans and the Blueshirts to Ireland's fragile democratic future. This strategy is called 'militant democracy', a term invented by Karl Loewenstein in 1937 to describe restrictions on civil and political freedom to contain fascism.[41] The most recent example of militant democracy was the withdrawal by several Irish universities of an invitation to speak to Nick Griffin MEP, leader of the

British National Party. Arguably, de Valera's version of militant democracy went further than the containment of republican and fascist threats. His 1937 constitution sought to reconcile popular sovereignty with Catholic social teaching, creating a conservative and distinctly sectarian state. The Irish constitution is not secular, since there is no separation between Church and state. It has resulted in major abuses of Catholic social power identified in the Ryan Report (2009), the Murphy Report (2009) and the Cloyne Report (2011) into clerical child abuse. But more fundamentally it circumscribed Irish democracy and repressed civil society – which was dominated throughout most of the twentieth century by the clergy.[42]

Modernisation, Sustainability and Political Fiction

The adoption of the project of modernisation from the 1960s onwards, involving entry into the European Community (now EU) in 1973, was to relocate Ireland's development trajectory within the global context, creating a new political fiction. It set the scene for the emergence of the Celtic Tiger economy, which became a metaphor for Ireland's reimagined development as a global urban society within the European Union. The debate about modernisation is essentially about models of development in this globalised context. As Ireland has moved from under-development through development to post-development – within the historical trajectory of the Irish state (founded in 1922) – new debates have emerged about the meaning and relevance of sustainability. The issue of the benefits of development, represented as 'good change' in public discourse, has been challenged by alternative models based on the goal of sustainable development. Following the emergence of the global economic crisis brought about by the collapse of international financial markets during 2008, new questions are being asked about the role of the state, as it seeks to deal with the consequences of market failure. Three models of development emerge in this modernisation debate, as illustrated in the table below.

Models of Development[43]

MODEL	IDEOLOGY	STRATEGY	GOAL	LOCATION
Market-led	Capitalism/ Neoliberalism	Modernisation	Globalisation	Economy
State-led	Social Democracy/ Marxism	State planning	Social equality	Politics/ Government
Community-led	Democracy/ Civic Republicanism	Citizen participation	Sustainable development	Civil society

The market-led model has been the dominant one in the age of globalisation, shaped by neoliberal ideology. But its hegemony has been challenged by the crash in 2008 and the requirement that the state save the market from total failure. The state-led model largely disappeared with the waning of socialism after 1989. The community-led model offers the only politically acceptable alternative to the market-led model in the contemporary world. This does not mean that the state-led model of development won't work. Up to the 1960s there was a concern in the West that the planned economy was more effective than the market-led model. Furthermore, the Chinese party-state model challenges the Western narrative of development based on the free market, representative democracy and the rule of law. The community-led model of development offers a new political fiction based on citizen participation and sustainability in a project that promises to rewrite the grammar of politics. It invites us to rethink the nature of modernity as an imaginary act. Cornelius Castoriadis in his book *The Imaginary Institution of Society* (1987) has argued that radical politics needs to move beyond the socialist (Marxist) exclusive preoccupation with capital. He redefines modernity as a struggle between the radical democratic project of autonomy (i.e. personal freedom to determine one's own future without structural manipulation) and the institutional project of mastery by the disciplinarian state. Writing about Castoriadis's theory, Gerald Delanty says that 'the focus on creativity offers an alternative theorisation of modernity echoing the idea of *homo faber* (man the maker) in Aristotle and Marx: the idea of society as an artefact created by human beings'.[44] New social movements within a reinvigorated civil society are playing a central role in reimagining political grammar in terms of being active citizens involved in a struggle for autonomy. Arguably, this is the progressive political fiction of postmodernity. This is a community-led model of development, based in civil society and inspired by the civic republican tradition of democracy that engages the citizenry in the polity, with the goal of sustainable development.

Sustainable communities provide a metaphor for deepening democratic politics that challenges previous ideologies of state or market dominance. It finds its most powerful expression in the New Bolivarianism that has reshaped the politics of Latin America – the first world region to disavow neoliberalism. But is it possible to reinvent Ireland's politics around the ideal of sustainable communities? Proposals from the Green Party in the last coalition government (2007–11) to devolve political decision-making to local communities suggests that the base of Irish democracy can be broadened. But in a global society we are left with the paradox of the placelessness of power and the powerlessness of place. This is the fundamental challenge that the idea of sustainable communities faces as a model of development, in a David and Goliath struggle for power.

Barack Obama in the *Audacity of Hope* (2008) built a presidential political platform around the generation of a new kind of politics. This is a politics that draws on the Ancient Greek tradition of civic republicanism, based on the ideal of sustainable democratic communities. In other words, the *agora*. President Obama has utilised his experience as a community organiser in Chicago to reinvigorate the concept of citizenship. His slogan 'yes, we can' invites the public to reimagine its relationship with the polity. The extraordinary political success of the Obama 2008 campaign was to create new political fiction at a time when Americans (and the rest of the world) were looking for change. President Obama, an advocate of reconciliation and participation, dreamt of a new Athens to replace the Sparta of the Bush administration – revitalised global democracy versus imperial military hegemony. This may be a Utopian vision that is at odds with *realpolitik* but it resonates with global progressive opinion. Political judgement will be passed on Obama's success or failure during 2012 in the presidential elections. His modest stimulus package, rescue of the banks and failure to reverse welfare reform have undermined the hope that the Obama presidency would be radical and transformational.

The Republic of Crisis: Apocalypse Now

Francis Ford Coppola's 1979 epic war film *Apocalypse Now* (an adaption of Joseph Conrad's novella *Heart of Darkness*) depicts modern war as a descent into primal madness. Set in the Vietnam War, it tells the story of war-weary Captain Willard (Martin Sheen) being dispatched to assassinate AWOL Renegade Colonel Kurtz (Marlon Brando) – secreted in the Cambodian jungle, where he is rumoured to have established himself as a local godhead. Kurtz's genocidal dictum 'Drop the Bomb: Exterminate them all', graphically illustrated by human heads mounted on stakes outside his compound, provides a hallucinatory Wagnerian quality to a film in which the insanity of the individual mirrors the insanity of the Vietnam War. The director struggled to find an ending to the film. This became a metaphor for the film itself in which reality and fantasy are merged. There is no purpose. Consequently, there can't be an end – at least not an end with a point, since futility on a grotesque scale has no point!

In a sense *Apocalypse Now* reflects the contemporary crisis that Ireland (arguably the most globalised country in the world) has inherited. It is hard to see an end to the crisis. Austerity (which makes recovery very difficult, if not impossible) is the officially supported policy in Dublin and Brussels. Yet, it doesn't seem to have a point – other than an ideological point. All of the escape routes have been closed off by the markets. The crisis has become political paralysis.

Slavoj Žižek argues in his book *Living at the End Times* (2011), that global capitalism is fast approaching its terminal crisis. He identifies the Four Horsemen of the Apocalypse as the worldwide ecological crisis; imbalances within the economic system; the biogenetic revolution; and exploding social divisions and ruptures. He characterises public reaction to this economic Armageddon in psychological terms as stages of grief: ideological denial, explosions of anger and attempts at bargaining, followed by depression and withdrawal.

Žižek's apocalyptic prediction of the end of global capitalism is not new. It is an end of civilisation thesis that has been around for half a century. It was propounded originally by Harvard professor Daniel Bell in his famous book *The End of Ideology* (1962) which claimed that the modernist project was exhausted and the acceptance of 'managed capitalism' was the only available political choice. The 'grand narratives' or 'big ideas' of the modern age were bankrupt. History was, after all, unchangeable. The future would be conservative. We have reached the ideological terminus of historical development, according to Bell. Similarly, Francis Fukuyama's book, *The End of History* (1992), claimed just that – the great ideological debates of the previous two centuries were over and liberal democracy in the form of market capitalism was triumphant. Socialism and transformative views of history were dead. Both Bell and Fukuyama and their many imitators in the millenarian preoccupation with 'endisms' were somewhat premature in their announcements. It is certainly true that the Western tradition of Enlightenment rationalism and belief in progress are in crisis. Whether this proves to be a terminal crisis remains to be seen. Both Bell and Fukuyama may be wrong in assuming that the future will be liberal and Western in the shape of American values. The Japanese philosopher Takeshi Umehara has observed that 'the total failure of Marxism . . . and the dramatic break up of the Soviet Union are only the precursors of the collapse of Western liberalism, the main current of modernity. Far from being the alternative to Marxism and the reigning ideology at the end of history, liberalism will be the next domino to fall.'[45] Islam laid down a dramatic challenge in the tragic events of 11 September 2001, when religious fanatics struck the heart of American economic and military power – the World Trade Center and the Pentagon. It has been followed by the erosion of civil liberties in the West that threatens the fabric of liberal democracy. This reflects a crisis of trust in democracy. Moreover, what we may be witnessing, as security increasingly dominates the agenda, is the end of politics as a forum for open debate, which is the crucible in which democracy flourishes. Tariq Ali comments from the vantage point of a lifelong political radical on the left of the spectrum:

> This closure of politics and economics produces fatal consequences. A disempowered people is constantly reminded of its own weakness. In the West a common response is to sink into the routines that dominate everyday life. Elsewhere in the world people become flustered, feel more and more helpless and nervous. Anger, frustration, despair multiply. They can no longer rely on the state to help. The laws favour the rich. So the more desperate amongst them, in search of a more meaningful existence or simply to break the monotony, begin to live by their own laws. Willing recruits will never be in short supply. The propaganda of the deed – the homage paid by the weak to the strong – will endure. It is the response of atomised individuals to a world that no longer listens, to politicians who have become interchangeable, to the corporations one-eyed in the search for profits and global media networks owned by the self-same corporations and locked into a relationship of mutual dependence with the politicians. This is the existential misery that breeds

insecurity and fosters deadly hatreds. If the damage is not repaired, sporadic outbursts of violence will continue to intensify.[46]

Ali's point is that Islamic terrorists in their 9/11 attack on the World Trade Center were asserting the primacy of religion over trade – God over capital and ultimately Islam over the Western tradition of modernity.

Ireland is at the epicentre of this global crisis. While we successfully ended the terrorist war in Northern Ireland through the 1998 Belfast Agreement, economic hubris has created a new crisis of unparalleled proportions. During our enthralment to the imaginary Celtic Tiger, arguably we became self-absorbed subjects (consumer citizens) rather than active citizens engaged in society. It was a perfect fantasy land – beyond the reach of reality, in which we borrowed from the future in a wager that we lost.

In post-Celtic Tiger Ireland, we are experiencing what Žižek calls the '*real* real', which he likens to the horror in a horror film. The line between politics and fantasy has become blurred in our contemporary reality. This presents Irish citizens with a series of questions:

- How can we overcome being subjects?
- How do we restore content to our republican imaginary?
- How do we deal with the destruction of the Celtic Tiger inheritance?

The answers must be based on an attempt to reclaim political reality. First, we must discover the difference between truth and falsehood. Second, we are challenged to explore new republican models and narratives in search of answers. Third, we need to reinvent politics in the form of a critical citizenship based on inclusion and participation, in which the self and others interact in a new narrative of the republic. Finally, we need to rediscover society in the form of sustainable communities, populated by *real* people.

How can this be done? The new Irish President, poet and intellectual Michael D. Higgins, in his book *Renewing the Republic* has set out an agenda:

> I believe we must now promote a positive vision of what it means to be a citizen in Ireland. This citizenship should be based on equality and respect, with a basic level of rights and participation – a citizenship floor – below which no one should be allowed to fall. We need to move away from radical individualisation towards a radical kind of inclusion.
>
> Inclusion means valuing diversity in all its forms and challenging exclusion wherever it occurs. No one in our society should experience the destructive effects of discrimination, isolation or rejection.
>
> Inclusion means celebrating solidarity by recognising the aspirations, concerns, creativity and potential of every citizen, regardless of the age, orientation, capacities or means. Inclusive citizenship also brings shared responsibility – a life that goes beyond the self to include those around us and, indeed, the generations yet to come.[47]

The Irish President advocates a creative society constructed from the bottom up:

The creative society cannot be imposed from above; it is built on creativity made possible by sustainable communities. Properly respected, the cultural space can be an invitation to push the boundaries of the possible – enfranchising us all in our capacity for living, and enriching the social and economic life of the nation.[48]

He argues that the alternative is Žižek's Apocalypse:

Should the adjustment in economic and social assumptions prove to be incapable of being made, we probably face an unmediated confrontation between the excluded and those who chose to be unconcerned. Such a point is the one at which the dark prescriptions of Slavoj Žižek become relevant. Around the world there is evidence that such an outcome is achieving momentum, and some support.[49]

President Higgins concludes with his own apocalyptic warning:

We are drifting to a final rupture between the economy, politics and society. If it happens, the ensuing conflict will not be mediated through trade unions, political parties or social movements. It will be a naked confrontation between, on the one side, the wealthy getting wealthier, and the poor getting poorer; between the excluded and the powerful; between the technologically manipulated. It will be a conflict as raw as any in history of private accumulation between, on the one hand, consumers, and, on the other, the excluded poor, who no longer have any norms of citizenship that they share or which would mediate their conflict.

Public participation is now falling in every institution of civil society. The norms of a shared life have little opportunity of being articulated. That is the inescapable other side of the coin of globalisation, which is the unaccountable economy on a world scale. That is why it is necessary for the Left to outline the case for a new and vibrant citizenship that can vindicate such values as solidarity, community, democracy, justice, freedom and equality. These values can be achieved by giving them a practical expression in a new theory of citizenship.[50]

The challenge that President Higgins has presented is essentially about the need for a new political fiction to take the narrative of the Irish Republic forward. It is very clearly framed within the language of civil society: community, inclusive citizenship and sustainability.

Arguably, President Higgins's vision of a political rupture generated by bottom-up forces within civil society points to the social left, as opposed to the political left, as the drivers of change in post-politics society. The Occupy movement (now experiencing suppression in New York, London and Dublin) is the most visible contemporary manifestation of the social left as an actor in post-politics. In response to the eviction of the protestors from the grounds of St Paul's Cathedral the *Guardian* (29 February 2012) declared on its front page:

> You cannot evict an idea. Such is the message of defiance from Occupy. But it is not entirely true. For the whole point of Occupy is that it's not just an idea bouncing around the internet. Occupy is stubbornly about the physical reality of space. Others may write books and

organise seminars. Occupy puts up tents. It takes up
space. It is there.

Sarah van Gelder likens the Occupy movement to the Arab
spring and argues that its name identifies the cause of the current crisis: 'Wall street banks, big corporations, and others
among the 1% are claiming the world's wealth for themselves
at the expense of the 99% and having their way with governments.'[51] What is refreshing about the Occupy movements
is their determination to link their political critique of capitalism to practical welfare initiatives aimed at the socially
excluded. Despite their chaos they genuinely represent a
search for truth.

President Higgins's concept of a 'creative society' has been
taken up by the Cork Occupy movement as a philosophical
basis of its protest:

> A hugely important aspect of the protest was the involve-
> ment of Cork Community Art Link, who brought a real
> creative and artistic colour to the demonstration. This
> combines the importance of our presence on the South
> Mall in the heart of the city with an appreciation of the
> need to move in more creative directions, opening up the
> Occupy movement to all. This is about making the move-
> ment accessible and welcoming to all, and bringing that
> together with the principles of equality and democracy
> that are central to what we do. In a time where there is
> such an overwhelming amount and range of advertising
> constantly being forced down our throats, we need to
> work in ways that really engage with people, and the
> wide and open nature of the Occupy movement is bring-
> ing something really new to the table.

Creative protests such as the Parade are testament to a DIY ethic producing our own culture, one that can be defiant through creativity, but this shouldn't be seen as the be-all and end-all of how we're to organise ourselves for this fight. We should not feel bound to the past to feel we owe today's struggle to those who've come before us – we should try to see ourselves within the tradition of human beings standing up for potent ideas of justice, equality and dignity. How we interpret that challenge of building a new society should be across the whole spectrum of human capacity – the creative and cultural shouldn't be seen as opposed to the political, to the practical task of organising and mobilising in cooperation with one another, against those whose interests are currently served by our rights being stamped on.[52]

The Occupy movement is part of a new political fiction that is creating a participative democratic narrative in which citizens are becoming actors in making their own history. It suggests that we are experiencing 'the democratisation of democracy' in response to the invisibility of autocratic power that seeks to mould contemporary political reality – and fails.

A 'Second Republic': A New Political Fiction?

A new political fiction requires a new grammar that is both emancipatory and republican. The challenge for the community-led model is to forge a new social and cultural grammar, which can deepen democracy. That involves confronting global hegemonic forces 'by the initiatives of grassroots organisations, of local and popular movements that endeavour to counteract extreme forms of social exclusion and open up new spaces for democratic participation'.[53] It also involves addressing Weber's 'iron cage of bureaucracy', which undermines democratic practice by subordinating the citizen to the bureaucratic state apparatus.[54] In turn that involves challenging the hegemonic conception of representative democracy (thin) by participatory democracy (thick) in a new synthesis that realigns politics to civil society in a project of demodiversity, based on greater citizen engagement in politics.[55] To put it concisely, the idea of sustainable community is the late-modern *agora,* where the citizen can democratically challenge oligarchies of wealth (capitalism) and power (bureaucratic state).

Peadar Kirby and Mary P. Murphy in their book *Towards a Second Republic* (2011) have proposed a complete restructuring of Irish institutions, economy and society. It presupposes that there was a 'First Republic', which Fintan O'Toole, citing Samuel Beckett, suggests may be a farcical idea, albeit one rooted in the Marxist Democratic Programme (1919).[56] It was of course the stillborn child of the Irish Revolution. The Second Republic movement has argued the case for a citizens' assembly. The Fine Gael–Labour government, elected in 2011, promised a 'democratic revolution'. A constitutional convention was presented as the means to achieve this goal. While the aspiration of the government to reimagine Irish politics is very impressive, so far plans have been more limited. Abolishing the Seanad is a controversial proposal since it arguably will constrain democracy. Limiting the tenure of the President from seven to five years is another proposal that is being considered. More radically the government has indicated its willingness to lower the voting age – empowering young people. This is welcome and progressive. But the real test of the proposed constitutional convention will be in its composition (what will be the level of citizen participation?), process (will citizens be empowered to set the agenda?), outcome (contractarian, i.e. pro-business, or solidaristic, i.e. pro-society?) and the status of its recommendations (will it be consultative or binding?). Finally, if it is to produce a republican constitution there must be separation between Church and state. Otherwise, there will be no 'Second Republic' as there was no 'First Republic'!

Linda Connolly and Niamh Hourigan have demonstrated the capacity of Irish social movements to bring about transformative change.[57] Arguably, change will not come through the political-party system, which is still constrained by the historical over-hang of militant democracy that has limited public debate. Trust is more likely to be embedded in civil society. But, as Peadar Kirby and Mary P. Murphy demonstrate, Irish civil society is very diverse: ranging from neoliberal (wedded to traditional voluntarism, building social capital and restoration of economic competitiveness); through social democratic perspectives driven by the values of equality and solidarity; to environmental orientations (concerned with sustainability, planetary citizenship and ecological justice).[58] It is possible that some civil-society actors could coalesce around the concept of a social left, based on a shared vision of critical citizenship founded on the principles of social inclusion and democratic participation, as a republican strategy. If we are to imagine a Second Republic in which the population genuinely feel like citizens as opposed to subjects, then there will need to be a core set of principles. Ten principles for critical citizenship are set out below:

Ten Principles for Critical Citizenship

1 Campaign for social justice – reject growing inequality:
   a Inequality causes poverty
   b Inequality causes social conflict
   c Inequality ruins lives
   d Inequality is a product of a market society
   e Inequality is based on oligarchy and is the antithesis of democracy.
2 Seek to 'democratise democracy' though public accountability, e.g. the banks, the political class, multiple ownership of property, links between politics and business, clientalism, etc.
3 Challenge monopoly of knowledge in information society – 'another world is possible'.
4 Demand the state upholds the planning laws, based on the principles of proper planning and sustainable development.
5 Broaden the political debate beyond a preoccupation with narrow economic concerns to social justice and sustainable community development. We can survive the crash by reinventing solidarity.
6 The creation of participatory democratic spaces at grass-roots community level that values the citizens' 'lived experience'.
7 Social action provides information and empowerment which empowers the citizen to know and understand what is going on in an increasingly changing society, based on cyber democracy – 'Think Global, Act Local'.
8 Build 'poor peoples'' social movements that challenge political parties' monopoly of power.

9 Promote 'Rights Talk' as the basis of critical citizenship – why should anybody be poor?

10 Build a strong democracy in Ireland based on 'thick' participation rather than 'thin' representation – reinvent Irish democracy.

'Up the Republic' now has the ring of a funeral dirge for a dead political project. The undertakers are here in the form of the troika (EU, ECB, IMF). They are grave, respectful and even understanding of our misery – as good undertakers should be! The grief reaction among the citizens for their lost sovereignty varies from denial through anger to despairing acceptance. There is a rupture with the past, but with no clear vision of the future that isn't apocalyptic. In the circumstances, the president has gently reminded the citizens that they have the power to construct their own future. His democratic vision is for a bottom-up renewal. He wants us to forge our own political fiction, in which we once again become actors in making our own history. We are invited by the president to deepen our democracy, think for ourselves, and shape our own destiny. Oddly, this sounds strangely counterintuitive. Like Benjamin Barber's caged animals, we don't like to leave the comfort of the cage even though the President has opened its door. Somehow, we remain mesmerised like the characters in Haruki Murakami's novel *IQ84*. But there are voices of protest. The Occupy movement has attracted public support because its members dared to step outside their personal cages and enter the public sphere. But of course we are told that it is private space and they must be moved on. They are making democratic noises, which the authorities judge to be an unreasonable provocation of the citizens. Despite their public support, their protest is being suppressed.

The Occupy movement resembles those campaigns for the right of association that gave birth to democracy during the eighteenth and nineteenth centuries. That resulted in the twentieth-century welfare state, the good society that benefited citizens. It too is being suppressed, however successful and compatible with a burgeoning economy. Social justice is a forbidden language in the twenty-first century. Our gentle undertakers – those global civil servants – point towards the cages, where the living dead are to be consigned. Up the Second Republic!

7

Republican Reflections on the Occupy Movements[1]

PHILIP PETTIT

What do you say to thousands of young people who gather in frustration at a political system that has utterly failed them? Is there anything to say that can reach the depth of their wholly understandable outrage at the disappearance of jobs and the collapse of prospects?

As someone associated in an unusual way with the 2004–11 government of Spanish Prime Minister José Luis Zapatero, I cannot avoid that question. Asked to report on the performance of that administration in the 2004–8 parliament, in particular its fidelity to the republican principles I espouse, I gave it a high mark. So what do I say four years later?

In thinking about the future of Spain under the Zapatero government – indeed under any government – I made two serious mistakes. I was naive about the reliability of the international financial system in providing the infrastructure that would enable the government in a country such as Spain to provide for its people's economic welfare. And I failed to realise how far the country's options for responding to a downturn of economic fortunes would be restricted by its membership of the eurozone.

I continue to commend the performance of the Zapatero government for its attempts to equalise the position of women in society, for its regularisation of the status of many illegal immigrants, for the law of dependency that it established in protection of the vulnerable, and for the introduction of same-sex marriage. And I still commend it for the independence that it gave to the national broadcaster, for the greater degree of transparency that it brought to government business and for establishing Spain in the role of a model international citizen.

All of these initiatives were important steps towards the realisation of what I see as republican goals. The republican ideal is that of living in freedom, without being subject to the dominating will of an individual or body that is capable of interfering without licence in your central life choices. As an ideal of justice, it holds out the prospect of a society in which people are resourced and protected against private domination in the enjoyment of such choices. As an ideal of democracy, it offers the promise of a regime in which the government that has responsibility for justice is not itself publicly dominating, being forced to operate on accepted, popular terms. And as an ideal of international relations, it directs us to the prospect of a world in which no peoples are dominated by other peoples or by multinational or inter-national bodies.

Many of the Zapatero initiatives were explicitly designed to advance such goals and are signal, hopefully lasting, achievements. But now is not the time for praise. Now is a time for taking stock and thinking about where we go from here. So what are the lessons that have been taught by the painful experiences of the last three or four years? In particular, what are the lessons for those who espouse broadly republican ideals? I concentrate on lessons for the relationship between government and the economy, though I recognise, as I mention in the conclusion, that there may be wider and deeper lessons to be learned as well.

Riding the Tiger

The crisis showed us all that the reliance of governments on the international financial system amounts, in an old phrase, to riding the tiger. All governments depend on the bond market for financing national projects, especially within a fixed currency area such as the eurozone; this is no more surprising than the fact that homeowners rely on mortgage providers for purchasing their apartments or houses. And all governments depend on the banking system and stock market, of course, for the capital that nurtures job-creating enterprises. This dependence makes for a serious vulnerability to the performance of the international financial system.

The system on which our governments depend – in my image, the tiger that they ride – is often presented as a body of individuals with a concerted will of their own: a cadre of international financiers and bankers that acts with a single, self-aggrandising aim. It would be nice if things were like that, for such an entity would then offer a lightning rod for our outrage, a target for our resentment, an agency that we might expect to be able to censure and hold to account. But alas, as always, things are more complicated.

The tiger that our governments ride is a more wayward and untameable beast than the body imagined in such a conspiracy theory. Its movements are dictated by motives no less self-seeking and callous than those projected in that theory. But they are dictated from a thousand or more sources, making the performance of the tiger an unpredictable precipitate of multiple inputs. The behaviour of this tiger is as directionless and thoughtless, and often as turbulent, as the shifts of wind in a storm.

A number of countries, particularly in Europe, are now exposed to the worst of those winds. An imported financial crisis has led to unemployment; unemployment payments to an increased government deficit; the rise in that deficit to bond-market uncertainty; and this uncertainty to increased borrowing costs. The fear of a further increase in costs has inhibited the potential of the government to respond to unemployment by Keynesian, pump-priming methods of economic stimulation, since they require budget deficits. And the constraints of the eurozone have made it close to impossible for the government to manage the crisis by devaluing the currency or defaulting on its debt. We are in the midst of a perfect storm.

How should European countries respond to this experience? How, more generally, should the peoples of the world respond? Do we have the capacity to assert ourselves democratically against the tiger of the financial system? Or are we forever subject to the whims and moods of a capricious beast?

Two Radical Responses

There are two extreme responses that the financial crisis and its aftermath have provoked. One is to say that all will be well if our governments stop trying to anticipate and deflect the movements of the tiger by propping up and bailing out the bodies that they judge too big to fail. This approach, exemplified in the stance of the Tea Party in the United States, amounts to pre-emptive surrender in face of the profit-seeking ventures of credit and capital. It gives government the task of law and order and calls for the abdication of the state in the sphere of production, commerce and employment.

This first response would downsize and marginalise government, letting the market rule unimpeded in the financial and material economy. The second radical response would recommend the very opposite. It would support a rejection of dependence on the sort of beast that the international financial system constitutes. Where the first approach would give the tiger free range, this would simply kill the animal. Those attracted to the response complain that so long as the tiger survives, we all live at its mercy. They recommend that we should reject dependency on impersonal market forces and reclaim our status as a democratic people, our standing as rulers of our individual and collective lives.

Because they are simple, these two responses have a natural attraction at a time of extreme crisis. It is comforting to think that all will be well if we can only liberate the power of the market or if we can only reassert our will as a people. But because the responses are simplistic, we should back away from both.

The Mistakes in These Responses

The first response puts its faith in the invisible hand of market-based adjustments, oblivious to the fact that it is governments who fix the laws under which titles of ownership are established, rights of property and trade are determined, the money supply is controlled, and the very capacity for incorporation that is exercised in the formation of banks and companies is defined. There is little plausibility or attraction in the ideal it hails. It would license a plutocratic regime in which markets allow enormous concentrations of personal and corporate wealth and the polity does nothing about restraining the power of those thereby enriched.

The second approach puts its faith in a more attractive object than the first, appealing to the sense of our collective power as a democratic people; it is populist in character rather than plutocratic. But this approach is equally blind to blatant fact. It suggests that we can rely on democratic decision-making to call an economic and financial system into being, relying on centralised planning or co-ordination, all on its own, to establish a viable system of credit and a functional market. And that is wholly implausible.

The creation of an economic and financial system requires a people and a government to recruit private sources of wealth and investment in the enterprise of building a prosperous society. And this means building with what Kant called the crooked timber of humanity. It requires acknowledging the imperfect motives and the limiting constraints of people's psychology and sociology and devising institutions that can survive in the presence of such more or less fixed parameters. Even the most democratically inspired institutions will fail unless they are able to take root in the human environment that these parameters define.

This human environment relates to democratic progress in the building of viable institutions much as the natural environment relates material progress in the technological use of the earth. The natural environment offers us rich resources of nutrition and energy but these resources are scarce and, as we now know to our cost, extremely hard to sustain. In parallel, the human environment promises us rich prospects of production, trade and employment but access to these prospects is also problematic. Their availability depends on how much confidence individuals and groups can be brought to invest in one another and on how much credit they can be persuaded to extend.

As a species, we have done many things surprisingly well in building a society that copes with the limitations of natural and human environments. The technologies accumulated in agriculture and industry have transformed the natural environment and bent it to our human will, enabling us to do more than scratch a bare living from the soil. And the ideals and institutions elaborated in our political and democratic practice hold out at least the possibility of a human environment in which we can claim shared responsibility for collective arrangements and can enjoy equal respect under those arrangements. This is the ideal of a democratic republic in which we can each walk tall, conscious of being sufficiently resourced and protected to be able to make our own way in the world – conscious, in effect, of enjoying a freedom that gives us independence from the will or domination of any individual or group.

If we are to do well on the technological front, achieving material progress, then we must clearly work within the limitations of the natural or physical environment. And if we are to do well on the institutional front, achieving democratic progress, then we must work equally within the constraints imposed by the psychological and sociological realities of human life. Long tradition teaches us about those realities. It counsels us that power corrupts, for example, and that those we empower should always be held accountable. It teaches us that no one is proof against temptation, so that no one should be given unconstrained opportunity for self-enrichment. And it teaches us that everybody's business is nobody's business and that in general, as Aristotle observes, people will look after their own property better than they will look after what belongs to all. We ignore these constraints at our peril when we offer proposals for democratic, institutional design.

The populist fallacy is precisely that of ignoring constraints of this kind and imagining that we can construct the great society without heed to the recalcitrance of the human material, the crookedness of the human timber, with which we build. It may not be as salient a fallacy as the plutocratic counterpart but it is just as dangerous. Thus it would encourage us to be complacent about the possibility of building a system of confidence and credit, which any flourishing democracy requires, without having to worry about its compatibility with the often uncongenial instincts and limitations of our human make-up. It would foster the illusion that there is a new, secular Jerusalem within our immediate, collective reach: that all it requires to get there is good will.

The Lesson of the Financial Crisis and its Aftermath

The looming shortage of fossil fuels, the manifest danger of relying on nuclear energy and the threat of climate change have made us all aware of how fragile are the technologies whereby we maintain synergy with our natural environment. And the financial crisis, I would say, teaches a parallel lesson in the human domain. It has shown us how fragile are the institutions whereby we promote successful government and preserve democratic control over our lives. In particular, it has demonstrated the ease with which institutional changes in the organisation of banking – the deregulation pursued with reckless abandon over the ten years preceding the crisis – can jeopardise the existence of the confidence and credit on which our democracies rely for the economic welfare of their citizens.

The deregulation that was introduced prior to the financial crisis was prompted by a disastrous indifference, on a par with the populist indifference just described, to the Kantian counsel of recognising that the timber of humanity is crooked. Consider the developments whereby those in the financial sector were allowed to blur the lines between high street and investment banking, to lend and invest on the basis of an ever smaller asset base, to divide and package debt obligations so that risk became utterly opaque, to allow for unsustainable levels of insurance against default, and to perpetrate a popular illusion that the temporary growth thereby stimulated was based on solid economic achievement. Whether or not these developments were promoted by the financial sector on a good-faith basis, they created a milieu in which the desire for quick, often fabulous, profits generated a frenzy of risk-taking and visited a tragedy on people worldwide.

None of us can contemplate with analytical detachment the ravages that the self-seeking few, operating within the newly deregulated environment, imposed on the rest of humanity. None can contemplate those ravages without moral indignation at the fact that only a tiny percentage of those few have had to pay a legal or even an economic price for their activity. And none can contemplate the ravages without extreme outrage at the realisation that most of the few have gone on to thrive and prosper, even as the many have had to face unemployment, austerity and downright poverty. The thing beggars belief.

But while the performance of financial operatives may beggar belief, on reflection it ought not to be very surprising. Over two thousand years ago Plato invoked the ring of Gyges to suggest that few of us would prove virtuous, were we able to wear a ring that gave us invisibility and impunity in the pursuit of our own pleasures. It is a sad fact of human nature that while many of us might not be corrupt, not many are incorruptible; when opportunity offers not many are capable of resisting the temptation to make a quick buck. The timber may not be rotten but it is crooked. Given the amazing opportunities that individuals and organisations in the financial sector enjoyed under the new deregulation, it should probably not shock us that those opportunities were exploited to maximum advantage.

Beyond Plutocracy and Populism

How then should we respond to the financial crisis and its aftermath? We should certainly avoid the iconoclastic urge to seek the demolition of either the governmental or the financial system. There is no case for advocating the abdication of democratic responsibility in the manner of the plutocratic response or for denying the need to ride the tiger of an independent financial system in the manner of the populist. The tiger is not to be given free range and the tiger is not to be hunted down and killed.

The response required, in a third alternative that our metaphor suggests, is to rein in and regulate the tiger: to put it to work for democratic ends, under restrictions that make sure it serves those ends. The challenge is to devise a regulative regime in which the financial system can continue to provide us with resources of credit without giving financial insiders the opportunity or incentive for activities that endanger the overall, common good.

This is a democratic and not just a technocratic challenge. It will certainly require technical expertise to identify means whereby a financial system that has novel instruments at its disposal can still be regulated and harnessed to the common good. But it is up to a responsible parliament and a contestatory citizenry to explore the strengths and weaknesses of different proposals and to maintain oversight of whatever proposal is eventually enacted.

How can a contestatory citizenry function in a role of this kind? The Italian-Atlantic tradition of republicanism suggests that if citizens are to exercise the contestatory control that democracy requires, then they must divide the civic labour of contestation between them, with different groups specialising in different areas of governmental activity; here as in other areas power must be dispersed. Contemporary society is too complex to enable the virtuous citizen, or even the body of virtuous citizens as a whole, to interrogate government on every front. It is essential for the proper invigilation of those in power that different civic associations can monitor the decisions of the authorities in different areas of policy-making, can muster the best available expertise in assessing what the authorities decide, and can hold them to effective, public account.

The 15-M movement in Spain, and the Occupy movements in other countries, have been important in giving expression to the insistence of the people at large that government should live up to their expectations on the economic and related fronts. But if it is to have a lasting impact on how government is pursued, then it must generate more specialised associations for the interrogation of government policy. Democracy is hard, often boring, work and it is vital that the democratic energy behind these movements is channelled in such directions. Otherwise it is likely to be as evanescent in its impact as a New Year's Eve fireworks display.

But while the challenge identified is democratic rather than just technocratic in character, it engages democracy on the international as well as the national front. The financial crisis began in the United States and spread elsewhere via the exposure of financial houses in other countries to the complex and opaque risks manufactured in America. Moreover, the austerity programme imposed in the aftermath of the financial crisis is the artefact of a skittish, international bond market and a determination on the part of a range of countries, particularly those in the European Union, to assure the market that neither they nor the countries they bail out of trouble will resort to pump-priming methods of economic stimulation.

The international nature of the challenge, like the technocratic, does not mean that it is not truly democratic in character. But it does mean that if people are to address it seriously in the contestatory mode I envisage, then they have to do so via civic associations that reach across boundaries. Fully alerting governments to the urgency of popular demand might be better achieved by marches across Europe than by mass gatherings in national squares. And the dubious case for pan-European austerity might be most effectively interrogated and tested by the trans-national, non-governmental organisations that such marches would support.

None of us who applauded the performance of government – any government – in the years prior to the financial crisis can be complacent about what has transpired since then in countries such as Spain, let alone countries such as Greece and Portugal and my own native Ireland. The experience of these countries is humiliating for any commentator who celebrated government success. We thought and said that things were going well but all the time there was a perfect storm in the making.

Apology aside, however, there are three points emerging from the previous discussion that I would like to emphasise. First, the achievements of the Zapatero government in those years should not be overlooked; they remain important and, I hope, lasting. Second, the failure of the government to provide for the employment prospects of its people should not prompt us to lurch into either of the iconoclastic positions I described; it should alert us to the importance of governmental regulation over the financial system and of democratic invigilation of the regulatory regime established. And third, the democratic challenge to government in the area of financial regulation and economic policy should be taken to the European level, not just left at the national; the civic associations on which it depends must assume a cross-country, EU-wide profile.

This essay has concentrated on the failure of government on the financial and economic front, since the stimulus to the 15-M and the Occupy movements has been the collapse in the jobs market. But the challenges that civic associations can make on government in furtherance of important goals are not limited, of course, to the financial front. The complaints generated by the movement run much deeper, casting doubt on the character of existing democratic parties, for example, and on their claim to be able to give voice to popular demand. But here too, if the movement is to make a permanent impact on public life, it has to get serious about issues of institutional design. It has to be able to generate proposals for change and it has to be able to command a hearing for those proposals in the popular press and within the political parties, in the parliament and at the polls. I trust that it will be able to generate discussion and open up decision on these wide-ranging matters. To the extent that it succeeds, democracy will be the winner: democracy in Spain and, by example, democracy in other countries too.

8

Law, Poetry and the Republic

THEO DORGAN

It is a fundamental duty of the state to manage the economy in order to provide for the common good. In so far as we are self-constituted as a republic, that duty is a solemn obligation conferred by the citizens acting in concert as citizens of the republic. The state, considered as the apparatus of governance in its entirety, derives its authority and legitimacy from the citizens who in their totality as free men and women constitute the republic; the right of the state to discharge the duties and obligations of a sovereign government is no more and no less than the devolved right to exercise the prior sovereignty of the republic.

It follows that the ceding of economic sovereignty is also an undermining of the sovereignty of the republic. The state, in so far as it takes its instructions from an external power, can no longer claim co-identification with the republic, an instrumental fiction that has proved useful up to now. In the most absolute sense possible, the continuing existence of the republic as a sovereign entity has been called into question.

What is to be done with our poor battered republic is not just an open question; it is a question that keeps on opening out into further questions, so much so that one begins to wonder if we'll ever find a way to get started on the process of rebuilding.

It seems to me we are still at the diagnostic stage, still trying to get a grip on the extent and nature of what is wrong before we can formulate even tentative proposals as to what is to be done. It may even be that rebuilding will prove impossible, in which case we shall find ourselves looking at a profound rupture, at the refounding rather than the reformulation of the republic and hence the state.

It is still an open question whether rebuilding is even possible; it may well prove to be, when all the analysis is complete, that we need to start over again from an entirely new set of assumptions as to what kind of state is needed to provide for the republic, for the common good in the twenty-first century.

One thing we can say for certain: piecemeal reform of an ad hoc kind is likely to leave intact what we might call the armature or infrastructure of the state, its accumulated burden of law, language and custom.

The state apparatus derives its ultimate authority from that regular consultation with the will of the people that we are pleased to call the representative democratic process. In theory, it works like this: we the people choose representatives freely, and those representatives, acting on our behalf, choose a government. Our primary influence on who forms that government is fatally circumscribed, in most instances, by a kind of a priori sleight of hand: strictly speaking, we cast our votes to select an individual as our representative, but in all likelihood that representative will have a prior allegiance to a party and a policy, and should that party enter into government, our representative will almost invariably find herself or himself disposed if not actually constrained to put party allegiance before the expressed interests of those people who elected her or him. No longer able (or perhaps willing) to act as a direct representative of his or her constituency's wishes, the individual deputy finds himself or herself co-opted by the unquestioned supposition that in voting for that individual we are, in effect, giving a free hand to his or her party to pursue its policy goals. Even when there are grounds to believe that the people *in toto* do not approve of a particular policy, the party in government will claim that it has a free hand until the next election, and that the individual deputy must in effect surrender his or her direct responsibility to a particular cohort of electors in favour of the party's will.

Once it enters into office according to law, the government assumes, crucially, responsibility for ensuring the continued operation of that corpus of laws it inherits, and it acquires the power both to amend existing laws and to promulgate further laws.

In effect, the government enters into possession of the law, and into ownership of the language of law. This further fuels the inexorable alienation of the government from the people.

If party allegiance is the first dilution of the contract between we the people on the one hand and the aggregate of our chosen representatives on the other, then the second dilution comes from a profound misunderstanding. Naively, a majority of the people believe, might always have believed, that there is a necessary connection between law and justice understood as fairness; that the state is concerned with delivering justice by means of policy and the law.

Neither the possessors nor the enforcers of law are under this illusion.

Bertrand Russell was of the opinion that: 'Law in origin was merely a codification of the power of dominant groups, and did not aim at anything that to a modern man would appear to be justice.' The late and unlamented J. Edgar Hoover believed that: 'Justice is incidental to law and order.'

When the citizen looks at the law, even when she hopes to benefit from it, she is always looking upward, towards the apex of a pyramid of power, towards that small handful of people who, in effect, own the law.

This is the dynamic underpinning the well-known anarchist slogans: 'Don't vote, it only encourages them', and 'No matter who you vote for, the government always gets in.'

Who makes the law? The naive believe that government makes the law, and instrumentally, though to a very limited extent, this is true. It is more useful, and in a broader sense more true, to say that the state makes the law, and we should always bear in mind that the incumbent government is no more than a part of, perhaps not always the most powerful component of, the state.

What is a law? Let us agree to speak of it for the moment as a directive arising from desire, embodied in language.

That desire, which is in essence a desire of governance, is a desire of the state.

The state desires that we refrain from murdering one another, for instance. In order to inhibit murder, the state frames a set of prohibitions in language, and a consequent set of punishments for transgressors of those prohibitions. These prohibitions make the transition from desire to instrument once they are embodied in language.

The state might equally wish explicitly to permit some action or other, and from time to time, when it is considered desirable for one reason or another, the state will frame a law that permits some action, or calls something into being. These permissions, too, will appear in the world framed in language, framed as a particular kind of text.

These texts, these directives, we call laws. We are accustomed to thinking of laws as relatively simple exercises in language. A law says, for instance: You may do this or, you may not do this other . . . I am not at all sure that this process is anything like as clear-cut and straightforward as it seems. In fact, these instruments in language are complex phenomena.

Firstly, in order to promulgate this law, the state must have the authority to do so. In our small republic, setting aside the historical processes that brought the state into existence, this authority derives from the constitution. It is by virtue of authority deriving from the constitution that the state is empowered to speak to us in the laws.

To be sure, laws are framed by the government of the day, which derives its immediate authority to make and enforce laws from the democratic election process, but the validating matrix of any given law is the constitution.

Thus, the first test of whether or not a law is a true law is its constitutionality; that is, the concepts and meanings that can be said legitimately to inhere in the law must be put through a linguistic process that tests whether or not there is agreement between the language of the law and the language of the constitution.

A law, then, is framed in a particular voice; the law speaks to us *de haut en bas*. Law must be founded on authority, and the language of lawgiving necessarily derives from precedent, by which I mean here linguistic precedent.

A law, to put it simply, cannot employ arbitrary language. Moreover, it would be rare indeed if a law could be successfully framed in colloquial language – imagine, if you will, a law against murder that said, simply, 'Ah here, you can't be going around killing people.'

The framers of laws are hedged around by inherited prohibitions, constrained by linguistic precedent, limited to a specific instrumental vocabulary, syntax and grammar.

Here is a major source of the unease most people feel in the face of the law. On the one hand, the state derives its authority under the constitution from the people. Without their consent to be governed, the people owe no allegiance to the state, nor can the state presume to frame laws and expect them to have and take effect. The constitution itself, which stands behind the state in its framing of laws, derives *its* authority from the people, too. The constitution, put to us as a proposal framed and expressed in words, takes effect with our assent as authority in language. Yet the language of law, as the language of the constitution, might as well exist in a different universe as far as the daily language of the people is concerned. The linguist Ferdinand de Saussure distinguished between two aspects of the use of language, aspects to which he gave the terms '*langue*' and '*parole*'. '*Langue*', to put it very simply, is official language, bourgeois and conservative language if you like. '*Parole*' is the common speech of everyday life.

Law is always and everywhere '*langue*'. It aspires to the qualities of fixedness: of fixed definitions, custom-enshrined usage, precedent, singularity of meaning. Law, if I might put it like this, aspires to a kind of marmoreal perfection; it aspires to the condition of language carved in stone.

'*Parole*', on the other hand, is flux and swerve, a busyness of constant renewal, a thing of tones and shades of meaning, inventive, protean, multilayered, a hare jinking through a field as opposed to a horse dreaming of its apotheosis in bronze.

All societies ruled by law will continue to accumulate laws in the light of Zeno's paradox, always approaching by smaller and smaller increments towards that unreachable state of perfection where everything that can be permitted has been defined and provided for, everything to be forbidden has been accounted for.

Laws, taken in their accumulation through time, tend towards a world view where life can be framed and conducted in the light of fixities and definites – which is so much at variance with life as we actually experience it that there is and must be a constant necessary tension between life and law.

Law, as I am framing it here, is hieratic, and every *hieros* must have its servants and hierophants – in this case its enforcers and explainers.

Because law in our time has the status of constituted mystery, as religion once had, in many places still has, the language of law has become a reserved language, and must therefore have its interpreters if it is to be made intelligible to us the people. These interpreters, seen horizontally, evaluate one another in accordance with each individual's skill at interpreting, parsing and deploying the language of the law. Because of the intrinsic stasis or tendency towards stasis of the whole system, there is also a vertical distribution of adepts, with the implicit assumption that those most versed in the law will occupy positions closest to the apex of the mystery, and that conversely those entering into the service of the law will do so at a level where the appropriate language must be painstakingly and laboriously acquired.

To those of us, on the other hand, who encounter the law as litigants or defendants, law presents itself as a closed system that needs to be interpreted for us and to us. In a real and even unremarkable sense, the language of the law is not our language.

So here is another plane of rupture: in the first place, the '*langue*' of law is in retreat from the normal flux of being and becoming in the social domain. Now, and still in the social domain, we find a priestly caste who, interpreting the law to us, are also by virtue of the same process possessors of the special domain of the law, a reserved mystery from which, *sans* interpreters, we are necessarily excluded.

Now the purpose of law is, of course, the ordering and regulation of society. You might say law is the means by which social relations enter into the domain of form, and the opposite of form is chaos. Any one individual might, from time to time, be able to live with a certain amount of chaos in the day to day; we have long since learned that society without laws will rapidly descend into, as Hobbes puts it, 'a ceaseless war of all against all'. This does not mean, however, that the boundary can ever be fixed or definite; we should think of it as a tide line, perhaps, a definite frontier whose line is always, to a certain small degree, in doubt.

It happens that social order in a normal social democracy is founded in law, and law is founded in, has its being in, language. The particular forms in language we use to contain the vital energies of lawgiving are few, and aspire to the immutable. Rhetorically, they tend to the declarative and, inside those parameters, towards the twin dynamics of permitting and forbidding. In this particular sense, the language of law is a kind of written and spoken organised withdrawal from history – in the sense that history as we live it consists of the unregulated and protean arrival of new facts from the future, and law is a permanent attempt to govern the present from the safety of the past.

You may well sense by now the uneasy ghost of Plato hovering offstage, rehearsing his lines in a worried murmur. Plato considered that reality, though he would not have used the term, is vertically structured, with the ideal forms at the top of the pyramid, the reality quotient of phenomena becoming thinner and more diluted as we descend all the way down to the muddled level of the everyday. In Plato's world view our task as humans desirous of becoming enlightened is to work our way by reason and clarity of thought upwards out of the fog into the rarefied empyrean, the high clear air of the ideal forms.

The higher we get, of course, the closer we approach to the Ideal Forms, the more measured our thoughts and our language become. We seek, then, the absolute, the frozen, the fixed and definite, that which is out of time – and to the extent that humans are capable of participating in this sacred order, it must be by virtue of language that itself remains unchanging. You might say, in Plato's world it is indeed possible, at least thinkable, to have the final word.

This divine achievement is, of course, reserved in our fallen world for the most exalted judges alone – but then as so many of their lordships will tell you, like the Gods of Olympus, their lordships, axiomatically, are never wrong.

If it were merely the case that the language of law and the language of society are at all times in a state of tension, that would not be so bad, provided of course that this tension could be constituted as a living dialectic. This, unfortunately, is far from the case. The process is, in fact, asymmetric: laws accumulate, and as they accumulate, so the power of the state accumulates. As the power of the state accumulates, the social space for unencumbered action necessarily contracts. As the space for free action contracts, so *parole* turns mutinous, retreats from the sphere of the state, grows and mutates under pressure from the constantly arriving future. Eventually, a schism is created between the state and its language, on the one hand, and the people with its multiplicity of *paroles* on the other. Just as asymmetry in wealth and power generates a social chasm, so, too, this social chasm is reflected in the gap between *langue* and *parole*, or, as it then becomes, the gap between the language of the state and the languages of the people.

I do not mean here that the language of the state is a professional dialect, of the kind that tends naturally to grow in any defined profession. The medical profession has its dialect, its shorthand; so, too, does engineering, shipping, policing, factory work, teaching and so on. It's an inherent tendency in language to exfoliate in specialist vocabularies and patterns, habits, of usage. But such occupational dialects are no more than *paroles* of kinship, subsets of the wider shared *parole* of a given society at a given time.

That there is a dialect peculiar to all who work in the law, many of us have observed; and in so far as this is a normal, a conventional thing, it is a harmless phenomenon.

The problem arises when this specialist dialect forms a particular relationship to the language of law as deployed by the state. In effect, it leads to the emergence or creation of a caste whose private domain is the law – in brute terms, to a common interest between lawgivers and interpreters of the law, which acts, over time, to increase the alienation of the citizen from the law, and hence from the state.

It comes to the point where a small but powerful consortium of interests comes to identify itself with the language of law, and hence to identify the law with itself. This caste, I should say, is not confined to the lawyers, judges and lawmakers; as the state class grows, its language begins to metamorphose into the language of politics, more precisely the language of governance. Not the laws themselves, to be sure, but those particular and specific habits of language – with this profound difference: where the language of law attempts to enshrine concrete concepts, definable precepts and principles, the language of the state tends towards emptiness, towards an illusory ideal of the state as instrument and embodiment of achievable total control.

This growth outward from law continues and makes terrible the already evacuated relationship between personhood and the language of law; just as the actual citizen, the individual whose consent is notionally necessary for governance to have authority, is nowhere present as himself or herself in the codex of laws, so also that individual ceases to be real in the edicts of governance. Thus a citizen patient in a hospital becomes a customer of the health service, and the civil servant, employed by us acting in common in order to serve us as citizens, discovers that in fact she serves the state, and that the citizen standing before her is no longer a citizen person but a customer, a client, a cipher in the calculus of state management.

What begins as a notion of necessary austerity in language develops a dark twin, a merciless and instrumental language of governance. This process, of course, is not confined to the upper echelons of the state, to the lawmakers and lawgivers: it attracts its adherents and cheerleaders – some of them, the Gardaí, say, the upper echelons of the defence forces and the upper reaches of the civil service, by reason of professional contiguity, but others, too, by reason of appetite or affinity, including political journalists and commentators, academics, and – not least of these parasites on power – persons of wealth and standing having a vested interest in closeness to the state.

I began by saying that law is a directive arising from desire, embodied in language. In our system, the desire may crystallise in one of three places: the courts might decide that an existing law is inadequate in its relation to a particular circumstance, and require of the Oireachtas that it remedy a deficiency by amendment, or that it cause a new law to be written to meet the circumstance; the Oireachtas, more practically the cabinet, might cause a law to be written for a specific purpose in order that it be passed by the Oireachtas; or, in obedience to an obligation arising from EU membership or other international affiliation, the Oireachtas might cause a law to be written, and subsequently enacted, in accordance with or in fulfilment of that obligation.

The actual writing of the law, the embodiment of desire as a directive in language, is the task of the parliamentary draftsmen and women.

These men and women are heavily constrained by precedent, in other words by custom and tradition. They will, inevitably, turn inward to the language of existing law for their vocabulary, syntax and grammar. They will strive for a cold lucidity; they will strive to eliminate any and all possible ambiguities of meaning; they will reach for a language that has no home in our hearts or in our daily speech, a language whose permanent tropism is towards the imagined cold perfection of the idealised unchanging state.

This process takes place within the civil service, notionally a body of men and women employed, as the name implies, to serve the *civis*, that is, to serve the people. The more proper name, at this point in our evolution as a republic, would be the state service. In the *Irish Times* on 22 April 2011, Eddie Molloy contributed a fascinating article, the core argument of which was that 'The country desperately needs a technically qualified, ethical, accountable public service, one that will place the public good ahead of the preferences of the incumbent government whenever officials are faced with hard choices between the two.' Mr Molloy, as he plainly states, does not believe that we have such a service at present.

I agree with him, of course, as any sane person would, but I do not underestimate the difficulties that root-and-branch reform will encounter should we ever embark on that course, not least the difficulty of transforming the habits of speech and writing, by which I mean the habits of thought, that permeate the state service.

And these habits, this habitual stance in language, are deep-rooted. In 1975, the poet Michael Hartnett, in Section 4 of 'A Farewell to English' wrote:

So we queued up at the Castle
in nineteen-twenty-two
to make our Gaelic
or our Irish dream come true.
We could have from that start
made certain of our fate
but we chose to learn the noble art
of writing forms in triplicate.
With big wide eyes
and childish smiles
quivering on our lips
we entered the Irish paradise
of files and paper-clips.

Such is the flexibility, the multivalence of language in the service of poetry that no reader will take this as a literal description, but few will fail to recognise what Hartnett describes and most of us will understand very well what he means. The 'Irish paradise of files and paper-clips' is the Four Courts as much as it is the Department of Finance; it is in any case a vivid invoking of the state as we the citizens encounter it.

Hartnett's poem is, of course, cast in a very different register of language, a register in which allusion, affective use of words, colour and tone are deployed to evocative effect as spurs to the imagination. His language is, in a word, passionate.

Aristotle tells us that 'the law is reason free from passion', and just as we wish our laws to be reasonable, so also we would wish them uninflected by some transitory passion. Our laws, almost all of them, are at the very least reasonable – and therein lies a considerable difficulty, for, as Aristotle also reminds us, 'Whereas the law is passionless, passion must ever sway the heart of man.'

Some passions are of the moment, and often it is a good thing that we do not take steps to act on those passions in the civic arena. But there is such a thing as shaped and controlled passion; there are passions that need to be actively encouraged, and constantly renewed – the passion for justice, for instance, for equity, for liberty.

Our problem is this: how do we frame our laws and governance so that the dry bones of the law and the day-to-day tedium of the state's ordinary business are constantly animated by these and other desirable civic passions?

In a settled society, provided the laws are reasonable and provided the state acts always within the law, momentary random dissatisfactions can be subsumed into the overall sway of things.

But, as we build up the corpus of law and the habitual behaviour of the state on the one hand, dissatisfactions begin to accumulate on the other side of the scales in equal measure, so that the state tends inevitably to withdraw farther and farther into its citadel of language, into a condition of mind engendered by the increasing remoteness of its perfected language – and the farther the state withdraws, the more we begin to distrust it.

In confronting the state through its laws and in that denatured language of governance which derives from the desiccated language of the laws, the citizen is denied not only his naive belief that law, and hence the state, is concerned with justice; he is denied, perhaps more fundamentally, a relationship with the state in which passion can find expression in dialogue. He or she finds that there is no pulse at the heart of the state, no governing passion restrained by moderation in language. Where there was once the fiery and passionate dream and promise of a republic, now there is only an arid landscape, picked over by weary souls who, perhaps unknowingly, are constantly tempted genuinely to despise us for our native dreams – above all, for our naive belief that the state exists for the promotion of the common good.

When Hartnett says, 'We could have from that start/made certain of our fate', he is saying a great deal. Among other things he is reminding us that our infant republic, at the handing over of power, could have chosen differently, could have looked beyond the inherited practice of civil administration, the inherited apparatus of law and its customs of governance; but of course we did no such thing. We took on, unquestioned, the burden of the common law as it had evolved in Britain, with all its precedents and preconceptions, never once asking if this was an appropriate tradition for our people, in our time. Never once asking if this was the proper frame for our future. We took on the British civil service tradition, not just in its forms of management and administration but in its entire suffocating weight of custom and practice. The beggars, to invoke Yeats, changed places indeed, but for the majority of the population the lash went on. Now there might well have been sound pragmatic reasons for doing this as a temporary measure, if only to buttress a fragile new Free State by providing it with an administrative apparatus in a time of transition, in a time of war. But of course this isn't what happened. We embraced the Irish paradise, its files, paper-clips and language, with relish. And stopped there.

For the vast majority of people, the harp replaced the crown on police stations and on the letterheads of the state – and that was all. There was no pretence that the state would be founded on consultation with the people, no attempt to conduct and direct a broad-ranging first-principles public debate on what form the state should take, what values its laws and its legislature should embody and profess. The passion of revolution, such as it was, found itself quietly extinguished in a decisive manoeuvre by a managerial class many of whom were already waiting and poised in the wings.

When I say with Hartnett that 'we embraced the Irish paradise', I should perhaps qualify that 'we'; the truth is, of course, that with residual exceptions, the architects of our new state were in the main second-generation revolutionaries and enduring functionaries of the previous administration. We forget or elide a simple but profound truth: the War of Independence was conducted largely by the urban and rural poor, officered and led in the main by the lower middle class. The lawgivers and managers of the new Free State were cut from a different cloth; they edged out the rough men with a practised ease, as is always the case. First come the dreamers and poets, and the poor who do the fighting and dying; then come the smooth men, the silky judges and lawyers and administrators. And, of course, behind these respectable men, the hard-eyed executioners when they are needed.

In time, those of the revolutionary generation who survived into politics had the hard edges sanded off them by the ceaseless murmuring abrasions of what was in essence an unaltered and seemingly insurmountable process of governance. As the Normans became *Hiberniores Hibernii*, so too the men and women who had overthrown imperial rule made themselves comfortable in the corridors and in the assured language of enduring functional power. Prisoners of the unaltered and unaltering state.

There was, there remains to this day, a sense of helplessness at the heart of government. As if stasis were fore-ordained and inescapable.

In his magnificent book-length poem *The Rough Field*, published in 1972, John Montague sets up a kind of counterpoint to his own words, a recurring series of quotations that question and inflect his own imaginings.

Two of these are set one above the other, by way of introducing the section entitled 'Patriotic Suite', first published by the Dolmen Press as a pamphlet in 1966. The first is from poet and ethnic-cleanser Edmund Spenser, speaking of Ireland: 'They say it is the Fatal Destiny of that land, that no purposes whatsoever which are meant for her good will prosper.' It is a perception to chill the blood, inasmuch as its prophetic power, whatever its provenance, rings as true today as it did during the barbarous Elizabethan conquest.

Spenser, who gives no authority for this fatalistic observation, was of course sent to rule over a sizeable portion of the province of Munster, and did a pretty good job of ensuring that neither the good nor the people prospered under his steely eye.

The second quotation is from Friedrich Engels: 'The real aims of a revolution, those which are not illusions, are always

to be realised after that revolution.' If there were revolutionary aspirations in the Rising and in the War of Independence,
I would argue that they were quickly suffocated in the lore,
language and precedents of that *mentalité* of governance we
so easily and unquestioningly took on ourselves.

It is a truism, and often by recent commentators held
against them, that the revolutionaries of our proto-republic
were visionaries and romantics – as if this were self-evidently
a bad thing. In so far as visionaries and romantics embarked
on revolution are more likely to be driven by song, story and
poem than by political analysis, there is a certain sting in the
charge. But without Davis and Ferguson, and behind them Ó
Rathaille, Ó Súilleabháin, Ó Bruadair and the anonymous
makers of the song tradition, how should we have risen, how
should we have struck, as we did, for liberty? Where, in a
phrase, should we have found that passion of the heart? The
great singer Frank Harte once observed that the winners write
the histories and the losers make the songs – without those
songs, poems and stories, how should we have remembered
ourselves, how should we have formulated a better dream of
who we yet might be?

It is a pity that Pearse, McDonagh, Collins, de Valera and
Markievicz were not well versed in the theoretical projection
of the post-revolutionary future; it is a tragedy that the only
revolutionary theorist among those freedom fighters came to
his end prematurely, strapped to a chair in the execution yard
of Kilmainham Gaol.

Well, our republic was not arrived at by a process of cold
reasoning. Yeats might well have nurtured, for a brief while,
the hope that England would keep faith, and we have many
among us who persist in that fond delusion still, but the
Rising happened, the War of Independence happened, and we

are the direct inheritors of those irrevocable, inescapable passionate gestures.

Julius Caesar had sage advice for revolutionaries: 'If you must break the law, do it to seize power: in all other cases observe it.' Ireland's tragedy is that, having broken the law to seize power, we immediately reinstated that very law we had overthrown. There is no more poignant symbol of this self-defeating revolution than Collins commanding those borrowed batteries that shelled the Four Courts. We live with that legacy still, and whether or not we aim to reform or refound our republic, we would do well to square up to this monumental fact.

In Section 4 of 'a Patriotic Suite' Montague celebrates the nobility of the founding dream:

Symbolic depth charge of music
Releases a national dream;
From clerk to paladin
In a single violent day.
Files of men from shattered buildings
(Slouch hat, blunt mauser gun)
Frame the freedom that they won.

The bread queue, the messianic
Agitator of legend
Arriving on the train –
Christ and socialism –
Wheatfield and factory
Vivid in the sun;
Connolly's dream, if any one.

But Montague is too good, too true a poet, to leave it at that. He goes on in the third and final stanza to say this:

> All revolutions are interior
> The displacement of spirit
> By the arrival of fact,
> Ceaseless as cloud across sky,
> Sudden as sun.
> Movement of a butterfly
> Modifies everything.

The revolution that we never had is that interior revolution. Because we did not change in our spirits, nothing of any substance was ever displaced by the arrival of a new set of facts. We failed, if I might put it very simply indeed, to change our minds.

We failed to change our language.

In the poems and the songs and stories there are more durable maps of memory than in all the edicts of the state. Perhaps we need to find new ways to re-insert these memories in our narrative of who we most deeply and truly are?

I would not underestimate the difficulty. In her poem 'A Child's Map of Dublin' (1991), Paula Meehan's opening stanza charts an exclusion process that has only accelerated since Montague wrote 'Patriotic Suite':

> I wanted to find you Connolly's Starry Plough,
> the flag I have lived under since birth or since
> I first scanned nightskies and learned the nature of work.
> 'That hasn't been on show in years,' the porter told us.
> They're revising at the National Museum,

all hammers and drills and dust, conversion to
an interpretive centre in the usual contemporary style.

I believe that our present crisis stems from a double failure: the failure of the revolutionary generation to establish a true republic, and our inevitable consequent ongoing failure to imagine a new state from inside the facts and the language of the present state.

Hannah Arendt says:

Predictions of the future are never anything but projections of present automatic processes and procedures, that is, of occurrences that are likely to come to pass if men do not act and if nothing unexpected happens; every action, for better or worse, and every accident necessarily destroys the whole pattern in whose frame the prediction moves and where it finds its evidence.

Change, in other words, meaningful change, will require some considerable accident or some profound, history-breaking action.

As with predictions, so with proposals: projected solutions couched in the present language of politics can at best offer a kind of battlefield triage to keep the patient alive for the moment. The real problem is to find a mould-breaking gesture, a departure into some new language, which offers a whole new life, perhaps a whole new kind of life, for the patient.

If we are to imagine a new republic, we are constrained to do so from outside the walls of the state – and we would do well to remind ourselves of Bob Dylan's useful phrase: 'To live outside the law you must be honest.'

The language of public life in Ireland today is a language of subservience to authority when it is not a bullying on the part of the state. Cringing before the displeasure of our new colonial masters, our governments have inflicted on us suffering and sacrifice into the fourth or fifth generation so that a political and banking system brutally indifferent to our needs and desires may be saved from its own excesses.

Dress it how you like, neither the last nor the present government can credibly claim that its first, governing loyalty is to the people of Ireland.

I think again of Michael Hartnett, and his excoriating, prophetic vision:

> I saw our governments the other night –
> I think the scene was Leopardstown –
> horribly deformed dwarfs rode the racetrack
> each mounted on a horribly deformed dwarf;
> greenfaced, screaming, yellow-toothed, prodding
> each other with electric prods, thrashing
> each other's skinny arses, dribbling snot
> and smeared with their own dung, they galloped
> towards the prize, a glass and concrete anus.
>
> I think the result was a dead heat.

Not, I agree, the language of statecraft or diplomacy – but a living language, a language capable of telling and carrying truths. A language far closer to the truth of what is than any number of government press releases, or post-ministerial *mea culpa*s.

I doubt that I need to, but perhaps I had better make it explicit that I am not suggesting for a moment that the language of law can ever be spoken or written as poetry is spoken and written. I do want to say, forcibly, that unless the language of governance breaks with the dead weight of the language of law and moves decisively closer to the fully inclusive *paroles* of song, poem and story, then the gap between governor and governed can only, and surely must, become that deep chasm out of which chaos will come swaggering one dark night.

Poetry is, among other things, passion embodied in living language; there is room for reason, and for unreason, too, but above all else poetry is disciplined language in the register of human passions. Poetry is the living language raised to the power of imagination.

Is it beyond us to found a dialogue between state and people in a living language?

The poet's business is with the dignity of the human soul in language, and whether it be the hard tyranny of persecution or the soft, insidious tyranny of willed indifference, the one thing government from above will not abide is language that insists on the irreducible human dignity of the citizen.

If the language of governance, and hence the practice and obligations of government, derive from the inherited corpus of law, and if the language of law derives from and gains its authority from the language of the constitution, and if you grant me that piecemeal reform is little more than a holding action in the face of looming chaos, then our task is a very simple one: we must rewrite the constitution.

We must change our language.

It has been done before, in a post-colonial state; it has been done, it is being done, in our time.

In post-apartheid South Africa, they faced up to the challenge of a new jurisprudence as a concomitant of facing up to imagining a new politics.

In a landmark case concerning the issue of whether or not certain benefits should be extended to Mozambican refugees, Justice Yvonne Mokgoro introduced, in parallel with the Kantian ideal of 'the Kingdom of Ends', the concept of *ubuntu*. The word translates, more or less, as 'humaneness', according to the scholar Drucilla Cornell, on whose description of that landmark judgment I am drawing here. Cornell tells us that Mokgoro stated the following:

> Generally, *ubuntu* translates as *humaneness*. In its most fundamental sense, it translates as personhood and morality. Metaphorically, it expresses itself in *umuntu ngumuntu ngabantu*, describing the significance of group solidarity on survival issues so central to the survival of communities. While it envelops the key values of group solidarity, compassion, respect, human dignity, conformity to basic norms and collective unity, in its fundamental sense it denoted humanity and morality. Its spirit emphasises respect for human dignity, marking a shift from confrontation to conciliation.

In a later part of the judgment, Justice Mokgoro goes on to say: 'In the Western cultural heritage, respect and the value for life, manifested in the all-embracing concepts of *humanity* and *menswaardigheit* are also highly priced.'

Cornell brings two towering figures to our attention, Justice Mokgoro and the former Constitutional Court Judge, Justice Laurie Ackermann, champion of the proposal that human rights are grounded in the moral idea of dignity, itself an idea he derives from German idealism. Between them, if I understand Cornell here, they can be said to propose a synthesis, a co-existence, between the rights of the individual and the rights of community; both ideas, says Cornell, 'appeal to the principle of humanity as the basis of legality'.

It is not without significance, I think, that this new jurisprudence feels free to draw on the plurality of languages available to the new state. It is not without significance that the new South Africa is respectful in its postures towards both the old and the new, towards high culture, including elements of the inherited legal culture of the former state, and towards the demotic cultures of the powerless.

The choice, as these learned judges recognise, is to make it new or to fall back into the disempowering language of the former regime.

To step outside your language is to step into a particular liberty; it is also to experience that vertigo, familiar to the poet, that Michael Hartnett expressed when he wrote: 'I have poems to hand, it's words I cannot find.' I would not deny the difficulty of what I am proposing. The language we employ in all its registers is overwhelmingly an inherited language, and the very fact that the language of law endures as it does suggests that to some extent at least it possesses an adequacy, an aptness for its purpose, that we should take very seriously into consideration. It is not as if, by will and *fiat*, we can imagine a wholly new language into existence – but that is by no means what I am suggesting. The task is to find and imagine a register in language that steps between liberty and vertigo, that conserves what serves and provides, it may be, for states of mind and being that we are only beginning to imagine. Above all else, perhaps, a register of language that embodies and renders active a reconciliation between passion and reason.

So, very simply, we must find the words. The old words will not do. The old language must be mined and sifted for what is good in it, and there will be a great deal, I am sure. But, only so much of what has brought us here will serve.

Lawyer and politician, poet and citizen, we face a common task. To build a right republic we must find the right words.

References

'DO YOU KNOW WHAT A REPUBLIC IS?': THE ADVENTURE AND
MISADVENTURES OF AN IDEA
Fintan O'Toole

1 *Irish Times*, 19 November 2011.
2 *Irish Times*, 2 March 2012.
3 *Irish Review* (Dublin), vol. 3, no. 29 (July 1913), pp. 217–27.
4 *Irish Worker*, 22 August 1914; *Workers' Republic*, 18 March 1916.
5 Brian Cowen, speech at Georgetown University, Washington DC, 21 March 2012.
6 Ernest Renan, *The Poetry of the Celtic Races and Other Studies*, translated by William G. Hutchison [1896], Kennikat Press, Port Washington, New York, 1970, pp. 66–75.
7 Dáil Éireann debates, vol. 1, 21 January 1919.
8 *Irish Times*, 5 June 1935.
9 *New York Times*, 31 October 1937.
10 James Loughlin, *The British Monarchy and Ireland*, Cambridge University Press, 2007, p. 345.
11 Elizabeth Keane, *An Irish Statesman and Revolutionary*, I.B. Tauris, London, 2006, p. 52.
12 'An Irishman's Diary', *Irish Times*, 19 April 1949.
13 Thomas Paine, *The Works of Thomas Paine, Esq.*, London, 1792, p. 105.
14 Maurizio Viroli, *Republicanism*, Hill & Wang, New York, 2002.
15 Edward Stillingfleet Cayley, *The European Revolutions of 1848*, Smith, Elder & Co., London, 1856.
16 Quoted in Viroli, *Republicanism*, p. 89.

17 Viroli, *Republicanism*, p. 12–13.
18 Joe Lee, *Ireland 1912–1985: Politics and Society*, Cambridge University Press, 1989, p. 646.
19 Heinrich Böll, *Irish Journal*, Northwestern University Press, Evanston, IL, 1994, pp. 109–10.
20 John Cooney, *John Charles McQuaid: Ruler of Catholic Ireland*, O'Brien Press, Dublin, 1999, p. 97.
21 I make these arguments myself in *Ship of Fools*, Faber and Faber, London, 2009.
22 P. W. Joyce, *English As We Speak It in Ireland*, M. H. Gill & Son, Dublin, 1910, p. 312.

THE REPUBLIC AS A TRADITION AND AN IDEAL IN IRELAND TODAY
Iseult Honohan

1 James Harrington, *The Commonwealth of Oceana and A System of Politics* [1656], Cambridge University Press, 1992, p. 8.
2 Philip Pettit, *Republicanism* [1997], Oxford University Press, 1999, p. 71.
3 Hannah Arendt, *The Human Condition*, Anchor Books, New York, 1958, p. 210.
4 Niccolò Machiavelli, *The Discourses* [1531], edited by Bernard Crick, Penguin, Harmondsworth, 1983, p. 253.
5 For example, Tom Garvin, 'An Irish republican tradition?' in Iseult Honohan (ed.), *Republicanism in Ireland: Confronting Theories and Traditions*, Manchester University Press, 2008.
6 Margaret O'Callaghan, 'Reconsidering the republican tradition in nineteenth-century Ireland', in Honohan (ed.), *Republicanism in Ireland*.
7 Cécile Laborde, *Critical Republicanism, The Hijab Controversy and Political Philosophy*, Oxford University Press, 2008; Iseult Honohan, 'Tolerance and non-domination' in Jan Dobbernack and Tariq Modood (eds.), *Hard to Accept: New Perspectives on Tolerance, Intolerance and Respect*, forthcoming.
8 James Bohman, *Democracy Across Borders: From Demos to Demoi*, MIT Press, Boston, MA, 2007; Máire Brophy, *Intervention and Sovereignty: A Republican Approach*, unpublished Ph.D. thesis, University College Dublin.

9 Margaret Canovan, 'Trust the people! Populism and the two faces of democracy', *Political Studies*, no. 47 (March 1999), pp. 2–16.

10 Cécile Laborde, 'The Culture(s) of the Republic. Nationalism and multiculturalism in French Republican Thought', *Political Theory*, no. 29 (October 2001), pp. 716–35; Laborde, *Critical Republicanism*.

CIVIC VIRTUE, AUTONOMY AND RELIGIOUS SCHOOLS: WHAT WOULD
MACHIAVELLI DO?
Tom Hickey

1 For a more complete account of liberty as non-domination, see Iseult Honohan's contribution to this volume.

2 The scholarship associated with Quentin Skinner, Philip Pettit and others is often referred to as neo-republicanism. See for instance, Philip Pettit, *Republicanism: A Theory of Freedom and Government*, Oxford University Press, 1997; Quentin Skinner, *Liberty before Liberalism*, Cambridge University Press, 1998.

3 Machiavelli suggested that 'just as good morals, if they are to be maintained, have need of the laws, so the laws, if they are to be observed, have need of good morals'. See Niccolò Machiavelli, *The Complete Works and Others*, ed. and trans. Allan Gilbert, Duke University Press, Durham, NC, 1965, p. 493.

4 Will Kymlicka is one who objects to civic republicanism on this basis. He insists that 'civic republicanism refers to the view that the best life – the most truly human life – is one which privileges political participation over other spheres of human endeavour . . . [I]t is inconsistent with liberalism's commitment to pluralism, and in any event is implausible as a general account of the good life for all persons.' Will Kymlicka, *Politics in the Vernacular: Nationalism, Multiculturalism, and Citizenship*, Oxford University Press, 2001, p. 297 n. 6.

5 See John Rawls, *Political Liberalism*, Columbia University Press, New York, 1996.

6 For an interesting overview from a republican perspective, see Cécile Laborde, *Critical Republicanism: The Hijab Controversy and Political Philosophy*, Oxford University Press, 2008.

7 These were the words of Bernard Stasi, President of the Commission, as quoted by Laborde. Ibid., n. 133.

8 The dissident republican intellectual Séan O'Faoláin decried this approach in the literary periodical *The Bell* in the 1940s. See Séan O'Faoláin, 'To What Possible Future', *The Bell*, April 1942, pp. 1–9, as quoted in Mark McNally, 'Séan O'Faoláin's Discourse of "The Betrayal of the Republic" in Mid-Twentieth Century Ireland', in Jeremy Jennings and Iseult Honohan (eds.), *Republicanism in Theory and Practice*, Routledge, London, 2005, pp. 79–94.

9 This view is associated in particular with Aristotle. John Rawls draws a distinction between the civic republicanism of Machiavelli and de Tocqueville on the one hand and Aristotelian 'civic humanism' on the other. He claims the former to be compatible with his political liberalism (i.e. 'neutral' between conceptions of the good life) while the latter understands 'man as a social, even political, animal whose essential nature is most fully realised in a democratic society' and accordingly takes political participation to be 'the privileged locus of the good life'. See Rawls, *Political Liberalism*, p. 206.

10 Neo-republican scholars such as Pettit and Skinner would distance themselves from this Aristotelianism, and draw a distinction between so-called neo-Roman and neo-Athenian republicanism.

11 See Iseult Honohan, 'Educating Citizens: Nation-Building and its Republican Limits', in Jennings and Honohan (eds.), *Republicanism in Theory and Practice*, pp. 199–207, which has influenced my ideas in this area. Honohan develops these themes in her contribution to this volume.

12 Honohan further argues in this vein that virtuous republican citizens must expand their perceptions to become aware of 'multiply reiterated interdependencies'. This requires citizens to understand the broader social and political arrangements within which they live their lives and enjoy their liberty. This involves 'countering assumptions of individual self-sufficiency and misconceptions about the impact of government and the effects of non-participation'. See Honohan, 'Educating Citizens', p. 205.

13 Machiavelli believed that the different factions that gained power 'never organised [Florence] for the common benefit, but always for the advantage of their own party' which led to an absence of shared political trust, and ultimately, domination. See Machiavelli, *The Complete Works*, p. 296.

14 Sara Shumer, 'Republican Politics and its Corruption', *Political Theory*, vol. 7 no. 1 (February 1979), pp. 15–16.

15 On the idea of public reason, see John Rawls, *The Law of Peoples: with 'The Idea of Public Reason Revisited'*, Harvard University Press, Cambridge, MA, 2001, pp. 131–80.

16 Rawls explains the idea with the simple illustration of Servetus, who 'could understand why Calvin wanted to burn him at the stake'. Similarly it is understandable why some or many individuals might want to coerce other individuals on the basis of their own innermost beliefs, but it is a different matter for those other individuals to reasonably accept those reasons as legitimate.

17 *Mozert v. Hawkins County Board of Education*, 827 F.2d 1058 (6th Cir.1987).

18 For analysis of the case in light of civic education in the liberal state see, Stephen Macedo, *Diversity and Distrust: Civic Education in a Multicultural Democracy*, Harvard University Press, Cambridge, MA, 2000, pp. 157–65.

19 *Mozert*, p. 1062.

20 Rawls, *Political Liberalism*, p. 200.

21 This distinction, which is so fundamental to the argument made by neo-republicans, is discussed widely in the literature. For a comprehensive analysis, See Philip Pettit, 'Law and Liberty', in Samantha Besson and Jose Marti (eds.), *Legal Republicanism: National and International Perspectives*, Oxford University Press, 2009, pp. 39–59.

22 Eamonn Callan, *Creating Citizens: Political Education and Liberal Democracy*, Oxford University Press, 1997, pp. 152–61.

23 Ibid., p. 153.

24 Ibid.

25 Ibid., pp. 153–4.

26 Steven Macedo makes this argument, but from the standpoint of political liberalism rather than republicanism. See Stephen Macedo, 'Liberal Civic Education and Religious Fundamentalism: The Case of God v. John Rawls?', *Ethics*, vol. 105 no. 3 (April 1995), pp. 468–96.

27 Its report, published in May 2012, is to inform the reforms that are to take place in school patronage in the coming years. For a brief critique, see Tom Hickey, 'A Thought Experiment for Ruari Quinn' at www.humanrights.ie (accessed August 2012).

28 See *Information on Areas for Possible Divesting of Patronage of Primary Schools*, Department of Education and Skills, Dublin, 2010.

29 On this argument, see chapters 4 and 5 of Eoin Daly, *Religion, Law and the Irish State*, Clarus, Dublin, 2012. See also Eoin Daly and Tom Hickey, 'Religious freedom and the "right to discriminate" in the school admissions context: a neo-republican critique', *Legal Studies*, vol. 31 no. 4 (December 2011), pp. 615–43.

30 Aristotle, *Nicomachean Ethics*, trans. Terence Irwin, Hackett, Indianapolis, IN, 1985, p. 35.

31 The most recent figures suggest that 87 per cent of those living in Ireland describe themselves as Catholic. See Central Statistics Office, *Census Reports: Population classified by religion for relevant censuses from 1881–2006*, Central Statistics Office, Dublin, 2006.

32 I am guided on these arguments by the work of Ian MacMullen. See Ian MacMullen, *Faith in Schools? Autonomy, Citizenship and Religious Education in the Liberal State*, Princeton University Press, NJ, 2007, pp. 169–75.

33 On this issue, see Tom Hickey, 'Domination and the Hijab in Irish Schools', *Dublin University Law Journal*, vol. 31 (2009), pp. 127–53.

34 This point is made by Ian MacMullen.

CITIZENS OR SUBJECTS? CIVIL SOCIETY AND THE REPUBLIC
Fred Powell

1 Charles Baxter, 'Behind Murakami's Mirror', in *New York Review of Books*, 6 December 2011, pp. 23–5.

2 John Ehrenberg, *Civil Society*, New York University Press, NY, 1999, p. 91.

3 Jonathan I. Israel, *Radical Enlightenment*, Oxford University Press, 2001, p. 259.

4 Russ Leo, 'Caute: Jonathan Israel's Secular Modernity', *Journal for Cultural and Religious Theory*, vol. 9 no. 2 (summer 2008), p. 76.

5 Ibid., p. 77.

6 Israel, *Radical Enlightenment*, p. 285.

7 Ibid., pp. 295–327.

8 Jonathan I. Israel, *The Revolutionary Mind*, University of Princeton Press, NJ, 2010, pp. 180–85.

9 Nicholas Phillipson, *Adam Smith: An Enlightened Life*, Allen Lane, London, 2010, p. 157.

10 Ehrenberg, *Civil Society*, p. 96.

11 Fred Powell, 'Civil Society Theory: Paine', in Helmut K. Anheier, Stefan Toepler and Regina List (eds.), *International Encyclopaedia of Civil Society*, vol. 1, Springer, New York, 2010, pp. 438–42.

12 David Dwan, *The Great Community*, Field Day, Dublin, 2008, p. 14.

13 John Keane, *Tom Paine: A Political Life*, Bloomsbury, London, 1995, p. 324.

14 Alexis de Tocqueville, *Democracy in America*, ed. Richard D. Heftner, Mentor, New York, 1956, p. 202.

15 Howard Zinn, *A People's History of the United States*, Harper-Collins, New York, 1999, p. 218.

16 Dwan, *The Great Community*, pp. 63–5.

17 Cited in Chris Hann and Elizabeth Dunn (eds.), *Civil Society: Challenging Western Models*, Routledge, London, 1996, p. 4.

18 Antonio Gramsci, *Selections from Prison Notebooks*, ed. Quintin Hoare and Geoffrey Nowell-Smith, Lawrence and Wishart, London, 1971, p. 12.

19 Hann and Dunn, *Civil Society*, p. 5.

20 Ibid., p. 8.

21 David G. Anderson, 'Bringing Civil Society to an Uncivilised Place: Citizenship Regimes in Russia's Arctic Frontier', in Hann and Dunn (eds.), *Civil Society*, p. 99.

22 Ibid., p. 100.

23 Fred Powell, *The Politics of Civil Society: Neoliberalism or Social Left?*, Policy, Bristol, 2007, p. 206.

24 Jean L. Cohen and Andrew Arato, *Civil Society and Political Theory*, MIT Press, Cambridge, MA, 1992.

25 Ibid., p. 9.

26 Harold Pinter, *Art, Truth, Politics*, Nobel Lecture, 2005.

27 *Guardian*, 8 December 2005.

28 John Keane, *The Life and Death of Democracy*, Simon and Schuster, London, 2009.

29 Benjamin Barber, *Strong Democracy: Participatory Politics for*

a New Age, University of California Press, Berkeley, CA, 1984,
p. xvii.

30 Ibid., p. 20.

31 Thomas Prugh, Robert Constanza and Herman Daly, *The Local
Politics of Global Sustainability*, Island Press, Washington, DC,
2000, p. 10.

32 Ibid. p. 220.

33 Iris Marion Young, *Inclusion and Democracy*, Oxford University
Press, 2000, pp. 9–10.

34 Ibid., p. 54.

35 Ibid., p. 55.

36 Bill Cooke and Uma Kothari (eds.), *Participation: The New
Tyranny*, Zed Books, London, 2001.

37 J. P. O'Carroll, 'Cultural Lag and Democratic Deficit in Ireland',
Community Development Journal 37 (1) (January 2002),
pp. 10–19.

38 Clifford Geertz, *The Interpretation of Culture*, Huntington,
London, 1975.

39 Ferdinand Tonnies, *Community and Association*, Routledge and
Kegan Paul, London, 1955.

40 Terence Brown, *Ireland a Social and Cultural History*, Fontana,
London, 1981, p. 41.

41 Patrick Macklem, 'Militant Democracy, Legal Pluralism, and the
Paradox of Self-determination', *International Journal of Constitutional Law*, vol. 4 no. 3 (July 2006), p. 488.

42 Fred Powell, *The Politics of Irish Social Policy 1600–1999*, Edwin
Mellen Press, New York, 1992.

43 Fred Powell and Martin Geoghegan, *The Politics of Community
Development*, A. & A. Farmar, Dublin, 2004, p. 17.

44 Gerald Delanty, 'Modernity and Postmodernity', in Austin
Harrington (ed.), *Modern Social Theory*, Oxford University Press,
2005, p. 276.

45 Cited in Samuel Huntington, *The Clash of Civilizations*, Simon
and Schuster, London, 2002, p. 306.

46 Tariq Ali, *The Clash of Fundamentalisms*, Verso, London, 2002,
pp. 3–4.

47 Michael D. Higgins, *Renewing the Republic*, Liberties Press,
Dublin, 2011, p. 21.

48 Ibid., p. 22.

49 Ibid., p. 62.

50 Ibid., p. 116.

51 Sarah van Gelder, *This Changes Everything*, Berret–Koeler, San Francisco, CA, 2011, p. 1.

52 *Occupy Cork*, issue 3, 2011, p. 11.

53 María Clemencia Ramírez, 'The Politics of Recognition and Citizenship', in Boaventura de Sousa Santos (ed.), *Democratizing Democracy*, Verso, London, 2007, p. 238.

54 Max Weber, *Economy and Society* [1919], trans. Ephraim Fischoff et al., ed. Guenther Roth and Claus Wittich, University of California Press, Berkeley, CA, 1968.

55 Barber, *Strong Democracy*.

56 Fintan O'Toole, *Enough is Enough: How to Build a New Republic*, Faber and Faber, London, 2010, p. 21.

57 Linda Connolly and Niamh Hourigan, *Social Movements and Ireland*, Manchester University Press, 2006.

58 Peadar Murphy and Mary P. Murphy, *Towards a Second Republic*, Pluto, London, 2011, pp. 217–18.

Index

FLATTERLAND

IAN STEWART
FLATTERLAND

LIKE **FLATLAND** ONLY MORE SO

MACMILLAN

First published 2001 by Macmillan
an imprint of Macmillan Publishers Ltd
25 Eccleston Place, London SW1W 9NF
Basingstoke and Oxford
Associated companies throughout the world
www.macmillan.com

ISBN 0 333 78312 3

1 3 5 7 9 8 6 4 2

A CIP catalogue record for this book is available from
the British Library.

Typeset by Florence Production, Stoodleigh, Devon
Printed and bound in Great Britain by
Mackays of Chatham plc, Chatham, Kent

CONTENTS

v

FROM FLATLAND TO FLATTERLAND

Sometimes writers get a bee in their bonnet – an idea that buzzes around for years until one day it suddenly crystallizes. Yes, it's easy to crystallize a bee: you just have to get the right mix of metaphors. *Flatterland* is a crystallized bee. Let me tell you how it came about, and why.

In 1884, in Victorian England, a headmaster and Shakespearean scholar named Edwin Abbott Abbott – that's right, two Abbotts – wrote a classic of scientific popularization called *Flatland*. Written under the pseudonym 'A. Square', it tells of a world of two dimensions, a flat Euclidean plane that came straight out of the geometry texts of that period. Abbott would have used them in his school. The inhabitants of Flatland are geometric figures – lines, triangles, squares, pentagons ... The rather narrow Victorian attitudes of A. Square are shattered by rumours of the Third Dimension, confirmed by a visitor from that extra-dimensional realm who is named The Sphere.

Flatland reprinted within a month and has never been out of print since. Its appeal has survived all intervening scientific and social upheavals. It exists in numerous editions, and several writers have published sequels or derivative works, such as Dionys Burger's *Sphereland* and Kee Dewdney's *The Planiverse*.

Flatterland is another.

The scientific purpose of *Flatland* was serious and substantial. Abbott's sights were focused not on the Third Dimension – familiar enough to his readers – but on the Fourth Dimension. Could a space of more than three dimensions exist? Where would you *put* it? Abbott softened up his readers' resistance to such an outlandish notion by making them imagine how a Flatlander would respond to the outrageous suggestion that a Third Dimension could exist.

He had a second purpose, a very different one: to satirize the rigid social structure of Victorian England, with its hierarchies of status and privilege – especially the lowly status accorded to women. To this purpose he made the females of Flatland mere one-dimensional lines, inferior even to the slimmest of isosceles triangles, and vastly inferior to the circular Priesthood. *Flatland* was – and still is – a very subversive book. Some supporters of female emancipation misunderstood Abbott's satire, and in the preface to the second edition he was forced to explain that A. Square

> has himself modified his own personal views, both as regards Women and as regards the Isosceles or Lower Classes . . . But, writing as a Historian, he has identified himself (perhaps too closely) with the views generally adopted by Flatland, and (as he has been informed) even by Spaceland Historians; in whose pages (until very recent times) the destinies of Women and of the masses of mankind have seldom been deemed worthy of mention and never of careful consideration.

So there! Abbott was, in fact, a social reformer who believed in equal educational opportunity for all social classes and genders; Flatland's narrow-minded social system is his cry of frustration.

The Fourth Dimension was hot intellectual property in Abbott's day. His interest in it came a decade before H. G. Wells's celebrated science-fiction story *The Time Machine*, which was serialized in the *New Review* (1894–5) and published as a book by Heinemann in 1895. Wells, like any good science-fiction author, based his tale on a solid dose of scientific gobbledegook, which in this case is supplied by the Time Traveller:

> 'But wait a moment. Can an *instantaneous* cube exist?'
> 'Don't follow you,' said Filby.
> 'Can a cube that does not last for any time at all, have a real existence?'
> Filby became pensive.

'Clearly,' the Time Traveller proceeded, 'any real body must have extension in four directions: it must have Length, Breadth, Thickness, and – Duration . . .

'. . . There are really four dimensions, three which we call the three planes of Space, and a fourth, Time. There is, however, a tendency to draw an unreal distinction between the former three dimensions and the latter, because it happens that our consciousness moves intermittently in one direction along the latter from the beginning to the end of our lives . . .

'. . . But some philosophical people have been asking why *three* dimensions particularly – why not another direction at right angles to the three? – and have even tried to construct a Four-Dimensional geometry. Professor Simon Newcomb was expounding this to the New York Mathematical Society only a month or so ago.'

Wells's reference to Newcomb reminds us that in the late nineteenth century higher-dimensional geometry was all the rage among mathematicians, especially Arthur Cayley (1821–95) and J. J. Sylvester (1814–97). Sylvester emigrated to the States and became a major founding figure of American mathematics. Some of the ideas about higher dimensions were introduced into physics by Hermann Minkowski (1864–1909), and were among the things that led to Relativity, the brainchild of (among others) Albert Einstein (1879–1955).

I'm giving you the dates to make it clear that *Flatland* is slap in the middle of all this. Abbott was a prolific writer, with some sixty books to his credit, though none of the others are remotely similar to *Flatland*. He was a passionate educator, and evidently understood the difference between serious science and solemn science. His fascination with some of the cutting-edge science of his day, in conjunction with these attributes, gave the world a classic.

At the start of the twenty-first century, mathematics and science have moved a long way from where they were at the end of the nineteenth. The Fourth Dimension is mild indeed compared with the mind-boggling inventions of geometers and physicists – spaces with infinitely many dimensions, spaces with none, spaces with fractional dimension, spaces with finitely many points, curved spaces, spaces that get mixed up with time, and spaces that aren't really there at all. The *respectable* reason for allowing that bee in my bonnet to crystallize is that there is ample scope to play Abbott's game again in a new context – indeed, in lots of new contexts.

I must confess, however, that there is a less respectable reason too. I'd been toying with writing some sort of sequel, and I'd got it into my head that since *Flatland* was about the adventures of A. Square, the update ought to follow the adventures of one of his modern descendants. We know that A. Square had children, because Abbott tells us so – but he doesn't tell us what the 'A.' in 'A. Square' stands for, and that bothered me. At this point, my thoughts were distracted by the sudden realization that I *knew* what Mr Square's first name must have been.

Obviously, the 'A.' stands for 'Albert'.

British readers will immediately appreciate why this has to be so. There is a popular TV soap called EastEnders – I'm not a fan myself – I don't like soaps – but things seep out into the general 'extelligence', and EastEnders is one of them. Anyway, this particular soap is set in a fictitious region of London centred around 'Albert Square'. There is no real Albert Square in central London, but there is an Albert Hall, an Albert Memorial, and an Albert Embankment. Albert was Queen Victoria's consort, and she loved him dearly, so London is littered with Alberts. Abbott was writing in Victorian times, satirizing Victorian values . . . the name *fitted*.

Now, there may not be an Albert Square in real central London, but there is a Grosvenor Square, a Berkeley Square (in which, according to the song, a nightingale sang . . .) and a Leicester Square. Suddenly the family tree of the Square dynasty was falling into place – Grosvenor, Berkeley, Lester . . .

What of the womenfolk? On Flatland, women are lines – and it followed just as night followed day that my central character should be female, and her name should be 'Victoria Line'. Vikki for short. There are Victorias all over London, too, including a main-line train station. The Victoria line is an underground railway line (the 'tube', or subway) linking Victoria Station to Euston Station, another main-line train station. So Victoria Line it was. Another underground line, the Jubilee line, gave me Vikki's mother, Lee.

Crazy, but it crystallized the whole bee into a book. Everything came to me in a rush. Young Vikki is Albert's great-great-granddaughter, a thoroughly modern young woman in a society rather like Britain and the US in the early sixties, but with a dash of Internet thrown in for narrative lubrication. Flatland's male-dominated Victorian culture is beginning to crumble as its women break away from their traditional restraints. Vikki finds an old notebook, Albert's original manuscript of *Flatland*, and is bitten by the 3D bug – much to her parents' consternation. Unknown to them, she tries to follow in her ancestor's vertex-steps (squares have vertices, but no feet) into the expanded universe of the Third Dimension . . . and she succeeds.

Now all I needed was to equip her with a guide. Dante had his Virgil to conduct him through the *Inferno*; A. Square had his Sphere . . . but Vikki would need a more versatile guide, familiar with dozens of mathematical and physical spaces . . . For weeks I grappled with this problem, until one evening I remembered a children's toy – a rubber-skinned inflatable orange ball with horns, plus two eyes and a broad grin painted on the front. The child sits on the ball, grabs the horns, and bounces across the floor. The toy was called a Space Hopper (the grin is that of an alien from Outer Space). Evidently, a Space Hopper is ideally suited to hop from one mathematical space to another . . . and I had my guide.

After that, all I had to do was choose *which* spaces were important enough to include, and I did that with an eye on the frontiers of today's mathematics and physics. Oh, yes – I also needed a title. I hope you can excuse the train of thought that led me to choose what now seems inevitable for a *Flatland* sequel – *Flatterland*.

Please pardon my temerity in attempting this add-on to a classic. You will see at once that I can't use Abbott's elegant Victorian prose style – modern times demand modern cadences. The original, fortunately, is untainted by my irreverence (re-read your copy: I promise that not a word has changed!).

I.S.

Coventry, July 2000

1

THE THIRD DIMENSION

Seen from space, it was a strange world, with the austere beauty of a page from Euclid. In fact it *was* a page from Euclid, geometry made flesh: a sprawling, humming world of two-dimensional shapes. Flatland. A land of lines, triangles, squares, polygons, circles . . . people, of their own kind. They lived polygonal lives, ate polygonal food, drank polygonal drink, made polygonal love, bore polygonal children, and died (polygonally) in a two-dimensional universe – and never thought it the least bit curious. Their flat world was all they could see, all they could hear, all they could feel. To them, it was all there was.

As long as nothing disturbed that perception, it was *true*.

But times were changing in Flatland.

The house was dowdy and unfashionably pentagonal, but in an excellent location: just along the street from the Palace of the Prefect. It had been in the Square family for almost 150 years, and was now beginning to show its age. Nonetheless, it was a comfortable dwelling, with the typical large Flatlandish entrance hall, seven rooms for the male members of the household, two apartments for the females, a study, a large room that once had housed servants but was now used as a kitchen, with a dining alcove, and a musty, cluttered cellar. It had separate doors for women and men – for safety reasons, women being rather sharp if encountered end-on. In the hall a middle-aged woman swept up after her two untidy square sons and her neat and lineal daughter, waving her body from side to side so that the males wouldn't accidentally blunder into an endpoint and cut themselves. She found it a comfortable life, though hardly a fulfilling one, and on the whole she was content with her lot.

In the cellar, her daughter Victoria was anything but content with hers. Flatland was a sexist subtopia in which women, seen by their menfolk as simple-minded one-dimensional creatures, performed only menial tasks. Even the lowest of the males, the isosceles triangles, had higher status, and each generation of males made sure everything stayed that way. Not exactly deliberately . . . well, not consciously . . . well, not with *malice*, anyway – they really thought it was the only option . . . Well, most of them. It just never occurred to the men that Flatland society might order itself differently. And it certainly never occurred to them that their most cherished beliefs about Flatland society might be based on prejudice and unchallenged assumptions. How could it be? In Flatland, your position in society was determined by how many sides you had and how regular your perimeter was. It was an objective test, hence unquestionable.

At the top of the tree were the Circles, priesthood-cum-nobility: glorious, almost transcendent beings – perfection made flesh. And the biggest bunch of snobs you could imagine. They weren't even true circles, just polygons with an awful lot of sides. Like many aspects of Flatland, their name was a polite fiction. Behind the rigid façade of Flatland society, however, the winds of change were starting to whine. They had begun as a gentle breeze when the Six-Year War between the Axials and the Alignment had thinned the ranks of Flatland males and thrust women into the munitions factories and the civil service. To the surprise of the men, and the quiet satisfaction of the women, the lineal ladies carried out what had previously been men's jobs with aplomb – maybe too much aplomb. There were mutterings in the Halls of Power – but the catenary was out of the bag, and no amount of effort would ever get it back again. As the decades passed, the breeze had stiffened to a howling gale, as the advance of technology brought with it inevitable social spin-off.

If Vikki Line had her way, the gale would soon become a roaring hurricane. Not that she disliked boys, you understand – as long as they knew their place. Once they stopped flaunting their vertices and comparing how many edges they had, some of them were even quite nice. In fact, that was what had brought her into the dusty recesses of the cellar: she was hoping to find some old discarded clothes of her mother's to wear to the disco that evening. Roger Rectangle was taking her on a date, the retro look was all the rage, and she was hoping to find a few items that would put a kink in the other girls' endpoints.

So far, all she'd found was a motheaten dishcloth and a box of her father's old string vests. (Literally: most Flatland garments were flexible lengths of string, which Flatlanders wrapped round themselves and secured with sticky tabs, leaving their faces uncovered.) Vikki had a feeling that her mother Jubilee would throw a fit if her daughter tried to go out wearing a string vest, however chic.

She noticed a cluster of rectangular boxes in a corner. One of them was battered and fraying at the corners, which looked promising; but she couldn't reach it easily, so she tugged at one of the nearer boxes. With a crash, the mildewed cardboard disintegrated and the contents scattered across the cellar floor.

'Victoria? *Victoria!* What was that? Are you all right, dear?'

She sighed. 'Yes, Mother. An old box came to bits, that's all.'

'Oh. Well, it sounded like a herd of ellipses. Do be careful, dear. And clear up any mess you've made.'

'Yes, Mother.' Vikki started to pick up the junk that had tumbled across the cellar floor, stuffing it back into the now rather battered boxes. She had almost finished when she noticed a tattered book. (More properly, it should be described as a scroll, for on Flatland books are written on lines, not flat sheets, in a kind of Morse code; and the way to store a line compactly is to roll it into a spiral . . . I can't keep explaining this kind of thing to you, my Planiturthian readers. So if I use a Planiturthian term that seems not to make sense, for instance, having Vikki – who is a *line*, for heaven's sake – pick something up or carry something, you'll just have to assume that there is some Flatland equivalent.)

Anyway, the book, for so we shall call it, had skated behind some cracked crockery, and nearly escaped her attention.

Curiosity impelled her to roll the book open. Even in the cellar, she had no difficulty seeing it, for in Flatland light manages to make its way into every nook and cranny. Where it came from was a complete mystery – even to the greatest savants, even at the end of the twenty-first century – but its ubiquity had an architectural consequence: houses did not need windows.

The book was handwritten, in an old-fashioned script. The title page bore the words *Flatland, a Romance of Many Dimensions*. The author was identified as *A. Square*. At first she thought it was some kind of child's primer on the geography, history, and sociology of Flatland, but as she skipped through the text it began to mutate into something darker and more personal. It was almost like a diary, except that it was not arranged by date. A bit past the middle she did come upon a date, however:

> *From dreams I proceed to facts.*
> *It was the last day of the 1999th year of our era. The pattering of the rain had long ago announced nightfall, and I was sitting in the company of my wife, musing on the events of the past and the prospects of the coming year, the coming century, the coming Millennium.*

Why, that would make the book almost exactly a hundred years old! Vikki read on, hoping for more clues. The weird narrative told of a Stranger, a Circle who could change size – a stranger from Space. It was some kind of science fiction novel, then. A lot of the boys seemed to be into that kind of thing. A phrase caught her eye:

> *You see, you do not even know what Space is. You think it is of Two Dimensions only; but I have come to announce to you a Third – height, breadth, and length.*

Ah. They'd done this in physics. Space was two-dimensional, of course – how could it be otherwise? But there was a sense in which you could think of time as a third dimension, thereby getting a three-dimensional 'spacetime continuum'. It wasn't *real*, of course, just a mathematical invention – and she found the idea rather pointless because you couldn't draw pictures of three dimensions, anyway. Face it, you couldn't even draw pictures of *two* dimensions – you had to project real space down onto a line if you were going to draw a picture. That was how the visual sense worked. Sculpture, though – that was genuinely two-dimensional, like the tactile and auditory senses. So a *moving* sculpture could be considered three-dimensional – and that was what the Stranger in the book was. A moving sculpture that spoke: what a strange idea!

She read on, and became confused. Whatever the Stranger's three-dimensional Space was – and only now did the significance of the capital letter become apparent – it was not the conventional three-dimensional spacetime continuum from her physics lessons. In the Stranger's mind, the Third Dimension wasn't time! What, for instance, could be made of this passage?

> *You are living on a Plane. What you style Flatland is the vast level surface of what I may call a fluid, on, or in, the top of which you and your countrymen move about, without rising above it or falling below it.*
>
> *I am not a plane Figure, but a Solid. You call me a Circle; but in reality I am not a Circle, but an infinite number of Circles, of size varying from a Point to a Circle of thirteen inches in diameter, one placed on the top of the other . . .*

Above? Below? On *top?* If A. Square had been writing about the spacetime continuum, surely he would have used words like *before, after.* These terms – she could try to infer their content from their context, but the inference didn't really work – were outlandish, meaningless nonsense words.

Vikki Line tucked the curious book away inside her edgebag, an accessory that had become very fashionable indeed, and not only among the young. Even males were wearing them, though they called them 'sidesacks' to distinguish them from effeminate edgebags. She would take a closer look at the book later on. Right now there was a more pressing problem: finding something suitable to wear to the disco.

※

'I don't understand why you young people insist on wearing your parents' old cast-offs', her mother fussed. 'You know, your father gave me that jacket just after we got married. It used to fit me then. The colour suits you, dear, I must say.' Only a few generations ago, Jubilee would not have been able to make such a statement – the rule had been 'any colour as long as it's grey'. But the old colour prejudice, fallout from the political sabotage of the Universal Colour Bill, was slowly dying out (indeed, dyeing out), except for a continuing prohibition on body-paint – and even that was coming under fire with the new fashion for tipstick among upper-class young women.

'It really needs an iron, though, dear,' Jubilee fussed. 'Would you like me to—'

'New clothes are so *ordinary*, Mother. I want to look different.'

'Different from what, dear?'

'Well, just . . . different. Like all my friends.'

'Different but the same, then, dear?'

'Ohhhh! You're making fun of me again!'

Her mother smiled (Flatland women do this by wiggling their front vertex in a special way). Vikki took the treasure away to her own little room, along with her other discovery. She kept her clothes in there, and her personal belongings – a Parallelogram Bear and a dilapidated My Little Polygon which she had long ago outgrown but kept for sentimental reasons; a tape-player with hundreds of cassettes; letters from her friends; schoolbooks; and – her pride and joy – one of the new Home Computers, complete with key-strip, tape-reader, printer, and scanner. It had a 2D graphics accelerator, and twenty megs of RAM. Bundled with it had been a 'free gift': a tiny electronic Personal Disorganizer, in which she kept contact information for her friends and an extensive diary. It communicated with the computer by invisible light. Not only that – once she'd saved enough money she was going to add a modem, persuade Daddy to rent an extra phone link, and surf the InterLine. It wouldn't be hard to persuade him: all she had to do was to stay on the phone to her friends for hours and burst into tears and tell him he was ruining her life if he dared interrupt to make his own calls. Her friend Dilly had tried it on *her* dad a month ago, and a second phone connection had been installed within a day.

The Flatland phone system, by the way, was a triumph of technical ingenuity. In a two-dimensional world, you can't lay a network of cables without trapping people between them – there's no underground and no overhead. But you can avoid cables altogether and use radio waves of a frequency to which most things in Flatland, especially houses and people, are transparent. With enough repeaters scattered around to boost fading signals back up to full strength and shunt messages past radio-opaque objects, the system worked surprisingly well. Fortunately, Flatlanders seemed to be unaffected by the radiation that sleeted through them, though some consumer groups were beginning to worry that overexposure to the phone system might be contributing to an epidemic of inflamed centroids.

At the very moment that Vikki was thinking about her father, he arrived home from work. Grosvenor was a huge, good-natured square . . . well, actually he had gone a bit trapezoidal in his middle age, mostly because Jubilee was such a good cook. As usual, he had picked up their young sons Berkeley and Lester from primary school on the way home. Grosvenor gave Jubilee and Victoria a homecoming kiss and flopped against the big sofa in front of the fire. The soft, slightly springy cushions closed snugly around three of his edges. (The distinction between sitting on/in/against a piece of furniture and *wearing* it was often rather fuzzy in Flatland.)

The boys shot off into the yard, to play until dinner was ready.

'Vikki, love, be a dear and bring me a beer, will you? It's been a bisector of a day at work.'

Typical. But thoughts of an extra phone link stopped her saying what was on her mind: *get your own beer, Dad.* Instead, she padded off obediently and brought him back a rectangle of lager from the freezer.

He popped the tab at one end and sucked. 'Thanks, sweet-centre.' *Well, at least he's expressed gratitude.* 'Like the shoes. Nice jacket, too, love: it suits you.'

'It's the one you . . . I mean, yes, it does, doesn't it? I found it in the cellar.'

'I keep meaning to clean that cellar out', said Grosvenor. 'Nothing but a heap of useless junk. Some of it's been in there for generations. Give the lot to Boxfam, that's what we ought to do.'

Talk of junk reminded Vikki of her discovery. Innocently, she said, 'That reminds me, Dad: I found a funny old book in the cellar. It looks really really interesting.'

'A book, eh? Well, that cellar holds an awful lot . . . bound to be a few books down there—'

'It was handwritten, like a diary. By someone called A. Square.'

Her father sat bolt upright and popped out of the enveloping sofa. His beer slipped from his grasp and the fire hissed as a few errant drops hit it. '*What?*'

'It was all about some weird Stranger from the Third Dim—'

Grosvenor's face turned an angry shade of grey. 'Victoria Line: don't you ever mention that phrase in this house! God, I thought the family'd got rid of that pernicious little diatribe fifty years ago!'

Vikki didn't understand what she'd done wrong. 'But Dad, it's just an old—'

Jubilee, ever the calm one, touched her daughter's side affectionately. 'Wait till the boys have gone to bed, Victoria. Then your father will tell you a piece of family history.'

Grosvenor stared at his wife in horror. 'Lee, are you sure that now is the right—'

'She's old enough to know the Facts of Life, Grosvenor dear, *and* how to deal with them on a practical basis. So she's old enough to know the truth about her great-great-grandfather.'

The Facts of Life bit was news to Grosvenor, and it threw him completely. 'Dammit, Lee: great-great-grandad Albert's already caused this family too much grief!'

'Is that what the "A" stands for, Dad? Is the book by *Albert* Square? Was he my great-great-grandfather? What *is* the Third Dimension, Dad?'

'Victoria, I've just told you not to—'

'Grosvenor, it's too late. We can't hide our past from our own daughter', said Jubilee. 'And it was all so long ago. Times are changing. She has a right to know. And you *did* promise—'

Grosvenor Square sagged back against the sofa. 'Yes, but I thought she'd be a bit older than this before I had to . . . Yes, yes, I'll tell her. I'm just finding it hard getting used to having a young woman in the house instead of a little girl, OK?'

'After dinner,' insisted Jubilee, driving home her advantage, 'as soon as the boys have gone to bed.'

Grosvenor was a beaten man. 'Yes, Lee – after dinner. As you say.'

Jubilee was already dishing out the food into semicircular bowls. Vikki rushed to the door and flung it wide open. '*Berkley! Les! Grub's up!*'

❋

Faint sounds of childish prattle were wafting from the boys' bedroom. Ignoring them, Grosvenor took a deep breath and tried to find the courage to peel the wraps off an ancient – and, he had hoped, forgotten – piece of Square family history.

Jubilee saw her husband was having trouble, and offered a simple solution. 'We don't talk about great-great-grandfather Albert because he died in prison, Vikki.'

'*Lee!*'

'There's no point in beating about the bush, Grosvenor. Albert *did* die in prison.'

'Yes, but he wasn't a criminal.'

'Did I say he was? Tell Vikki what he did to get himself imprisoned.'

'Uh – well, you see, Ancestor Albert . . . Lee, do I *have* to do this?'

'Yes.'

Grosvenor grunted, accepting the reality of his position. 'Very well. Vikki, Ancestor Albert was . . . he was the black shape of the family, so to speak. He . . . he got some ridiculous nonsense into his head about what he called the Land of Three Dimensions. It was an imaginary world, different from ours, and he would have been all right if it had *stayed* imaginary, but his . . . his mind went. He became convinced it was real. He claimed that he had received a visitor from the Land of Three Dimensions, which he called The Sphere.'

'What a funny word. Was the Sphere the Stranger I read about in Albert's book?'

'It was. Albert even claimed he had visited the Land of Three Dimensions himself, with the Sphere as his guide.'

'Wow! Hey, that's really neat!'

Grosvenor sighed. *The naive enthusiasm of youth . . .* 'A hundred years ago, Vikki, saying things like that got you sent to prison. For heresy, because you were contradicting the Priests, and because anyone who claimed to have visited another world must be a madman.'

'Oh.'

'So you see, sweetcentre, it's not something the family is proud of. To make matters worse, Albert's unfortunate brother was imprisoned too, supposedly because he witnessed something – a

Visitation, some such nonsense.' He paused, gulped for air, found none that helped. His voice came out half-strangled: 'Do you *really* want all the neighbours to know that two of your ancestors were lunatics?'

Vikki wasn't sure. Being imprisoned for your beliefs was kind of romantic, like being a freedom fighter. And as for witnessing a Supernatural Visitation, that was *cool*. 'Crumbs, Dad, that was a hundred years ago.'

'The taint still lingers, Vikki. If your friends found out about old Albert, you might find that some of them weren't your friends any more. I admit that people aren't as obsessed by religion as they were in 1999, but they're still unhappy about any hint of mental instability.'

You mean they're still just as narrow-minded and unimaginative as they ever were, thought Vikki. It was a sobering thought.

'Did you read Albert's book, Vikki?'

'Only a few bits and pieces, Dad. I just . . . glanced at it.'

Grosvenor sighed with relief. 'Good, at least it hasn't had a chance to taint you too.'

'It looked kind of . . . interesting. I was going to read the rest of it later.'

'*No!*' The cry was instant and automatic. 'Sorry, love, but I don't think it's suitable material for you to read – or anyone else.'

Vikki felt this was an infringement of her Polygonal Rights. 'Why not?'

'Look what it did for Albert,' said Grosvenor, a wry smile flitting across his florid features. 'Think what it might do for you, for us . . . In your room, is it? Go and get it for me, there's a good girl.'

Vikki didn't like the sound of that. 'But Dad, it's a historical document!'

'A hysterical document, more like. I'll get it, then. Where did you put it?'

Vikki gave her mother a pleading look. 'Mum! He's going to destroy it! Can't you stop him?'

Jubilee gave a negative shake of her endpoints. 'I'm sorry, but your father's right, dear. Best not to wash our dirty strings in public. What's done is done, let's not dwell on the past. You had to be told about Albert because at some stage his name might come up, and you need to know how to react. But you *don't* need to read the rubbish that put him in prison. It's not fit for a young lady, anyway.'

Oh, Mum, if only you knew some of the books I've read . . . But Vikki could tell when she was beaten. 'Wait here, Dad, Mum: I'll go and get it. Give me a few minutes, though, OK? Just to be alone with my thoughts. I promise I won't try to read any of it before I bring it to you. Trust me? Please? Give me *some* dignity?'

Her father nodded, her mother gave a smug smile. Vikki slunk out of the room, defeated.

'That was very hard,' said Grosvenor, 'I feel awful. Do you think we should—'

'She said to trust her, dear. So we shall.'

'Of course. Lee, you're so sensible about these things.'

They waited. After a quarter of an hour, Vikki was back. With a sulk, she put the book on the table in front of her parents.

Grosvenor rolled it partly open, checked the title, sampled a few lines here and there to be sure it was the authentic copy. There was trust – and there was *trust*. 'Should have been burned long ago,' he said. Then he tossed it into the fire. 'Time you got yourself ready for young Roger, the lucky dog. Go out and have some fun.'

Vikki watched, damp-eyed, as the flames turned her great-great-grandfather's life's work into smoke and ashes. 'Anything you say, Father.'

2

VICTORIA'S DIARY

Wunday 25 Septober 2099
It's been a day of lefts and rights, Dear Diary, and I'm still reeling from the shock. I have a – get this – infamous ancestor! Isn't that absolutely ORTHOG? My great-great-grandfather Albert was a religious heretic who got himself slung in the pokey for his beliefs – and let me tell you, they are *wild*!!!!! I hardly know where to BEGIN!!!!! Basically, they're about . . .

Victoria stopped, unsure of the best way to convey the essence of Albert's heresies to the encrypted Diary in her Personal Disorganizer.

After Grosvenor had burned Albert's book – *what about freedom of speech, Dad? What about freedom from censorship?* – she had fled to her tiny room, snuggled up against the thin cushion that served as the Flatland equivalent of a bed, and sobbed her heart out until she heard her father tipvertex away from the door of her room. She had continued sobbing for a few minutes longer, letting the level fade, until finally she stopped. Then she had put on a bit too much tipstick, found a skirt that was just a little more daring than Dad normally allowed her to wear to discos, slipped into Mum's wonderful – though, she now noticed, slightly smelly – old jacket, grinned wickedly, snivelled until her mascara ran, and emerged into the communal hall for an inspection from her mother. Jubilee noticed the streaks of mascara, admonished Grosvenor for upsetting his sensitive little daughter, and hauled young Victoria back into her room to do a proper repair job on her lineliner. Ten minutes later Grosvenor was still looking sheepish, and Roger had arrived to escort her across town to the disco as arranged. The skirt was not mentioned: Grosvenor knew when he was on a hiding to nothing.

It had been a successful evening, and Roger brought her home again with five minutes to spare. Best to show willing. She said goodnights to her parents, and retired to her room.

Within seconds she had switched on the Personal Disorganizer and accessed her Diary. There was so much to tell before she forgot.

. . . Basically, they're about a new kind of universe. That's right, a whole new UNIVERSE. And what thrills me to the core, Diary Dear, is that Old Al actually WENT there!!!! Of course, Dad made me hand Al's book over to the Authorities – namely, HIM – I should've known he'd do that, the ancient book looked much too interesting for me to be allowed to look at it, let alone KEEP it. And, entirely predictably, he burned it.

Fortunately, Dad doesn't know how to work my computer, and he certainly doesn't know how to crack Most Excellently Private Encryption, so I am free to reveal to you a few things of which my dear Papa knows not one whit. (MEMO: find out what a whit is.) I did promise not to read Al's subversive pamphlet during the fifteen minutes that Mum and Dad left me alone in my room to console myself about the impending loss of major historical data, and you will not be surprised to hear that I KEPT that promise, me being a good little butter-wouldn't-melt-in-her-trisectors young lady of horrendously decent upbringing.

However, I didn't promise not to . . .

Victoria broke off typing. Best to check if the file was intact before looking foolish in front of her own Diary.

She booted up the computer and checked.

It was.

. . . I didn't promise not to read it LATER. Now, you may well ask: how could I read a book that Father had burned? (Go on, humour me.) Ah, since you ask, Diary Dear: that is the oh-so-very clever part. You see, instead of spending those vital fifteen minutes snivelling about having to give way to Higher Authority, as Father no doubt imagined I was doing, I spent them scanning Al's magnum opus into my cute little computer. I now have two copies in the machine, three more backups on tape, and yet another backup in my Personal Disorganizer, so Albert Square's seditious screed is safe for posterity!!!! (meaning me). I now intend to read it from vertex to vertex, and I shall faithfully record my discoveries in YOU, Diary Dearest. But be patient with me, for I must make sure my parents don't catch me reading it, otherwise there will be convex hull to pay. OK?

Now, to more personal things. Let me tell you about racy Roger!!!! He really is one of the cutest quadrilaterals I've dated in absolutely AGES and he really knows how to show a girl a good time . . .

＊

The days passed, and the topic of Ancestor Albert and his cranky beliefs was dropped by all concerned. Roger Rectangle fell out of favour and was replaced by Trevor Trapezium. Grosvenor felt this was a backward step, what with Trevor being even less regular than Roger, but he consoled himself that by saying nothing he was demonstrating how modern and unprejudiced he was. It was what you *were*, not your perimetral geometry, that mattered. But deep down he hoped that eventually his daughter would find a nice pentagon, get married, and present her parents with oodles of grandchildren – Hexagons, preferably – like any respectable young lady should.

The young lady's thoughts, though, were elsewhere. The lure of the illicit was proving irresistible, sucking her further and further into her ancestor's wild fantasies . . .

＊

Twoday 26 Septober 2099
Dear Diary,

I've become irrationally convinced that old Albert didn't make up his story at all. I'm certain as Squares fit in the Woods that the Sphere was REAL!! My evidence is that the whole tale is *much* too imaginative to have been invented – certainly not in the intellectual climate of the previous century. Albert generally portrays himself as a boring, rather ho-hum sort of guy – which he *is*. He has enormous difficulty taking on board even the simplest 3D concepts, such as a cube. But a cube, Al my friend, is just a line's worth of squares, just as a square is no more than a line's worth of lines. That much seems evident even to me (though I suppose I'd better concede that we did the cube in physics: it's the space-time diagram of a square that persists for an interval of time). So Albert must have got his outlandish ideas from *somewhere*, and the best place to get outlandish ideas from is Outland – somewhere *external* to Flatland. And if there is such a place, why shouldn't it contain a line's worth of circles – admittedly of various sizes – which is what his friend the Sphere seems to have been?

Spheres, then, exist – if only in some Flatonic realm of higher ideals. So does *The* Sphere, I am sure – and in a far more concrete realm. 'Space', it was called in the book. And if The Sphere visited Albert, why shouldn't one of its descendants visit *me*?

The only problem seems to be attracting its attention. And that is a real pig.

Nevertheless, I'm writing computer programs to analyse Albert's treatise, in search of hidden messages. Surely he would have left some clues for others to follow in his vertexsteps.

◈

As Victoria's obsession with Albert's book grew, she began to spend more and more of her time in her room, working away on the computer. Grosvenor noted this tendency with approval. 'I do believe Vikki is growing up', he confided to his wife one evening after their daughter had rushed off to her room, saying she had some urgent homework to do for a test. 'I *knew* that computer would have educational value.'

Jubilee wasn't so sure. In her experience, when a girl of Vikki's age suddenly developed new habits, that was the time to start worrying. But there was no point in disturbing Grosvenor's equilibrium unnecessarily. She would keep a quiet eye on her daughter, just to set her mind at rest.

By now Victoria could pretty much recite *Flatland* by heart. She had also learned to mistrust it, having noticed some absurdities. The most glaring was Albert's solemn declaration that from generation to generation there was an almost certain progression towards ever greater regularity. '*It is a Law of Nature with us that a male child shall have one more side than his father, so that each generation shall rise (as a rule) on step in the scale of development and nobility. Thus the son of a Square is a Pentagon; the son of a Pentagon a Hexagon; and so on.*' What utter rubbish! Why, for a start, what of her brothers Lester and Berkeley, square sons of square Grosvenor? And a moment's thought about the evolutionary history of Flatlanders, which had been going for at least a quarter of a million generations, was enough to tell you that something was wildly amiss in Albert's confident statement. For if he were correct, by now every male in Flatland would be a near-perfect Circle with a quarter of a million sides! Even the most lofty of the Priests probably had less than a hundred.

What *had* he been thinking of? She could think of a few possibilities. First, of course, the modern concept of Deep Time and a vast evolutionary history hadn't really gained common currency until a generation after Albert wrote his book, so the error wouldn't have been so glaring then. Probably Albert had taken the *aspirations* of his class and cast them as a Law of Nature – for it was as certain as anything could be that in his time ordinary Flatlanders were desperate to rise at least one level in their rigid, class-ridden society. So the occasional rare 'success' – judged by the standards of the period – had somehow become elevated to the undeserved status of Natural Law. That 'as a rule' was the giveaway. The truth – she had done this in biology some years back – was more prosaic. Most male children had the same number of sides as their fathers. A tiny proportion had fewer, usually just *one* fewer. A roughly equal proportion had an extra side; a very tiny proportion indeed had two or more extra sides. This 'random walk' of polygonal sides had, over time, led to a small number of 'Circles', while the overwhelming bulk of the population were equilateral triangles, squares, pentagons, or hexagons. This, at least, was what happened among the regular classes. With the irregulars, mainly triangles, a similar story was played out but with changes to the lengths of the sides.

Perhaps Albert had just exaggerated the truth to flatter his readers? Or was he mouthing a conventional wisdom that pretended people's hopes were reality? Certainly he was suppressing a lot of things that his society presumably found to be unmentionable in polite company: there was, for instance, no mention of starchildren – polygons so hideously deformed that their sides *overlapped*, so that a pentagonal father might have a star-shaped pentacle for a son. Colloquially known as '2½-gons', such children seldom survived more than a few years.

All this paled beside an even more pertinent observation: what about the female contribution to their offspring's genetics? Albert's male-default blinkers had prevented him from even asking the question. But even though a woman's form might be a line segment, there were clearly lines *and* lines.

And it was while lying in front of her bedroom fireplace, thumbing through the book in search of clues to this strange puzzle, that Victoria made a major discovery.

❁

Threeday 27 Septober 2099
I HAVE FOUND SOMETHING!!!!!

Last night, rereading Albert's treatise for the hundred-and-umpth time, I noticed some *very* faint chicken-tracks, after the end of the book itself. The cunning old swine had written them in tiny characters and very faint ink, but my scanner is rather good at enhancing contrast. After southloading some image-processing software from the InterLine I enhanced them further, and – lo and behold – they're a list of numbers separated by dots and slashes:

18.3.1.12 | 6.12.2.90 | 2.6.2.69 | 16.1.3.20 | 20.14.1.29 | 4.1.2.15 | 19.1.3.1 | 19.1.3.2 | 8.1.1.3 | 11.2.1.28 | 12.2.1.2 | 6.13.2.40 | 18.2.1.3 | 7.3.4.28 | 12.11.1.13 | 11.2.1.14 | 14.2.1.28 | 14.2.1.18 | 18.15.2.18| 3.1.1.1 | 18.1.4.10 | 4.1.4.16 | 4.1.3.29 | 18.20.1.6 | 6.1.2.32 | 22.2.3.15 | 22.2.3.17 | 13.6.3.21 | 13.6.3.35 | 13.6.3.16 | 21.4.2.17 | 13.6.4.15 | 1.3.2.20 | 21.7.3.58 | 21.7.3.59 | 9.4.4.16 | 16.1.3.27 | 3.3.1.11 | 3.3.3.15 | 1.2.1.11 | 5.5.2.26 | 5.12.4.13 | 7.4.3.24 | 3.3.2.4 | 3.3.1.11 | 12.3.3.34 | 8.1.1.7 | 7.1.1.20 | 14.1.1.18 | 3.3.1.24 | 1.2.1.15

and there's a good bit more in similar vein which I've stored in the computer.

It must be a coded message (cliché, ho hum). No, *not* ho hum, this is *exciting*! If Albert took so much trouble to include this funny message, it *has* to be important. And for some reason he wanted to keep it secret from the casual reader. Why? Well, I have an idea about that. After all, *I* am an anything-but-casual reader. The message is for people like me: people who are looking for truths even deeper than those recorded in *Flatland*. People so obsessed by the Third Dimension that they might just be able to find an almost unreadable message.

You're saying I just got lucky? Diary Dear, that is an extremely cynical and accurate remark, and because of it I shall stop writing this very instant. Shame on you.

❀

Victoria took to spending even more time in her room. Jubilee, growing ever more suspicious but having no idea what she should be suspicious *about*, searched the room every day while her daughter was at school, but found nothing untoward. Though there were lots of scribblings with numbers and letters all over them – mathematics homework, by the look of them.

❀

From Vikki's Notescroll directory

- It can't be an alphabetical code, because it includes numbers like 90, and our alphabet only has 73 symbols.
- I've tried all of the decryption software that I can southload from the InterLine, without result. It's not a transposition cipher, nor is it a polyalphabetic one. And public-key crypto wasn't invented in Albert's day, so it's not that, thank God. It can't possibly be a one-time scroll: it *has* to be decipherable, or else Albert wouldn't have put it in his book. But it's only intended for people who are willing to put in plenty of effort to decode it, that's for sure.
- The numbers break into groups of four: 18.3.1.12, then 6.12.2.90, and so on. Why?
- The groups involve different ranges of numbers. The first in each group only goes up to 22. The second is usually small (like 2 or 3) but occasionally goes as high as 15. The third is

always small: the highest is 4. The fourth, though, sometimes gets up towards a hundred. This *has* to be significant.

- It must be based on some *key*. Probably a standard text. I have tried *Polygon With the Wind, Parallels Lost, A Tale of Two Circles*, the *Complete Works of Shakesquare*, and sundry religious texts – all without success. What book would Albert have chosen? I am baffled.

- Idiot. There is one obvious book – *Flatland* itself. But what do the numbers *mean*?

- *Flatland* has 22 chapters. The first number in each group never exceeds 22! I do believe . . .

- *Yes!* It has all become clear. The first number in each group of four refers to a chapter, the second to the numerical position of a paragraph within that chapter, the third to a sentence within that paragraph, and the fourth to a word within that sentence.

How crass! Anyway, after a few recounts I have cracked the code, and the SECRET MESSAGE reads:

O Learned traveller who aspire to follow me the method is perplexing and perilous do not reveal your intentioned The Sphere can be summoned by drawing diagrams so as to be seen from Third Dimension semicircle circle two isosceles triangles touch without their bases two rectangles with a common side and . . .

❋

Fourday 28 Septober 2099
Albert's message is now clear to me, though his grammar is sometimes a bit overstretched – I suspect because he had trouble finding the exact word in his book, and settled for something close enough to be comprehensible. Most of the message is an extensive and unfortunately somewhat ambiguous series of instructions for constructing some quasi-geometric diagram. It must have some cabalistic significance, because at first glance it seems to be completely structureless.

I've got some sticks and I've dumped them on my bedroom floor. The result is my best guess at the outlines the secret message so cryptically described.

[Added later: My diagram, I now understand, looked roughly like this when viewed from the Third Dimension:

However, I had got the third symbol upside down, thanks to a misinterpretation of Al's ambiguous instructions. And he claimed to be a mathematician! In mathematics, Albert old fruit, the keyword is precision, *OK?]*

I am now wondering *where* to place my diagram so that it will be visible from the Third Dimension. I'm totally baffled – Al's message gives no clue.

[Added much *later: It hadn't then dawned on me that* every-where *– including the insides of my cupboards and* the insides of me *– is visible from the Third Dimension. Yes, I'd read the bits where old Albert said just that, but they hadn't registered. Idiot.]*

I'm absolutely shattered, Diary Dear, and it's time I got some beauty sleep. The rest of the puzzle must wait until tomorrow.

3

THE VISITATION

With so many things whirling round and round inside her head, Victoria had difficulty getting to sleep. Eventually she dozed, but her sleep was troubled with strange dreams. Somewhere in the nogonsland between 'asleep' and 'awake', with her mind drifting but half-aware, she began to hear a voice. At first it was faint – no discernible words, just a speech-like intonation, barely above the threshold of perception – but slowly it became louder and louder . . . until, with a start, she came fully to her senses.

An atavistic tingle ran along her length, and a sentence from Albert's book came unbidden into her mind: *'I became conscious of a Presence in the room, and a chilling breath thrilled my very being.'*

The Sphere! It must be somewhere nearby! Hovering just a short distance away from Flatland in that enigmatic Third Dimension! At this very moment it was experiencing a panoramic view of her house, her room, and her own internal organs. Including, she realized with shock, her dinner in the process of digestion. How yucky! Albert had never mentioned this, although he'd been surprisingly northfront about the visibility of his insides: no doubt he'd considered this particular aspect of three-dimensionality just a little *too* gross to put in his book.

The voice came again, and this time she understood its words. 'Excuse me? Someone called?' Then, suddenly, incredibly, before her eyes, a dot appeared in the middle of the room, like a very short woman except that its shading was more like an extraordinarily tiny circle.

It was orange.

It did not enter through the doorway: it was just *there*, when a moment earlier that place had been unoccupied. Was this The Sphere? She'd expected it to be larger. But then, Albert had said that The Sphere was composed of Circles of many sizes, shrinking right down to a point, so some would have to be extremely tiny.

A little way off a second dot appeared, which also expanded to a small orange Circle. Were there *two* Spheres? A double visitation?

The disembodied voice spoke again. 'Hello? Is anyone at home? Did you want something?' Then a third orange Circle, somewhat larger than the others but still smaller than a typical Circular Flatland adult, *grew* into the space between the first two:

Three Spheres? How many were there? Why were they all clad in orange garments? (Were they Buddhists? Is that why they were budding?) Could there be an entire *herd* of Spheres lurking just . . . *below* (above?) the homely plane of Flatland? *What else was out there?*

It was a chilling thought, but there was no question in her mind that she must respond, quickly, while there was still a chance. If the Spheres made no contact, they might never return. Fortunately the house, being rather old, had thick walls. In a voice that she hoped could be heard by the Spheres but not by her parents, she said, 'Yes, it was me, I'm at home.' Feeling very foolish, and realizing that what she'd said didn't convey a great deal of information, she added: 'My name's Vikki Line, and I . . . I want to meet a being from the Third Dimension.'

The three Circles did something very complicated and merged together like pools of liquid, turning briefly into a shape that her sense of shading told her must be something like this:

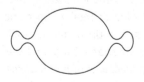

Then, so fast that she couldn't follow the movement, it expanded like a balloon into a fairly normal-looking Circle. The only difference was that the Circle didn't stay quite the same width all the time – it made her feel slightly giddy to watch it.

'Is that *all*?' said the Visitor. 'Only the *Third* Dimension?'

Vikki felt that the Third Dimension would be a good start, but Albert had waxed lyrical about even more esoteric realms, so she chose her words carefully. 'As many dimensions as you prefer, sir, as long as it's more than two.'

'Then you're in luck,' said the Visitor. 'When it comes to dimensions, I'm as versatile as the next being.' There was a pause, and he added, 'Well, more so, since *you* are the next being, and you're a Flatty.'

This didn't sound very polite, but it seldom pays to point out such social nuances to transcendent beings from another universe. 'Excuse me, sir, but are you a Sphere?'

Her stomach vibrated to the sounds of deep laughter. 'Me? A Sphere? Nothing so prosaic, I'm delighted to say.'

'Um, then . . . what are you?'

'I,' the creature declaimed proudly, 'am a Space Hopper.'

'That's a very strange name,' said Vikki, before she could stop herself.

'Not at all,' said the being, 'it's a very good name.'

'Why?'

'Because – isn't it obvious? Because I can hop spaces.'

❊

Fiveday 29 September 2099
It took a while to sort out what the Space Hopper meant by that, Diary Darling. For a time I thought that by 'space' the creature meant 'gap' – as we would refer to the space between two buildings, say.

Not a bit of it.

To the Space Hopper, a *space* was an entire world! More than that, it was an entire self-contained UNIVERSE. Flatland is one kind of space, and Albert's freaky Spaceland is another kind of space. But that's just the tip of the iceangle. Al himself talked of Lineland, with its smartarse King, and the complacent God of Pointland: '*Infinite beatitude of existence! It is; and there is none else beside*

It.' And he dropped heavy hints of *'mysteries yet higher . . . Extra-Solids . . . and Double-Extra Solids . . .'*

Now: you and I may find this kind of stuff way out, but to the Space Hopper it was kind of boring. Extra dimensions? Yesterday's news. He – I'll call him a he, even though we haven't discussed Space Hopper Gender Issues . . . for all I know they have seven sexes or none . . . Anyway, he sounds like a male, and he's into far heavier stuff than that. One-and-a-quarter dimensions, would you believe? Infinite dimensions. Bent space and rippled space and space that blows itself up . . . Space that's just disembodied dots, space that isn't really space at all. This is one seriously spaced-out guy, ha ha.

And when he calls himself a Space Hopper, able to 'hop spaces', what he seems to mean is that he can hop BETWEEN spaces. Only there isn't any Between, just the spaces themselves. Or maybe there is a Between (I reckon he's a bit confused about this) and they all live inside some kind of Grand Unified Metaspace (or GUM) known as the Mathiverse. Look, I don't understand this buzz any more than you do, Diary Dear, so there's no use asking me for clarification. Not yet, anyway.

We ran out of chat time rather suddenly when Lee woke up and I heard her snooping outside my room. But The Space Hopper says he'll visit me again tomorrow night. And this time he'll bring a Virtual Unreality Engine.

At least, I think that's what he said.

※

Jubilee Line was getting very worried indeed. Modern morality was all very well – no, actually it *wasn't* all very well at all, it was far too lax, though she acknowledged with a certain wistfulness that she had been born a generation too soon – but Grosvenor would have a fit if he found out that his dear sweet Victoria was entertaining a man in her room in the early hours of the morning.

There was no doubt in Jubilee's mind. She had woken up, and heard muffled voices coming from somewhere in the house. At first she'd thought it might be burglars, and she'd sneaked out of her room with every intention of stabbing the intruder with her sharp rear end. She had neither fears nor qualms about this: all Flatland women were armed and dangerous by virtue of their needle-sharp lineal geometry, and they were trained from birth to use this natural advantage if it became necessary. Criminals had no rights in Flatland – rights were what you got if you agreed to abide by the common legal code, and you couldn't have things both ways. But as she sneaked closer to the source of the sound, it resolved itself into a conversation between an unknown male (she could tell by the voice) and her daughter! Her worst fears were being confirmed; she'd known Vikki's change of habits had to be a symptom of some kind of improper behaviour.

It was that computer, without a doubt. She never should have let Grosvenor buy the thing. Not that there'd been any way to stop him once he'd got the idea into his head, however damnfool it was.

She tiptipped closer. Suddenly the voices stopped, but not before she heard Vikki agree to meet the stranger in her room the following night. *Well, we'll see about that!*

As quietly as she could, Jubilee made her way back to her own room. Silence once more descended on the Square household. But now it was a *thoughtful* silence.

※

Vikki *had* heard right. The thing that the Space Hopper was going to bring was indeed a virtual unreality engine, or VUE. It would, he said, 'blow her mind'. Not literally – despite its ungainly appearance, the gadget was perfectly safe, because most of it existed only in the metareality of the Mathiverse. More precisely, the Space Hopper explained, the VUE would expand her mental horizons. Take her mind to new places. Change her point of VUE. She was about to become a Space Traveller, and the VUE was to be her Space Suit. With its extradimensional terminals plugged into the delicate tissues of her brain – an easy operation, since her brain was protected only against interference from North, South, East, and West, not from Up or Down – she would be able to experience each of the bizarre spaces of the Mathiverse *from the inside*. The Space Hopper had no need of such prosthetics: he could transport himself from one space to another using only the Power of Imagination. A Flatland mind, though, would need technological assistance to overcome its own inherent limitations.

So absorbed had Vikki and the Space Hopper become in installing the drivers for the VUE and customizing her user-preferences that they failed to hear Jubilee's approach. Through the solid door, Lee could hear their discussion clearly. Whatever they were doing, phrases like 'reinsert your floppy' sounded distinctly immodest and unladylike.

When the strange male urged Vikki that it was time to 'go for it', Jubilee could no longer restrain herself. Outraged, she threw open Vikki's door, and charged into the room, her infinitely thin needle-point waving threateningly. Ahead was her daughter, frozen by the suddenness of the intrusion . . . and a remarkably handsome Circle wearing the most ghastly orange cloak.

Jubilee skated to a halt, confused. At least her daughter had *taste* – more than she could say about the man's dress sense. Jubilee wondered how Vikki could have met this gorgeous hunk. But no good ever came of affairs with the upper classes – they'd just get you segment and dump you. With a shrill cry of 'You swine! You ought to be circumscribed!' Jubilee launched herself backwards at the intruder, intending to give him a brand new diameter. But he just seemed to slide away from her infinitely sharp tip. She *thought* she heard Vikki's voice saying 'Don't worry, Mother . . .' Then, silence.

Vikki, and her high-bred paramour, were gone.

With growing horror, Jubilee searched every corner of the room. She *knew* they hadn't gone out by the door, and that was the only possible route. They'd vanished.

Eventually, Grosvenor woke up to find his distraught wife peering hopelessly behind every piece of furniture and every child-hood toy in their daughter's room, sobbing her midpoint out.

❋

Virtual Unreality, Vikki had decided, was *cool*. Agreed, it took a bit of getting used to – but once you'd mastered the knack of seeing new geometries in their own terms, instead of expecting them to have the same properties as the space you were familiar with from birth, you could begin to appreciate their novelty. And it certainly made you realize just how limited your familiar concept of space was. Having the VUE made all this a lot easier: without it, you'd have to rely on your imagination. In Virtual Unreality you could *experience* what others could only dream about. She now understood how Albert had felt when his flat world had suddenly expanded into the glorious realm of solidity, literally opening up new directions. And the true form of the Space Hopper was now visible to her, with his twin horns, manic grin, and bulging body. He wasn't one circle, or two, or three. All the while she had been trapped within the confines of Flatland, all she had been able to see of the Space Hopper was a two-dimensional cross-section. As he moved up or down (words to which she could finally put a meaning), his cross-section changed. As he rose through the plane of Flatland, what she had seen was this:

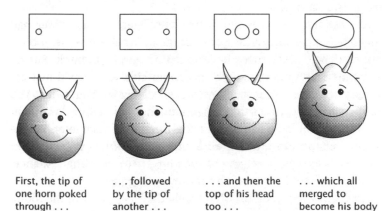

First, the tip of one horn poked through . . .

. . . followed by the tip of another . . .

. . . and then the top of his head too . . .

. . . which all merged to become his body

Even the complicated shape she thought she had seen, if only for a moment, now made sense: it was a slice through the level where the horns joined the bulbous lump of the creature's body.

So *this* was what Albert had seen! Not with a shape as complicated as the Space Hopper, though, just a straightforward Sphere:

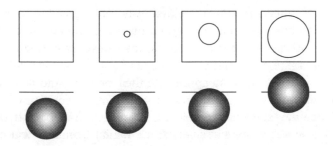

As the Sphere rose towards the plane of Flatland, not yet inter-secting that plane, it was invisible. As its surface began to pass through that plane, it appeared – from nowhere, it seemed – as a single point, which became a small circle, then a larger one, then ... When the 'equator' of the Sphere aligned itself with the plane of Flatland, the circular cross-section had the same diameter as the Sphere itself – but what a woefully inadequate representation this single circular slice was! And if the Sphere continued to rise, its cross-section would shrink back down to a point, and then vanish.

✹

What is the Mathiverse?

The Mathiverse transcends Time and Space ... it transcends Intelligence and Extelligence ... it transcends Thought; it transcends Transcendence itself. Within it – and 'within' is definitely the wrong word, for concepts such as 'inside' and 'outside' apply to individual Spaces, not to the unfathomable reaches of the Mathiverse – are not just all Spaces and Times that *have* existed, or all Spaces and Times that *will* exist, or even all Spaces and Times that *could* exist. It also contains (wrong word, again) all Spaces and Times that could *not* exist, if only as a grim warning of the dangers of the nonexistent.

The Mathiverse contains all numbers.

The Mathiverse contains all shapes.

The Mathiverse contains all geometries.

The Mathiverse contains all vectors, matrices, permutations, combinations, integrations, separations, projections, injections, surjections, bijections, semigroups, transformations, relations, functions, functors, functionals, algebraic group schemes, super-manifolds, *K*-theories, *M*-theories, *M*-sets, power sets, subsets, supersets, and plain, ordinary, common-or-garden sets.

The Mathiverse contains all data structures.

The Mathiverse contains all processes.

The Mathiverse contains all formal descriptions of logical structures.

The Mathiverse contains all informal descriptions of illogical structures.

If one day somebody managed to invent a new kind of *thing*, one that wasn't a Space and wasn't a Time but somehow belonged in the same category (and, now that you mention it, the Mathiverse contains all categories) . . . anyway, if somebody did what I've just said, then whatever they came up with would have been present in the Mathiverse all along. (Except, as you've guessed, 'would', 'have', 'been', 'present', and 'in' are the wrong words, and so are 'all' and 'along'. We can probably accept 'the', though.)

Space Hoppers use the name 'Planiturth' to refer to the world that you, dear reader, inhabit. Planiturth is *not* the same as what old Albert had called 'Spaceland' – but there is a close connection. Spaceland is an abstraction that captures some of the essence of Planiturthian geometry, but Planiturth is *real*. Planiturth has a history as well as a geography, and its relation to the Mathiverse is complex and convoluted.

Even philosophers (a special breed of the creatures that live on Planiturth, generically known as Peoples) do not doubt that Planiturth is intimately associated with the Mathiverse – *of* it but not *in* it, so to speak (not that 'in' . . . but we've been through that already, sorry). In a sense, the Mathiverse is a creation of the combined mentality of the Intelligences of Planiturth. It is a Planiturthian mental construct. Despite which, it has its own kind of reality – it is *so* real that every atom of Planiturth's universe dances to its tune. The very rules by which Planiturth's universe runs are drawn from the Mathiverse.

Or so the Planiturthians think, anyway.

It is a deep philosophical conundrum. Does Planiturth's universe *really* obey rules that come from the realms of the Mathiverse? Or is that an illusion born of Planiturthian prejudices? Is Planiturth's universe built from *mathematics*? Or is mathematics built by the minds of Planiturthians? Planiturthian mathematicians would like to think that their universe is built from mathematics, but that's only natural, after all. Planiturthian physicists would like to think that the Planiturthian universe is built from physics. Planiturthian biologists would like to think that the Planiturthian universe is built from biology. Planiturthian philosophers would like to think that the Planiturthian universe is built from philosophy. (Let me tell you a secret: it is. The fundamental unit of the Planiturthian universe is the *philosophon*, a unit of logic so tiny that only a philosopher could hope to split it.) Planiturthian greengrocers would like to think that the Planiturthian universe is built from carrots and potatoes. Planiturthian taxi-drivers have the definite opinion that the Planiturthian universe is built from opinions, and they are prepared to say so at length. And Planiturthian beauticians would like to think that the Planiturthian universe is built from beauty, and in this belief they may be closer than all the others, for whatever attributes the Mathiverse might have, beauty is paramount among them.

Mathiversian beauty is, of course, an acquired taste.

The Planiturthians are unique among the creatures of (but perhaps not *in*) the Mathiverse in that they are not sure which Space (or Time, or Spacetime, or . . .) they really belong to. Long ago they thought they inhabited Spaceland, a rigid 3D universe; Time was simply something that passed, a separate 1D process. This was the Clockwork Universe of a famous People named Isaacnewton: Absolute and Uniform Space ticking to the beat of an Absolute and Uniform clock, and decorated with Absolute (but definitely *not* Uniform) Matter. Spaceland is a genuine part of the Mathiverse, but the Planiturthians have now decided – correctly – that they don't actually live in Spaceland at all. They live, perhaps, in Curvyspace. Or is it in Waveworld? Or are they gambolling in the Quantum Fields ('gambling' might be a better word since these fields are made from *probabilities*). The Planiturthians aren't really sure, and about every ten years they completely change their minds.

Mind you, Flatlanders will shortly have some rethinking to do, too.

＊

Sixday 30 Septober 2099
We've been exploring Spaceland! (Planiturth, too, but that's a lot more complicated.) Like Flatland, it's a *Euclidean* space (as I now know to spell it). When the Space Hopper first said that word, I asked him what a 'yuke' was and why it needed a lid. He hummed and hawed for a while, and then said that somewhere in the humongitude of the Mathiverse a Planiturthian being known as Euclidthegreek first mapped out the geometry of worlds like Flatland.

I find this a questionable assertion, to say the least, since according to all the history books Flatland was first mapped out by an explorer named Marco Polygo. Still, I rely on the Space Hopper to conduct me from space to space safely, and it is best not to annoy him.

Anyway, Diary Dear, it's amazing what an extra dimension can do for you. Not just Spheres and Cubes and Pyramids and things – face it, those are pretty obvious extensions of Circles and Squares and Triangles. A Flatlander, shown a sequence of cross-sections, could get quite a fair idea of what they're like. But there are MUCH more interesting things in Spaceland, things that are completely outside the Flatland frame.

Some of them are simple. In Flatland, if you hammer a nail right through a plank of wood, it falls to bits:

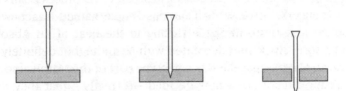

This DOESN'T happen in Spaceland. And they can use *wires* to connect telephones, without trapping everyone in the tangle they create. They put the wires UNDER (a new word I've learned that means 'in the Down direction') the places where people walk.

Some are subtle. My absolute FAVE is a widget they call a KNOT. This is a loop of string, like a Circle, but it sort of runs through its own inside!!! The result is that it tangles up in a way you can't rearrange into an ordinary Circle. Flatland is just too low-dimensional to allow knots.

The Space Hopper says that even Spacelanders (well, actually he called them 'Planiturthians', he says there's a subtle distinction but he refused to talk about it until later) don't actually have a very good feel for 3D – they have trouble with *knots*, for instance! This, he says, is because their eyes really see only in 2D. They see a 2D *projection* of an object, not the entire object ALL AT ONCE. So it's surprisingly easy to shake their intuition about the space they live in.

For instance, here's a teaser that the Space Hopper asked me. Take a Spaceland cube, of unit side (that's a fancy way to say 'one thingy each way' where the 'thingy' is some standard unit of measurement, OK?) and cut a hole through it (without it falling apart, like a plank would in Flatland) with a square cross-section, so that another cube can be pushed through the hole. Got that? Right – here's the question. What's the largest size of cube that can be made to pass through such a hole?

I know what you're thinking, Diary Dear. Obviously you can't push a larger cube through a smaller one. But that's a Flatland way of thinking. What you have to realize is that the second cube might be pushed through at a slant. With the *right* slant, you can push a cube of side 1.06 through a cube of side 1. You cut it like this:

Each black dot is ¼ of a unit from the nearest corner of the cube

Each grey dot is ³⁄₁₆ of a unit from the nearest corner of the cube

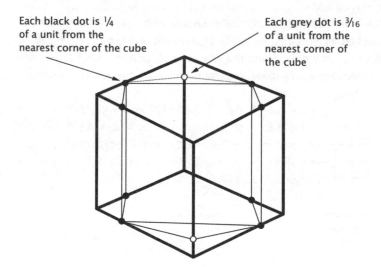

So in Spaceland, you can push a bigger cube through a smaller one! (Not many people know that.)

On the other hand, there are *some* things that Spacelanders THINK they know – and it turns out they're RIGHT – but it's not so easy to PROVE they're right. One of the most amazing is all about how greengrocers stack oranges . . .

*

'It's called the Kepler problem, and it's one of the oldest unsolved Planiturthian mathematical problems,' said the Space Hopper. 'At least, it *was* until someone solved it. Then it was one of the newest *solved* Planiturthian mathematical problems.'

'How old was it? Before some Planiturthian solved it, I mean?'

The Space Hopper scratched one of his horns. 'In the Planiturthian calendar it goes back to the year 1611. That's 1711 in Flatland dates – by a strange coincidence, Flatland time runs exactly 100 years ahead of Planiturthian time. And it was solved in 1999 their time, so it lasted 388 years!'

'What's it about?'

'The best way to stack spheres. Tell me, Vikki, how do greengrocers stack fruit in Flatland? Round fruit like . . . well, roundfruit?'

That was an easy one. As a small child, Vikki had always enjoyed a visit to the greengrocer's hexagonal shop with its neatly laid out clumps of fruit. The squarefruit, of course, were always packed in squares, because that way they fitted exactly. But the roundfruit were packed in a honeycomb pattern. That left gaps, but you had to leave gaps, and in this arrangement the gaps were as small as they could be:

Squarefruit fit together tightly like this

You **could** pack roundfruit like this . . .

. . . but **this** way you get more of them in a given space

Flatlanders liked both arrangements, because the first was based on squares and the second on hexagons. (If you can't see the hexagons, look at any circle and the circles that surround it. There are six of them, and their centres form a regular hexagon.)

'Quite right,' said the Space Hopper when she told him this. 'But how do you *know* that the hexagonal pattern is the most efficient?'

'Experiment?' suggested Vikki.

The Space Hopper shook his horns. 'No, that's not a proof. It's one of those cases where the answer is "obvious", but proving the obvious is difficult. It took the Planiturthians until 1910 to do that – and even then the proof outlined by Axelthue is rather sketchy. A really solid proof didn't turn up until Fejestóth found one in 1940. So don't be too unhappy that you couldn't tell me why the hexagonal pattern is the most efficient way to pack circles in the plane. It's hard, however obvious it may seem.

'Spacelanders have fruit too. They have bananas, which are long thin ellipsoids – usually bent – and they have spherical ones, like oranges. And, just as in Flatland, every Planiturthian greengrocer *knows* the best way to pack oranges. How do you think they do it?'

This was a good test of Vikki's mastery of the VUE, and she created lots of virtual spheres in mid-air and started fiddling with them. Eventually she stopped. 'How about this?'

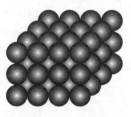

You **could** pack oranges like this . . .

'That would be good with cubefruit,' said the Space Hopper. 'But even in Flatland, the way you pack squarefruit isn't the way you pack roundfruit. You've arranged each layer in squares. Try again.'

'Um . . . Oh, I see! I can make lots of hexagonal layers and stack them vertically on top of one another!'

. . . but **this** way you get more of them in a given space . . .

'Better – but you're still thinking like a Flatlander. You can do better still.'

'I don't see how.'

'Try shifting the layers so that the bumps in one layer fit into the dips in the previous one. You're putting bumps against bumps.'

Vikki thought about this for a moment, then she rearranged her virtual oranges into a more efficient packing:

. . . and **this** way you get even more of them!

'Fantastic!' said the Space Hopper. 'That's the one I want! As I mentioned, it's the arrangement that every Planiturthian greengrocer knows fills space most efficiently. A Planiturthian mathematician and mystic called Johanneskepler knew it too, in 1611 – or, like the greengrocers, he thought he did. It's certainly a very efficient way to pack spheres in 3D. But is it the *best* way? That's another question altogether.'

'Does it really matter? After all, if I'm a greengrocer, I don't really care as long as I don't waste too much space.'

'And if you're a Planiturthian, as long as the pile doesn't collapse. Quite right – and that's one reason why the greengrocers *don't* "know" the answer. What they know is the answer to a slightly different question. They build their piles of oranges on a flat surface, and mostly they want to find a method that avoids avalanches. But in a way it *did* matter to Johanneskepler that this arrangement is the best, though he didn't realize it at the time. What he wanted to understand was snowflakes.'

'Surely he didn't want to stack snowflakes?' asked Vikki, puzzled.

'No. It's easy to stack snowflakes: it's called a snowdrift. Though that doesn't stack them very efficiently. No, Johanneskepler wanted to understand why snowflakes are six-sided. You see, he wasn't very rich (being a mathematician), and he needed to give his sponsor – who rejoiced in the name of Johnmatthewwackerofwackenfels –

a New Year's present. So he wrote him a book called *On The Six-Cornered Snowflake*, in which he tried to work out why snowflakes had sixfold symmetry. And he traced it to a packing problem.'

'But you just said—'

'Ah. Not a problem about packing snowflakes together. A problem about packing together whatever tiny units of *stuff* a snowflake is made from. Johanneskepler didn't have the modern concepts, but what he was asking about was the atomic structure of ice crystals. He figured out that *if* ice was made of tiny spheres – not quite right, but close enough – and *if* those spheres packed together as closely as possible, then the "crystal lattice" of ice would have a hexagonal structure. Just like the hexagonal packing arrangement for oranges. And the second "if" was spot on, because atoms pack together in whatever arrangement makes their energy lowest, and basically that means close-packing.'

Vikki knew that 'atoms' were very small particles – well, particle-like things – out of which all matter was made: they'd done this in Physics. And she knew about crystals. They were made from atoms arranged in a regular lattice pattern, a grid. In this respect, Flatland was just like Spaceland, except that there were 17 types of crystal lattice in Flatland, as compared with 230 in Spaceland. So what the Space Hopper was telling her all made perfect sense – for once.

'Anyway,' the Space Hopper went on, 'there was a period of nearly four hundred years when the Kepler conjecture – that the arrangement of staggered hexagonal layers is the best way to pack spheres – was something that "most mathematicians believed, and all physicists knew". But you can imagine that if a similar problem in 2D wasn't solved until 1910, then its 3D analogue would prove to be a lot harder – and it was. Lots of Peoples tried, and failed. Then, in 1999, a Planiturthian mathematician named Thomashales finally proved that the physicists had been right all along. (This greatly disappointed some of the mathematicians, who were vaguely hoping that the physicists would turn out to have been wrong. Fat chance!) His proof was *huge*: he turned the problem into a vast number of calculations and then got a Planiturthian computer to do the sums. The idea is to start with an arrangement that's *not* packed into staggered hexagonal layers, and show that by rearranging some of the oranges you can improve the efficiency.

Because in principle there are many possible ways not to have staggered hexagonal layers, you have to do this in an awful lot of cases. But Thomashales managed to organize a *huge* calculation to deal with every possibility.'

Sevenday 1 Noctember 2099
Planiturth, and its Spaceland geometry, are BRILL. I'm having my mind stretched in a dozen directions at once, and they're all fascinating. But tonight I'm feeling a bit sad – homesick, really. My parents must be terribly worried. Thing is, I'm having a lot of fun, and I don't want to go home JUST yet – but it would be nice to get some kind of message back to them to say I'm OK.

Maybe there's a way to tap into the Flatland phone system from here. I'll ask the Space Hopper tomorrow.

A HUNDRED AND ONE DIMENSIONS

Wunday 2 Noctember 2099
I've been MUCH too busy to phone home.

Compared with Flatland, Diary Dear, the Planiturthian universe is a riot! For starters, it's got a HUMONGOUS number of Spheres – well, they're more or less that shape – which range from huge balls of fire called *stars* to tiny balls of ice known as *setalights*. No, Diary Darling, I haven't the foggiest *why* they call them that – I guess because you have to set them alight to warm them up. (It'd be a better name for the stars, really.) Anyway, the Space Hopper has been having a whale of a time buzzing all over the place, showing me all the tourist attractions like Black Holes and Oooooooooort (I *think* that's the spelling) Clouds . . .

I'd call it a whistle-stop tour, except we never *stop*. Or whistle.

The Planiturthian universe, I now know, contains a vast range of shapes that I've never seen before. Some are GIGANTIC: spiral things called galaxies, clusters of galaxies, superclusters . . . right up to rippled skeins of matter millions of light years across. (A light year sounds like a unit of time but it isn't: it's a very big unit of distance indeed, the distance light goes in a year. And in the Planiturthian universe, light *sizzles*.)

On a smaller scale, most of the Planiturthian universe seems to be made of rocks. Of every conceivable shape and size. And many inconceivable shapes and sizes. Except – most of the Planiturthian universe is uninhabited, but every so often you find *living creatures* of one kind or another. Even intelligent beings like US (though not as beautiful and *far* less perfect). Almost without exception the inhabitants of the Planiturthian universe (oh, yes, there's lots) are convinced that they are the ONLY life-forms in the whole of Space. The Space Hopper says that when it takes light several centuries to get to your nearest neighbour, then it's hardly surprising that you should think you're the only lifeform in the whole of Space. I think the Space Hopper is much too willing to tolerate poor imaginations, but that's just the opinion of a humble Flatlander.

One of the smaller spheres (it would be tempting to call it Roundworld, but there are SO MANY round worlds here, and anyway its inhabitants refer to it as Planiturth, so I shall too) is quite a fun place. I've told you about it before, but now I've had a crash course in Planiturthian Studies. Lots of these medium-sized Spheres are littered with common – though distinctly nongeometric – shapes, such as rocks, mountains, canyons, volcanoes, and clouds. Planiturth is smothered from pole to pole with far more unusual structures: swamps, trees, plants, animals, and curious vaguely star-shaped things with five protuberances that call themselves *Peoples*. Like this:

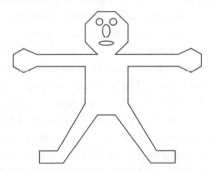

The Peoples of Planiturth are just as complacent about living in a 3D world as we Flatlanders are about living in a 2D one. Most of them are convinced that there is no such thing as the Fourth Dimension. The Space Hopper says that they're right, but for the wrong reason.

I wonder what he means by that? Tomorrow, I'll ask him. Right now, I'm worn out. I do wish I could phone home. Maybe I can build a transmitter!

※

'They're right, Vikki, because there is no such thing as *the* Fourth Dimension. And they're wrong, because there are lots of different Fourth Dimensions – not to mention Fifth, Sixth, or even a Hundred-and-First – many of which they experience in their daily lives, but fail to recognize.'

Vikki found it hard to believe that anyone could experience a Fourth or Fifth Dimension and not know it, and said so.

'It's a question of being sensitive to what you're actually experiencing,' explained the Space Hopper. 'They've got it into their heads that "Fourth Dimension" has to mean a fourth direction in *space* – by which they mean their usual 3D space. Well, naturally if you go looking for a Fourth Dimension in a 3D space you won't find it, any more than you could find a Third Dimension in Flat . . . *Well*, actually, that's not quite—'

'You're saying they should look for a Fourth Dimension *outside* their own space? *You* may be able to hop spaces, but for the rest of us it's not so easy, you know.'

The Space Hopper wiggled impatiently. 'Sometimes. Not always. It may be just a question of looking at their own space in a different way. But instead of us just talking about it, let's see what a People has to say about it.' He made some adjustment to Vikki's VUE, and the universe turned inside out . . .

An infinite series of folds unfolded, and Space stabilized. Vikki sat still for a moment until she stopped feeling sick.

They were sitting at the side of a rutted dirt path in the middle of beautiful, rolling countryside. Beyond it was a field full of fluffy white things on sticks that made 'baaaa' noises and copied each other a lot. From the distance came a curious sound, a kind of rattle-buzz-hum. Then, along the path, bouncing erratically from one rut to another, came A Machine. It rolled along on two big Circles, and a People sat precariously on top of it.

'A Bicirclist,' whispered the Space Hopper. 'We're very fortunate: you don't often see them in this habitat.' He bounced up and down, and the Bicirclist promptly left the path and toppled into a ditch. There was a silence, followed by a stream of Planiturthian invective. The Bicirclist climbed back onto the road and stomped towards them.

'*Why did you—* Oh, I say, are you two part of some promo or something? How on Earth do you squeeze into those costumes? Are you dwarves? That squarey thing is amazing, it looks so thin that from the edge it seems to vanish altogether! Some kind of optical illusion? Must be.'

'Not at all,' said the Space Hopper. 'We are visitors from a different Dimension.'

The Bicirclist clutched its belly and laughed heartily. 'I know,' it said, 'you're students, aren't you? Is it Rag Week? This is some kind of practical joke.'

The Space Hopper turned to Vikki. 'You see?' She nodded.

'Why do you think it's a joke?' asked the Space Hopper.

'Because there aren't any Extra Dimensions,' said the Bicirclist. 'There's the usual three, and that's it.'

'Really?' said the Space Hopper. 'Just suppose, for instance, that your comfortable, solid, 3D space were in reality just an infinitely thin slice of a far more glorious 4D continuum.'

'*Slice?*' said the Bicirclist, incredulously. 'How can a solid space be a slice?'

'Let me tell you about a place called Flatland . . .' the Space Hopper began.

＊

The Bicirclist was extremely patient.

In the circumstances.

＊

'So you see, a Flatlander must face much the same question: since the plane is all there is, how can it possibly be a slice of *anything*?' For the dozenth time, the Space Hopper had launched into his favourite argument. 'By analogy, in what sense is a plane *thin*, when it extends infinitely far along both of the possible dimensions North–South and East–West? There is no other direction for it to be thin *along*. It's thin along the Up–Down direction? These words have no meaning. Show me "Up" and I might believe you – but you can't show me "Up," not if we remain in Flatland. In the same way, you Spacelanders may have difficulty comprehending that your solid 3D space might indeed be an infinitely thin slice of something bigger.'

'But that's just an analogy.' The Bicirclist was getting really into his stride now, and his face was flushed and animated. He waved his protuberances a lot. 'The difference is that I can *see* there's more to Space than just a plane. But I can't *see* there's more to Space than . . . Space.' Before the Space Hopper could tell him yet again that this was because his perceptual apparatus was too limited, the Bicirclist quickly conceded part of the argument. 'I suppose it might be a part of something bigger that we can't perceive,' he said, 'I grant you that. But whatever it is, it can't be *thin*.'

'Oh, but it can', the Space Hopper contradicted. 'Agreed, your space is very thick (though probably not infinitely so) along the three dimensions of North–South, East–West, and Up–Down. But there could be a fourth dimension, Chalk–Cheese, and along that direction your supposedly thick space might be no more than a filmy slice. Though the "film" would be three-dimensional, of course. Travel a trillionth of a micrometre Chalkwise or Cheesewise, and you would move out of your homely Space altogether!' And he scratched a rough diagram in the dried mud at the side of the path:

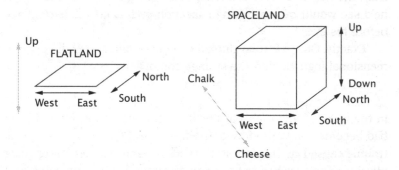

'It's not very convincing,' said the Bicirclist. 'I don't quite see where the Chalk–Cheese line *goes*.'

'Yes, well . . .' The Space Hopper writhed with embarrassment. 'I . . . yes, I admit it's not possible to draw a convincing fourth dimension on a two-dimensional path – but then, even to represent a *third* dimension requires the convention that a slanting line doesn't actually reside within the picture.'

'I guess.'

'So we just need a further convention, that another kind of slanting line doesn't reside within 3D Space.'

'Mmmph.'

The Space Hopper could see that the Bicirclist was still unconvinced. 'OK, then: replace "Chalk" with "Past" and "Cheese" with "Future".'

'I don't catch your drift, old chum.'

'Isn't your present world separated by a trillionth of a second from its future, and likewise from its past? *Time* is an example – but not the only one – of a Fourth Dimension. And along the time direction, your present world is wafer-thin!'

The Bicirclist disputed that time could be a dimension, but as usual all he really did was argue that it wasn't a spatial dimension, which was reasonable but irrelevant. The Space Hopper turned to Vikki. 'Wouldn't it be nice if one day a Hypersphere could convince him of the existence of a Fourth Dimension, merely by appearing from thin air within a locked room, growing from a point to a small sphere to a larger sphere, and then shrinking back to nothingness.'

'Or maybe he could get a visitation from a Hyperspace Hopper from the Fourth Dimension!' said Vikki. She paused. 'Of course, all he'd see would be a puzzling collection of spheres, changing size before his eyes.'

'Exactly. Only a Virtual Unreality Engine could reveal the extradimensional logic behind the strange contortions.'

＊

In the wake of Victoria's baffling departure, the Square household had become a very gloomy place indeed. In Grosvenor's mind, the trouble caused by his ancestor's old book and his daughter's inexplicable departure had to be connected somehow. He felt guilty that his hasty burning of the ancient document was what had upset Vikki and caused her disappearance, and to avoid admitting this – to himself or anyone else – he alternated between raining curses on old Albert for bringing the family into disrepute from the far side of the grave, and denouncing Vikki for the same offence from its near side. These episodes, in turn, were punctuated by long periods of stony-faced silence on the whole issue – which, he would declare, was just something they should put behind them. 'The girl was no good, Jubilee,' he would say, 'always obstinate and headstrong. I don't know how she vanished, and I don't know where she went, and I don't *care*! The family must move on.'

The boys, Les and Berkeley, had been told that their sister had been offered a really good job in Numerica, a distant region of Flatland, and had been forced to leave abruptly before it was offered to someone else. They appeared to accept this explanation, but Jubilee could tell they were only half-convinced.

She herself had gradually come to a very different view from the one that her husband professed to hold. She was puzzled by the manner of Vikki's sudden disappearance, and the more she thought about it, the less certain she was that her daughter had, in fact, been involved in a secret liaison. She had searched Vikki's room and found nothing incriminating; she was starting to wonder if her daughter had been an innocent victim of events that neither she nor Grosvenor understood. And she couldn't help sensing echoes of Albert's strange visitations. Just what *had* been in that old book?

Grosvenor had notified the police, of course, but he'd had to conceal some of the story because officialdom would have thought he was nuts if he'd told them she'd vanished into thin air. So he just said she'd run away. Now, a daughter of Vikki's age disappearing in a huff was hardly unusual, and technically Vikki was an adult, responsible for her own actions and her own decisions. In the absence of any signs of foul play, the police were privately regarding her disappearance as a typical flight from the family home by a young woman in search of personal liberty. They put Vikki on their missing persons list, and that was pretty much all they did.

Jubilee knew that her husband's real feelings were very different from those he dared to express, and she hoped he would eventually be able to admit as much. She was worried that when Vikki turned up again – and she had an exceptionally strong hunch that it *would* be 'when', not 'if' – then Grosvenor would blow his northedge and cause an irreparable rift.

Secretly, Jubilee also hoped that her daughter was having fun – otherwise she had caused an enormous amount of trouble for nothing – and when everything started to overwhelm her, she tried to lose herself in housework and looking after the boys.

It was a very difficult time for them all, and the atmosphere in the spacious old house was strained and awkward. Still, they coped.

'If Time were a dimension,' said the Bicirclist, 'you ought to be able to travel *along* it, like you can with the dimensions of Space.'

'You can,' said the Space Hopper. 'You can travel forwards at one year per year.'

'No, I mean travel back and forth at will.'

'Ah.' The Space Hopper turned to Vikki and whispered, 'Should I reveal that we Space Hoppers are also Time Hoppers?' He turned back to the Bicirclist. 'Travelling through Time is more difficult than travelling through Space because the temporal metric is far more compressed—'

But the Bicirclist wasn't listening. 'Time travel – like that bloke in the story by H.G. Wells. Which, by sheer coincidence and narrative imperative, I've got in my saddlebag.' He rummaged in a small bag attached to the rear of the Bicircle and extracted the book triumphantly. '*The Time Machine*, that's what it's called.' He opened the book and thumbed through the first few pages. 'Wells's Time Traveller opens the story by arguing that an *instantaneous* solid body is just as much a mathematical fiction as a line or a plane: "Clearly," the Time Traveller proceeded, "any real body must have extension in four directions: it must has Length, Breadth, Thickness, and – Duration". Having argued that material bodies are really four-dimensional, Wells's Time Traveller then springs his trap. "There is no difference between Time and any of the three dimensions of Space except that our consciousness moves along it," he says, and drops dark hints that he has overcome this particular limitation.'

The Space Hopper had a good grasp of Planiturthian history, especially when it came to Space and Time. 'Do you know that within ten years of *The Time Machine*, a People called Alberteinstein invented the Theory of Relativity? And another named Hermann-minkowski formulated Alberteinstein's ideas in terms of the geometry of four-dimensional spacetime?'

'Nope.'

'Well – the idea of time as *the* fourth dimension came into vogue, and in this world it's never quite gone away again. But the truth is far stranger. Your world has not just four dimensions, but five, fifty, a million, or even an infinity of them! And none of them need be time. Space of a hundred and one dimensions is just as real as a space of three dimensions.'

'Rubbish!'

'Not at all. Why, take that Bicircle of yours. It has at least seven dimensions.'

'Really? Then show me some.'

'I will if you bring it over and hold it upright.' The Bicirclist obliged. The Space Hopper bobbed across to the Bicircle. 'You'll grant that its current shape is three-dimensional?'

'Of course.'

The Space Hopper nudged the Bicircle's handlebars through a small angle. 'There! A Fourth Dimension!'

The Bicirclist laughed. 'Don't be silly! You just moved it in 3D.'

'Yes, but it changed shape.'

'Nonsense!'

'No, it really did,' said Vikki. 'If it had stayed the same shape you could make it fit into its current position by a rigid motion. But that bit with horns on had to turn while the rest didn't. *That's* not a rigid motion!'

'Oh. I suppose you could put it like that. But if it moved through a new Dimension, in what direction does that Dimension point?'

'In the Turn-The-Handlebars direction,' said the Space Hopper, 'which is different from the Turn-The-Front-Circle direction, which is different from the Turn-The-Back-Circle direction, which is different from the Turn-The-Pedals direction. That's four new dimensions, in addition to the original three. You've got a seven-dimensional bicircle.'

✦

Twoday 3 Noctember 2099

I really must phone home soon. But the Space Hopper says that this will be difficult, because of system incompatibilities. Apparently, if I want to phone home then it's best not to do it from here.

Well, Diary Dear, eventually the Space Hopper managed to explain in what sense the Planiturthian People's Bicircle is Seven-Dimensional. It's all to do with *variables* – quantities that can change. 'Dimension' is a geometric way of referring to a variable. Time is a nonspatial variable, so it provides *a* fourth dimension, but the same goes for temperature, wind-speed, or the number of termites in Tangentia. The position of a point in three-dimensional space depends on three variables – its distances East, North, and Upwards relative to some reference point. By analogy, anything that depends on four variables lives in a four-dimensional space, and anything that depends on 101 variables lives in a 101-dimensional space.

In fact, ANY complex system is multidimensional. The weather in a typical Flatland back garden depends on temperature, humidity, two components of wind velocity, barometric pressure – that's five dimensions already! I didn't know we had a 5D garden before! An economy with a million different commodities, each having its own price, lives in a MILLION-DIMENSIONAL space!!

No wonder economies are hard to control!

*

Vikki was dreaming . . .

She dreamed she was floating in the darkness above a world that looked much like Flatland must have been before Life evolved – a featureless, uniform, white surface. But *something* lived on the surface, for she could hear it muttering to itself: 'Painting the dot, painting the dot, red paint, red paint, round and round; painting the dot, painting the dot, red paint, red paint, round and round . . .' over and over again.

In her dream, she came closer, and discovered a curious little antlike creature, with pot and paintbrush in hand, going round and round in a spiral. It had started by painting a small dot, and then it had gone round the edge making it a bit bigger, and it had carried on until by now the dot was really quite big. And still the tiny creature laboured away, painting its world a brilliant crimson.

She watched, and the rim of the red dot got bigger and bigger, until she could only see a small part of it. And as it got bigger, it got straighter and straighter.

And the little ant continued painting, and continued muttering to itself, 'Painting the dot, painting the dot, red paint, red paint, round and round . . .'

Vikki was amused and contemptuous at the same time. *Silly beast*, she thought. *Doesn't it know that the world goes on for ever? It will never finish its red dot!* She didn't say this – and even if she had, she doubted the little animal would have heard, so engrossed was it in its task. And then something funny seemed to have happened, for the ant was now going round and round inside a white circle. It had painted itself *inside* a shrinking hole in its red dot.

This made astonishingly little sense.

And still the ant persevered, until finally it was completely surrounded by a vast expanse of red, and was balancing on tiptoes (not that ants have toes, but that's what it looked like) inside a white dot that was smaller than its own body. It put down its pot and brush, and its endless chant changed into 'Painted the dot, painted the dot, time for a rest, time for a rest, let the paint dry, let the paint dry; painted the dot, painted the dot, time for a rest, time for a rest . . .' Until the paint *did* dry. And then—

Then, the ant picked up its pot and brush, and began circling the white dot, chanting, 'Painting the dot, painting the dot, white paint, white paint, round and round . . .' And the white dot grew, and grew, until she could only see a small part of it. And as it got bigger, it got straighter and straighter . . .

She was intending to ask the Space Hopper what it meant, but when she woke up, she forgot. There was so much to do, so many spaces to hop . . .

The next night she had a different dream – a nightmare. She dreamed that *she* was an ant, in Spaceland this time. In one hand she held a small red ball, in another a pot of red paint, and in a third (ants have six limbs, remember) a brush. And she was singing a little song: 'Painting the ball, painting the ball, red paint, red paint, round and round, painting the ball, painting the ball, red paint, red paint, round and round . . .' And as she sang she applied layer upon layer of thick paint to the ball. The red ball got bigger and bigger until she could only see a small part of it. And as it got bigger, it got flatter and flatter.

And Vikki continued painting, and continued muttering to herself, 'Painting the ball, painting the ball, red paint, red paint, round and round . . .'

And then . . . something funny seemed to have happened. For Vikki was now going round and round inside a spherical hole. She had painted herself *inside* a shrinking hole *inside* the ball.

She was trapped!

At which point she woke up in a cold sweat.

This time, she remembered the dream, and told the Space Hopper all about it.

*

'You were dreaming you were inside a 3-sphere,' said the Space Hopper.

'You mean there's something sensible behind it? I thought my mind had just made up some kind of nonsense.'

'Not at all. Exotic dreams are a common side-effect of using a VUE. It's entirely sensible.'

'It looked just like Spaceland.'

'Yes, 3-spheres do, Vikki. If they're big enough. It's a trap a lot of people who paint balls fall into. It's amazing how often they have to be dug out with pneumatic drills.'

'What's a 3-sphere, Hopper? What was happening?'

'Let me put it this way, Vikki. The mathematics of multidimensional spaces is based on generalizations from low-dimensional spaces. For example, every point in Flatland, a 2D space, can be specified by two coordinates, and every point in 3D Spaceland can be specified by three coordinates. And a point in 4D space ought to correspond to a set of four coordinates, and a point in nD space ought to correspond to a list of n coordinates. So n-dimensional space itself (or n-space for short) can be thought of as the set of all such lists.'

'Is space really a lot of lists?'

'Mathematicians don't worry about what things *really* are. They just want to find effective ways to work out what they can do.'

'Oh.'

'Now, the same kind of mental trickery leads to formulas for distances in n-space, angles, and the like. From there on, it's a matter of imagination: most sensible geometric shapes in two or three dimensions have straightforward analogues in n dimensions, and the way to find them is to describe the familiar shapes using the algebra of coordinates and then extend that description to n coordinates in whatever way seems most obvious.

'A circle in the plane, or a sphere in 3-space, consists of all points that lie at a fixed distance from a chosen central point. The

A HUNDRED AND ONE DIMENSIONS ∘ 49

same idea applies to *n*-space. The set of all points that lie at a fixed distance from a chosen point is known as an (*n*–1)-dimensional *hypersphere*, or an (*n*–1)-sphere for short.'

'Why the minus one?'

'Ah. The dimension drops from *n* to *n*–1 because ... well, because it makes sense. You see, a circle in 2-space is a curve, which is a 1D object, and a sphere in 3-space is a 2D surface. A *solid* hypersphere in *n* dimensions is called an *n*-ball. So Planiturth is a 3-ball and its surface is a 2-sphere. This kind of stuff is a bit prosaic, but once you've set it all up you can happily talk about a 9-cone in 11-space whose base is a 4-sphere and whose axis is a 5-plane. Or whatever.'

'And ... you said I was trapped inside a 3-sphere?'

'Yes. The ant in your first dream, you see – it was really on the surface of a very big 2-sphere. It started painting at the north pole, and by the time it had worked its way down to the equator, the edge of its red dot was looking pretty close to a straight line. Actually it was a gigantic circle, but you couldn't see that, you were too close to it. Then, when the ant had painted its way south of the equator, it was painting itself inside an ever-shrinking circle, surrounding the south pole. So it waited for the paint to dry, and then it started again with white paint, working its way northwards. A very hard-working ant, was it not?

Painting the dot . . .
painting the dot . . .

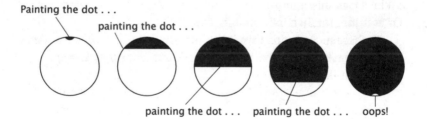

painting the dot . . .   painting the dot . . .   oops!

'Your second dream was what would happen if you did the same kind of thing inside a 3D analogue of a 2-sphere – that is, a 3-sphere. The ball represented its "north pole". As you painted the ball, and it got bigger, you were actually filling the northern "3-hemisphere" with paint, and eventually you passed the equator.

From then on it was only a matter of time before you got yourself trapped inside an ever-shrinking 3-ball centred on the "south pole".'

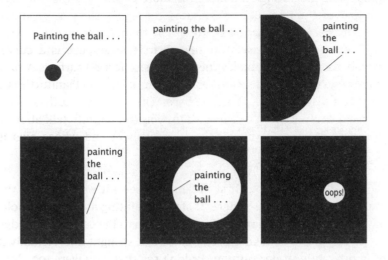

'This multidimensional geometry is weird stuff,' said Vikki. 'But it has its own kind of logic, doesn't it?'

'It certainly does. It makes so much sense that after a while you get used to the geometric language. But you can always do the algebra to *check* it makes sense, if you're worried.'

'Actually, what worries me is something quite different,' said Vikki. 'Does this multidimensional stuff let you do anything *useful*? Or is it just intellectual fun and games?'

The Space Hopper's grin became even more manic than usual. He must have done something to her VUE, because suddenly everything went dark.

❊

Something went *whizzzzzzzzzz!* past her ear, and she ducked. It left a streak of blazing white light like a meteor. Moments later, another streak shot past, and another. As her eyes became accustomed to the dark, she realized that white streaks were all around her.

'Where are we?'

'We are in the Land of Dotcom,' said the Space Hopper.

'And what are those whizzy things?'

'Let's find out.' The Space Hopper produced a boxlike device and held it up. As the next white streak shot past, its trajectory suddenly bent through a hairpin curve and it sizzled straight into the end of the box. 'Got it!' shouted the Space Hopper, proudly. 'Now, let's see just *what* we've got.'

There was a little window in one side of the box, and when Vikki looked through it she saw little red letters, forming words. They scrolled past her eyes:

Mrs Smoggrimble, HI. Thanks for your e-mail of 14 January. We have consulted our files and regret to inform you that we can find no record of any payment for the crate of poodle dye that was delivered to you. Unless the invoice is settled in full within 30 days we will HAVE TO SUE. :-)

'What's all *that* about?'

'It seems that Mrs Smoggrimble thinks she has paid for a crate of poodle dye but her supplier begs to diff—'

'I can see that. I mean: what does it signify? How does it relate to those whizzy things?'

The Space Hopper bounced delicately. 'Ah. It *is* one of those whizzy things.'

'How can a whizzy thing that streaks past at the speed of light be made of *words*?'

'Because those whizzy things are messages. Just think of them as very rapid messages, like someone who talks very fast. A used cardioid dealer, say.'

'Hopper, we've got e-mail in Flatland,' said Vikki dismissively, 'but I was asking about the uses of many dimensions. Instead of answering, you're showing me an e-mail message. Why can't you stick to the point for once?'

'I *am* sticking to the point, Vikki. Messages can be thought of as points in multidimensional space. Modern digital communications use sequence of 0's and 1's to encode information. For example, here they might encode the letter M as 10010, R as 11100, whatever. So the message you read would be coded as a string of binary digits, starting with 10010 11100. Let's just think of those first ten digits. You can think of the string as a Point in a ten-dimensional

Space, whose coordinates are either 0 or 1. The first coordinate determines the first digit, the second coordinate determines the second digit, and so on.

'Now, the trouble with digital messages is that interference can cause errors. Say the message is sent out looking like 1001011100, but arrives as 1001010100, where the seventh digit has changed from 1 to 0. If you get a lot of that kind of thing the message might be received as:

Mr Snogthimble, oi. Thinks fur you re-mail of 174th canary. We have insulted your flies and piglet to infoom you that ?XX**?? grind on reword any playmate for the cart of noodle eyes that was undelivered you. Unload the thin ice is speckled in fool within 03 dogs we well. Love to Sue. :-(

'. . . which would be confusing.'

Vikki laughed. 'I can see that. So what do you do? Get rid of the interference?'

'Nope, usually impossible. But there's a clever trick: error-detecting and error-correcting codes.'

'How can you detect an error if you can't understand the message you receive?'

'If you can't understand it, Vikki, then probably something is wrong. But the idea is cleverer than that. For instance, you could detect (but not correct) any isolated error if you coded every message by replacing every 0 by 00 and every 1 by 11. Then a message such as 110100 would code as 111100110000. If this is received as 111000110000, with an error in the second pair of digits, you know something's screwy because the pair 10 should never occur.'

'Oh. I see. But you can't tell whether it should have been 00 or 11.'

'I'm coming to that. Suppose you code 0 as 000 and 1 as 111. Then any isolated error can be corrected as well as detected. Suppose your received 111000101111, say. What was the message before the error got made?'

'Uh ... 111000111111. Easy! But what's that got to do with thinking of a message as a point in a multidimensional space?'

'Ah. For that, we need to journey into one tiny corner of Dotcom. I hope you don't mind feeling cramped.'

The VUE reset, the world changed. As far as she could tell, it now contained exactly four points:

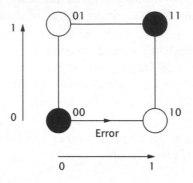

'Welcome to the Double-Digit District,' said the Space Hopper.

'This is a *district*?' asked Vikki.

'Certainly. I admit it's a bit sparse, but there's a reason. We're in a digital space. It has very few points, but, far more importantly, it has a *metric* – a concept of *distance*. Each white point is one unit away from each black point, and each point is *two* units of distance away from the other point of the same colour.'

'Don't you mean root two?' said Vikki. 'Isn't the diagonal of a square—'

'Aha! In Flatland, yes. In the Double-Digit District, no. Here diagonals don't exist – so you have to go along the edges.'

'Oh.'

'The Double-Digit District is the essence of the error-detecting code I just mentioned. Think of two-digit segments of the coded message – valid segments 00 and 11, and invalid ones 01 and 10. By thinking of the digits of these segments as coordinates relative to two axes (corresponding to the first and second digits of the segment respectively) we get the geometry of the Double-Digit District. The valid segments 00 and 11 are at opposite corners of the square, so they are *two* units of distance apart. Any isolated error changes them to segments only *one* unit of distance away, at the other two corners – but those are not valid segments.'

'Oh, I see. So because each valid segment is surrounded by invalid ones, you can tell when something's gone wrong.'

'As long as you don't get two errors in one segment, yes. But in the Double-Digit District, the invalid segments are adjacent to both of the valid ones. So different errors can lead to the same result. That's what makes it an error-*detecting* code, but not an error-*correcting* one.'

'Fine. So how do you correct errors using a code?'

'The most obvious way to get an error-correcting code is to move into Triple-Digit Territory. If we use segments of length three and encode 0 as 000 and 1 as 111, then the segments live at the corners of a "cube" in a finite 3D space. Any isolated error results in an adjacent segment; moreover, every invalid segment is adjacent to only *one* of the valid ones.'

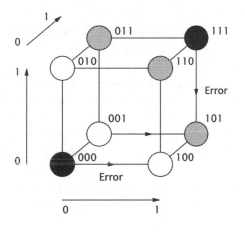

Fourday 5 Noctember 2099

Dear Diary,

You'd think that a Space consisting of isolated points would be exceptionally dull.

Not a bit of it. Especially the multidimensional ones. And the amazing thing is, the InterLine wouldn't work without them. Every message sent to or from a computer would be corrupted – I *like* that word, sounds very streetwise, doesn't it? – by noise.

The Space Hopper says that it all works because of a gadget called a Hamming metric. I rather assumed this was some kind of incompetent actor until he explained that it was a beautiful, simple idea for turning coding theory into geometry.

You see, on Planiturth – I've already told you why we can't really get away from that Place, have I not? – this approach to code messages was pioneered by a People named Richardhamming in 1947. In the geometric imagery that stemmed from his original algebraic ideas, codewords of length *n* correspond to the corners of an *n*-cube – a hypercube in *n*-dimensional space. Single errors correspond to moves along an edge of the *n*-cube; double errors correspond to moves along two successive edges, and so on.

The Hamming metric tells you the *distance* between two codewords – how many single-digit changes it takes to convert one into the other. In fact, it's just the distance between them measured along the shortest path *formed by edges of the hypercube*. Each edge has length 1 unit, so in the Hamming metric the opposite corners of a square are 2 units apart, not √2 units apart as they would be in Flatland . . .

Hamming hypercubes don't have diagonals, OK?

Now comes the clever part. Codewords 2 units apart in the Hamming metric can detect one error but not correct it. Codewords 3 units apart can correct one error or detect two, and so on.

Richardhamming and his successors discovered a whole *slew* of useful codes. And there's payoff in other areas of the Mathiverse, such as sphere-packing. Back to Johanneskepler and the six-cornered snowflake, OK? A lot of scientific problems, like crystal structure, boil down to finding efficient ways of packing circles in 2D or spheres in 3D. Now, you can ask the same questions in *n*D, and use the results to do things like number theory. In 1965 a Planiturthian People named Johnleech took an idea from another one called Marcelgolay, and discovered a really efficient packing of 23-spheres in 24D. No People has found a better one since! In fact, it's so efficient that it led to a solution of the kissing number problem in 24D.

No, Diary, don't be naughty. It's not like that *at all*.

The problem is this: what is the largest number of nonintersecting hyperspheres that can touch ('kiss', OK? Satisfied?) a given hypersphere? Planiturthians know the answer in exactly five cases: 1D, 2D, 3D, 8D, and an astonishing 24D. And how do they *know* such obscure factoids? Well, it's a very curious story. In 24D a whole heap of Planiturthian mathematicians managed, between them, to prove that the kissing number was at most 196,560. The proof was highly indirect and nobody knew if that number could actually occur. Johnleech's packing – amazingly – gave exactly the same number, so that was the end of the kissing number problem in 24D. (Oh, and the kissing numbers in 1D, 2D, 3D, and 8D are 2, 6, 12, and 240.)

❋

The Space Hopper must have dropped off for a snooze. When he awoke, Vikki was counting.

'One hundred and ninety-six thousand, five hundred and fifty-*one* . . . One hundred and ninety-six thousand, five hundred and fifty-*two* . . . One hundred and ninety-six thousand, five hundred and fifty-*three* . . . One hundred and ninety-six thousand, five hundred and fifty-*four* . . .'

'Vikki, what are you—'

'*Don't interrupt!* One hundred and ninety-six thousand, five hundred and . . . and . . . Um. Er, *one, two* . . . Bother!'

'You don't need to check it so laboriously,' the Space Hopper pointed out. 'The Planiturthians have calculated it, I'm sure they got it right.'

'I just wanted some practice with the VUE. You know, this gadget almost makes the Mathiverse *too* easy.'

'Except when you lose count.'

'Shh! That was a *joke*. I saw you were asleep and I started from one hundred and ninety-six thousand, five hundred and forty. But what I'm trying to say is, how would anyone visualize multidimensional spaces *without* a VUE? How do Planiturthians manage, for instance? Do they have VUEs?'

'Not yet. They're working on them. They're up to Virtual *Reality*. Virtual Unreality is some way off, as yet.'

'But this Johnleech People thingy must have . . . I mean, he surely couldn't have—'

'Ah. No, he didn't get the kind of image you perceive through the effortless medium of the VUE. *He* had to *think*. He had somehow to equip himself with *n*D spectacles. I don't know how he did it – probably a lot of algebra but thought of as geometry. But Planiturthians have taught me a few simple tricks, little more than analogies with 2D and 3D, which go a long way.

'Let's . . . I know, think of your ancestor! No VUEs in *his* day, I assure you. Yes, suppose that great-whatever-grandad Albert Square is sitting happily in Flatland, and wants to "visualize" a solid sphere. How does he do it?'

'Well, in his story he talked about the Sphere passing through the plane of Flatland, and moving perpendicular to it, so that what he saw was a series of cross-sections of the sphere.'

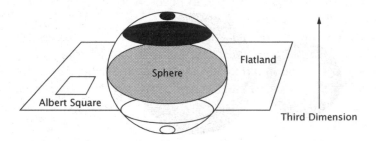

'Good! Yes, first he sees a point, which grows to form a Circle. The Circle expands until he is seeing the equatorial section of the sphere, after which it shrinks again to a point and then vanishes.'

'Well – look, actually old Albert saw the Circles edge-on – line segments with graded shading – but his visual senses *interpreted* this image as a Circle.'

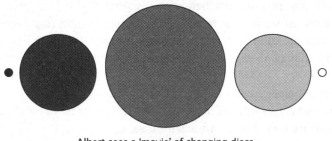

Albert sees a 'movie' of changing discs

He can also think of this as a static sequence of colour-coded frames

'Don't be pedantic. Anyway, by analogy a Planiturthian can "see" a 4D-ball – a solid hypersphere in 4D-space – as a point which grows to form a solid 3D-ball, expands until it reaches the equator of the 4D-ball, then shrinks back to a point, and finally disappears.'

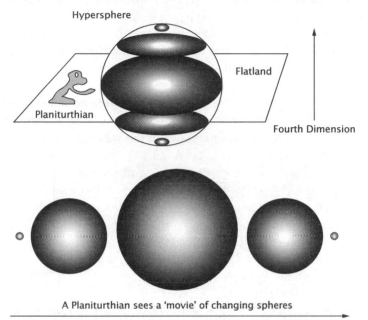

A Planiturthian sees a 'movie' of changing spheres

He can also think of this as a static sequence of colour-coded frames

'So in both cases the extra dimension is really represented as *time*?'

'You could say that, Vikki, yes.'

'Well, my physics teacher kept insisting that while time is *a* third dimension, it's not *the* third dimension', said Vikki heatedly. 'Mind you, he also said that there was no *real* third dimension at all, and thanks to the VUE I now realize that's nonsense. Nevertheless—'

'Nevertheless, using time is all very well, but the problem with time is that it has a life of its own. I met Time once, and it definitely did have its own life, I can assure you. Quite an interesting one, but *it could never go back*. Time is always moving in one direction – into the future. What we want is what Herbertgeorgewells's Time

Traveller allegedly invented – a way to move at will up and down along some substitute for a fourth dimension.

'One of the Planiturthian tricks is to imagine a fourth dimension as a *colour*. Imagine displacement along a fourth dimension to be colour-coded, say from blue to red, with all possible shades of purple in between.'

'Why?'

'The advantage of using colour is that it doesn't imply some particular physical quantity, such as time. Planiturthians are very used to the idea that *any* quantity can be colour-coded.'

Vikki could relate to that. 'Same on Flatland. Well, depends on the era. Colour was freely available at the time of Chromatistes and the Colour Revolt, and in those days colour was used with tremendous freedom and creativity. Then came the backlash, of course. It was the stupidity of the Revolutionists and their Universal Colour Bill that did it. Typical totalitarian attempt to impose some kind of uniform code of practice – and of course they got it all wrong. Imagine trying to have Women and Priests painted with virtually the same colours! Endless confusion, and it led to a massacre with the Suppression of the Chromatic Sedition.'

'Yes,' said the Space Hopper. 'I remember that.'

'*You* remember! How old *are* you?'

'In the metaspace of the Mathiverse, time has no meaning. I have no age – I simply *am*.'

'Oh. Anyway, the idea of using colour as a form of decoration couldn't be suppressed for ever, and much later, after the Six-Year War, some daring young women pioneered a new colour-conscious fashion. We've never really looked back, actually. Anyway, what I'm really saying is – you're right. Colour is a pretty arbitrary way to represent something.'

'I'm glad you agree, Vikki,' said the Space Hopper. 'Now, where was I – oh, yes. Anyone wishing to visualize a fourth dimension, say, can mentally equip themselves with a Colour Machine instead of a Time Machine. Merely by depressing a simple pedal they can imagine themselves moving at will along the red–blue axis.

'At each stage they "see" a 3D cross-section of 4-space corresponding to that colour. As the colour varies, they can mentally "stack" these images. Different sections that seem to overlap in 3D but have different colours don't really overlap, because they exist in different "levels" of 4-space. In the same way, two Planiturthian cars that pass through a crossroad will collide only if they occupy the same position *at the same time.*'

'So . . .' said Vikki, 'if Albert used a Flatland Colour Machine to think about a 3-ball, he would imagine a blue point which grows to a disc and gradually becomes tinged with more and more red. The disc reaches its maximum size when it is a beautiful purple, 50 per cent blue and 50 per cent red. As it reddens further the disc shrinks, and eventually becomes a red point, after which it vanishes.'

'Correct.'

Vikki had a moment of inspiration. 'Hopper! I've just realized! A Planiturthian could visualize a 4-ball in the same way! They start at the blue end, where they see a single point. As they depress the pedal, moving in the red direction, that point turns into a purplish-blue ball, and gets bigger. When they reach the halfway mark they see a solid purple ball. Further into the red, the ball shrinks again, and turns redder. Finally they see a single red point, which then vanishes.'

'Very good. Now, it is well known that Planiturthians have problems visualizing knots. Can you tell me how they could use a Colour Machine to visualize how to untie a knot in 4D *without breaking the loop?*'

'Um. I guess they . . . yes, yes, I can see! When Planiturthians look at a knot, they see places where the string seems to cross itself. It doesn't really, of course – that's just an effect of perspective. But those apparent crossings tell them the shape of the knot. At each crossing, one bit of string goes underneath – I'll call that bit an "underpass". And another bit goes over the top – an "overpass". Anyway, what the Planiturthians ought to do is imagine a blue loop, tied in a trefoil knot, say. Near one of the crossings they imagine grasping the overpass bit of the loop, and they pull that bit out *along the red direction.*'

The Space Hopper bounced gently as he contemplated this idea. 'Yes. So nearby sections of the loop have to turn various shades of purple, in a graduated way, to maintain continuity?'

'Sure, Hopper, sure. But most of the loop can stay blue. Now they push the purple overpass down *through* where the underpass is. It *looks* like they intersect, but actually they don't, because the underpass *is still blue*! Things that intersect must do so at a point with a common colour (the fourth coordinate) as well as a common spatial position (the other three coordinates). And now they can safely release the colour-pedal and return that loop back to the blue region of 4-space. The end result is as if they'd just pushed the overpass down through the underpass. So the loop is no longer knotted.'

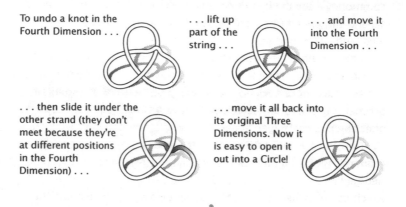

To undo a knot in the Fourth Dimension . . .

. . . lift up part of the string . . .

. . . and move it into the Fourth Dimension . . .

. . . then slide it under the other strand (they don't meet because they're at different positions in the Fourth Dimension) . . .

. . . move it all back into its original Three Dimensions. Now it is easy to open it out into a Circle!

*

Fiveday 6 Noctember 2099

Well, Diary Mine, multidimensional Spaces are a lot of fun, and coding theory shows they can be useful.

And it doesn't stop there.

According to the Space Hopper, a solar system or an economy can be viewed as a multidimensional space. I admit it sounds unlikely: the Planiturthian solar system, for instance, is just a lot of rather big rocks trundling around in ordinary 3D space. But the Space Hopper says that appearances can be deceptive – or rather that they can be absolutely correct, but irrelevant.

The way he sees it, every body in the Planiturthian solar system needs three coordinates to specify its position. So with nine planets, that's 27 coordinates – and anything that has 27 coordinates necessarily lives in a 27-space! In fact you really need a 54-space, because positions alone don't tell you what the planets are doing. You need to know their *velocities*, and that's another 3 coordinates per planet.

And if you include the asteroids . . . well, you're looking at TENS OF THOUSANDS of dimensions!!! And, that, he says, is what makes celestial mechanics so hard.

I thought he was joking, but he's deadly serious. 'The Curse of Dimensionality,' he calls it.

So, Big Hairy Deal, a solar system has oodles of dimensions. Kind of esoteric, though. But – get this – an economy has *millions* of dimensions! Each dimension corresponds to the price of some commodity – say the first dimension is the price of oxagons, the second the price of hogsagons, the third the price of squarrel-feed, and so on. And that, he tells me, is what makes economics even harder than celestial mechanics.

No, that's not meant to be a joke, either.

Ah, Diary my Old Friend, I know what you're thinking. MultiD geometry provides an elegant reformulation, yes – but does it offer any practical advantages?

The Space Hopper says 'yes'. He says that, thinking about economic problems multidimensionally led a Planiturthian called Georgedantzig to some weird idea called the 'simplex method', which can find the most profitable combination of goods that a factory ought to produce. Allowing possessors of said method to make oodles and oodles of money!

Could physical space *really* have more than three dimensions? After all, how can you fit the fourth dimension in? Everything's filled up already.

Well, of course that's what Ancestor Albert's book was about. Physical reality has many interpretations, and the one presented to us by our sense organs need not be the only possibility. Our universe could be just one of an infinite variety of universes that might have happened instead, so that we occupy just a wafer-thin slice of a vast multiverse.

Mindboggling, isn't it?

＊

'So now we've visited all the possible spaces?' asked Vikki.

'Whatever makes you think that?'

'Well, Hopper . . . we've done 0D and 1D and 2D and 3D and 4D and all the way up to a millionD, and I can kind of see how it would go from there and I don't think we really need to visit the rest. What else is there?'

'There's a lot more to spaces than just their dimensions,' replied the Space Hopper. 'But even if we stick to dimensional variations, there's plenty more to find out about. What about one-and-a-quarter-dimensional space, for a start?'

Vikki stared at him as if he were mad. 'But you can't possibly have one and a—

5

ONE AND A QUARTER DIMENSIONS

'—quarter dimensions!' said Vikki in bewilderment. But even as she spoke, she experienced that by now so familiar psychic discontinuity, and her VUEpoint shifted. There were times when she wished the Space Hopper wouldn't take her every statement as a challenge, to be demolished by conveying her to yet another weird space. However, it seemed impossible to stop the fat bouncy little creature with the thick orange skin from reacting to questions with actions. It was certainly a striking teaching technique, high on drama and nervous energy – but there were times when she would have preferred a more relaxed approach.

She stared through the nonexistent realm of metaspace as if it weren't there (which it wasn't, not in any sense of *there* that could be understood by mortal creatures). Where metaspace wasn't, there seemed to be – a forest.

'The Fractal Forest,' the Space Hopper announced proudly.

'It's very ... beautiful,' said Vikki. And it was. There were gnarled trees, and spiky-leaved bushes, and thick clumps of fern. Snow was falling, and every surface was picked out in soft, diamond-studded icing.

'So what's with the forest, Hopper?'

'Look at the fern, Vikki.'

She tugged at a frond. 'It's ... Hopper, it's just an ordinary fern. Intricate, pretty – so what?'

'Use the VUE. Look *closely*.'

'Well, what I see is a lot of fronds lined up on both sides of the stalk ... and each frond is *also* a lot of smaller fronds lined up on both sides of a tinier stalk. That's what makes ferns ferny, isn't it?'

'Closer than that.'

'OK . . . each smaller frond is a lot of even smaller fronds lined up on both sides of an even tinier stalk . . . and . . . oh. This one doesn't stop, does it?'

'No. It goes on doing that for ever. It's not a *real* fern: it's a mathematical idealization of fern structure. The trees and bushes have the same infinitely fine repeating structure. And so, oddly enough, does the snow.'

Vikki readjusted her VUEfinder. Hovering in mid-air, sparkling and crisp in the unremitting light of VUE-enhanced imagination, was a single snowflake.

It was the sort of snowflake that would appeal to a Flatlander, made – so far as she could tell – from an endless series of eversmaller equilateral triangles. There was a big triangle, with three smaller ones placed on its sides to make a six-pointed star . . . then there were (she counted) twelve smaller triangles, placed on the edges of the star to make a more elaborate star. *Then* there were (she lost count five times and gave up) a *lot* of even smaller triangles placed on the edges of that new star. When she Cranked up the magnification of her VUE it became clear that the sequence of triangles didn't stop there: the closer she looked, the more of them she saw. The edge of the snowflake was crinkled, and there were crinkles on the crinkles, and crinkles on the crinkles on the crinkles.

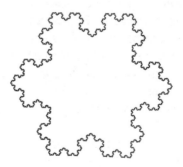

The snowflake spun gently in the brilliant light, like a tossed pancake in low gravity. 'Enough of that', said the Space Hopper, and twiddled some extradimensional knob or lever or metaspatial demon, freezing the snowflake in one position. 'In the Fractal Forest, geometry goes on for ever and dimensions come in fractional amounts. The edge of this snowflake, for instance, has *approximately* 1.26186 dimensions. It's not *exactly* one and a quarter, I accept, but if you really want I can certainly show you a shape that—'

'Whoa there, Hopper! Let's just back up, OK?'

'Sorry? You have a problem?'

Vikki tried to pull her scattered wits together. She had a feeling that only part of her discomfort was the psychic dislocation caused by the Virtual Unreality Engine. 'Look, dimensions can't be fractions.'

'Tell that to Helge the Snowflake, then,' said the Space Hopper. A quizzical eye opened at the centre of the six-pointed star. 'Sorry, Helge, but you've got another unbeliever.'

'Just my luck,' said the snowflake glumly, 'I should have known. It always happens to me. Every Tim, Dick and Harriet who wanders into the Fractal Forest always ends up on my doorstep sooner or later – and it's usually sooner.'

'It's because of your inherent simplicity and elegance,' said the Space Hopper, 'plus your parents chose an attractive name.'

The snowflake's edges fluttered in acknowledgement of the compliment. 'I suppose so. But it's still a great burden to have to bear, you know. If I had a penny for every time my circumference has been measured, I'd be able to retire to some nice fractal forgery of an island and spend my time sunbathing on its infinite beaches.'

'Are you a *real* snowflake?' asked Vikki.

'No, no, not at all. If I were, then I wouldn't be able to sunbathe – I'd melt.' The snowflake paused, as if gathering its wits. 'However, I do share a real snowflake's sixfold symmetry, and if anything I am even more intricate, but my bodily form is *much* too regular for a true snowflake. Think of me as a visual pun.'

'The Space Hopper said you had 1.26186 dimensions,' said Vikki. 'I think that's rubbish.'

The snowflake scratched its edge with one frilly corner. 'I think someone discovered that rubbish has about 2.8739 dimensions,' it told her, apparently in all seriousness. 'Of course, it does depend on how you crush it, but—'

'I meant, you were *talking* rubbish.'

The snowflake looked offended (though you'd have to be an

expert to spot such nuances of expression). 'Me? Rubbish? Perish the thought! You'll get nothing from me but the most sparkling insight. But *my* dimensions are two, just like many of your fellow citizens. You, of course, are one-dimensional.'

'But—'

'Ah! The dimensions of my *boundary* are 1.26186, whereas your boundary, if I'm not mistaken, has exactly zero dimensions. Let me check . . .' (it began counting on its vertices) '. . . one, two, three . . . mmmm . . . mmnnnhmmm . . . hmmmhmmm . . . *zero.* Right.'

'My boundary consists of two points', said Vikki.

'Correct! And a point is zero-dimensional, and the same goes for any finite set of points. Including two.'

'Zero dimensions, I can understand. It's really just a convention – it fits the sequence cube/square/line/point. But 1.26186 dimensions? That's nonsense. The number of dimensions something has is the number of different *directions* it points in – the number of numbers needed to specify a point in it. You can have one direction, or two, but you can't have 1.26186 directions. Can you?'

'Of course not, Vikki,' said the Space Hopper. 'But you know what mathematicians are like – always meddling. No sooner does one of them come up with a definition of dimension in terms of directions, when some other smartarse has to improve on the idea by finding a completely different definition that gives the same answer when the dimension of a space is a whole number, but works for other spaces too. More general, you see, which to a mathematician means "better". Except that with the *new* definition, you can get fractions.' It swelled slightly with excitement. 'They were Planiturthians, those mathematicians . . . Can't say I was surprised. Whole-number dimensions . . . well, to be truthful, those had been around since the time of Euclidthegreek, at least in principle. But a Planiturthian called Henripoincaré pushed the idea about as far as it can be pushed. According to Henripoincaré, *every* shape, however weird, has some whole number of dimensions. As long as you allow infinity, of course . . . oh, and minus one.'

'*Minus one?*'

'Sorry, don't be nervous. That's just a convention. The only –1D set is the empty set.'

'Which is?'

'Nothing at all. If you draw a picture of it, it's blank.'

'Let me see if I'm getting this right,' said Vikki. 'According to this Hairypunkarray—'

'Henripoincaré.'

'—every shape has a whole number of dimensions.'

'Correct.'

'But you just said that Helge the Snowflake has 1.26186 dimensions.'

'No, that's my *boundary*—' Helge protested.

'Boundary, schmoundary. Whatever, it's not a whole number.'

The Space Hopper bobbed in agreement. 'Yes, but that's because another Planiturthian disagreed with Henripoincaré. *His* name was Hausdorffbesicovich, and *he* had quite a different idea about dimensions. He reckoned that it wasn't a matter of more dimensions meaning more directions – it was more dimensions meaning filling space more effectively. More crinkly, so to speak. You might call it "crinkliness" instead of "dimension", but of course mathematicians wouldn't do that, because the name wouldn't sound impressive enough. And, to be fair, there's another reason. You see, on all the usual spaces like the 2D plane or 3D space or even 101D space, the Henripoincaré-dimension and the Hausdorffbesicovich-dimension are the *same* – they're 2 or 3 or 101, as you'd expect. So both notions *generalize* the "number-of-directions" version of dimension.'

'Unfortunately,' said the snowflake, 'they generalize it in two incompatible ways.'

'Yes – but that's maths for you. As far as mathematicians are concerned, the more kinds of dimension you invent, the happier they are. And if some kinds are incompatible with one another, you can have a lot of fun finding out why and when. So now there's the box-counting dimension, and the similarity dimension, and the information dimension, and—'

'*Stop!*' Vikki lowered her voice to more normal levels. 'You've already told me enough dimensions to last me a lifetime. But you still haven't explained how Helge can have 1.26186 dimensions.'

'Haven't I? Dear me, no, I haven't.' The Space Hopper was momentarily embarrassed. 'Uh . . . well, the easiest way to see *that* is to use the similarity dimension.' The Space Hopper waved his horns like a conjuror, and a piece of card materialized between them. He laid the card flat (in metaspace, you appreciate) so that it seemed to be hovering in thin air. With a flourish, an entire pack of similar cards appeared, and the Space Hopper fanned them out. 'Now, Vikki: how many of these do I need to make the original square twice as big?'

'In what sense?' she queried, having learned caution. The Space Hopper asked too many trick questions!

'By fitting them together. Look, let me show you the answer and you'll see what I mean.'

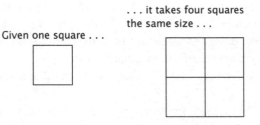

Given one square . . .

. . . it takes four squares the same size . . .

. . . to make one twice as big

'Right, I get it,' said Vikki.

'It works with triangles, too. Four copies *also* make a triangle twice the size.'

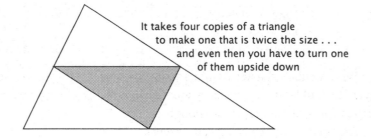

It takes four copies of a triangle to make one that is twice the size . . . and even then you have to turn one of them upside down

'Of course.'

'What about cubes?'

'Cubes?'

'Do four cubes make a cube twice the size?' The Space Hopper twitched his horns, and four identical cubes materialized in her VUEfield.

'Um . . . no. They do make a sort of square slab, but it's too thin to be a cube.'

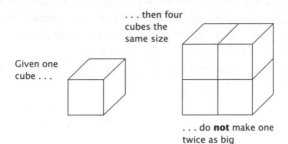

Given one cube . . .

. . . then four cubes the same size

. . . do **not** make one twice as big

'So how many more—'

'Four! If we make a *second* slab, and fit it behind the first one, we get a cube twice the size of the original.'

'Excellent. But why?'

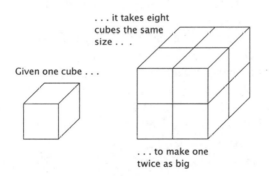

Given one cube . . .

. . . it takes eight cubes the same size . . .

. . . to make one twice as big

'Well, a cube's thicker than a square, so you have to have two layers to double the thickness. A square has no thickness, and twice zero is zero, so one "layer" is enough.'

The Space Hopper grimaced. 'Yeeesss . . . but there's a better way to say that. What do you mean by "zero thickness"?'

'Um . . . it's not thick.'

'True. But in what *direction* isn't it thick?'

'The one in which it's . . . *oh*, I see what you're getting at. The cube has an extra *dimension*, which I've been calling "thickness", but the square doesn't.'

'Precisely. The cube is 3D, but the square is 2D – like the triangle.'
'I see.'

'Now, 4 is the *second* power of 2 – its square. Whereas 8 is the *third* power – its cube. So what's the common pattern?'

'In order to double the size of a shape, the number of copies you need is 2 *raised to the power of the dimension.*'

The Space Hopper grinned manically (∪). 'So if the dimension is 1?'

A line can be made twice the size by joining two copies together

'You need 2 to the power 1, which is . . . 2. *Two* copies. Oh, right!'

'And if we wanted to multiply the size by three, how many copies would we need? Here's a hint: three copies for a line, nine copies for a square, and twenty-seven copies for a cube. So the general pattern this time is?'

'3 raised to the power of the dimension.'

'Fine. Which, by a roundabout route, brings us to the snowflake.'

'I'm glad you haven't completely forgotten about me', Helge the snowflake muttered.

'Not at all, my friend. Show Vikki here one of your edges. Not your entire perimeter, that's a bit complicated. Just one section of it.' The snowflake did so. 'Lovely and crinkly, isn't it?'

'Beautiful,' said Vikki. The snowflake blushed with pride.

'And the interesting thing is, you can make that crinkly edge three times the size by fitting *four* copies together. Yes?'

'Absolutely. So?'

'What power of 3 makes 4, Vikki?'

'Well, um . . .' She racked her brains, and then realized it was another of the Space Hopper's trick questions. 'There isn't one.

The first power of 3 is 3, which is too small, and the second power of 3 is 9, which is too big. And after that, they just get bigger still.'

'What about the one-and-a-halfth power?'

'That doesn't – oops, yes, it does. We did this in maths. The halfth power is the square root. So the one-and-a-halfth power is . . . the cube of the square root?'

'Correct. And that is?'

'Sorry, I'm not that good at mental arithmetic.'

'OK, I'll tell you: it's 5.19615. Roughly. But unfortunately, that's—'

'Still too big. We want to get 4.'

'OK. So what about the one-and-a-quarterth power?'

'Um . . . that's the fourth root of the fifth power, right?'

'Right. Value 3.94822.'

'Which is close.'

'As you say. In fact, we can get a lot closer. The 1.26186th power of 3 – which you could work out as the 100,000th root of the 126,186th power of 3 – is *extremely* close to 4. And by going to more decimal places, you can get as close as you like. The exact number, in fact, is log 3 divided by log 4, where "log" is the logarithm.'

'So you're saying that—'

'The dimension of Helge's edge is very close indeed to 1.26186. Like I told you.'

There was a long silence. 'It's not *really* a dimension, is it?' asked Vikki. 'It's just come sort of measure of – crinkliness – that happens to be equal to the usual dimension when you have a simple sort of space.'

'Fair enough,' said the Space Hopper. 'Complicated shapes like the snowflake or the fern, whose "dimension" in the crinkliness sense is a fraction – or to be strict, just differs from its dimension in the Henripoincaréan sense – are known as *fractals*. Roughly speaking, a fractal is a shape that has detailed structure, no matter how much you magnify it. Physical examples are rocks, clouds, trees, coastlines – as long as you don't magnify them to the scale of atoms, of course. Mathematical fractals can be scaled up for ever and still have intricate structure; real fractals can be scaled up *a lot* and still have intricate structure.

'And if you want to be very precise, you can always call the crinkliness measure the *fractal dimension*. Then there's no danger of getting confused and trying to find one-quarter of a direction.'

*

'Fractals must be very rare,' said Vikki.

'Why?' asked the Space Hopper.

'All that detail. Unusual.'

'Funnily enough,' the Space Hopper told her, 'it's pretty much the other way round! Nearly all mathematical shapes are fractal. Having a whole number of dimensions is what's rare. Think of it this way: if you pick a number at random – a decimal, not necessarily a whole number – then the chance of it *being* a whole number is very small indeed. Most numbers have something after the decimal point.'

'True – I hadn't thought about it that way. So what do some of the other fractals look like?'

'I'm sure the Snowflake would be happy to let us meet some of his friends here in the Fractal Forest.'

'Delighted to be of assistance,' said the Snowflake. 'You can usually find them hanging around among the leaves and in between the tree-roots . . . Yes, here's a very close friend of mine. Like me, he's based on triangles.' And he introduced them to Sierpiński Gasket, who was made out of triangles with triangular holes, which cut it into more triangles, also with triangular holes. He soon dug up Sierpiński Carpet, who was very similar but with square holes instead. And an energetic search revealed the very impressive Menger Sponge, who was like the Carpet but made from a cube.

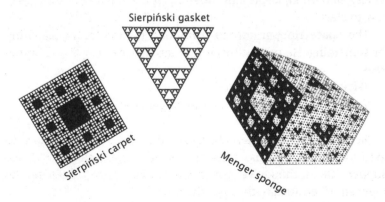

Sierpiński gasket

Sierpiński carpet

Menger sponge

'Fractals like these,' the Space Hopper explained, 'are *self-similar*. Like a fern, they're made up from lots of smaller copies of themselves – that's what makes it easy to work out their fractal dimension. Have a go!'

'Um . . . Sierpiński Gasket is made from three copies, each half the size?'

'That's right. So his fractal dimension is $\log 3/\log 2 = 1.5850$. Whereas Sierpiński Carpet is made from eight copies, each one-third the size—'

'—so his fractal dimension is $\log 8/\log 3 = 1.8928$. I can do it too! Good job my Personal Disorganizer has a built-in scientific calculator!'

'And Menger Sponge is made from 20 copies each one-third the size, so his dimension is $\log 20/\log 3 = 2.7268$.'

'I see what you mean: the bigger the fractal dimension, the "thicker" the shapes seem to get.'

'That's the general idea, and it's what gives intuitive meaning to the fractal dimension.'

Vikki watched as the Snowflake, Gasket, Carpet, and Sponge wandered off and disappeared behind the infinitely crinkled vegetation of the Fractal Forest. 'Are all fractals self-similar?'

'Definitely not,' said the Space Hopper. 'Those are just the easiest ones to understand. But there are lots more. They have a fractal dimension too, which is usually not a whole number, but it's nothing like as easy to calculate.'

'It must be very difficult to find a shape that has structure on *all* scales,' said Vikki, 'especially when it's not self-similar. I don't see how to start!'

The Space Hopper turned from side to side, as if searching for something. He peered towards a gap between two fractal pine-trees.

'What are you looking for?'

'I'm trying to remember the way to Quadratic City.'

'Why?'

'Because there's somebody there who will show you how to specify a shape that has structure on *all* scales,' said the Space Hopper. 'OK, I think I've got my bearings. Follow me!' and he bounced off erratically through the trees.

'Who?' asked Vikki, wriggling along behind him.

'The Mandelblot.'

*

Sevenday 8 Noctember 2099

As we made our way through the beautiful landscape of the Fractal Forest, Diary Mine, the Space Hopper told me the story of the Mandelblot.

For the record, here it is.

Seems that the Mandelblot was originally called the Gingerbread Boy. Baked from gingerbread, but unusually articulate for a cookie. He changed his name when he grew older. After he was first baked, he ran away. He came to a river, and there was a fox snoozing beside it.

'Please, Mr Fox, take me across the river,' said the Gingerbread Boy.

'I am the Fox Pup, and the wise person listens to me,' said the Fox, who had an eye for a bargain, especially if the bargain was a free lunch. 'Hop onto my back and I'll swim across.'

So the Gingerbread Boy hopped onto the Fox Pup's back. But as the fox swam further out into the river, he began to sink. 'Hop onto my head,' said the fox, 'and you'll keep dry.' So the Gingerbread Boy hopped onto the fox's head. But still he sank. 'Hop onto my nose,' said the fox, 'and you'll keep dry.' So the Gingerbread Boy hopped onto the fox's nose.

And as the fox sank further, the Gingerbread Boy hopped onto the very tip of the fox's nose. And then the tip of the tip, and the tip of the tip of the tip . . . until the fox began to get very frustrated. 'How long do you intend to keep this up?' the fox demanded, in an irritated voice. 'How do you expect me to get lunch if you keep hopping onto ever finer scales of my nose? I may have to dip my nose completely into the water if this carries on.'

But the Gingerbread Boy kept hopping on to the tip of the tip of the tip of the tip of the . . . tip of the tip of the tip of the fox's nose. Because he knew that the fox wouldn't submerge his whole nose in the water. *Why not?* you are asking, Diary Dear. Because he didn't like soggy gingerbread. And the fox got seriously frustrated, and again he asked the Gingerbread Boy how long he intended to keep hopping along his nose, and when he planned to get to the end (where, of course, the fox could open his mouth and gobble him up).

'I'm awfully sorry, Mr Fox,' said the Gingerbread Boy, 'I'm afraid I'm never going to reach the end of your nose. You see, before I can get to the end, I have to get halfway to the end. And before I can get halfway to the end, I have to get a quarter of the way to the end. And before I can get a quarter of the way to the end, I have to get an eighth of the way to the end. And so on. So I can't even get started—'

But the Fox Pup had heard that one. 'Listen to me, young man,' he told the Gingerbread Boy sternly, 'I've hung around the Mathiverse a lot, and I've come across Zeno's paradox before. I don't believe a word of it. For a start, you're *already* nine-tenths of the way along my nose, and if your argument were correct, you wouldn't have been able to get that far.'

'Oh, all right, then,' said the Gingerbread Boy, 'let me put it this way. After I've got nine-tenths of the way along your nose, but before I can get to the tip, I have to get ninety-nine hundredths of the way along your nose, yes?'

'Well . . . yes,' admitted the Fox Pup.

'And after I've got ninety-nine hundredths of the way along your nose, but before I can get to the tip, I have to get nine-hundred-and-ninety-nine thousandths of the way along your nose, yes?'

'Well . . . yes,' conceded the Fox Pup, who hadn't encountered this variation before.

'So it's clear I can *never* get to the tip of your nose.'

'Let me get back to you on that,' said the Fox Pup. By then he had nearly reached the far shore, though he was too busy counting on his paws to notice, and the Gingerbread Boy trotted along to the very tip of the fox's nose and hopped off.

'Hey!' complained the fox. 'I thought you said you couldn't do that?'

'I lied,' said the Gingerbread Boy. 'The sequence is convergent.'

❋

Vikki waited, but the Space Hopper had finished.

'Was that *it*?'

'Yes.'

'That's a very stupid story!'

'Well, it was a very stupid fox. Anyway, I was just passing time until I could locate the – and there he is! Hey, Mandelblot!' And the Space Hopper bounced up and down in excitement.

The Mandelblot was a very funny shape, a cross between a cat lying on its side and a cactus:

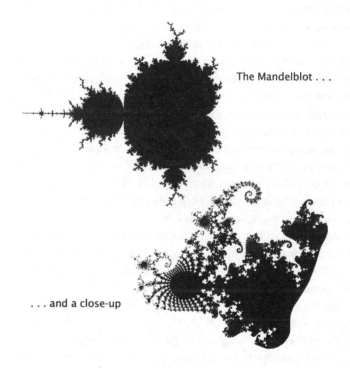

The Mandelblot . . .

. . . and a close-up

And the closer Vikki looked, the more complicated the Mandelblot's shape seemed to be.

'He's a fractal?'

'Indubitably. One of the best. But no, to anticipate your next question – he's not self-similar.'

'Why is he that shape?'

'He was made Taxi Controller, in charge of Quadratic City's taxi service, and he tells the taxi drivers whether they can get out or not.'

'That,' said Vikki, 'is as clear as mud.'

'It's quite a long story,' said the Space Hopper, 'but better than the one about the Fox Pup and the Gingerbread Boy, I promise. Come with me, and I'll ask the Mandelblot to explain—'

'Everything in Quadratic City,' began the Mandelblot, 'is based on squares. 'Why, the city itself is nothing more than a square grid.'

'How big?' asked Vikki.

'Well, from the *outside* it's about the size you'd expect for a city, but on the *inside* it's infinitely big. It's a plane, just like your home-world – yes, I can see you're a Flatty, we don't often get nonfractal folk like you in the Fractal Forest, you know.'

'Does it have pentagons and circles and things like that?' It wouldn't be the *same* as going home, but it might substitute. She still missed her family and friends – she really must persuade the Space Hopper to overcome those alleged system incompatibilities and find a way for her to phone home, or at least send a letter . . .

'Not as such, no. Mostly it has roads . . . and taxis. And taxi-drivers, of course. Both of those are points.'

'Oh.' Not at all like home, then.

'The roads are always straight lines, and there are two kinds. Streets run east–west, and Avenues run north–south. There's exactly one Street and one Avenue for every point in Quadratic City: they form a coordinate grid. So, for instance, if you get a taxi on the corner of 2.4 Avenue and 1.7 Street, and want to go to the corner of 5.6 Avenue and 3.8 Street , then the taxi-driver immediately knows that he has to go 3.2 kilometres east and 2.1 kilometres north.'

'That's a neat idea,' said Vikki. 'Fix it so's the street names tell you where you are.'

'Yes. Mind you, most of the names of the Streets and Avenues are pretty long. I *hate* it when I have to go to π Street or $\sqrt{2}$ Avenue. But that's a minor inconvenience when you consider how easy it is to navigate.

'The two main thoroughfares are 0 Street, otherwise known as Real Road, and 0 Avenue, the Queens i Way. That's "i" as in the Square Route of Minus One, you appreciate. They cross at Grand Central Station, the exact centre of Quadratic City. Taxis start out from Grand Central Station, and try to get out of the city.'

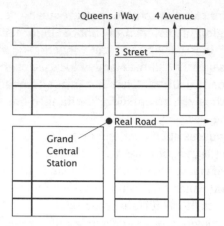

'But I thought the city was infinitely big on the inside?'

'So it is. They're allowed to take infinitely long to escape, you see.'

'But—'

'You'll see in a minute when we look at taxis 2 + 3i and –0.1 + 1i.'

'Those are registration numbers?'

'Very good.'

'They're strange.'

'Very sensible, actually,' said the Mandelblot. 'Each registration number is in the form $A + Bi$, where A and B are numbers. And on any journey, taxicab $A + Bi$ is licensed only to travel from its starting point to whichever intersection is A units to the east (or A units to the west if A is negative), and B units to the north (or B units to the south if B is negative).'

'Let me see if I've got that,' said Vikki. 'Suppose I'm in taxi 2 + 3i. Starting from Grand Central Station, I can make a trip to the intersection of 2 Avenue and 3 Street.'

'That's right,' said the Mandelblot, 'and from there your next trip in taxi 2 + 3i takes you to the intersection of 4 Avenue and 6 Street.'

'OK. And then you can get to the intersection of 6 Avenue and 9 Street, and then the intersection of 8 Avenue and 12 Street, and then the intersection of 10 Avenue and 15 Street, and so on.'

'You got it,' said the Space Hopper. 'The Avenues go up in twos, while the Streets go up in threes.'

'Now,' said the Mandelblot, 'when I said the taxis are trying to *escape* from Quadratic City in infinite time, what I really meant was that they want to follow a path that eventually gets them outside any finite region of the city. An "unbounded" path. So taxi $2 + 3i$ *does* escape.'

'Hold it!' said Vikki. '*Any* taxi eventually escapes!'

'Except for taxi $0 + 0i$. That just gets stuck at Grand Central Station. Which is why my predecessor in this job was just a point. Dot, her name was.'

Vikki found this statement enigmatic, to say the least.

'Look,' the Mandelblot went on, 'the Taxi Controller's job is to make a map of Quadratic City that tells customers arriving at Grand Central Station which taxis can take them out of the city.'

'Nearly all of them,' Vikki pointed out.

'Yes, but someone has to tell them not to jump into the back seat of taxi $0 + 0i$. OK, OK, it was an easy job when Dot did it, but not any more. What Dot did was to introduce a systematic way to map out which taxis could or could not escape. Start with a blank map of Quadratic City. Pick a taxi, $A + Bi$, say, and colour the intersection of A Avenue and B Street *white* if taxi $A + Bi$ eventually escapes, but *black* if it doesn't. Do that for every possible taxi, so every point on the map is coloured either black or white. Then all you have to do is look at the map to see which taxis to avoid.'

'If I'm following you, then the only point that gets coloured black is Grand Central Station itself, corresponding to taxi $0 + 0i$ – the only one that never escapes.'

'Exactly. That's why they called her Dot.'

'Ah,' said the Space Hopper, 'I wondered whether—'

'Another worry!' Vikki butted in. 'Escaping from Quadratic City is all very well, but surely if you've just arrived at Grand Central Station, you might want to see some of the sights before you leave.'

'Mmmmmm . . .' The Mandelblot gave this idea some thought, as if it had never occurred to anyone before. Finally, he said, 'You don't know Quadratic City.'

But Vikki considered this an evasion, and persisted with her line of questioning. 'Suppose I've taken taxi $2 + 3i$ to 2 Avenue and 3 Street, and I want to go back to Grand Central Station. What do I do?'

'Hop out and hope that taxi $-2 - 3i$ can get to you, of course! Or if that one can't manage it, take a two-trip ride on taxi $-1 - 1.5i$. Use some initiative!'

'That won't work,' Vikki objected. 'Neither of those taxis can ever get to 2 Avenue and 3 Street. Not starting from Grand Central Station.'

'True.' The Mandelblot looked crestfallen. 'I forgot to tell you the other thing that taxis can do, that's why. After Dot had made her map, the city authorities took a look at the result and decided that they needed a more effective taxi service, something that would give the tourists an incentive to stay a while. (God knows why, mind you.) So they decreed that taxis could make a different kind of trip in between their regular "A east, B north" ones. They're allowed to *square*. In fact, they have to. Each regular trip must be followed by a square trip.'

'Why?'

'No point in following it with a *round* trip, is there? And each square trip must be followed by a regular trip. And they start with a square trip.'

'What's a square trip?'

'Well, that's an interesting question. The easiest way to answer it is to say that if you're on X Avenue and Y Street, then squaring takes you to $X^2 - Y^2$ Avenue and $2XY$ Street. Look, don't blame me, it's the city authorities who thought that one up. See, suppose you're what I call a *real* taxi, one with a license plate like $X + 0i$. So the dot on the map that corresponds to it is where X Avenue meets Real Road, get it? Then when you square, you go to $X^2 + 0i$, which is where X^2 Avenue meets Real Road. That's why it's called *squaring*. It tells you how the Avenues change when you go along Real Road.'

'Oh.'

'*But*, notice that X^2 is always positive, so those intersections all lie to the *east* of Grand Central Station. What if you want to go west?'

'No idea.'

'That's the cunning part – the city authorities weren't totally nuts. Suppose you choose a taxi with license plate $0 + 1i$, that's plain i for short. On the corner of 1 Street and the Queens i Way.'

'Why is it called that?'

'Because points on it correspond to license plates $0 + Y$i, and it doesn't go to Brooklyn.'

'Oh.'

'Anyway, if you work out the square for taxi i you get the intersection of $0^2 - 1^2$ Avenue and $2 \times 0 \times 0$ Street, which is the intersection of −1 Avenue and Real Road. So the square of i is −1, in effect. Every point along the Real Road has a Square Route, and not just the ones to the east of Grand Central Station.'

'That's cool!' said Vikki.

'And at that point I inherited Dot's job, didn't I?' said the Mandelblot. 'And it's a zillion times harder, let me tell you! See, what *I* have to do is map out which taxis escape from Quadratic City if they start at Grand Central Station and keep alternating a square trip with a regular "*A* east, *B* north" trip.'

'And that's hard?'

'Think about it. Suppose you get in taxi −2 + 0i. Where does that take you?'

'Let me work it out . . . we start at Grand Central Station, so the first square trip take us to – Grand Central Station?'

'Yes. The square of $0 + 0$i is $0 + 0$i.'

'That's silly. Why waste a trip?'

'It puts a few minutes on the clock – kind of entry fee.'

'*Then* the first regular trip takes the taxi to −2 Avenue and 0 Street. Followed by another square, which takes it to 4 Avenue and 0 Street. Then a regular trip . . . ending up at 2 Avenue and 0 Street. And then another square, which gets it to – oh!'

'Problem?'

'It goes back to 4 Avenue and 0 Street!'

'Agreed.'

'And then it just hops for ever between 4 Avenue and 0 Street, and 2 Avenue and 0 Street, doesn't it?'

'Right.'

'So – it never escapes?'

'Exactly. Which means I can take the map, and I can colour −2 Avenue and 0 Street *black*. But you see, that's only one point on the map. There are infinitely many points. But for most of them the calculation doesn't work out so nicely. Try taxi 2 + 3i, since we were talking about that, and see how its itinerary changes with the new rules.'

So Vikki got out her Personal Disorganizer, and programmed its shopping spreadsheet to do the calculation, and this is what it told her:

Trip	Avenue	Street
START	0	0
Square	0	0
Regular	2	3
Square	−5	12
Regular	−3	15
Square	−216	−90
Regular	−214	−87
Square	38,227	37,236
Regular	38,229	37,239
Square	74,713,320	2,847,219,462

'Looks like it's definitely escaping,' said Vikki. 'I wasn't sure at first, but now that the numbers are getting so big—'

'Yes, but how can you be *certain*?' wailed the Mandelblot. 'You can't keep calculating for ever!'

'Surely,' the Space Hopper protested, 'once the numbers get big enough, the taxi *has* to escape? Can't you prove that?'

'Well, yes, I thought of that,' said the Mandelblot. 'It's a bit complicated, but you can. Turns out that as soon as a taxi gets more than 2 kilometres from Grand Central Station – as the crow flies – it will always escape. But some taxis take an awfully long time to get that far, you see. Here's one of the first taxis I was told to sort out when I started the job. Have a go at taxi −0.1 + 1i.'

Vikki tipped that into her Personal Disorganizer, and got this:

Trip	Avenue	Street
START	0	0
Square	0	0
Regular	−0.1	1
Square	−0.99	−0.2

Regular	−1.09	0.8
Square	0.5481	−1.744
Regular	0.4481	−0.744
Square	−0.352742	−0.666773
Regular	−0.452742	0.333227
Square	0.0939353	−0.301732

'I don't *think* that one's escaping,' said Vikki. 'The numbers are staying fairly small . . . all of them seem to be within 2 kilometres of Grand Central Station.' She stopped. 'On the other tip, they're not repeating, either, and I doubt they will. Still – I'll guess it never escapes.'

'*WRONG!*' shouted the Mandelblot with glee. 'Keep calculating!'

'Nothing much happening yet – oh, hang on, *now* they're getting quite large . . . and now the numbers are gigantic. So it does escape.'

'You're beginning to see how hard it is to be sure what colour some points on the map ought to be,' said the Mandelblot, 'and sometimes it's a lot worse than that. In fact – ' (he lowered his voice for a moment) – 'the calculation might have to go on for longer than the lifetime of the universe!'

'Which universe?'

'Any universe. As long as you like. Or longer. To tell the truth, whether a general point gets coloured black or white is algorithmically *undecidable*.'

'Which means that no computer program can be guaranteed to give an answer,' added the Space Hopper, helpfully.

'That must have made your job pretty difficult,' said Vikki.

'Difficult? It was impossible! So . . . I *cheated*. But don't tell anybody! I found a rule of thumb that gives a good approximation to the answer, and I used that. Keep following the taxi for a hundred trips: if at any stage it gets further than 2 kilometres from Grand Central Station, then you definitely know to colour the corresponding point white. *Colour all the others black.* Some points will be given the wrong colour if you do that – the ones that were *going* to escape, but slowly. However, only a tiny proportion are like that. And it's just not worth the effort to be more accurate, because the eye wouldn't be able to tell the difference anyway.'

'That sounds a reasonable approach to me,' said Vikki. 'Pragmatic.'

'That's my feeling – but *don't tell my boss*, OK? I might lose my job if she finds out.'

'It's a promise. Not a word shall I breathe. Anyway, what answer did you get?'

'Me. The Mandelblot, I call it, when I want it to sound posh.'

'You mean you're that weird cactus-cat shape because that's the answer?'

'Yes, just as Dot was a dot when *that* was the answer. But I'm far more complicated. In fact, I'm a fractal. Well, my *boundary* is. Look very closely and tell me what you see.'

Vikki cranked up the VUE and zoomed in on the edge of the Mandelblot. 'Sort of cactusy blobs . . . decorated with their own cactusy blobs . . . now it's spirals . . . then sort of – *seahorses*? More spirally things . . . twirly curly curlicues . . . now it's like the branches of a tree . . . Gosh, it *is* complicated, isn't it?'

'Infinitely complicated,' said the Mandelblot, proudly. 'Now, take a look right . . . *here*.'

'It's – my word, it's a tiny copy of you!'

'Perfect, I'm told, in every detail.'

'But the Space Hopper said you're not self-similar.'

'I'm not. Some bits of me – rather rare ones – are small copies of me, though they're all very slightly bent. Most bits, though, aren't. So I'm not made out of small copies of myself. And that means I'm not self-similar.'

'What's your fractal dimension?'

'You mean the fractal dimension of my boundary?'

'Yes.'

'It's exactly 2.'

Vikki was disappointed. 'I expected something like 1.7729 or whatever. A fraction.'

'Ah, but my boundary is a curve. Yet it has the same fractal dimension as a solid disc, or a square. So actually that's very interesting. Because intuitively a curve ought to have dimension 1–'

'It does, in the Henripoincaréan sense,' the Space Hopper interjected.

'Thank you. Anyway, in the fractal sense, the dimension is 2. Which is as big as you can get for a curve in the plane,' the

Mandelblot pointed out proudly. 'So that's *very* remarkable and unusual.'

Vikki turned to her companion. 'Space Hopper, this is fascinating, but is there any serious *point* to it? What's it all about?'

'Dynamics,' said the Space Hopper, 'rules for moving taxis around, if you wish. More to the point, rules for moving *anything* around. Any system that changes as time passes, and isn't subject to random influences, must obey some kind of repetitive *rule* that governs everything it does. That rule is its *dynamic*. If we gave the taxis a different rule for the trips they were permitted to make, we'd get different kinds of dynamic. And almost all important systems change over time. Populations of animals or bacteria, the positions of planets, the weather . . . they're all like the taxis of Quadratic City.'

'So what does the Mandelblot tell us, then?'

'That a very simple mathematical rule can lead to incredibly complicated behaviour,' replied the Space Hopper. 'Isn't that amazing?'

'I guess . . . But doesn't that mean that trying to understand dynamics in terms of rules is a waste of time?'

'Not at all!' said the Mandelblot heatedly. 'Can't you see how beautiful I am?'

'Sorry, but what's beauty got to do with anything—'

'Pattern!' shouted the Mandelblot. 'Structure! I may be infinitely complicated, but I'm made from layer upon layer of intricate pattern!'

'That's right,' said the Space Hopper. 'What the Mandelblot tells us is that something which seems very complicated may in fact arise from simple rules. So the trick is to understand the rules, not the complicated behaviour that follows from the rules. And if you didn't know there *were* any rules for the Mandelblot, you'd still be able to tell there must be some, because of the patterns. He's not a random mess, you see.'

'I'm not any kind of mess,' protested the Mandelblot.

'Sorry, never meant to suggest you were,' said the Space Hopper. 'What I mean is, instead of all this telling us that rules aren't any use because they can lead to complexity, it tells us that we can hope to understand complexity by finding out what the rules are.

But, to do that we have to be sensitive to new kinds of pattern, such as fractals. New types of pattern can lead us to new types of rule.'

Vikki felt she *ought* to be impressed by this, but wasn't sure exactly why. The dilemma must have showed on her face, because the Space Hopper tried again. 'The Planiturthians have a name for rules like that, Vikki. It may be an exaggeration, but it shows how important they can be.'

'And what name is that, Hopper?'

'Laws of Nature.'

'Heavy,' said Vikki. 'Philosophical. And all based on a city that's so featureless, the only thing new arrivals can think about doing is getting out again.'

'Well, if you feel like that, we'd better go and visit somewhere else.'

That sounded a good idea to Vikki. 'Somewhere *fun*, Hopper? Where there's a lot going on?' *Somewhere to take my mind off home.*

The Space Hopper wiggled its antennae, searching for inspiration. Then its face lit up in a ∪. 'I know just the place!'

6

THE TOPOLOGIST'S TEA-PARTY

An instant – or a lifetime – passed. Vikki had no way of telling how much time had elapsed, since time had no meaning in metaspace ... What she experienced was not a transition, but a shift of attention. Her Virtual Unreality Engine reconfigured itself, and she was ... *elsewhere.*

Using her VUE-enhanced senses, she tried to come to grips with her new surroundings. It was difficult, for nothing stayed still. Strange bendy plastic shapes drifted silently past, shrinking and swelling, rippling and undulating, twisting into grotesque pretzel-like forms, writhing and intertwining like very friendly surreal baroque worms. Even the ground beneath her endpoints heaved and pulsated like a living creature, sprouting elaborate protrusions and then sucking them back into its weird alien landscape. It was disturbing, yet oddly beautiful.

'Here we are,' said the Space Hopper proudly.

'Where?'

'Topologica,' replied the Space Hopper, 'the Rubber-sheet Continent, which doesn't so much drift as *stretch* ... We have entered the realm of topology, from which rigidity was long ago banished and only continuity holds sway. The land of topological transformations, which can bend-and-stretch-and-compress-and-distort-and-deform' (he said this all in one breath) 'but not tear or break. You'll find plenty to occupy you here. Look, someone's coming to meet us already.'

Vikki was about to ask what such a place might be good for when she looked up to see a small, rather nondescript creature sauntering towards them through the ever-changing hills and valleys of the restless landscape. It carried some kind of bag. Even though the creature seemed to be dawdling, it reached them surprisingly quickly.

And promptly went to sleep.

Vikki stared at the snoring animal. It had a fat little body, a sharp nose with whiskers, tiny ears, and a long thin tail. She poked it, being careful to fold her tip back on itself like a hairpin to avoid spiking the curious beast. It continued to snore, and where she poked it her curled-up tip left a dent. The animal had a texture like dough.

'Meet the Doughmouse,' the Space Hopper whispered. Then he shook his horns in irritation. 'I don't know why I'm whispering. A Doughmouse can sleep through just about anything . . .' his grin broadened into a ∪ '. . . except a "**WAKE UP!**" . . .' the Doughmouse shot to its feet and the contents of the bag it was carrying scattered everywhere '. . . call from a Space Hopper. Doughmouse, you have company.'

'Oh, hi . . .' The Doughmouse gave a gaping yawn, and began to curl up again.

'I said, **WAKE UP!** Be polite this time, and *stay* awake.'

'I'll dough my best,' said the sleepy creature.

'Hopper, you've made the poor little thing spill everything,' said Vikki, her latent maternal instincts aroused by the animal's big round eyes and doleful expression. 'Let me help you pick them up.' The bag was marked 'Doughnut Disturb', and several dozen ring-shaped tubes of cooked dough had spilled out onto the ground.

Moments later, they had contorted themselves into the cups from a twelve-piece tea-set. Chinese willow pattern.

'Doughmouse,' said the Space Hopper, 'allow me to introduce my friend Victoria Line.'

'Dilated to meet you,' said the Doughmouse, swelling alarmingly as if to prove it. Vikki's maternal instincts were about to vanish, but then it shrank back to its previous size. 'Er . . .' The Space Hopper had told it to be polite, and the Doughmouse was a very literal-minded creature. What was the height of politeness when meeting a stranger? Ah, yes! It turned to Vikki and bowed. 'Would both of you care to join me—'

'Join you to what?' asked the Space Hopper. 'That's not a topological transformation!'

'—for tea?'

'That's very kind of you,' replied Vikki, ignoring the byplay, 'but your tea-set has only cups, Mr Doughmouse. No saucers, no plates – and no teapot! I'd say it's a very poor service.'

'And that's a very poor joke,' said the Doughmouse, 'also a very old one. And you're a very forward young lady. Only just arrived, and already you're criticizing my crockery.'

'Vikki is a visitor from Flatland,' the Space Hopper said.

'Oh well, that explains it,' the Doughmouse stated with a shrug. 'Very elegant people, Flatties, but rather rigid in both their geometry and their thinking. And yet ... here you are, Victoria, consorting with me and the Space Hopper, so perhaps you've got more imagination than your fellow geometrymen. I wonder, though, if you have enough imagination for *this*! You criticized my tea-set, and here is my answer!' And with that, the Doughmouse tipped out two dozen ball-shaped doughnuts. Then he turned the bag upside down and jiggled it, muttering to himself, until the bag disgorged the most peculiar doughnut Vikki had ever seen.

It had two holes.

The Doughmouse looked expectantly at her.

After a few seconds' stunned silence, she realized she was expected to react. 'Sorry, but I don't ... what I see is a dozen cups and 25 doughnuts, of which 24 have no hole at all and the other is so very badly made that it's got two. It still isn't a tea-set!'

The Doughmouse gave the Space Hopper a meaningful look. 'It is if you think like a topologist. Let me present my wares in a way that makes sense to your Euclidean eyes.' He held up one of the round doughnuts, and as she watched it flattened itself into a thin pancake, for all the world like a lump of pastry being rolled flat. The pancake's rim tilted and its edge contracted. With a final silent hiccup, it settled into its new shape. The Doughmouse placed the now-transformed doughnut beneath one of the cups.

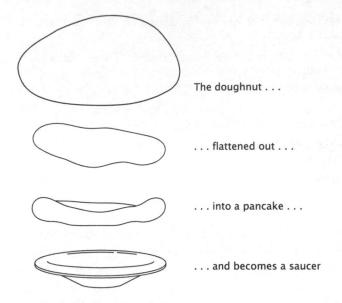

The doughnut . . .

. . . flattened out . . .

. . . into a pancake . . .

. . . and becomes a saucer

'A saucer!' cried Vikki.

Eleven more doughnuts changed into saucers. Twelve more expanded to about twice their size and became plates. Only the two-holed doughnut remained doughnutty.

'Well . . .' said Vikki, half-conceding. But not yet. 'Where's the teapot?'

The Doughmouse used its whiskers to gesture towards the two-holed doughnut.

'That? *That's* not a teapot! Teapots don't have two holes!'

'Really?' replied the Doughmouse.

'No. The tea would trickle out.'

'Oh dear, just my misfortune to bump into a teapot expert! Well, I'm sure you know best. But tell me: does a teapot have a handle?'

'Of course. Otherwise you couldn't pick it up,' said Vikki, getting angry now. The Doughmouse was so *obtuse*.

'So there must be a hole between the pot and the handle for you to put your hand through?'

'Hand?'

'Sorry, I forgot you're a Flatty. Your manipulatory vertex.'

Vikki hadn't thought of the aperture as a hole before, but she had to admit that it was just as much a hole as the one in a doughnut – which wasn't actually *in* the doughnut . . . it was more a place where there could have been dough . . . but . . . there wasn't.

'All right, I accept that in that sense a teapot has one hole. But your doughnut has two . . .' Her voice trailed off. 'Oh! A teapot has a hole in the top!'

The Doughmouse gave her an enquiring stare. '*That's* not a hole.'

'Yes it is! It's a hole for putting the tea into the pot.'

'Ah, but that "hole" only goes *in*. It doesn't come out again.'

'Nonsense!' said Vikki. 'A hole in a wall can go in but come out again. A hole that goes in and does come out again is called a *tunnel*.'

'Terminology, terminology,' muttered the Doughmouse, 'why does everybody get hung up on *terminology*? It's enough to send a body to sleep . . .' It emitted a tentative snorelet, and the Space Hopper administered an admonitory kick. 'Ow! Uh – in Topologica, a hole that only goes *in* isn't a hole at all. It has to come *out* again. Somewhere else.'

'Then why didn't you say what you meant?'

'I did say what I meant – you just didn't *hear* what I meant . . . but don't get me started on the meaning of words, young lady, it's been done. Tell me, when you pour the tea, how does it get out of the pot?'

'Through the spout,' said Vikki. Really, the creature was *extremely* annoying.

'So there has to be a hole in the spout to let the tea out.'

'That's a tube, not a hole!'

'A tube,' said the creature carefully, 'is just a long, thin hole.' It coughed in a self-important way. 'In Topologica, the Rubber-sheet Continent, "long" and "thin" have no significance. A hole is a hole, whatever its size or shape. Though I should be careful how I say that. What do you make of *this* doughnut?' It held up a semitransparent, strangely convoluted mass of dough:

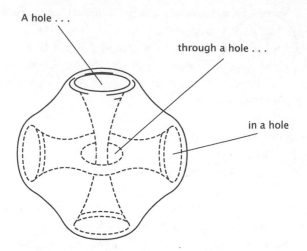

A hole . . .

through a hole . . .

in a hole

'It's a . . . no, it's more of a . . .'

'It's a hole-through-a-hole-in-a-hole,' proclaimed the Dough-mouse.

'That doesn't make a hole lot of sense—' Vikki began, and then stopped. Because actually, it did. Suddenly everything that had been happening *was* starting to make a weird kind of sense. The Doughmouse wasn't as stupid or as annoying as he seemed. 'Hole' was just a rough-and-ready way to describe something infinitely more subtle: *topology*.

'You're telling me that the hole where the tea goes into the pot, and the spout where it comes out, are really just the two ends of the *same* hole?'

'Exactly! So now you can see how my two-holed doughnut turns into a teapot. Think of it as two doughnuts joined together, like Siamese twins. First, I pinch one twin down to make a handle on the side of the other. Then I flatten the bigger one out to make a disc with a small hole. I bend the disc up into a cup-shape, and then stretch it further and shrink the edge of the cup so that it's teapot-shaped. Finally, I pull out the region immediately around the hole into a tube, stretch that to the right length, and bend it into a spout shape – oh, and while I'm at it, I tidy up the shape and position of the handle. Done!'

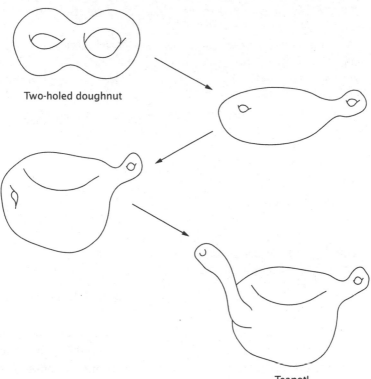

Two-holed doughnut

Teapot!

Topologica, thought Victoria, *is a* very *strange continent. I must be careful. Things aren't necessarily what they seem. I wonder if* – she picked up one of the cups and nibbled gingerly at the rim.

Sweet dough crumbled into her mouth.

She looked inside the teapot. It was full of tea, and none of it seemed to be leaking out. She poured some tea into her half-eaten cup, expecting the cup to soak it up and turn into a sloshy mess. It didn't. It sat there, like normal tea in a normal cup.

'All geometric forms in Topologica lead multiple existences', said the Space Hopper, who had guessed what she was worrying about. 'Mathematically, any shape is topologically identical to anything you can continuously deform it into. But to the inhabitants of this particular world, the *physical* properties of shapes depend on what you use them for. "Context-dependent", that's the phrase.'

'Oh.' Vikki began to pay more attention to the tea, rather than the cup. 'Yuck! There's no milk!'

'An omission that can easily be remedied,' said the Dough-mouse. 'I happen to know that just over the brow of the next hill there lives a cow who will sell us a bottle of milk at a very reasonable price.'

'What is the name of this beneficent beast?' asked the Space Hopper.

'Moobius.'

'And its milk comes in . . .?'

'Klein bottles.'

The Space Hopper sighed. 'I rather thought so.'

*

Wunday 9 Noctember 2099
Whatever next, Diary Dear? A talking cow, would you believe? Not that it *looked* much like a cow – but, after all, a doughnut doesn't actually *look* much like a teacup. Even so, this was a very singular cow . . .

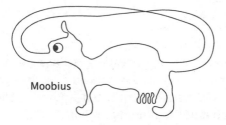

Moobius

*

Victoria wasn't particularly bothered that Moobius the cow was two-dimensional – because, after all, so was she. Nor was she bothered by its extraordinarily long tail, which could wrap all the way round to touch its face. She was a little disturbed, though, when she realized that the cow's tail was glued to its nose. Or, rather, that tail and nose merged seamlessly into each other:

Was the creature *really* a cow with its tail attached to its nose? Might it instead be an elephant with its trunk attached to its bottom? Either way, she wasn't sure she wished to pursue the matter. However, even the remarkable appendage, whatever it was, was less disturbing than the extremely loud music that seemed to be coming from somewhere inside the cow. They had heard the music growing ever louder as they approached the animal, but for a while they had assumed it must be coming from somewhere else. Now it was clear that the music definitely originated inside (or, the creature being two-dimensional, *on*) the cow itself. At first it had seemed to be coming from the head, but then it migrated to the stomach. At the moment it seemed to be concentrated near the cow's rear end. It was some kind of military march – mostly brass and drums.

'Hello!' shouted Vikki, trying to make herself heard over the din.

'Eh?' said the cow.

'Sorry, but your music is making an awful lot of noise!'

'You'll have to speak up,' said Moobius, 'my music is making an awful lot of noise.'

Vikki put her moth close to the cow's ear and yelled, 'Can't you put a stop to it?'

'Good heavens, no,' said the cow. 'That would be terribly orienting.'

'Surely you mean "disorienting"?'

Moobius shook its head. 'I know what I mean.'

'Well, can you turn it down a bit so that we don't have to shout all the time?'

'I suppose so,' said the cow, somewhat miffed. It jiggled around for a moment, and the noise of the band faded to a low *clickety-clackety-boom*. 'I'd be nothing without my band,' said the cow. 'It's essential to my existence.'

Vikki decided that this was yet another aspect of Moobius the cow that might best be left unexplored, but the Doughmouse must have felt otherwise. 'Oh no it isn't,' it said.

'Oh yes it is!' the cow responded, quick as a flash.

'Oh no it isn't!' Vikki felt that the quality of debate might be improved, but there was no doubting the level of commitment.

'Oh no it isn't!'

'Oh yes it is!'

'Oh yes it is!'

'Oh no it isn't!'

'Oh no it isn't!'

'Oh yes it—'

'*Hold it right there*,' Vikki interrupted, replaying the conversation in her head 'I don't think I *quite* followed that—'

'Let me explain,' said Moobius in a patronizing tone of voice. 'First *he* said "Oh no it isn't" and then *I* said "Oh yes it is" and then *he* said—'

'Not at all,' the Doughmouse objected, '*you* started the argument by saying that it was, though not in those words, and then I made the reasonable point that it wasn't, to which you responded without a single *whit* of justification that it most assuredly *was*, and then—'

'*Eeeeeeeeek!*' Vikki's scream stopped them both. She gathered her breath and tried to calm herself. 'Uh . . . Doughmouse: first you started out saying that Moobius's band *isn't* essential to its existence.' She turned to appeal to the Space Hopper for support, but it seemed to have wandered off. 'Uh . . . when Moobius disagreed, you repeated what you'd said before. But then . . . well, Moobius changed his mind and *agreed* with you, but you promptly changed sides and said that the band *is* essential to Moobius's existence. Then Moobius agreed with *that*, too, but all *you* did was go back to your original position!'

'Sure. But then Moobius changed his mind again—'

'*And so did you!* You were both being completely inconsistent! Don't either of you know which side you're on?'

They stared at her. 'I know which side *I'm* on', said the Doughmouse.

'Which?' demanded Vikki.

'The inside,' said the Doughmouse.

'The *what* side?'

'And you are on the outside,' the Doughmouse added in a helpful tone.

'Uh . . . then what side is Moobius on?'

'Both,' said the cow. 'Well, actually there's only one, and it's on me.'

'You're both talking utter rubbish,' said Vikki.

'Not at all,' said the Doughmouse. 'Haven't you heard the phrase "a side of beef"?'

'Yes, but—'

'Well, that's what Moobius is. A side of beef. Whereas I—'

'Yes?'

'—am an inside of a Doughmouse. And you—'

'*What about me?*'

'—are nearly beside yourself with rage. And I recommend that it remains "nearly", my dear, at least until you visit a space with the property of bilocation.'

With an effort, Vikki took a deep breath before trying to reboot the conversation. 'Moobius. Is. An. Entire. Cow. A side of beef is half a cow, that's why it's called a *side*. If you slice a cow in half from nose to tail – excuse me, Moobius, nothing personal – you get *two* separate sides of beef. One from the left side and the other from the right side. Even Flatland butchers know that, though our cows are mostly oxagons, you know. Er – a cross-breed between hexagons and octagons,' she added apologetically.

'No hoctagons?'

'Well, no, but there's a hogsagon, which yields excellent bacagon—'

'*Keep to the point!*' shouted Moobius. 'I assure you that I am a *single* side of beef.'

'Rubbish!' said Vikki. 'Nothing has only one side.'

'Well, actually, *nothing* has no sides at all—'

'And *you* were telling the Doughmouse to keep to the point! Of course you've got two sides. Why, even from here I can see that part of you is on the far side and the rest is on the near side.'

The cow grimaced. 'Yes, I *know* that, you pigheaded Flatty, but—'

Vikki made an effort and kept her temper. 'So you've got two sides, Moobius.'

'Only . . . locally. Um . . . you know, what I could really do with is a hosedown. Can you fetch that hose over there, Doughmouse? And since the young lady is so clever and knows so much about bovine anatomy, she can hose me down on *just one side*. Yes?'

'Well – I really don't see why *I* need to do it, but in order to prove my point, OK.'

The Doughmouse came back with a dog collar. 'Got it.'

'No, that's a—'

'In Topologica, nothing is what it seems.'

'No,' said Moobius, 'nothing *isn't* what it seems, because if it's nothing then there isn't anything to *seem*.'

'Oh, do shut up!' snapped the Doughmouse. He handed Vikki the dog collar. 'Grab one end, Victoria.'

'It hasn't got any ends.'

'Yes it has, they look like edges. Grab an edge.' And she did . . . and the Doughmouse pulled . . . and pulled . . . and pulled . . . and the short fat cylinder of the dog collar became longer and longer and longer, and thinner and thinner and thinner, until she found herself holding the end of a hose. She just managed to point it away from herself before a spray of water shot out.

'Hose me! Hose me!' yelled the cow. 'But only on one side, remember!'

'Easy!' said Vikki. First, she peeped round the back to make sure that there was a second side to the cow's face: there was. Then she sprayed water all over the side of the face that was nearest to her. Slowly she worked her way along the flank of the cow until she reached the tail.

'Carry on,' said the cow. 'You haven't finished yet.'

'I know that. But there's only the tail left to do.' Vikki worked her way back along the cow's tail, checking that the near side was dripping wet but the far side was dry, but about halfway along she found she was having to contort her body to get at the correct side of the tail. 'Hey, Moobius?' she called out. 'Your tail's twisted, did you know that?'

'Tell me about it!' said the cow.

The Doughmouse started to yawn again, and looked round in a vague sort of way for something soft to sleep on. It took the teapot out of its bag, did something to make it grow a good deal bigger, climbed in, and pulled the lid over its head.

Vikki kept on spraying water over Moobius, being careful to keep the far side dry. 'Nearly done, coming back to the nose – hold it.'

'Now what?'

'I'm back to your nose – but it's *dry*!' She glared at it. 'Moobius, have you been sneakily drying yourself while I've been hosing your tail?'

'Not a bit of it,' protested the cow. 'Try looking on the other side.'

'It's – it's dripping wet! Are you playing a trick on me?'

Moobius nodded. 'Yes.' Then it shook its head. 'But not in the way you mean.'

'Can't you ever make up your mind?'

Moobius gave her a level look. 'I always thought that my mind made *itself* up, and only told *me* about it later. But the wet "side" of my face really is the one you started washing, I promise.'

'Then what – *oh*. The twist. In your tail. It – it flips over so that the wet side runs into the dry side. I see it all now. If I keep going I'll spray the whole of your *other* flank, and then go along the *other* side of your tail . . . and finally get back to where I started. The twist makes your two sides join together.'

Moobius nodded. 'Which means that what you thought were two different sides are actually just different parts of the *same* side. So, like I kept telling you, I've only got one side. And I'm not on it: it's on me.'

'Whereas I—'

'Have two separate sides,' said the Space Hopper, reappearing from nowhere with two new companions. 'These guys were looking for the Doughmouse – Vikki, where'd he go?' A resonant snore boomed from the interior of the teapot. 'Oh. You shouldn't have let him go in there. Now we'll have a terrible time waking him up.

'Anyway, *you* have two separate sides because you've got edges that keep your sides separate.'

Vikki thought about this. True, an edge can separate one side of a flat surface from the other, but the Space Hopper's argument had a flaw. 'Moobius has edges, too.'

'*Edge*,' the Space Hopper corrected. 'Run your eye along it. What you think ought to be two separate edges *also* join up seamlessly.'

'Because of the twist. Again.'

'Of course. Every good tail has to have a twist, you know.'

'Um – I think that's "tale"', said Vikki.

'Tail, tale, so what? It's the *twist* that matters—'

'—so you'll only get one side of beef out of me', Moobius finished.

*

... and that, Diary Dear, is how two people can hold a really interactive but one-sided conversation.

Moobius went on to say that the reason we were getting so confused is that the word 'side' has several meanings. It's not really a question of how many sides a cow has: it's *orientations* that matter.

I'll see if I can explain. Moobius has a resident band – mostly brass, but when I looked closely I saw that there's a drummer with a gigantic bass drum. It always carries the drum on its left – well, what Moobius says is its left. When I first saw it, that's where the drum was.

But when the band marched all the way along Moobius's body, back along its tail, and returned to its starting-point, the drum was on the *right*.

I'd been watching it closely. The drum never switched sides.

Then it clicked. The band doesn't live *on* Moobius. It's *in* it. Like an ink drawing that's soaked right through to the other side. Now, *locally* – that is, near any given place – Moobius has two sides, just like any other surface. But globally – taken as a whole – the twist in its tail makes the two sides join up. As a result, there's no sensible concept of left/right. As the drummer goes round the twist – Diary, stop laughing, you know what I mean – his apparent orientation gets flopped over, so left becomes right and right becomes left.

The Moobius band is nonorientable, that's the point.

And Moobius isn't the only such surface. There's an even weirder nonorientable surface, which Moobius keeps her milk in. A Klein bottle.

The Space Hopper told me why it's called that. It's a Planiturthian name, you see. A mathematician's *joke*. In one region of Planiturth, called Germany – no, not because it has many germs, Diary Dear – the word *klein* means 'small'. But size doesn't matter in Topologica, so that's a red herring. And a Germany-People called Felixklein invented a nonorientable surface in 1882. Unlike Moobius, it had no edges – it was a *closed* surface. Basically, it's a tube that bends round and joins up to itself, like a doughnut.

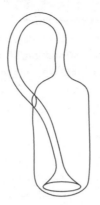

But as it bends round it kind of passes through itself and turns inside-out, so the surface all joins up.

Weirder still, it only passes through itself if you try to embed it in 3D. In 4D it *doesn't*.

Now, the Space Hopper has a private theory about the name *Klein bottle*. He thinks it was originally *Klein's surface*. In Felixklein's day, Germany-People were forever inventing new surfaces and getting them named after themselves. For instance, there was a People called Ernstkummer and he invented *Kummer's surface* – which in Germanyspeak is *Kummersche Flache*, the '-sche' being a possessive ending and *Flache* meaning 'surface'.

So, the Space Hopper reckons, the name started out as Kleinsche *Flache*, Klein's *surface*. But it *looks* like a bottle, and the German for bottle is *Flasche*, so . . .

QED, as we Flatlanders say.

※

The two new creatures the Space Hopper had brought with him had come to join the tea-party. Make it more sociable, he said. Vikki thought this unlikely, though she politely kept the thought to herself. One of the creatures was a very angry-looking horse. The other carried what seemed to be a bottomless bucket of mud, and kept building mud huts with it.

'Who are they?' whispered Vikki.

'The Harsh Mare and the Mud Hutter,' replied the Space Hopper. The two creatures climbed into the teapot to join the Doughmouse, waking it up, and all three began to bicker. Their voices rose and fell.

'I know they *seem* a bit intimidating,' the Space Hopper continued, 'but that's because they *are* intimidating, so it's OK to be intimidated by them, right?'

'But I don't want to be intim— *What the convex hull is that?*'

Another extraordinary inhabitant of Topologica was trotting towards them across the bouncy surface of the Rubber-sheet Continent. Its head, if head it was, was adorned with antlers, if antlers they were ... they seemed to branch and entwine and

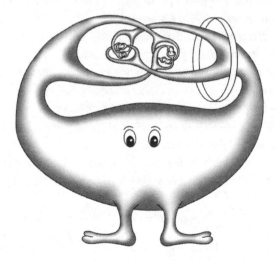

branch and entwine ... and the closer the curious beast got to them, the finer the branches became.

A red sweatband was wound between them.

'Wow!' said the creature, skidding to a halt. 'A tea-party? Great! And visitors from Out-a Space, too! Hi, Hopper – how's tricks?'

'An old friend,' the Space Hopper whispered by way of explanation. 'Whatever you do, don't take him seriously.' He turned to the new arrival and spoke in a more normal tone. 'Vikki: meet my old buddy Alexander the horned sphere.'

'You're a sphere?' Vikki found this difficult to believe. Alexander surely wasn't *the* Sphere: Albert would undoubtedly have mentioned the horns.

'Hey, baby, yeah!' boomed Alexander.

'Er, in a manner of speaking,' the Space Hopper qualified.

'Yeah. My inside is topologically the same as the inside of a Sphere – but my outside is topologically different from the outside of a Sphere. Dig?'

'That doesn't make any sense at all,' said Vikki.

'Sorry to contradict, babe, but it does. You're forgetting the difference between the intrinsic topology of a space, considered on its own, and what happens when it's embedded in another space. Intrinsically I'm a Sphere, but extrinsically I'm not.

'It's the horns, see?' Alexander went on. 'From the inside, pushing out a horn doesn't make me any less spherical. So pushing out lots of horns, even infinitely many, doesn't either. But when seen from the outside, the horns tangle up, whereas the outside of a sphere isn't tangled at all. I'll prove it. Try to remove my sweatband.'

'Uh . . .' Vikki began. Those horns looked *sharp*. Fractal, even.

'Go on, try,' the Space Hopper encouraged her, 'give it a tug.'

Vikki tentatively pulled on the sweatband, but she couldn't dislodge it from its loop around the horns. 'It's . . . stuck!'

'"Homotopically nontrivial" is the phrase ya want, babe, but ya dead right. But . . .' The horned sphere's horns started to shrink back into its body. 'If I now turn myself into a bog-standard sphere . . . Try again, kiddo.'

By now the horned sphere had turned into a perfectly round ball. The sweatband was wrapped round it somewhere close to what a Planiturthian would have called the Tropic of Cancer.

Vikki reached over and, without the slightest difficulty, lifted it off.

'See? My *inside* topological shape never changed, but now I've got a null-homotopic sweatband!'

'Uh?'

'It can be pulled off, OK? So my outside topology *has* changed.'

'Indisputably', said Vikki.

The bickering inside the teapot stopped, and the Harsh Mare

poked her nose over the edge. '*You* may not dispute it, madam, but *I* will dispute *anything!*'

'No you won't,' came the voice of the Mud Hutter.

'Yes I will,' insisted the Harsh Mare, ducking back into the teapot. *Snore*, the Doughmouse contributed to the debate. The bickering intensified.

'Oh dear,' said the Space Hopper, 'I think we may have outstayed our welcome. Time we went.'

And they did.

7

ALONG THE LOOKING-GLASS . . .

'This stuff about one-sided surfaces is all very interesting,' said Vikki, 'but it's just intellectual fun and games, isn't it? You can't really *use* it for anything.'

The Space Hopper gave a few thoughtful bounces. 'That depends on what you mean by "use",' he said. 'If you mean *direct* application, then maybe not. I did read once about someone using a Moobius band as a conveyor belt, because that way the wear on its surface was halved – but you could achieve the same thing by using an ordinary cylindrical belt and then turning it over to use the other side, so I can't personally see the point. Except perhaps a small saving on maintenance.'

'So you don't—'

'I don't think there are many *direct* applications. But most applications of maths are indirect. It plays out its roles behind the scenes. And there are plenty of ways to use topology. But you were talking specifically about one-sided surfaces. I *do* know one place where such things turn up naturally, and the associated ideas are certainly useful. Ready? Let's go!'

Vikki scarcely had time to prepare herself for the transition before her VUE reconfigured . . .

*

This was a bleak and oppressive world. A seemingly endless sandy desert stretched away in all directions. It was flat and featureless.

'I don't like this place,' said Vikki.

'Why not?'

'It feels lonely and unforgiving. And nothing's happening.'

'Not yet. Don't judge geometries by first appearances, Vikki. Some of the most beautiful geometries start out looking most austere. If you reserve judgement, you will find that this is a very elegant world indeed.'

'Hmmph.' Vikki was unimpressed. 'Where are we, anyway?'

'We have landed somewhere on the Projective Plain. And it's not as deserted as it seems. It's teeming with wildlife.'

'Wildlife? There isn't so much as an *ant*!'

'Not so. The Projective Plain is inhabited by lions.'

'Lions?'

'Projective lions.' The Space Hopper saw Vikki gasp, and her eyes flashed wildly to and fro. 'Don't worry – they're friendly. So friendly, in fact, that *any* two projective lions always meet.'

'Meet? Meet what?'

'Each other.'

'Meet each – *where?*'

'Somewhere. At some projective point – which is to say, at some location in the Projective Plain. Precisely where depends on the lions. Why, right now a lot of them are all meeting *here*.'

'Lions? Lots? Here?' Vikki's voice was edging upwards.

'Don't worry, they're harmless. Anyway, you're a lion yourself.'

'Pardon?'

'Victoria Lion.'

'That's Victoria *Line*, you buffoon!'

'Which, in the local jargon, is pronounced "lion". The difference is that *you* are a Euclidean lion – well, part of one, anyway – whereas *they* are projective lions. And it's a very significant difference, because in Flatland you can have parallel lions – sorry, *lines* – which never meet, but on the Projective Plain every lion meets every other lion at one, and only one, point.'

'Crazy!'

'Not at all. And to get back to your original question: just like a Klein bottle, the Projective Plain has only one side. And it's very useful, for example in art and perspective drawing.'

'To me it looks like an entirely normal plain – I mean, plane,' said Vikki.

'Yes, it does, and *looks* is definitely the word. But as we explore the Projective Plain and get to know the lions, you'll come to see that I'm telling the truth. This is a far stranger world than it appears.'

'It certainly is,' said Vikki. 'For a start, I can't see any lions.'

'You can't? Oh, my mistake – I forgot to adjust your point of VUE to make them visible. They are infinitely thin, you see. Well, they would be, wouldn't they?'

'Why?'

'Because they live in a desert and they're very friendly. So of course they don't get much to eat. And that makes them infinitely thin, so to the untutored eye they are completely invisible. But if I make the right adjustments to the VUE's settings . . .'

Suddenly a blue glow came into being – a long, thin line, stretching away to the distant horizon. Vikki turned, and it stretched away behind her to the horizon in *that* direction, too.

'That's a projective lion?'

'Apart from the artificial blue tinge, yes.'

'It looks just like an ordinary lion to me. I mean, "line".'

'It does, but it's not. Let me reveal another lion, and you'll see the difference immediately.' Now a thin red lion brightened into visibility.

Vikki stared at the two lions. They marched off to the horizon together. As far as she could see, they were perfect parallels. But the Space Hopper had said . . .

'I thought you said there were no parallel lions in the Projective Plain?'

'I did.'

'But these two lions *are* parallel!'

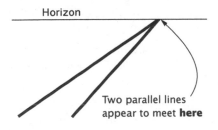

Horizon

Two parallel lines appear to meet **here**

'Really?'

'They don't meet anywhere!'

The Space Hopper did a double take. 'They don't?'

'No. They seem to converge as they go towards the far horizon, but that's an optical illusion.'

'It is?'

'Well, it would be on Flatland. I'd have thought that on the Projective Plain . . . oh, maybe not. New space, new rules.'

'Now you're talking. This space runs on projective geometry, not Euclidean geometry. Think how many paintings include the horizon as a genuine line. Why is that? One reason is that when artists want to paint a scene, they *project* that scene onto a flat sheet of canvas or paper. Another is that Planiturth is round, but even if it were an infinite Euclidean plane, they'd still draw a horizon – because if you looked, that's what you'd see. In effect, they draw lines from every object in the scene to their eye, and where that line hits the canvas, that's where they paint that object. It's like looking out of a window and tracing what you see on the glass. If the object is at infinity, in the projective sense, it may still correspond to a point on the glass – and if it does, you have to draw it to make the picture look right. So projective geometry is a good geometry for thinking about perspective.'

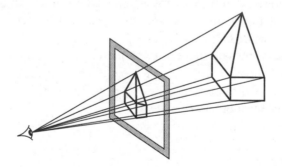

Vikki was assailed by an unexpected twinge of pain. 'Damn, I'm getting blisters on my endpoints from all this space travel. I'm going to take my shoes off.'

(You may be wondering why a line needs shoes – and if so, where she wears them. Well, shoes are a universal female attribute throughout the unbounded Mathiverse. They're an essential fashion accessory. Moreover, they always come in pairs – otherwise they would not be shoes. To be sure, the millipods of the Amazin' Basin have to wear five hundred pairs, but that's an extreme case. Victoria Line wore a normal pair of shoes: a left shoe for her front endpoint, and a right shoe for her rear one. She was always getting them mixed up, and that was a nuisance because then they didn't fit.)

She eased off her shoes and inspected her endpoints for blisters. The left end was fine, so she put that shoe back. But the right end was sore.

The Space Hopper made vague passes in the air, and a container of ointment appeared. He passed it to Vikki, and she massaged some into her sore foot.

'Let me ask you something, then,' said the Space Hopper, as if their conversation hadn't been interrupted. 'Is the horizon a genuine *line* in Flatland?'

'Yes.'

'Then where is it?'

'A long way away.'

'How far? If the horizon exists, then it must be in a definite place. So how far away is the point on the horizon where two parallel lines would meet – if they were extended far enough?'

'Well . . . at the edge.'

'It's a long way to the edge of a plane. Infinitely long. The place where parallel lines appear to meet is at infinity. In the Euclidean plane of Flatland, infinity doesn't exist. You can go as far as you like, but you can't actually *get* to infinity. So the horizon *looks* like a line, but it doesn't really exist. When the eye looks at parallel lines, they appear to meet. Parallel lines don't exist in the geometry of the visual system, so we need a new kind of geometry, one in which *any* two lines can meet. And that's what happens on the Projective Plain.'

Vikki found this hard to believe. 'Infinity can't exist. It's just an ideal concept.'

'Really? I think you'd better come with me. We're going lion-tracking.'

*

Twoday 10 Noctember 2099
What the Space Hopper meant, Diary Dear, is that we were going to follow the parallel lions and see where they met. In short, we

were going to walk to the horizon! Totally mad, I thought, just as usual: the poor creature doesn't have much of a brain anyway, and what it has seems to have flipped.

Wrong again! I'm beginning to think that the opposite is true: that the Space Hopper's bulbous head is *all* brain, and a first-class one at that. He just *behaves* like a nutcase, for dramatic effect.

Be that as it may, we followed the parallel lions, and something very funny started to happen. (Well, the first thing that happened was that I realized I'd left my right shoe behind. The ointment had been so effective, and my feet had felt so comfortable as a result, that I hadn't noticed.)

I pointed this out to the Space Hopper, but he said not to worry, we'd be back where we started shortly. That seemed unlikely, since we were heading for the horizon, but I've learned not to argue with him.

Anyway, as I was saying, something funny happened. You know that normally, when you walk towards the horizon, it just moves away from you – like a Planiturthian rainbow. But on the Projective Plain the horizon behaves quite differently. It stays where it is, and you get closer to it.

I first realized we were actually *reaching* the horizon when I heard the growling. At first it was so faint that my ears couldn't really focus on it, but slowly the noise grew until it was loud and clear.

I asked the Space Hopper what the noise was. Fool. 'Oh, that's the lions meeting!' it told me. 'Having a conversation.' And you know, when I listened really closely, I began to make out words. As far as I could tell, the lions' conversation went like this:

'Pleased to meetcha!'
'Pleased to meetcha!'
'Pleased to meetcha!'
'Pleased to meetcha!'

And so on. Not a very *interesting* conversation, I told the Space Hopper. 'But a very friendly one,' he said.

Then, suddenly, we straddled the horizon: the Space Hopper was on the far side, and I was on . . . well, you appreciate, Diary, that whatever side I am on is by definition the near side, and that's where I was.

We were there.

I told the Space Hopper that it was a funny edge that could be straddled. I mean, the bit he was standing on *shouldn't have been there*. Well, in his usual smart-alecky manner he insisted on pointing out that if it wasn't there, he wouldn't be able to stand on it . . . I hate that kind of conversation, don't you?

Well, things got a bit heated for a while, but the upshot of the conversation was that on the Projective Plain, the horizon exists, but it's not an edge. In fact, there *isn't* an edge. What there is, is—

*

'Infinityville,' said the Space Hopper, proudly.

There was a notice scratched in the sand. It bore the symbol ∞. Beneath it was written, POPULATION ∞.

'What's that figure eight thing?' Vikki asked.

'That's not a figure eight,' said the Space Hopper, 'it's the symbol for "infinity". And that's where we are.'

The sign changed: POPULATION ∞ + 1.

'Ah, a birth,' said the Space Hopper.

The sign flickered for an instant, then reverted to POPULATION ∞.

'Uh – a death?' asked Vikki, in a quiet voice.

'What? No, not at all. That would look like POPULATION ∞ – 1. But then it would change back to POPULATION ∞ again. You see, infinity *plus* one equals infinity, and infinity *minus* one equals infinity. Infinity, basically, is Where Things Happen That Don't. Which is why parallel lions meet there. The Projective Plain is very similar to Flatland, in a lot of ways, except for this business of parallel lions meeting. Which changes things a lot – for instance, "distance" doesn't make much sense.'

'Is that why we got to infinity so quickly?'

'Of course. Anyway, like I said, on the Projective Plain parallel lions always meet. And, like Flatland, they meet at just one point.'

Vikki digested this. 'Hang on. In Flatland, parallel lines meet at the horizon, which isn't a genuine line. Here, apparently, it is. But even so, in Flatland parallel lines meet at *two* points. One at one end, one at the other.'

'Not on the Projective Plain,' said the Space Hopper.

Vikki turned round. In the *far* distance she could see the two parallel lions converging. She looked at her feet (one still unshod):

the lions met a short distance away. Well, it looked short, but distance has no meaning on the Projective Plain . . . No matter. She pointed out the *other* meeting point for the parallel lions.

'There? No, that's not a second meeting point. That's the same place as here.'

'But it's not here. It's over there.'

'Yes, but over there is actually here. The ends of the lions are one, not two – look, all you have to do is use the zoom facility on your VUE and you'll see what I mean.'

Vikki boosted the magnification and inspected the second meeting point from close up. And what she saw was—

Herself.

Talking to the Space Hopper.

The other Vikki seemed to be inspecting something through the zoom facility of her VUE.

Wild!

'You're saying we're over there as well as over here?'

'No, I'm saying that over there *is* over here. It's the same point. We're just looking at it along two different directions. It's like seeing some object, *and* seeing it in a mirror. One ray of light comes straight from the object; the other ray *bends* when it hits the mirror. Or it's like a mirage, when you see the same object in different directions because hot air refracts light.'

'But you said that these lions are straight.'

'They are. But they still bend. On the Projective Plain, lions can be straight and yet close up. Like a circle – in fact, in a topological sense they *are* circles – except that these circles are *straight*.'

'I don't understand,' said Vikki in bewilderment.

'That's because I'm using Flatland words to describe a projective phenomenon', said the Space Hopper, pompously. 'Let's have another go.' He pondered for a few moments. 'OK. Mathematically, infinity is just an abstract construct, so we can endow it with any properties we want. I happen to want lines to meet at only one point. So I insist that the "two" points at infinity, at either end of a pair of parallels, are considered as the same. It may sound odd, but it works. It's sort of like bending the lines round into a circle, except that they stay straight.'

'Clear as mud!'

'Good. So we can think of the Projective Plain as the usual plane, *plus* a "line" at infinity, *plus* the rule that the opposite ends of pairs of parallels meet the line at infinity in the same point.'

'I just can't visualize it.'

'On the contrary, Vikki, it's how your visual system actually works.'

'Well, I'm having trouble getting it into my head in one piece. And it's not at all clear to me why the Projective Plain has only one side, as you say. The ordinary plane has two sides, top and bottom.'

'Yes, but the top surface and the bottom surface get joined together at infinity because of the rule about the endpoints of parallels being the same', said the Space Hopper. 'Don't try to think about it. Just follow me. We'll keep following the same parallel lions as before, in the same direction, and see where we get to.'

They trudged on. Now Vikki's shoeless vertex started to hurt. She was just about to complain when the Space Hopper called a halt. 'We're there.'

'Where?'

'You tell me. What's that lying on the ground?'

Vikki followed the line of his horns. 'My shoe!'

'So?'

'So we've come back to where we started! You're right, the lions here really do seem to go round in circles!' She glanced back to check: a pair of parallel lions led towards the distant horizon, met, and diverged again. With the zoom facility of her VUE, she could see herself standing next to one of her shoes. Shoes! She seized the accidental castoff and pulled it onto her bare right endpoint—

It wouldn't fit.

She inspected it.

'Hang on, this is a left shoe! The one I lost was a right shoe!'

'Have a look through the VUE,' said the Space Hopper. She did. In the distant image, she was definitely looking at a right shoe.

'What you see in the VUE is the same shoe as the one before your eyes,' said the Space Hopper.

'Then why has it changed into a left shoe?'

'It hasn't. *You* have changed into a left Victoria. Yes, I *know* you're a line, so that ought to make no difference, but you have a sense of left and right, and *that* has changed. Your left shoe has changed into a right shoe, and your right foot has changed into a left foot. It is as though you have passed through a mirror, but there *isn't* a mirror. The Projective Plain is a one-sided surface. We're not standing *on* that surface, as a Spacelander would stand: we are *in* the surface, like drawings inscribed upon it, but going all the way through, like ink on tissue paper. And the geometry of the Projective Plain means that when you slide an object along a lion until it gets back to where it started from, it returns as its own mirror image.'

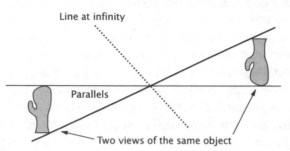

Line at infinity

Parallels

Two views of the same object

Vikki began to wail. 'I need another shoe! This one won't fit!'

The Space Hopper gave her a kindly look. 'You're tired, too,' he said. 'Give me the shoe, and wait here. I won't be long.' She watched as the Space Hopper headed off along the lions, back towards where they'd come from, carrying her unwanted, wrong-footed shoe. He dwindled into the distance . . .

. . . and tapped her on the shoulder.

She jumped.

'Sorry. I thought you'd see me coming.'

'I was still watching you *going*.'

'On the Projective Plain, coming and going are the same thing. Anyway, I've brought your shoe.'

'The same one?'

'Of course. You don't think I can create shoes out of thin air, do you?'

'Then it's useless. I've tried it and it won't fit.'

'Try it now.' She did. It fitted.

She gave the matter some serious thought. 'Oh! Now I see – if the shoe is carried *once* round a lion, it flips. But carry it round a second time, and it flips again—'

'Getting it back to where it was originally,' said the Space Hopper.

❋

Threeday 11 Noctember 2099
Dear Diary,

My experiences with the missing shoe have convinced me that the Projective Plain really does have only one side. It acts like a sort of mirror, but instead of going *through* the looking-glass, you go *along* one.

Moreover, the Projective Plain captures the geometry of *projections* – which are important. For instance, I now see that every time anyone takes a photograph, their camera *projects* the outside world onto the film. The Space Hopper says that by using projective geometry, you can compare a photograph with the real thing and work out where the camera must have been (no, don't ask me how, I gather it's a bit technical). So one-sided spaces are useful after all.

Funny old world, isn't it?

8

GRAPE THEORY

Flatlanders are so *emotional*, the Space Hopper thought. Vikki had gone off in a huff for no reason at all. Just because he was explaining the geometry of the Projective Plain in exquisite detail, that was no justification for being antisocial! Then it belatedly occurred to him that what he thought of as 'exquisite', others might well find 'excruciating'. For once, the bouncy creature felt depressed. He'd offended the little Flatlander by being overenthusiastic. He ought to do something to bring back the sparkle to her endpoints . . .

Of course – the very thing!

He scuttled over to where she was trudging along between the parallel lions. 'I don't know about you,' he said, 'but I could do with a drink. I know a *great* bar just a few paraspatial leaps away in the Mathiverse. Owned by a turtle, has his own vineyard, makes *great* wines – Chordonnay, Modulot, Quadrati, Rhombolo, Bouzo . . . Care to join me?'

Vikki perked up at once. A bar sounded a lot more exciting than a desert. And a paraspatial bar at that! Within a few minutes they were on their way to Running Turtle's, which was situated on a prime piece of surreal estate in one of the more fashionable zones of metaspace. Zone 999999999959, in fact – as prime as they come. Not only that, it had an excellent view of the Galois Fields, the Lakes of Wada, and the Devil's Staircase. They would be able to watch the tangent cones grazing.

❖

Elsewhere in the Mathiverse – not that there was a Where to be Else in – the Square family were settling down to their evening meal.

'I do wish Vikki would come home', said Lester, out of the blue.

Jubilee went rigid. It was the first time that Lester had mentioned his sister for weeks.

'What's it like in Numerica, Mum?' asked Berkeley, and Jubilee seized on the distraction like a drowning polygon being thrown a length of rope.

'It's very . . . numerical,' she said. 'They have very big houses and very big cars and they all eat very big meals.'

'Do they have very big cats and dogs?' asked Les, wide-eyed.

'Er – no. I think their cats and dogs are the same size as ours. And they're the usual star shape, too.'

'What sort of big meals do they eat? Giant oxagons?'

'Um . . . giant *lumps* of oxagon. In a bun. They call them hogsburgers, I think.'

'Surely it ought to be oxburgers, dear,' said Grosvenor. 'Hogsburgers ought to be made from hogsagons.'

'I think someone once told me,' said Lee tentatively, 'that hogsburgers are called hogsburgers because they were invented in a town named Hogsburg. Not because they're made from hogsagons. And the Hogsburglars happened to make their hogsburgers from oxagon meat, just to confuse everyone.'

'Well I never,' said Grosvenor. 'Never knew that.' He lapsed into silence.

'Is Vikki eating hogsburgers?'

'Of course,' said Lee. 'Just like any native Numerican.'

'Is she eating them right now, Mum?'

'Probably, dear.'

'And will Vikki be coming home soon, Dad?'

Lee saw the expression on Grosvenor's face, and tried to steer the conversation back to safer lines. 'Not *very* soon, Les, no. Not very soon.'

'Why not? Is she having too much fun?'

Whatever gave the boy that idea? Grosvenor thought.

'I'm sure she's having some fun, Les,' said Lee, 'but definitely not too much! No, she's got to stay there for quite a long time yet, because . . . er . . .'

'Because she's working very, very hard,' said Grosvenor.

'Yes, that's right,' Lee agreed. 'I'm sure that's exactly what Vikki is doing right now.'

*

Running Turtle's was, in fact, run by a large turtle, who poured the drinks and mixed the cocktails himself. It had a pleasant balcony with lots of small, cloth-covered tables, nicely sheltered from the afternoon breezes. The only mildly dissonant note was struck by the large number of small orange snails that were crawling over the patio, the railings, and several of the tables.

'Why is he called *Running* Turtle?' Vikki asked. 'He mostly stands still.'

'Listen.'

Vikki did so, and she heard the turtle muttering under its breath, '. . . makes seven hundred and ninety-six; *five* plus seven hundred and ninety-six makes eight hundred and one; *twelve* plus eight hundred and one makes eight hundred and . . .'

'He's adding things up.'

'Exactly. Keeping a running turtle.' Vikki kicked him.

Running Turtle had undergone an Out-of-Cosmography experience like Vikki – dislodged from his own universe by a random metaspatial fluctuation. He had decided that he preferred the Mathiverse to home, and had set up as a bar-owner in partnership with two other Mathiversian immigrants, Woolly Coati and the Chicken Mock Nugget (who organized the bar food).

It soon became clear that Running Turtle had a problem.

'Blasted Tetrahedro!' said Running Turtle in annoyance.

'Pardon? I don't speak Turtle, I'm afraid—' Vikki began.

'And blast the Enneagono, the Triangulo, the Trapezoidia, the Frustumo, the Chordonnay, and above all the Circumfrovese!' he added heatedly.

'What?'

'Grapes. I've got seven (. . . plus eight hundred and thirteen makes eight hundred and twenty . . .) varieties of grape that I need to test, to see which gives the best wine. I want to plant them in plots in my vineyard overlooking the Galois Fields. Unfortunately my hill is narrow, and I can plant only three (. . . plus eight hundred and twenty makes eight hundred and twenty-three . . .) varieties of grape on each plot of land. And I want to minimize the effects of different soils and different exposure to metaspatial illumination, too.'

'You've got *eight hundred and twenty* varieties of grape?'

'No, just seven (. . . plus eight hundred and twenty-three makes eight hundred and thirty . . .) just . . . just the smaller number I mentioned. I daren't say it, or I'll be forced to add it to the running total. It's a habit of mine, I just can't seem to—'

'In matters of viticulture,' the Space Hopper interjected pompously, 'good experimental design and hypothesis testing are essential to eliminate error.'

'I agree with every word I understand, my friend. And I've drawn up some requirements which I believe will achieve those aims.' With a flourish, Running Turtle produced a sheet of paper on which was written:

Seven varieties of grape are to be arranged in plots. Each plot contains exactly three different varieties. The following conditions must hold:
- Any two plots have exactly one variety in common.
- Any two varieties lie in exactly one common plot.

'Very clearly expressed,' said Vikki. 'What's the problem, then?'

'I can't find an arrangement that satisfies my conditions,' said Running Turtle sadly.

'Any ideas?' the Space Hopper asked Vikki.

'None,' she replied, brushing several of the tiny snails to the ground. 'Running Turtle, just be grateful your problem's not about geometry! This crazy Space Hopper will stuff your mind with parallels that meet at infinity, circles that are straight lines, and surfaces that have only one side!'

'Don't you think Running Turtle's problem sounds *geometric*, then?' asked the Space Hopper.

'Geometric? It's about grapes! Which reminds me – I'm hungry.'

There was a *whoosh*, and there appeared a stocky creature covered in feathers and with a rubber beak. It thrust a menu in front of her.

'Oh – thanks. Who are you?' asked Vikki, startled by the rapidity of the response.

'I am the Chicken Mock Nugget. Today's special is sugar-coated rat-on-a-stick followed by a choice of kipper blancmange or pond-weed pudding.'

Vikki made a face, glanced down the menu, and ordered a fruit salad, while privately wondering what she would find on her plate.

'Geometry can be about grapes,' the Space Hopper persisted. 'Mathematics is universal, and its truths apply in many different interpretations. As instance of which: suppose I replace "plot" by "line" and "variety of grape" by "point". Then the Turtle's conditions become:

> Seven points are to be arranged in lines. Each line contains exactly three different points. The following conditions must hold:
> - Any two lines have exactly one point in common.
> - Any two points lie in exactly one common line.

See? It's geometry.'

'Hmm,' said Running Turtle. 'But grapes, small and round though they may be, are not points. And plots of land, even if long and narrow, are not lines.'

'True – but irrelevant,' said the Space Hopper. 'We're talking about abstract properties of *arrangements* of objects, not the objects themselves. Logically, it makes no difference what *names* we call them. As the great Planiturthian mathematician David-hilbert said, the logical structure of geometry should make equal sense if the words "point", "line", and "plane" are replaced by "beer mug", "chair", and "table". Names don't matter.'

'I don't think I'd be happy if my beer mug were replaced by a point,' said Running Turtle.

'Look at what *kind* of geometry we've got here. Is it Euclidean?'

'Um – no', said Vikki. 'It's got to be a form of geometry in which there are no parallel lines. Because one of the conditions is that *any* two lines have a point in common. And that condition fails in Euclidean geometry.'

The Space Hopper nodded energetically. 'Right. But that condition holds in *projective* geometry. So Running Turtle's little problem is really about a Projective Plain. A *finite* Projective Plain. It *is* a geometric problem, but the geometry has finitely many points. Or, in this case, baby space hoppers.'

'*Baby space hoppers?*'

'They're the most suitable materials to hand. I could have used grapes, but I don't see any. And for some reason this patio is crawling with baby space hoppers.' He pointed at the things she'd thought were snails. 'Must be the breeding season, though nobody told *me*.' The Space Hopper made a low whistling noise and seven babies – they really *did* look like little shell-less snails, bright orange with tiny antennae – crawled up the leg of the table and arranged themselves in a semicircle in front of him.

'Baby space hoppers!' said Running Turtle in a hopeless voice. 'He's going to solve my wine problem using *baby space hoppers!*'

Numbers from 1 to 7 appeared on the sides of the space hoppers, as if by magic. 'These babies correspond to your seven varieties of grape: Tetrahedro = 1, Enneagono = 2, and so on. OK?'

Running Turtle nodded. He no longer had the energy to disagree.

'Now,' said the Space Hopper, addressing the babies, 'I want you lot to form yourselves into seven lines of three. Got that? OK, then. Right: numbers 1 and 2, just line up somewhere – yes, that'll do fine! Now, another of you – yes, number 6, I saw you volunteer – stand in between them. Good, that's one line of three. Now, number 3, you go and stand somewhere off to the side – that'll do nicely. Number 4, stick yourself in between 2 and 3. And number 5, stick yourself in between 1 and 3. Great, now that's *three* lines.'

'What about me?' squeaked number 7.

'Oh. Uh – just sit right in the middle, will you? Now, if numbers 4, 5, and 6 jiggle about a bit – stay in line with the other guys, OK? – then we ought to be able to get three more lines. Number 4: just shift along a bit so that you're in line with 7 and 1, but stay in line with 2 and 3, yes? Good. Number 5, you do the same kind of thing, in line with 7 and 2 as well as 1 and 3. And Number 6, you get in line with 7 and 3 as well as 1 and 2.

'Excellent! So now we've got six lines. Vikki, what's the seventh?'

'I can't see one.'

'No, I mean: if there was one, what would it have to be?'

'Dunno.'

'Remember Running Turtle's rules? Any two points lie on a line and any two lines meet at a point. Look at number 4. Which babies is he in line with right now?'

'Er – 7, 1, 2, and 3.'

'Not 5 or 6?'

'Well – he's in a line with either of them, of course, but there's nothing else in the same line.'

'So it seems, yes. Suppose numbers 4 and 5 form part of another line. It has to meet line 1–2–6 somewhere, according to Running Turtle's conditions. So where?'

'Well, it can't be number 1 because 1 and 5 already lie on line 1–5–3, and there can't be two lines that contain them. And it can't be number 2 because 2 and 5 already lie on line 2–5–7, and there can't be two lines that contain *them*, either. So that only leaves number 6.'

'Right.'

'Which won't work, because 4, 5, and 6 lie on a circle, not a line.'

'Right.'

Vikki looked pleased.

'And wrong. What did Davidhilbert say?'

'Something about beer mugs . . . oh. There's no reason why a "line" should *look* like a line.'

'No. Especially since it represents a plot of land. We just *deem* (lovely word!) points 4, 5, and 6 to form the seventh "line". And then, by a miracle, we find that Running Turtle's conditions are all satisfied.'

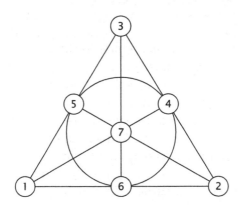

The Chicken Mock Nugget returned with Vikki's food. She was relieved to see that the fruit salad actually was a fruit salad. Raspberry and radish. The chicken sat down next to her.

'In terms of the original problem,' said the Space Hopper, 'I just list the triples of "points" on each "line", and this is what I get:

1–2–6
1–3–5
1-4-7
2–3–4
2–5–7
3–6–7
4–5–6

The numbers 1 to 7 are the varieties of grape. The list corresponds to the seven different plots, each containing three varieties. And both your conditions hold. "Any two plots have exactly one variety in common." Well, the first two plots, 1–2–6 and 1–3–5, have just 1 in common. Plots 2–3–4 and 4–5–6 have just 4 in common, and so on. "Any two varieties lie in exactly one common plot." That's true too. For instance, varieties 1 and 5 lie in 1–3–5, and in none of the other plots. And varieties 3 and 6 lie in 3–6–7 only. You can check them all if you really want to.'

The chicken wasn't quite sure. 'But the *curved* line isn't—'

'It has to be drawn in a curve, Chicken Mock Nugget, because the "points" and "lines" aren't *real* points and lines, they're varieties of grapes and plots of land! Look at the list! It works! Do you *care* that one "line" is bent?'

'Uh – no. It wouldn't stop Running Turtle planting those combinations of grape varieties, would it?'

'Not at all. Finite geometry is all about combinations, you don't actually *need* to draw diagrams.'

'Though the diagram does have its uses,' said Vikki. 'It's a lot easier to remember than a list. And you can *see* that it satisfies all three conditions. You don't really have to check everything so laboriously.'

'Great,' said Running Turtle. 'I'll tell Woolly Coati to get planting tomorrow. In the meantime, perhaps you and your lady-friend would join us in a relaxing wine tasting.'

*

Several bottles later, Woolly Coati happened to mention that he, too, had some grapes to test. 'I've got thirteen varieties, though, and my plots are larger: each can hold four different varieties. But I still want Running Turtle's two rules to hold.'

'Terrific!' muttered the Space Hopper, thinking rapidly. *Thirteen points, in lines of four, each pair of lines meeting in a unique point and each pair of points lying on a unique line. That's* another *finite Projective Plain!* 'Can do. But,' he added, determined to extract the maximum advantage, 'I'll only tell you if you let me tell it *right*. I want to explain where the answer comes from, as well as what it is.'

'Why?' asked Woolly Coati. 'All I want is the answer.'

'Answers without reasons are magic, not mathematics, Woolly Coati. And knowing where that answer comes from might help you solve similar problems later.' Woolly Coati reluctantly agreed, and everyone settled down for a long afternoon. The Chicken Mock Nugget brought nuts and olives, and the wine flowed . . .

'The starting point is the connection between the usual Euclidean plane and the Projective Plain,' said the Space Hopper. 'To get the Projective Plain you take the Euclidean plane and add an extra "line at infinity", which has one point for each *direction* in the Euclidean plane. If a bunch of parallel lines all point in the same direction, they are deemed to meet at the corresponding point on the line at infinity. Right?'

'I wouldn't dream of contradicting', said Running Turtle, downing a glass of full-bodied red.

'I should hope not! Now, to get a finite analogue of a Projective Plain we need to start with a finite analogue of the Euclidean plane. Vikki, does that ring any bells?'

'This Chordonnay is really, really goo— Oh, sorry, Space Hopper. You . . . said something?'

'Does "finite analogue of the Euclidean plane" ring any bells?' repeated the Space Hopper, a little testily.

'My head is ringing a bit, but no bells, Hopper, not one.'

'The Double-Digit District, Vikki! That was a four-point analogue of the Euclidean plane. Two coordinates – but only taking values 0 and 1, remember?'

'Oh, yes, those e-mail messages.'

'Four points forming a square,' said the Space Hopper, beginning to suspect that no one else was listening. 'Now, we have to decide what "straight lines" should be in such a geometry. That's easy: they're the sides of the square and its diagonals. Finally, we add a line at infinity. The top and bottom of the square are "parallel" in the sense that they don't meet. So we add to each a point at infinity. Similarly for the left and right sides. The diagonals form a third pair of parallel lines.'

'But the diagonals of a square *meet*,' Woolly Coati objected, staring into the far distance with his eyes crossed.

'Not on the grid, they don't,' said the Space Hopper. 'In *this* version of the Euclidean plane, only the four corners of the square exist. The diagonals don't meet at a corner, so the centre of the square doesn't count. Since they don't meet *on the grid*, I consider them to be parallel.'

'Fine by me,' said Woolly Coati, opening another bottle.

'Those three sets of parallels provide three extra points, forming a new line – "at infinity" – and we get a system with seven points and seven lines. Of course it's just a disguised version of the 7-point Projective Plain I talked about before.'

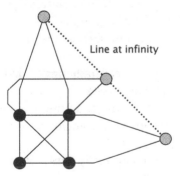

Line at infinity

'Wonderful!' yelled Woolly Coati. 'No it's not', he corrected himself. 'My plot has thirteen varieties, so it'll need thirteen points, not seven.'

'Don't worry, I'm coming to that,' said the Space Hopper.

'Soon?'

'*Fairly* soon . . . To get a 13-point Projective Plain we play the same game, but this time starting with a 3 × 3 grid of nine points. The lines in the grid come in sets of three "parallel" lines. The obvious sets of parallels are the horizontal lines 1–2–3, 4–5–6, and 7–8–9 and the vertical lines 1–4–7, 2–5–8, and 3–6–9. But there are two more sets, which "wrap round" – one consists of the broken diagonals 1–5–9, 2–6–7, and 3–4–8, and the other is made up of the broken diagonals 7–5–3, 4–2–9, and 1–8–6. Now all you have to do is add a "line at infinity" with four points, numbered 10–11–12–13, one for each set of parallels. And then . . . you get a 13-point Projective Plain!

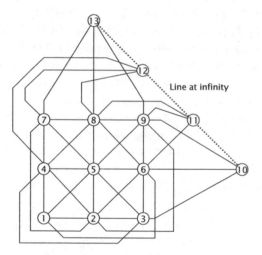

'If you want to, you can read off a list of thirteen plots, each with four varieties of grapes in it, to solve your problem, Woolly Coati.'

'That's amazing!' said the Chicken Mock Nugget. 'Let me try! I'll start with a 4 × 4 grid—'

'Whoops, no, you—'

'—I can do it! Don't interrupt, Hopper, I'll soon get the hang of this . . .'

Two hours later, the sun was beginning to set, and the Chicken Mock Nugget's eyes had a glazed look. The wine had long run out, but that wasn't the reason. 'It doesn't work,' he said finally.

'I either get too many points on lines, or not enough lines through points.'

'I was trying to tell you that hours ago,' said the Space Hopper. 'The method won't work with a 4 × 4 grid because 4 isn't prime. You have to use a square grid whose size is a *prime* number. You could start with a 5 × 5 grid, for instance, and you'd get six sets each containing five "parallel" lines. You'd end up with a Projective Plain containing 31 points arranged in lines of six.'

'Where dose numbersh come fum?' asked Vikki.

'Well, the number of points on each line, *not* counting one point at infinity, is called the order of the Projective Plain. And the total number of points, including all those at infinity, is one plus the order plus the square of the order. Each line contains one more point than the order, and the number of lines is the same as the number of points. So if the order is 2, there are three points on each line, and $1 + 2 + 4 = 7$ points altogether. If the order is 3, there are four points on each line, and $1 + 3 + 9 = 13$ points altogether. And so on.'

'Which – *hic!* – ordersh're possible, Hopper?'

'There are Projective Plains of any prime power order – 2, 3, 4, 5, 7, 8, 9, 11, 13, 16, 17, 19, and so on.'

'What about the rest?' asked Woolly Coati. 'Order 6, for instance?'

'The rest are tough. The Planiturthians have known for a century that there isn't a Projective Plain of order 6. You can't arrange 43 points in lines of seven while obeying the conditions that each pair of lines meets in a unique point and each pair of points lies on a unique line. So, Woolly Coati, if you'd had 43 varieties of grape to test, in plots that could hold seven varieties, you'd have been out of luck.'

'No I wouldn't, I'd have been rich.'

'I was speaking hypothetically.'

'So was I!'

The Space Hopper sighed, and battled on. 'There's been one big advance, which rules out orders 14, 21, 22, and infinitely many other values. But that still leaves a lot of orders unsolved – 10, 12, 15, 18, 20, and so on. It's a hard problem because the number of possibilities get very big. When the order is 10, for instance, there are 111 points, which have to be arranged in lines of 11 apiece. There's no way you could try every possible arrangement, life's just too short. However, a People named Lamthielswierczandmackay devised a computer proof that there isn't an order 10 Projective Plain. It took nine years, on and off. Now, here's an attractive challenge for you – the order 12 case is still open! Of course, an attack along the same lines would take ten thousand million times as long, but . . .' He noticed that his audience had gone to sleep.

How could they possibly doze off when he was telling such a gripping tale? Putting it down to the wine, the Space Hopper deflated itself to a comfortable girth, and joined them.

WHAT IS A GEOMETRY?

Fiveday 13 Noctember 2099
How am I feeling?

Somewhat overhung, Diary Dear, since you ask. Which is a remarkable condition for a Flatlander to be in. We usually suffer from stickouters, not hangovers. But I am definitely overhung, not outstuck.

I hadn't realized that finite geometries could have such a drastic physiological effect!

However, that's not why I'm writing this. I had a really important idea somewhere in the middle of the night, and I need to make a note before I forget it. Here is the idea:

WHAT *IS* A GEOMETRY, ANYWAY?

As you will instantly grasp, it is a stroke of sheer *GENIUS!!!* (she said modestly). You see, the Space Hopper has been so busy carting me round dozens of different geometries that until now it never occurred to me that something was missing. Namely, Diary my Pet, an Organizing Principle.

It was the finite projective geometries that did it. Until then, I'd kind of got it in my head that geometry was about spaces, and spaces were sort of continuous. Smeared-out sort of things, right? The kind of environment you could imagine things wandering around in.

Not just a small collection of dots.

Yes, I know the Space Hopper had taken me to the Double-Digit District and on to Triple-Digit Territory, but all that talk of distances along the edges made me think they were just particular bits of Euclidean space, with the emphasis on their corners. Now I see better. Only the relationships between those corners matter: the rest don't have to be present at all. We were looking at finite geometries then, too.

Anyway, some time in the last twelve hours I awoke from a rejuvenating snooze and realized that I now have no idea whatsoever of what a geometry is. So now I'm bugging YOU with it, Dearest Diary, in order to bug the Space Hopper with it once he, too, regains consciousness. Though, to judge by the Doughmouse-like snores emanating from his general vicinity, I wouldn't hold my breath.

❀

'You mean you haven't worked it out?' said the Space Hopper in incredulity. 'I show you all these marvellous examples of geometries – plane Euclidean, 3D Euclidean, nD Euclidean, fractal, projective, topological, finite projective – to name but a few – and you *still* don't know what you're looking at?'

'That's right. It's just a random grab-bag of unrelated stuff, as far as I can see.'

'Oh dear.' The Space Hopper looked downcast. 'I haven't done my job as well as I thought.' He rubbed his horns together (not easy) in search of inspiration. 'Hmmm . . . ah! Yes! We must temporarily return to the vicinity of Flatland!'

'You mean I can contact Mum and Dad?'

'I really don't think that would be wise at this juncture. It would only upset them, and it might get them into trouble with the authorities.'

'Oh.' Vikki wasn't sure whether to feel disappointed or relieved. Certainly she was having far too much fun to think of going home just yet. But it would have been nice to leave a message. On the other hand, what could she tell them? Anything she said would either have to be a lie, or be totally unbelievable.

A few hours later, subjective time, they hovered a short distance away from the Euclidean plane of Flatland, displaced from it along a metaspatial dimension that can best be captured by the word 'above'.

The Space Hopper had tactfully chosen a region remote from Vikki's house, so as not to risk making her feel homesick. This was somewhere on the edge of a city, and a crowd of polygonal Flatlanders – mostly equilateral triangles and squares, nothing very posh – were making their way through the streets.

'There,' said the Space Hopper. 'Do you see?'

'See what?'

'The essence of geometry.'

'No. All I see is a bunch of polys on their way to work.'

'You don't see a hint of a far-reaching principle that can unify all the different geometries we've visited so far?'

'If it's a hint, it's so subtle that it hasn't registered on my conscious mind, Hopper.'

'But you do see what happens to the polygons when they move?'

'Nothing happens.'

'*Brilliant!*' The Space Hopper bounced with joy. 'You've grasped it immediately! Oh, frabjous day!'

'What in the Plane are you gabbling about?'

The Space Hopper stopped bouncing and its face fell into a ∩. 'You mean – that was just a guess?'

'Hopper, I don't know *what* it was. An expression of ignorance, probably.'

'But you do see that the polygons can move without anything else happening to them?'

'I can't imagine what else *could* happen.'

The Space Hopper's ∪ returned. 'You'll retract that statement in a hurry once I've adjusted the VUEfield to include the part of Flatland we're looking at.'

Flatland . . . well, it *shimmered*. Suddenly, the polygons began to distort as they moved. What had previously been an entirely ordinary equilateral triangle *flowed* into a convoluted swirly shape. You couldn't even tell it was triangular. Squares turned into ellipses, Maltese crosses, and irregular hexagons with curved edges. Some shrank, some swelled to ten times their original size.

It was awful.

Vikki tried not to feel sick. 'Hopper! What are you doing to those poor people?'

'Don't worry, Vikki. They don't feel a thing. To them, everything seems normal. It's just the effect of the VUE. Now, tell me what *didn't* happen to them before when they moved.'

'They – they didn't change shape. Or size.'

'Correct. That's what happens to an object in Euclidean geometry when you *transform* it. Effectively you make it move, though technically that's not quite the same thing. Its shape and size are *invariant* under Euclidean motions. That means they don't change.'

The Space Hopper let Flatland slip back out of the VUEfield, and at once everything returned to normal. 'Watch closely. As each polygon moves, it is being *transformed*. Mostly what you're seeing is *translation* – the whole polygon just moves rigidly without any change of its orientation. But what about *that* one?' The Space Hopper pointed to a small pentagon that was spinning endlessly about its centre.

'That one? That's just a kid playing Dizzy.'

'That kind of transformation is called a *rotation*. And there's one more transformation, which Flatlanders can't actually do to them-selves. But, with a little bit of metaspatial help . . .' The Hopper leaned down, tucked the tip of one horn under a Hexagon that had stopped near a large public building, and neatly flipped it out of the Plane of Flatland altogether. Screeching in fright, he spun like a tossed pancake, and flopped back into the Plane, landing upside down.

'That's called a *reflection*,' said the Space Hopper. 'If you want to perform a reflection while staying in the Plane, you have to use a mirror. But if a third dimension becomes available you can reflect an object by rotating it in the extra dimension.'

'Oh, poor thing! He'll be most upset!'

'He was. Literally. And I can't leave him that way – all his internal organs will be back to front. All his molecules, too. He won't be able to get any nourishment from ordinary proteins. He'll starve unless I do something. So . . .' The unfortunate experimental subject was flipped out of Flatland a second time, reverting to his normal hand-edness. He fled down the street, yelling incoherently.

'If you perform a reflection twice, Vikki, you get back to where you started,' the Space Hopper pointed out. 'Isn't that fascinating?'

'Considering what you've just done to that poor Hexagon, I hope there's some *point* to all of this,' said Vikki in a menacing tone. 'He could have been a friend of mine.'

'Point? Oh, yes, very much so . . . What you've been looking at are rigid motions in the plane. Translations, rotations, reflections. Those transformations characterize the geometry of Flatland: the only meaningful geometric properties of Flatland are the ones that are *unchanged* after a rigid motion. Invariant. Properties like length, area, angle, and so on.'

'Oh.'

'Whereas in topology, say, the range of allowable transformations is far greater. Length, area, or angle are *not* topological invariants. They can all be changed by continuous transformations. They can change in projective geometry, too – but in projective geometry the permitted transformations are projections, so straight lines stay straight. "Straightness" is invariant in projective geometry. But it's not invariant in topology, because there you can take a straight line and bend it.'

Vikki mused upon this new idea. 'You're saying that . . . you can distinguish different geometries by their allowable transformations?'

'That's right.'

'But that still doesn't tell me what a geometry *is*.'

'No, but we're nearly there. Let me tell you about *groups*.'

※

Sixday 14 Noctember 2099
Another e-note for you, Diary Dear, before I forget. This mathematical stuff is very cute, but it's a pig to remember.

A space is a set of objects, conventionally known as *points*. But they don't have to LOOK like points, actually. The set of all triangles in the plane, for instance, is a space. Its 'points' are really triangles. It has six dimensions: two to specify the position in the plane of each vertex.

A transformation, I gather, is in effect a recipe for moving things around inside a space. 'Translate by seven units in a north-easterly direction.' 'Reflect in *this* mirror.' And so on.

Transformations can be combined with one another by doing first one, then the other. For instance, think of a square. Rotate it through 90 degrees, then through 180 degrees. That's two consecutive transformations. The result is the same as 'rotate through 270 degrees' – another transformation. According to the Space Hopper, the word for this is that the transformations form a *group* – meaning that the result of performing any two of them in turn is another one.

A geometry is a space together with a group of transformations of that space. For the 2D Euclidean geometry of Flatland, the space is a Plane and the transformations are rigid motions. For topology, the space is whichever topological object you're interested in, and the transformations are continuous deformations. For 2D projective geometry, the space is the Projective Plain, and the transformations are projections. And so on.

The legitimate geometric concepts, for a given space and transformation group, are the things that are *invariant* under all transformations in the group. Things like lengths and angles for Euclidean geometry; things like 'knotted' for topology; things like 'lying in a straight line' for projective.

This idea, apparently, was invented by Felixklein – yes, the Planiturthian who came up with the Klein bottle. Pretty clever guy, eh? What it means is that ALL of the geometries ever imagined turn out to be different versions of the same idea: groups of symmetries of some space. Now *that's* what I call an intellectual synthesis!

*

'How do the *finite* geometries fit into the Felixkleinian picture, though?' Vikki asked the Space Hopper. 'I don't see how you can *move* objects when space is a finite set of dots.' Another objection struck her. 'And what about fractals?'

'Ah. Those geometries are *also* associated with transformations. For fractals, the allowable transformations are lipeomorphisms.'

'Right, that makes perfect – sorry?'

'Lipschitz diffeomorphisms.'

'*OK*, that *explains* it! Well *done*, Hopper!'

'You're being sarcastic,' said the Space Hopper. 'Look, roughly speaking, a lipeomorphism is a transformation that lives somewhere between a topological transformation and a rigid motion.

Unlike a rigid motion, it can change distances, but there's a limit to how far it can stretch things, whereas there's no limit for topological transformations.

'The important thing is that the fractal dimension of a shape is invariant under lipeomorphisms. So a fractal is a geometry, and its fractal dimension is a legitimate concept within that kind of geometry.'

'I believe you. And the finite geometries?'

'There, the transformations are *permutations* of the points. They're ways to change the labels on the points – to rearrange them, if you like – while preserving the relation of "being in the same straight line". For instance, think about the 7-point projective plane. If I rearrange the points so that the labels 1234567 become 4736215, for instance—'

'Where did *that* come from?'

'A few straightforward but messy calculations, Vikki. Educated trial and error, if you like. Anyway, if you permute the labels like that, you find that every line transforms to a line.'

'I don't quite follow.'

'Well, 1–2–6 is a line. The permutation sends 1 to 4, 2 to 7 and 6 to 1. So 1–2–6 goes to 4–7–1, and that's one of the seven lines. You can check all seven if you want.'

Vikki did. He was right. 'Is that the only possible permutation that sends lines to lines?'

'Not at all. There are exactly 168 of them, as it happens.'

'That's a lot!'

'It is. It means that the 7-point projective plane is extremely symmetric – it has 168 symmetries.'

'I'm not sure what you mean by "symmetry",' said Vikki.

'Ah! That's the most important idea of all!' said the Space Hopper. 'What does "symmetric" mean in ordinary language?'

'Ummm . . . well-proportioned? Elegant?'

'Yes. Mostly, people use the word in a metaphorical sense. Sometimes they mean something more specific, though: that an object looks the same when viewed in a mirror. Like your Mother. Mathematicians call this "bilateral symmetry", and see it as the simplest example of a much more general concept.'

'That doesn't surprise me,' Vikki said, sniffing a little. The Space

Hopper, in his bumbling way, didn't realize that mentioning her family might make her feel unhappy. But, actually, it was comforting to talk about them: it reminded her that they still existed. Oh, and so *close* . . .

'Your father, for example, has eight symmetries.'

'That does surprise me. I didn't realize he had *any*.'

'Oh, yes. As long as you ignore fine details like where his eyes are, of course. His general *shape* has eightfold symmetry. Poor Planiturthians only have twofold symmetry – bilateral. And it's somewhat imperfect. Nonetheless, they make an awful lot of fuss about the "beauty of the human form" and suchlike. Well, no doubt it's beautiful to *them* – but to us Space Hoppers you can't beat a good fat bouncy blob with svelte orange skin, a pair of horns, and a cheeky smile.'

'Grin.'

'What's the difference?'

'Total visible area of teeth.'

The Space Hopper quickly changed the subject. 'To mathematicians, a symmetry – note the "a", we're talking specifics here – isn't a thing, it's a *transformation*. To be precise, a symmetry is a transformation that leaves an object looking exactly the same as it was before the transformation was performed. For instance, if someone rotated your dad through a right angle while you're looking the other way, you wouldn't notice any difference in his overall shape. So "rotate through a right angle" is a symmetry transformation of any Square.'

If a square is rotated through a right angle . . .

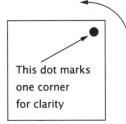

This dot marks one corner for clarity

. . . its appearance is unchanged

'Sometimes more than one such transformation exists. Then, the object has symmetri*es*, not just symmetry. That happens to be the case with your dad, because he's a Square. Every Square in the Euclidean Plane has eight rigid-motion symmetries. Can you think of any?'

'Well . . . let's see . . . "rotate through *two* right angles"?'

'That's right. If "rotate through one right angle" doesn't change the shape, then another "rotate through one right angle" doesn't either, and their combined effect is "rotate through two right angles". Any more?'

'"Rotate through *three* right angles"!' Vikki said, cheering up a little. That was an *easy* one. And the Space Hopper's enthusiasm was infectious.

'Very good. And that's the same as "rotate through one right angle in the opposite direction", of course.'

Vikki stared at him. 'Of course? But that twirls him the other way, and through a different angle.'

The Space Hopper's horns drooped disconsolately. 'Sorry. Silly me. I forgot to explain something extremely important about what a "transformation" is. The only thing that matters when describing a mathematical transformation is where everything ends up, relative to where it started from. The *route* it takes on the way is ignored.

'If your dad rotates through three right angles in one direction – let's call it "clockwise" to be specific, though it would look anti-clockwise if you viewed Flatland from the other side – then he ends up in a particular position, and we can tell what that position is by looking at his eyes, even if we can't tell by looking at his outline. If, instead, your dad rotates through one right angle in the anticlockwise direction, then again he ends up in a particular position, and again we can tell what it is by looking at his eyes. Not only that, it's the *same* position as the previous one! So in that sense the transformations specified by "rotate clockwise through three right angles" and "rotate anticlockwise through one right angle" are identical.'

Vikki said she understood. All that matters is how each initial point corresponds to where it ends up. Clear as mud.

'Any other symmetries?'

'Well – "rotate clockwise through *four* right angles"? No, hold it – everything ends up where it started if you do that. So that doesn't count—'

'Actually, it does. "Leave everything where it is" is a transformation, and it certainly can't change the shape! It's known as the *identity transformation* – from "identical", I guess. The identity is a symmetry of any shape whatsoever!' The Space Hopper's grin faded. 'But not a terribly interesting one. And quite often, the only one. When we say that a shape is *asymmetric* – without symmetry – what we really mean is that it is without any symmetry other than the identity. The identity is "trivial", you see. But in a precise theory of symmetry, we have to bear it in mind, trivial or not.'

'Why not rule it out? Define a symmetry to be any non-identity transformation that leaves the shape looking the same.'

The Space Hopper pursed his rubbery lips. 'Could do. But then you destroy one of the key properties of the symmetries of an object, the "group property": any two symmetry transformations carried out in succession lead to a symmetry operation. If the first transformation leaves the shape unchanged, and the second transformation leaves the shape unchanged, then doing them both in turn *must* also leave the shape unchanged. Yes? If you don't change the shape, and then you don't change it *again*, then you haven't changed it!'

'That's kind of obvious, isn't it?' asked Vikki.

'Sure. Obvious things can still be true – though often what *seems* obvious turns out to be false, young Victoria. The fact that two symmetries make a symmetry is both obvious and profound. It leads to a kind of "calculus of symmetry", known in the Mathiverse as group theory. But I'm getting ahead of myself: you've still only told me four of your dad's symmetries, and I reckon he has eight.'

'Can't see any others. I mean, "rotate through five right angles" is the same transformation as "rotate through one right angle", if I've understood what you've just told me.'

'Absolutely.'

'Then I'm stuck.'

'I think you may find that, on reflection, you're not.'

'But I am! I just told you so! More thinking isn't going to help—'

'That's not what I said. I said that I thought that *on reflection* you—'

'Oh! That was a clue, wasn't it? Reflection! If Dad stands in front of a mirror, his reflection still looks like a Square!'

'Yes – although with most mirrors, his position in the Plane changes. However, there are four mirrors which, after reflection, leave his outline exactly the same as before.'

'I don't see how that can be true. If he stands in front of a mirror, then his image will appear to be behind it. Wherever the mirror is. And if he stands behind it, there won't be any image at all.'

'Yes, but these are mathematical mirrors, not glass ones. You don't have to stand in front of them for them to reflect you. You could stand behind them and they'd still work.'

'That doesn't help either. If Dad stands behind a mathematical mirror, then his image will appear to be in front of it.'

'Right again. Now, think like a mathematician. Are "stand in front of" and "stand behind" the only possibilities?'

'Yes! Wait, wait, no! You could stand part-way across the mirror – some parts of you in front, others behind.'

'Yes. And if you're Grosvenor Square, and you want your mirror image to coincide with you, just where do you stand relative to the mirror?'

'Well – the mirror has to run through your middle,' said Vikki, 'or else the image pokes out differently from you, if you see what I mean.'

If a square is reflected in a mirror,
then it only fits its original outline . . .

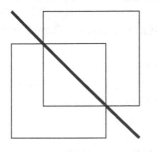
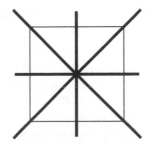

. . . for these four choices of mirror

'Very good. Will *any* mirror through Grosvenor's middle give an image that coincides with him?'

Vikki called up the VUE's menu-bar visualization routine to try a few thought experiments. 'Oh, no. The image can flop over into a different position, even when the mirror runs through the middle of the Square.'

'Right again. But are there any positions for the mirror where that doesn't happen? I'll give you a clue: what happens to the angle between one corner of the Square and the mirror, when the Square gets reflected?'

Vikki doodled with the VUE again. 'It *doubles*.'

'Correct. But if the Square's image fits on top of the Square, what can that doubled angle be?'

'Oh! A right angle!'

'Yes. Or two right angles, or three right angles – or no right angles, zero degrees.'

'So twice the angle between a corner and the mirror has to be a multiple of a right angle . . .' Vikki mused. 'And the angle itself must be a multiple of *half* a right angle – which is 45 degrees.'

'Beautifully expressed – I couldn't have put it better myself! So the possible angles between the mirror and a corner of the Square are 0, 45, 90, and 135 degrees. Where do those place the mirror?'

'Um. Zero degrees puts it . . . along a diagonal of the square. Then 45 degrees is . . . through the middle, parallel to two of the sides. Ah! And 90 degrees is the *other* diagonal of the square; and 135 degrees is through the middle, parallel to the other two sides.'

The Space Hopper waggled his horns in delight. 'So you've found – how many reflectional symmetries?'

'Four.'

'Which together with three nontrivial rotations and the identity makes . . .?'

'Eight. Like you said.'

'Good!' The Space Hopper bounced energetically up and down. 'So now we've established that Grosvenor has eight symmetries—'

Vikki interrupted. 'Hang on, you're hopping to conclusions.'

'I am?' The bouncing ceased.

'You told me to think like a mathematician. How do we know it's *only* eight?'

'Choose a corner. You can place it on top of any of the four corners, itself included. Having done that, there are only two ways to position the neighbouring corners: rotate the square, or reflect it about the diagonal through your chosen corner. That makes eight ways to reposition it.'

'It's obvious now you've told me. I withdraw my objection.'

*

Sevenday 15 Noctember 2099
Dear Diary,

I have just had a BRILLIANT idea!!! I now know *why* our ancestors placed so much weight on how many sides a polygon had, and how regular it was.

It's not really about the number of sides *as such*, and it's not regularity *as such*.

It's about SYMMETRY.

For the same reason that Dad has eight symmetries, every Pentagon has ten, every Hexagon twelve – the number of symmetries of a regular polygon is twice the number of its sides. A genuine Circle has *infinitely many* symmetries – no wonder the Priests were so snobbish! Of course, an approximate Circle, which is what they really were, has perhaps a hundred sides . . . but even so, that's *two hundred* symmetries, which is a lot.

On the other hand, a poor little Equilateral Triangle has only six symmetries – three rotations, three reflections – and an Isosceles Triangle has only two: the identity and a reflection. An Irregular Triangle of the 'criminal classes' has *only the identity symmetry.*

An interesting point for future reference, Diary Dear: Flatland women have *two* symmetries: the identity and rotation through 180 degrees. In fact – a technical caveat that may or may not be significant – there are *four* rigid motions in the Plane that leave a woman's form invariant. Two of them I've just described. The third is to *reflect* the Plane in a mirror that runs along the woman's length. And the fourth? Reflect in that mirror *and* flip her end over end. (I mean rotate her by 180 degrees. Didn't mean to sound risqué!)

So, with the exception of women – misunderstood, as always, by the male-oriented society of a century ago (and it hasn't changed MUCH, Diary Darling, as you and I both know) – anyway, with that exception, one's social position was determined almost entirely by *the size of one's symmetry group*!

This, of course, must be the result of sexual selection. The Space Hopper says the same thing happens on Planiturth – female birds prefer males with symmetric tails, for instance. As I understand the process, a symmetric form is an external sign of 'good genes' – an indicator of genetic fitness. Females that happen to mate with symmetric males (and vice versa, natch) have fitter offspring, so not only are genes for symmetry passed on to the kids, *so are genes for preferring symmetric mates.*

Astonishing. Suddenly the whole of our past snobbish society makes complete evolutionary sense. Bummer!

Except for the lowly role of women, who – as I've told you – are about as symmetric as a Square. Unfortunately, evolution treats males and females differently.

Until now.

We have nothing to lose but our genes!

10

PLATTERLAND

Vikki had the good sense to keep this particular insight to herself. She didn't want to get involved in gender discussions – she was having enough trouble coping with the challenges posed by the Mathiverse. And now the Space Hopper was determined to carry them away to pastures new.

Once more Vikki experienced the indescribable but unforgettable sensation of Space Travel. The Space Hopper grunted in satisfaction. 'Now *this* is a space I really like. Significant. This one will surprise you, and no mistake.'

So far every new space had surprised Vikki, so she couldn't see why the Space Hopper was more fascinated by this particular world than by the others they'd visited. But she had to admit that it was rather elegant. It floated directly below them, a perfect circle, glowing salmon-pink and lavender against the non-coloured backdrop of metaspace. It looked like a giant dinner-plate.

'Welcome to Hyperbolica,' announced the Space Hopper. 'You'll feel at home here: it's two-dimensional. Colloquially known as Platterland to us Space Travellers,' it added, confirming her mental image.

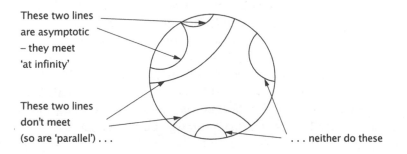

These two lines are asymptotic – they meet 'at infinity'

These two lines don't meet (so are 'parallel') . . .

. . . neither do these

As they descended towards the glowing disc, Vikki began to make out details. The growing expanse of the plate was criss-crossed with curved lines, which at first she took to be roads, until a series of smoke puffs drew her attention to the long vehicles that were making their way across the Platterland terrain.

The curves were railway lines. But there was something terribly wrong with them.

'Hopper, am I right in thinking that those lines are railway tracks?'

'Yes. From a distance they look like single lines, but up close like this they come in pairs.'

Unlike Spaceland trains, the ones in Platterland were running *between* the rails. So was the trail of smoke they left behind. But that made good sense to a Flatlander: in two dimensions, there wasn't an 'on top' direction. No doubt sections of rails, the wheels, and parts of the carriage walls could be dismantled when the train reached its destination, so that passengers could get in or out. That's how Flatlanders would handle such technological obstacles. The smoke could be let out the same way. Or maybe it would just fade away of its own accord . . . But one thing bothered her.

'If those are railway lines,' she said, 'then why are they curved? Surely they ought to be straight.'

'Trains can follow curved tracks, Vikki.'

'I know. But curved tracks hundreds of kilometres long must be terribly inefficient. Why aren't they following the shortest paths?'

The Space Hopper considered this carefully. 'I think they *are* following the shortest paths. The tracks look perfectly straight to me.' He was about to qualify this remark when Vikki objected.

'Straight? *Straight?* Rubbish! They're curved. All of them! They look like arcs of circles. Shouldn't railway lines be parallel? That is, unless the people here know how to manufacture trains whose wheels can get closer together or further apart, depending on the width of the rails. Here the pairs of rails meet at the edge!'

'As I was about to add when you interrupted, it all depends on what you mean by "straight" and "parallel",' said the Space Hopper, 'and "line", for that matter. Each railway track here has one straight rail and one rail that's equidistant from it but not straight.'

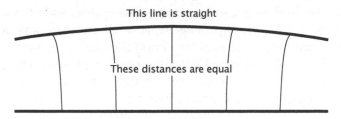

This line is straight

These distances are equal

This line is curved

'That's ridiculous.'

'No, not really. Since the equidistant lines aren't straight, they're not true parallels. On the other hand, some straight lines here *are* parallel – but not equidistant. In fact, technically speaking, the distance between parallel lines gets closer and closer to zero.'

'You mean they meet?'

The Space Hopper was baffled. 'Sorry? *Meet?* Where?'

'At the edge.'

'What edge? There isn't an edge!'

'The edge of the plate.'

Now the Space Hopper understood the source of her confusion. 'Ah. Yes, it does look like an edge, doesn't it? But Platterland has no edge. Or at least, if it does, none of the inhabitants can ever reach it. And appearances are deceptive. Some of the lines that look curved are actually straight, and the curves that seem to meet at the edge are really parallel straight lines. But, in this space, the distance between parallel lines is *not* constant. So if you drew a line at a fixed distance from a straight line, which is what you need to make a railway track, then the second line wouldn't actually be straight!' He saw Vikki's look of puzzlement. 'Mind you, if the distance is small, they look pretty much like straight lines do here. Which is to say – from *our* point of VUE – curved.'

'But the lines you're telling me are equidistant get closer together as they head towards the edge, Hopper.'

'Do they?' asked the Space Hopper in a quiet voice.

'Yes, they do!'

'You realize that if you're right, then the trains must shrink as they get closer to the edge? And they can't just get narrower, either, because if they did, they'd stop being train-shaped, and the natives would notice. So the whole *train* must shrink as it approaches the edge. The passengers, too.'

Vikki looked down at the Platterland rail network from her overhead VUEpoint. 'They *do*. Shrink, I mean. They get smaller and smaller the closer they get to the rim.'

'Really?' The Space Hopper's scepticism was palpable.

'I can see it with my own eyes,' Vikki protested.

The Space Hopper sighed. 'Haven't I told you over and over again not to believe what you see when you look at a space from the outside? As external observers we have a privileged position, which is denied to the inhabitants. To them, what they can perceive is what's real – and *all* that's real.' By now Vikki was looking a bit sulky, and the Space Hopper bounced apologetically a few times, his horns wobbling. 'Come with me *into* Platterland, and All Will Become Clear. I promise.'

Vikki's stomach lurched as the bottom dropped out of her universe. *Here we go again!* Platterland rushed up to meet them . . . There was a sound like supersonic suet pudding encountering a mountain range – then the world fell to pieces in total confusion.

＊

When Vikki's senses returned, everything seemed perfectly normal. Just as in Flatland, the Space Hopper had reverted to being a mere two-dimensional section of its Spaceland glory. At the moment it was roughly circular, though it shrank and expanded in an extremely disturbing, though rhythmic way. She realized that must be the Space Hopper's breathing.

Actually, things weren't *quite* normal. She felt . . . well, more *curvy* than usual, as if her endpoints had been sucked in. But she didn't feel any unusual compression of her internal organs. It was almost as if her central region had *bent*.

Platterland no longer looked like a plate. No matter how hard she tried, she couldn't see the edge any more. Everything just faded out into a distant haze.

They were standing on a footpath, not far from a level crossing. From out of the hazy distance came the mournful hooting of an approaching train.

They hurried over to the crossing. As they neared it, the barrier slid across to bar the way. Fortunately it was semitransparent, otherwise it would have blocked their view. The rails were semi-transparent too – and the barrier was actually a section of rail, which could be swung aside to let travellers pass when there were no trains coming.

With a sound like thunder the train surged past. When the train was far enough away for it to be safe to cross, the barrier opened. The Space Hopper led Vikki out into the middle of the track, and they stared at the departing train. The smoke had cleared, and she could see it perfectly well, even though the rails had appeared to curve when she had seen them from outside Platterland.

The Space Hopper 'rose' to a level where his eyes could see the train too. 'You're right,' he said. 'Look, the train's shrinking!'

Vikki laughed. 'Don't be silly. It's all perfectly normal. That's just perspective! The further away the train gets, the smaller it looks. It hasn't changed size in the least.'

'Oh?' said the Space Hopper. 'Are you sure?'

'Of course I am!'

'That's not what you said just now when we were privileged observers.'

'But then I could *see* – oh.' This was going to be embarrassing, she could tell.

'Exactly. And you can *still* see, but now you don't take what you see literally. So why did you take it literally before?'

Vikki blushed pale grey. 'Force of habit. But you do have to admit that it all seems perfectly normal now that we've entered Platterland.'

The Space Hopper gave her a mischievous look. '*Me? Have* to admit? Vikki, I am the Space Hopper – *I* don't have to admit *anything*!' He paused. 'But maybe you're right. Let's carry on along this path and see if we can find anything to change your mind. Or mine.'

The path led through a wood, with what looked like perfectly normal flatbushes and jomma trees. An edgehog scurried across the trail just ahead of them, and squarrels ran round the bases of the trees looking for nuts. At least, they *looked* like squarrels. Except there was something funny about them.

The Space Hopper began to shrink. As the circular cross-section of his fat body gave way to the twin circles of his horns, he sank below the plane of Platterland. Vikki just caught a faint cry of 'I'll be back momentarily' before the words floated away on the breeze. There was a flurry of activity and a muffled squeak. Moments later, the Space Hopper was back. Trapped between his horns was one very surprised squarrel.

The Space Hopper was triumphant. 'They're almost impossible to catch, these things. Unless you sneak up on them along an unexpected dimension. I used the nineteenth, did you notice?'

'Don't be silly. Anyway, what's so special about trapping a squarrel?'

'You tell me. Do you *see* anything special?'

Vikki gave the wretched animal a quick once-over. 'It's a perfectly ordinary squarrel, just like the ones in Flatland. It's small and furry, it's square, and it hoards nuts.'

The Space Hopper bobbed in excitement, so that he looked as if he was breathing very rapidly. 'Are you *sure* it's square?'

'Well, admittedly I can't see all its sides without walking round it, but I can recognize right angles when I see them. And when it was running round the tree, all *this* squarrel's angles looked right to me. And all its sides looked the same length, too.'

'I agree. They are. But did you count its sides?'

Vikki exploded. 'Now you really are being silly. If all the corners are right angles and all the sides are equal, it's *got* to be a square.'

The Space Hopper grinned. 'Sure?'

'Absolutely!'

'OK. Just indulge me. Keep an eye on the animal while I pirouette, and count how many sides it has. You can tell you've got back to the start when its nose comes round again.'

Vikki stamped her vertices in frustration – this was *such* a pointless game. 'Oh, if you insist. What a stupid idea! OK, start turning . . . One, two, three, four . . . five. See, it's a perfectly ordinary sq—*five*? Hang on, you're cheating. Turn round again. One, two, three, four, five. Again: one, two, three, four, five. Nuts. How are you doing that? This is mad! How can there be a five-sided square?'

'Maybe it's a right-angled pentagon,' the Space Hopper suggested, with a wicked ∪.

A squarrel

'Yeah, maybe – oh, you're awful. That doesn't help at all, it's just as bad. This is crazy.'

The Space Hopper bobbed in agreement, then stopped. 'On the other hand, Vikki, it may just be showing you that Platterland isn't quite as perfectly normal as it appears. After all, it *did* look a bit weird from the vantage point of Grand Unified Metaspace.'

'But you just said I shouldn't trust my eyes.'

'True. You really must learn not to take everything I tell you so seriously. But not right at this moment.'

※

Wunday 16 Noctember 2099
Diary Dear, you must believe me when I tell you that this Platterland space is as nutty as a squarerootcake. At first every-thing looks normal, and then when you take a more careful look it's all completely MAD. There are triangles here whose angles don't add up to 180 degrees, for instance. In fact they're ALL like that, though with the smaller ones you'd never notice. The area of a Hyperbolican triangle is proportional to the difference between the angle-sum and 180 degrees: if the sum is close to 180, then the area is close to zero! The bigger the triangle, the weirder it is: there are some triangles whose angles add up to *zero* degrees. Though apparently those aren't really triangles, just shapes made from three straight lines, because their vertices are on the edge, which doesn't exist . . .

I *think* that what saves my sanity is the belief that what counts as a straight line in Platterland is actually curved . . . but the Space Hopper insists that this is merely a parochial Flatland view, or more accurately a parochial *Euclidean* view.

※

'Think of it this way,' the Space Hopper was saying for the dozenth time. 'Imagine that Platterland really is a circle in Flatland, as your visual sense wants you to believe. What kind of fancy physics would make the Platterland railway lines and creatures behave the way they clearly do?'

'I haven't the foggiest idea,' admitted Vikki.

'Fog? Oh dear me, no, not fog. More like a touch of *frost*. Here's a clue: to you, everything in Platterland seems to *shrink* as it approaches the rim of the disc. What physical influence makes things shrink?'

Vikki thought about this. *Pushing* makes things shrink if they're elastic, but somehow she doubted that was the physical influence the Space Hopper had in mind. *Frost?* Frost is cold . . . Ooooh. Things shrink when they get cold, just as they expand when they get hot.

'Cold.'

The Space Hopper's thick orange skin wobbled in encouragement, like hyperactive blubber. 'Very good. Now, as I say, this is only an analogy. The inhabitants of Platterland don't actually feel any kind of cold. But suppose there is some kind of "temperature" effect of which they are unaware: the rim is very cold indeed, and the centre is a lot warmer. Imagine that the temperature falls away according to the distance from the centre—'

'How, exactly?'

'It doesn't matter much, but if you must know, the temperature should be the difference between the square of Platterland's apparent radius and the square of the apparent distance from the centre . . . anyway, assume that all objects shrink in proportion to this "temperature". At the rim, the temperature is zero, so objects shrink to zero size as they approach the rim. Got that?'

'Yes.'

'Fine. So here's my first question. How far is it from the centre to the rim, *as experienced by a Platterlander*?'

'It's just the radius of the disc . . . oh, no, because to them everything shrinks in accordance with the temperature. So let's suppose there is a Platterland creature that can take very big strides—'

'There is. It's called a bigstrider.'

'—and to keep the argument simple, let's imagine that when it starts from the centre its first pace takes it halfway to the rim, as it would appear to us.'

The Space Hopper grinned manically. 'Bigstriders aren't *that* big, but you're on the right lines. Keep going!'

'OK. Um . . . Because distances shrink as the temperature falls, its *next* stride takes it halfway from where it is to the rim – that is, three-quarters of the radius as we would see it. And the third stride also takes it halfway from where it is to the rim . . . seven-eighths of the radius. With the fourth stride, it gets to fifteen-sixteenths of the radius; the fifth takes it to thirty-one thirty-seconds, and so on.'

'Well . . .' said the Space Hopper, with a worried look. 'Your basic idea's right, but your numbers aren't. You're assuming that the temperature is proportional to the distance to the rim, whereas the correct temperature rule would give something distinctly more complicated. Never mind, though: qualitatively, you're smack on target. The length of the strides shrinks *very* rapidly as the bigstrider nears the rim. With your numbers, how many strides would it take to reach the rim?'

'Um . . . *Oh!* It never gets there!'

'Correct. And the same goes for the accurate numbers. Mind you, to our eyes it will appear to get *extremely* close if it keeps going . . . but the poor animal is taking tinier and tinier steps – again from our prejudiced viewpoint – so to *it*, the rim seems just as far away as ever.'

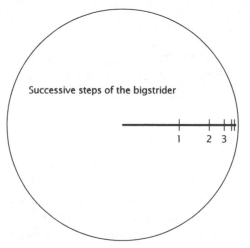

Successive steps of the bigstrider

Vikki had a sudden moment of insight.

'The rim is *infinitely* far away, then.'

'From the bigstrider's point of view, yes. And it's *his* world, so we ought to respect his viewpoint.'

Vikki thought about this. 'You keep saying that being outside a space gives us a privileged – and therefore potentially misleading – position. *We* perceive Platterland as a finite disc . . . but its own inhabitants perceive it as being of infinite extent.'

'Exactly.'

'But it's *really* finite, isn't it?'

If there had been any sand around, the Space Hopper would have gone and buried his head in it. And he was *all* head. But there wasn't any sand, so instead he just said, 'Let's go and ask them.'

*

They had landed in a rural part of Platterland, and it took a while before they encountered a native Platterlander. He had that same disturbing appearance as the squarrel. His angles were those of a hexagon, 120 degrees – but he had seven sides.

The Space Hopper introduced himself with a degree of politeness that Vikki had never heard from him before. 'Very formal, Platterlanders,' the Space Hopper whispered to her. 'They expect courtesy.' Then it turned once more to the hexangular heptagon. 'Please excuse my brief conversation with my fair companion, good sir,' he said. 'I was enlightening her with regard to the customs of your delightful country.'

'Ooh aar,' replied the heptagon. 'Tha's a real gennelmun an' no mistake. An' a stranger to these parts, ooh aar, that ye are.'

'That is most exceedingly perspicacious of you, sir. We are travellers from a distant land, visiting your beautiful and prosperous country for the first time. Such is our ignorance that we have many questions – but perhaps it would not be polite to ask.'

'Foire away,' said the heptagon. 'Oi'm bein' a fair bit more broadminded than most.' He paused. 'That's what comes from 'avin' a bigger 'ead than most, har-har-har!' Clearly this was a favourite joke, and equally clearly it was not to be taken literally – though with seven sides, the heptagon could hardly fail to have a big head.

'I'm curious about your weather,' Vikki began. 'Do you find it cold out here near the rim?'

'Cold? Why no, m'darlin', it's a glorious summer's day. But what's this faffle about a rim?'

'The edge of your world—' Vikki began, and stopped when the Space Hopper kicked her. He would have kicked her in the angle, but she didn't have one, being a Line. Not until now, anyway.

'Edge? You'm thinkin' of a *'awthorn* 'edge, p'r'aps? Not 'ere-abouts, Oi runs a *modern* farm mysen, an—'

Vikki couldn't restrain herself any longer. 'No, "edge" as in "boundary". Where the world ends.'

The heptagon broke into peals of laughter. 'The world 'as no *edge*, m'dear, as you can plainly see for yoursen, it bein' such a glorious day an' the pollution 'avin' been cleared by last noight's thundershower.'

Vikki ignored the Space Hopper's increasingly urgent kicks. 'But if you keep walking away from the centre, don't you eventually reach the edge of the world?'

'Har-har-har, funny joke. But what d'ye mean by *centre*, duckie?'

'The midpoint of the world,' said Vikki, 'the special place where everything is at its biggest.'

'Ah, you'm be meanin' Boondock, no doubt. That's the town where we sells our produce, 'bout two hours by schmule, that-aways. They got buildin's with more'n *foive* rooms in Boondock – that's what Oi calls *big*!'

'No, I mean the place that's different from any other, where objects reach their greatest size!'

The heptagon wrinkled one edge in perplexity. 'No such place,' he finally stated. 'Apart from the local lan'scape, every place on Oiperbolica is 'xactly the same as any other. And everythin' stays the *same* soize – wherever it moight be!'

'But—' Vikki began.

'I think my young companion is referring to the effects of perspective,' said the Space Hopper, diplomatically. 'Things look smaller when they're further away from you', it explained when the heptagon's edge began to cloud over in puzzlement.

'No,' Vikki protested, 'I mean that things really *are* smaller—'

'Nonsense!' said the heptagon. 'If fings changed soize as they moved aroun', nothin'd fit prop'ly any more.'

There seemed to be no answer to that.

＊

They had found an inn, The Sober Newt, and were arguing Platterland geometry over glasses of the local firewater. Grosvenor would have been horrified had he known, just as he would have been when Vikki had taken part in Running Turtle's wine tasting, but Daddy was a world away. If not several.

'I don't see the problem,' said the Space Hopper. 'After all, in Flatland, if you watch an object moving away from you, your eyes tell you it's shrinking. In fact, as it heads off into the infinite distance its apparent size shrinks to zero. So Flatland objects behave just like Platterland ones!'

Vikki wasn't having any of this nonsense. 'But on Flatland we know that really the object *isn't* shrinking. It's just the effect of perspective.'

The Space Hopper wasn't buying that. 'Hah! So when your eyes tell you that *Flatland* objects are shrinking as they move off to infinity, that's just an optical illusion. But when your eyes tell you that *Platterland* objects are shrinking as they move off to infinity, that's reality. Seems to me you're just choosing whichever interpretation suits you best. That's poor logic.'

'But Flatland objects *don't* shrink! If you walk away from somebody else, it may appear *to them* as if you're shrinking . . . but you don't feel yourself getting smaller. You're still the same size relative to your surroundings.'

'But the person watching you sees the surroundings shrinking too. So *of course* you wouldn't notice that you were shrinking.'

A look of horror passed over Vikki's edge. This was starting to sound quite convincing, if you took it at face value. 'You're just teasing me, aren't you?'

'No,' said the Space Hopper. 'I'm trying to put you into a Platterlander's frame of mind about Platterland.'

'I still think that's different. Look – on Flatland you can carry a ruler with you and measure your size. It stays the same, however far away you move.'

'That's because the ruler shrinks at exactly the same rate you do.'

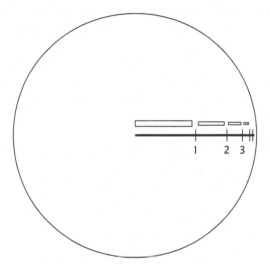

'Rulers can't shrink! Rulers are rigid.'

'So what happens if a Platterlander carries a rigid ruler with them as they head out towards the rim? Won't they notice that their size, as measured by the ruler, doesn't change?'

'But their rulers shrink! The temperature makes *everything* shrink.'

'Just as the temperature in Flatland makes everything shrink as it moves towards infinity?'

'Don't be silly. There's no temperature in Flatland – well, not like the one in Platterland.'

'How do you know?'

'We've never noticed one.'

'But the Platterlanders don't notice *theirs*, either. In fact, it's not real. It's just an aid for Flatland thinkers to understand Platterland geometry.'

Vikki's mind started to rearrange itself. Just like Topologica, Platterland was finally beginning to make its own kind of twisted sense. You just need twisted logic to appreciate the twisted geometry. It might *sound* crazy, but everything was perfectly self-consistent. '*Ooohhhh . . .* I *see.* You're saying that if rigid rulers can change their size as they move – whatever that means – then you can't rely on the rulers to measure distances accurately.'

'Nearly. Actually, I'm saying the exact opposite. Since the only way you can measure distances is by transporting supposedly rigid rulers around, you have to believe what they seem to be telling you. And on Platterland, what they tell you is that nothing *really* shrinks when it moves . . . and the world is indeed infinite in extent.'

Vikki saw the logic, but she still couldn't shake off the feeling that her own perceptions were the true reality, and said so.

The Space Hopper thought about that for a while. 'The trouble with perceptions,' he said, 'is that they're processed by brains. And brains have evolved short cuts in processing as an aid to survival. Often what we perceive is *different* from reality. If you switch your VUE to Spaceland mode, I can make that very clear to you.' He waited for her to do so.

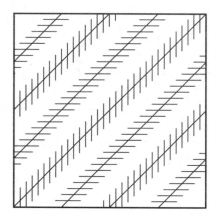

'Look at these lines – the long ones, not the short cross-hatchings. Tell me, do you perceive them as being parallel, or as converging?'

'Obviously they're converging.'

The Space Hopper agreed that it did look like that. 'Measure the distance between them. What does that tell you?'

'Um . . . Wow! It says they're really parallel! But they *look* . . . oh, I get your point now. They're not what they look like. The cross-hatchings fool the eye.'

'They fool the brain into misreading what the eye tells it. I'm not saying that your perceptions and senses are *false*, Vikki, just that there are some circumstances in which you can't trust them.'

❀

Twoday 17 Noctember 2099
Dear Diary,

The Space Hopper has explained the ridiculous geometry of Platterland in terms of an easily comprehensible Flatland analogy. I now see why the angles of triangles here need not add up to 180 degrees, and the right-angled pentagon of what counts for a squarrel in these parts now seems perfectly sensible. I remain vaguely convinced that Platterland's straight lines are really bent, but I now concede that, from a Platterlander's point of view, Flatland's straight lines can be considered bent too. It is dawning on me that what a universe looks like from the inside, and what it looks like from the outside, may be very different.

This, of course, is what the Space Hopper had been telling me for weeks. Stuck-up little twit!

❀

'But surely a "straight line" ought to be the shortest path between two points,' said Vikki. 'It is in Flatland.'

'Of course,' said the Space Hopper. 'So?'

'So, I don't see how a *curve* can be the shortest path.'

'Oh dear.' The Space Hopper's customary manic grin turned upside down, from a ∪ to a ∩. 'I thought we'd gone over this already. *They're not curves.* They look like curves to us, because we're on the outside. From inside Platterland, they're *straight*. And – I'm sorry, but they *are* the shortest paths.'

Vikki's head was swimming. 'I hear what you say, but I can't convince my eyes it's true.'

'Let's compare a line that looks straight to *us* with one that looks straight to *them*,' said the Space Hopper. 'What you have to remember is that rulers shrink as they get nearer what we see as the "rim". And our "straight line" lies nearer the rim than theirs. So when you try to measure the two lines, the ruler is shorter along our line than it is along theirs. It's a delicate calculation, but the extra length caused by the shrinkage outweighs the apparent loss of length caused by looking straighter (to us). See it now?'

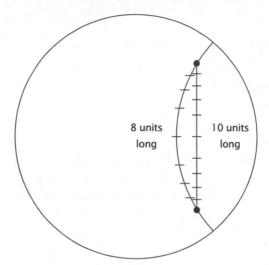

8 units long 10 units long

'I suppose so,' said Vikki. 'At any rate, I do see what you're getting at.'

'The relationship between intrinsic Platterland geometry and what we see when we observe their world from orbit is very elegant,' said the Space Hopper. 'We can characterize their straight lines rather neatly. To us, they are arcs of circles that meet the rim at right angles – at both ends. This is called *hyperbolic geometry*.'

'What's it good for?'

'Well, you'll recall me telling you that long ago on Planiturth there was a mathematician called Euclidthegreek. The most influential thing he did was to invent a brilliant way to formalize geometry – in fact, his method can be extended to any part of mathematics. His idea was to start by stating a system of *axioms*: basic assumptions that provide a starting-point for making deductions. You don't have to decide whether axioms are *true*: they determine the "rules of the game". If you dislike the axioms, you just don't play that particular game.

'Anyway, when Euclidthegreek laid down axioms for what in

those days was assumed to be the only possible kind of geometry –
in two dimensions, anyway – most of them were pretty simple
things: "any two points may be joined by a unique straight line".
And "any two lines are either parallel or meet at a unique point"
and "all right angles are equal". But one of them was a lot more
complicated.'

'What did that one say? Some right angles are more equal than
others?'

'No, no. It said, "given any line, and any point not on that line,
there is a unique line through that point that is parallel to (meaning
'does not meet') the given line".'

Given any line in the Euclidean plan

. . . and any point not on that line . . .

. . . there exists a unique line through that point that is parallel to the given line

'I see what you mean by "complicated" – but it makes sense.'

'It certainly seems to. And because it was complicated but made
sense, people wondered if it could be proved from the other
axioms. Because if it could—'

'The complicated axiom would be superfluous,' Vikki finished
for him. 'Which would be nice,' she added as an afterthought.

'Exactly. Now, a lot of Planiturthian People tried to do just that.
Guess what?'

'No idea.'

'They all failed.'

'OK, so Planiturthians are rotten at geometry.'

'Not at all. Some of them are brilliant. Euclidthegreek was. Mind
you, *most* of them are rotten at geometry . . . but that's true about
everything. Sports, music, painting . . . But I'm drifting away from
the point. Some of the most brilliant Planiturthian mathematicians
began to wonder if there was a *reason* why every attempt to prove
the parallel axiom failed.'

Vikki thought for a moment. 'But surely there *must* be a way to
prove it. I mean . . . why don't you just draw the new line equally far
from the original one at every point along its length? That'll do it.'

'Fine. They tried that one. The snag is, how do you know that what you've just described is a straight line?'

'Pardon?'

'How do you know that what you've just descri—'

'I heard you the first time. I just couldn't believe my ends. Of course it is!'

The Space Hopper's uncharacteristic ∩ became even more elongated. 'You think that's a good way to do mathematics? "Of course it is"? What about critical analysis? What about proof? What about logical rigour?'

'Yes, but this is obvious.'

The Space Hopper's ∪ returned, but now it was like the teeth on a shark. 'Really? Well, that's certainly what everyone on Planiturth thought – until they came across hyperbolic geometry. You see, in hyperbolic geometry, all Euclidthegreek's axioms are true—'

'I don't see how they can be, if the lines are curved.'

'I keep telling you, they're *not* curved. But you didn't let me finish. All Euclidthegreek's axioms are true *except* the parallel axiom. And that means you can't prove the parallel axiom from the others.'

'Why not?'

'Because, if you could, the same proof would show that the parallel axiom is valid in hyperbolic geometry. But it's not. Given any hyperbolic-line, and any point not on that hyperbolic-line, there are *infinitely many* hyperbolic-lines through that point that do not meet (which in Euclidean geometry is the same as "are parallel to") the given hyperbolic-line.'

Given any line in the hyperbolic plane . . .

. . . and any point not on that line . . .

. . . there exist infinitely many lines through the given point that do not meet the given line

'It's not about how the real world fits together, is it?' said Vikki. 'It's an abstract statement about the logical consequences of certain assumptions.'

'Exactly. If you spend your entire life in *one* space, you can perhaps be forgiven if you think it's the only space there is, and has the only geometry there is. We Space Hoppers know better: we've hopped between so many different spaces – and now, so do you, even though you're a Flatty with all the usual Flatty prejudices. There are *lots* of spaces and *lots* of geometries, all equally valid in terms of internal logic. And in this particular geometry, hyperbolic geometry, *nearly* all of Euclidthegreek's beloved axioms are valid. Just one isn't: the perplexing parallel axiom. So now you see *why* it's perplexing. *There is no proof.* So there's no point in looking for one.'

'I think I see. It's like trying to prove that the only possible geometry is that of Flatland. But we've seen several different ones already. To us – well, to *me* – the others all seem weird. But if you were used to them, they'd seem entirely natural.'

'Right. You got it.'

Vikki felt pleased. Then a new thought stuck her. 'Space Hopper, what is hyperbolic geometry good for?'

'Good for? What's Flatland good for?'

'It's good for us to live in.'

'OK, so hyperbolic geometry is good for Platterlanders to live in.'

'Yes, I see that. But why should a Flatlander *care*?'

The Space Hopper bounced in excitement. 'Well, one reason – maybe even be the *best* reason – is that Things May Not Be What They Seem.'

'Sorry?'

'You'll see. But not yet. First, you have to understand just *how* different geometries can be. Then, when I've got you softened up to the point where you really *don't* believe your eyes, we can think about the true shape of the Planiturthian universe.' Vikki began to protest, but the Space Hopper was adamant. 'No! Not yet! First, you must learn both patience and imagination.'

Imagination will be easy, she thought. *I've got a good imagination. But patience . . . that's not one of my virtues. In fact, to tell the truth, it's not one of my virtues AT ALL.* But she bit back her protest, since it would only make the Space Hopper's point all the more forcefully.

CAT COUNTRY

Of all the realms of the Mathiverse, there is none stranger than Cat Country. It is (until replaced by something else) the space in which all Planiturthians live – the space *from which they are built*. Yet it is so different from the space that they *perceive* themselves as living in that they find it bizarre in the extreme. Even their scientists find it difficult to understand what goes on in Cat Country. They can *calculate* what's happening, and they can carry out experiments to check their calculations . . . but when it comes to what it all *means*, even the scientists get confused.

You can tell, because if you ask questions about what it all means they stop behaving like scientists and either shout at you or turn into High Priests of some Cosmic Religion. Or both.

Cat Country is ruled by Superpaws, more usually referred to in terms of the owner of its intellectual property rights, an intensely curious Planiturthian named Erwinschrödinger. Not 'curious' in the sense of 'weird': Erwinschrödinger was surprisingly sensible considering what he was interested in. Curious in the sense of 'possessing curiosity'. Now, it is said that 'curiosity killed the cat', but Erwinschrödinger went one better. He killed his cat *and* kept it alive, all at the same time.

Not surprisingly, the poor beast is even more confused than the Planiturthian scientists.

Not surprisingly, the Space Hopper was determined to ensure that Victoria Line became intimately acquainted with Schrödinger's Cat.

Suddenly the universe seemed to be *growing*. Not just the space between things, but the things themselves. A piece of gravel that only a moment ago had been lying on the path became a boulder, then a rocky outcrop, then an unorthodoxly shaped mountain . . . Then it became too big to see as a single object at all.

Only the Space Hopper remained his usual size. And Vikki herself, of course.

'Why is everything growing?'

'It's not. We're shrinking.'

The surface of what once had been a pebble kept changing in surprising ways – sometimes rugged, sometimes rippled, sometimes smooth, and sometimes hairy, as if forests were growing on it. Funny clusters of bulbous things appeared, like balloons being blown up, but even they quickly became too big to take in. The pace of shrinkage slowed, then stopped. The surface of whatever it was they were now looking at became sort of lumpy, like dumplings floating in a thin soup. They were small dumplings, and the soup was so thin that it was scarcely distinguishable from empty space. The dumplings formed clusters, like bunches of grapes – but the gaps between the bunches were a lot bigger than you would ever see on a Planiturthian grapevine.

Not far away was a sort-of-beach, itself rather lumpy; and sort-of-waves rolled up towards it, creating iridescent rippled patterns that were hard to make out clearly. Try as she might, Vikki couldn't see where the waves *went*. They just kept coming towards the beach.

There would be time to sort out the waves later. Right now, it was the *lumps* that were bothering her. 'What are those?' Vikki asked. 'Those lumpy things. And why are they so . . . *fuzzy?*'

'Do you mean the round lumps, or the bunches?'

'The round lumps.'

'Those,' said the Space Hopper, 'are atoms. The bunches are molecules.'

Vikki knew about those. 'Atoms are what all matter is made from', she said. 'They're very tiny particles, and they're invisible—' No, *that* couldn't be right. 'Sorry, in*di*visible. And they combine together to form molecules, which is what chemical compounds are made from.' There were atoms and molecules in Flatland, much as in Spaceland, but the differences of dimension made Flatland chemistry a bit simpler than it was in Spaceland. The basic principles, though, were pretty much identical.

'That's what the Planiturthians used to think,' said the Space Hopper. 'Now they know better. Atoms aren't exactly particles, and they're not exactly indivisible. Look, I'll show you.' And he grabbed one of the dumplings and *squeezed*. Out popped three smaller round objects, also fuzzy: two the size of peas, and the other so tiny that only VUE-enhanced senses could see it at all. One pea was green and the other was yellow; the small object was pink. The Space Hopper explained that these were not their true colours – they didn't have true colours. The VUE had just been set to represent them that way.

'Let me just – *bother!*' yelled the Space Hopper. He flapped ineffectually at the yellow pea, sending it skittering through the interatomic soup, in which it momentarily left a faint trail, like ship's wake. They skittered after the errant pea, while the Space Hopper cursed under its breath.

Something small and circular loomed ahead. No, something *large* and circular. Improbably, in this space of fuzzy lumps, it was a perfectly sharply defined object. A bowl. Round the side was written SCHRÖD – no doubt there was more, but it was hidden from view. Inside the bowl was – catfood.

Fuzzy, lumpy, sometimes a bit *wavy* catfood.

The yellow pea plopped into the bowl.

'Good,' said the Space Hopper. 'We'd never have caught it if that hadn't happened.'

'Caught what?'

'The proton.'

'Come again?'

'The yellow pea. It's a subatomic particle called a proton. It's got itself trapped in a potential well. And unless I'm very much mistaken, the electron – the small pink particle – will be sticking to it. They do that, you know. When we first encountered them, those three particles were the parts of a deuterium atom. Now the neutron has been expelled, and the proton and electron have combined to make a hydrogen atom. It's very hard to stop those two joining up if they get the opportunity.'

'What *are* you waffling about?'

'Don't you take that tone with me, young Line. This is very basic stuff – subatomic particles and the Four Forces of—'

'*e*,' a tiny voice interrupted. It seemed to be coming from the pink particle.

'What was that?' said Vikki. 'Did something say "Eee"?'

'No, *e*.'

'Who are you? An electron?'

'Nearly. I am the Charge on the Electron. The fundamental unit of electricity.'

'Oh. I thought the charge for a unit of electricity was about 40p.'

'Not a *financial* charge,' said the Space Hopper. 'An *electric* charge.'

'Well, it would be, for a unit of electricity.'

'I mean, *it's not money*!'

'Oh.'

The Charge on the Electron lost its cool. 'No, not o! *e*! I keep telling you, but you don't listen. I may not be a financial charge, but I do have a value. My value is one ten-quintillionth of a coulomb.'

'That's not very much.'

'No, but there are an awful lot of us, I can tell you.'

❋

Threeday 18 Noctember 2099
Diary Dear, you're wondering why the Space Hopper made me spend so much time talking to that funny little Charge creature that lives on an electron.

The answer, in a word, is *particles*.

The answer, in a word, is *waves*.

Aha! I can tell, you're confused! You ask me one question, and I give you two answers. Which contradict each other.

Cat Country is like that.

❋

They sat on the seashore of Cat Country, watching the waves surge up the beach – and disappear. Unlike Planiturthian waves, they didn't roll back again.

It was caused, the Space Hopper claimed, by Quantum Tunnelling. Vikki saw no point in asking what that was. She sat, dangling her rear end in the . . . sea . . . and tried to sort out what she hadn't yet understood. 'What *is* an electron, anyway, Hopper?'

'It's a particle.'

'A very, very, very tiny piece of matter?'

'Yes. Smaller than an atom. And it's all in one lump – that's what "particle" means.' The Space Hopper thought about that and corrected himself. 'Used to mean.'

'Isn't *everything* made from particles? What else is there?' asked Vikki.

'Waves. Waves are very strange things. Think of water waves. They seem to be moving along quite fast – and they do roll up beaches, I admit. But if a wave was really a lot of moving water, the land would have flooded long ago. In fact, the water mostly moves up and down – but the hump that People *see* looks as if it's a thing that travels along. However, at each instant, that hump consists of *different* molecules of water. They just trade places. Until they hit the shallows, anyway.'

'But water is just a lot of particles, isn't it?'

'Yes. It's made from hydrogen and oxygen atoms, and those are made from protons, neutrons, and electrons. But water waves are *big*. At very tiny scales, there are waves that *don't* reduce to moving particles.'

'Such as?'

'Light. Light is a wave. Or, at least, that's what Planiturthian scientists had convinced themselves it was. They could even do experiments to prove it. And they thought that electrons were particles – they could do experiments to prove *that*, too.'

'What sort of experiments?'

'I'm sure the Charge on the Electron would be happy to demonstrate a particle experiment', said the Space Hopper.

'Happy? I'd be ecstatic!' said the squeaky voice. 'But I'll need some help. Give me a few minutes to set it up.'

The Charge on the Electron disappeared, and Vikki and the Space Hopper sat beside the quantum seashore watching the waves. The Charge soon returned, accompanied by thousands of identical particles, who were carrying several metal plates and a bottle of oil.

'Idiots! I said *two* plates, not dozens! Oh, never mind, just dump the rest and bring me two. Now, you lot start by lining up the plates, and the rest of you can open up the bottle and create some oil drops. As small as you can manage, please, and be quick about it!'

Soon all was as ordered. 'OK. Now, some of you sit on one plate, and the rest sit on the other one. I'll squirt a drop of oil in between, and you can play roller coaster like you usually do.'

'What on Flat—' Vikki began.

'The other Charges on the Electron are going to take rides on the drops,' the Space Hopper explained. 'That way they transfer electricity from one plate to the other. Now, suppose you could measure the amount of electricity very accurately. What would you expect to find if the electron is a particle?'

'I have no idea.'

'Let me put it this way: each electron carries a charge of one e. So could you detect a transfer of $0.5e$ from one plate to the other? Or $619.74e$?'

'Oh! The amount of electricity transferred always has to be a whole number times e!'

'Spot on, Vikki. And that experiment has been done, and that's the answer you get. If electrons were divisible, you'd get fractions of e, but you don't, so they're not. And that – everyone thought – means that electrons are particles.'

'I'll buy that. What about waves?'

'The important feature of waves is that when they interact, they *add up*. I'll just borrow some of those plates, and you'll see what I mean.' The Space Hopper waded into the sea with a couple of the plates, and set them on end with a small gap between them. Vikki noticed that as the waves encountered the gap, a series of semi-circular ripples formed on the other side.

'That,' said the Space Hopper, rather short of breath from lugging the plates around, 'is a diffraction pattern. It's a sure sign you've got waves.'

'We can *see* the waves,' Vikki pointed out.

'Yes, but *we've* got a VUE. Planiturthian scientists don't have that, but they can detect diffraction patterns even when the waves that make them are invisible. Now, let me add another plate, to make a second gap. To start with, I'll just block off the first gap. What happens?'

'Another series of semicircular ripples, Hopper!'

'As expected. Now I'll unblock the first gap, so that we've got two. *Now* what do you see?'

'Uh – it's rather complicated. A sort of bent chequerboard, that's the only way I can describe it.'

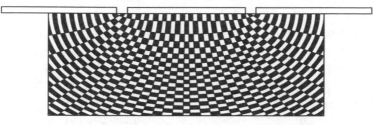

'What's happening is that when a peak of one set of semicircles meets a peak of the other set of semicircles, the two peaks add up to make an even higher peak; and when a trough of one set of semicircles meets a trough of the other set of semicircles, the two troughs add up to make an even *lower* trough. And if a peak meets a trough, they cancel out and the result is in between. That's what I mean by waves adding up. It's called *superposition.*'

'So if we see that sort of pattern—'

'—it's a sure sign of waves. Or, as I said before, so everyone used to think.'

'Used to?'

'On very small scales – down at the sizes we've been shrunk to by the VUE – matter is a bit weird. As Charge on the Electron will now demonstrate.'

'Why *me*? Why not one of the others?'

'You'll do it so *well!*'

'Aw – I *hate* this bit.'

Charge on the Electron stood back, took a run at the middle of the central plate, and hit it with what ought to have been a *splat*. But, Vikki couldn't help noticing, he didn't actually seem to get to the plate – he started to spread out. And then, on the *other* side of the plates—

He formed the bent chequerboard pattern that she had just learned to associate with waves.

'An electron is a wave?'

'Sometimes it feels like it,' said Charge on the Electron in a wavering sort of way. He slowly reassembled into a conventional rounded particle shape.

'It is like a wave,' replied the Space Hopper.

'How can a particle—'

'Behave like a wave? Good question. But it gets worse.'

'I rather expected that,' said Vikki.

'Everyone was convinced that light was a wave. They'd argued about it for hundreds of years, but the diffraction patterns and superposition experiments made it absolutely clear that light really was a wave. Until they looked at the photoelectric effect.' He cast around for inspiration. 'Ah. I knew these plates would come in handy. They're made of a special metal which emits light when . . . Charge on the Electron, will you oblige again, please?'

'Oh, no! I'll be bruises all over . . .' But there was no way out. Again he stood back, took a run at the middle of the plate, and hit it with what this time *was* a pretty convincing SPLAT. He bounced off.

As he did, a thin beam of light shone out of the plate, just for an instant.

'See, Vikki: the metal converts the energy of the impacting electron into light. So what would happen if he hit the plate *harder*?'

'Can't we go for softer?'

'Not yet.'

'You're a pig.'

'We'll get more light?' Vikki hazarded.

'Let's see.'

SPLAT!

'Ow!'

'Yes, you're right. OK, Charge on the Electron – *now* we'll try softer.'

'You rotter!' Splut.

'That's funny,' said Vikki, 'I didn't see any light at all.'

'Me neither,' confirmed the Space Hopper.

'But – we should have seen a fainter beam of light, surely? The lower the energy of the impact, the weaker the light – but it shouldn't just *switch off*.'

'If light is a wave, infinitely divisible, yes. But it did switch off. So what's the explanation?'

'Uh – well, clearly light isn't infinitely divisible.'

'Which means?'

'It's a *particle*?'

'That's what an extraordinarily wise Planiturthian named Alberteinstein was led to conclude. He deduced that light comes in tiny packets with a fixed amount of energy. They're called *photons*. That had already been predicted by a People called Maxplanck. The amount of energy in one packet – one *quantum* – of light is very tiny. It's equal to the frequency multiplied by *Planck's constant*, and that's incredibly small.'

'How small?'

'0.000000000000000000000000000000006.'

'OK, that's small. Space Hopper?'

'Yes?'

'Is light a wave or a particle?'

'Yes.'

'Both?'

'Sometimes one, sometimes the other. Well – sometimes *behaving* like one, sometimes behaving like the other. Particles and waves are things from classical physics – things we can observe on the human scale. There used to be a thing called the Complementarity Principle that said you could never catch light being both things at once, but that always seemed much too neat and tidy for me. A photon is a quantum object – why should it care which classical object it looks like? And, sure enough, I was right. But on the whole, it tends to resemble one or the other nearly all of the time.'

'And the electron?'

'That's both, too. You can call them wavicles if it makes you feel happier. Though most people now call them quantum wave-functions.'

'I don't think new names make a great difference. It still seems very weird.'

'That's because we normally live on the classical scale, and we see quantum effects only if we try very hard and use special apparatus. If we'd grown up on the scale of the Planck length, where wavicle physics applies, we'd think that a particle that could *only* be a particle was ridiculously unimaginative.'

'The world is made of wavicles?' Vikki asked, stunned by the newfound vision. *Solid matter wasn't solid.* It was all ripply!

'So the Planiturthians were led to believe. They realized that the wave nature of matter on small scales meant that everything was based on probabilities – on chance. In fact, a quantum wave *is* a wave of probabilities. The places where the wave is biggest – the probability peaks – are the places where the particle is most likely to be observed.'

'Why can't they just observe the entire wave?'

'Because of the Uncertainty Principle, discovered by Werner-heisenberg. If you try to measure the position of a particle, say, then you disturb its quantum wavefunction. In fact, you can't measure a particle's position and velocity at the same instant. Trying to observe one of them changes the other, randomly.'

Weird, though Vikki. Which was a good start. If you don't think quantum theory is weird, then you haven't understood it.

※

Fourday 19 Noctember 2099
The more I look into this particles business, Diary Dear, the more hairy the whole thing gets.

I'll start with *atoms*. When it comes down to it, the Planiturthian physicists have an astonishing habit of choosing really bad names. Like 'Relativity' for a theory where relative motion isn't relative and lightspeed is absolute. But new discoveries have to be given names, and those names have to be based on guesses about what will happen next. If those guesses are wrong, you're stuck with a bad name. I don't *think* that's what happened with Relativity, but it's certainly what happened with 'atom'. Which means *indivisible*, doesn't it, Diary?

Unfortunately, that's about as far from the truth as you can get. There are literally HUNDREDS of *subatomic* particles – *pieces of the indivisible!!!!* Proton, neutron, electron, photon . . . but those are just the best known. There are muons and tauons and neutrinos and pions and all sorts of others . . .

The list of fundamental particles is HUGE. It's hard to see how they can be fundamental when there are so many of them. But the irony of it is – so the Space Hopper says – that the best way to reduce the number of fundamental particles is to introduce a lot of extra ones.

This sounds mad, but it works because the old ones can be built up from the new ones. So when it comes to 'fundamental building blocks' you can keep to a fairly short, and very structured, list. Sort of sub-subatomic, then, if you catch my drift, Diary.

The most important of these sub-subatomic particles are known as QUARKS. (The name rhymes with 'corks', not 'marks', OK?) Protons and neutrons, for instance, are made by sticking quarks together. The proton is two *up* quarks plus one *down* quark; the neutron is two *down* quarks plus one *up* quark. The omega-minus particle – no, I dunno either – is three *strange* quarks.

It's like this: there are six 'flavours' of quark: *up, down, top, bottom, strange,* and *charmed.*

Quarks always come either in threes, or as a quark–antiquark pair. Mesons are like that, for instance. You never observe a solitary quark. How do they know that? Because quarks have charges that are ⅓ or ⅔ the charge on the electron. So if they occurred on their own, they'd stick out like a sore vertex.

*

Where there is catfood, there will be a cat. (Often the same one.)

Vikki looked anxiously around, but the animal was nowhere to be seen. She walked round the bowl of catfood. On the other side, it read 'INGER'.

'Why does the bowl say INGERSCHRÖD?'

'No, no, Vikki: that reads SCHRÖDINGER.'

'Manufacturer?'

'No.'

'Catfood advert?'

'No.'

'Logo?'

'No.'

'The cat's called Schrödinger?'

'No.'

'Oh.'

'Maybe the cat dings schrös.'

'Dings?'

'Rings like a bell.'

'Schrös?'

'Rather like shrews, I think.'

'Oh.' The conversation lapsed into an awkward silence. Finally, Vikki said, 'Space Hopper, you made that up! You have no idea what the name means, and there's no such thing as a schrö!'

'Don't complain to me,' said the Space Hopper. 'Actually, I do know where the name comes from, but here's the cat himself. You can ask *him*.'

'Where? I don't see him.'

'He's starting to materialize. Look over there – you can see the glum.'

'The *glum*? What's a glum?'

'The opposite of a grin. This is a very sad cat.'

A ∩ shape had formed in mid-air, near the bowl. It slowly solidified into a doleful and rather fat grey-and-white striped cat, which sat down by the bowl and began to eat from it.

'Excuse me—' Vikki began.

'Don't mention it,' said the cat in a mournful voice, and carried on eating.

'No, I mean I'm sorry to interrupt you—'

'Then don't!' snapped the cat.

'I *did* say "excuse me",' Vikki pointed out.

'And I told you not to mention it. Which you've just done. Again. Don't you ever *listen*?'

'You're a very strange cat,' said Vikki.

The cat stopped eating and stared at her. 'Look: you're an *observer*, right?'

'Sorry, what do you—'

'You're *observing* me, yes?'

'Well, if you put it that way. I suppose I am.'

'Then I can't be a strange cat,' said the cat. 'I'm only a strange cat when you *don't* observe me. When you're not looking, I'm totally weird. But you'll never *observe* me being weird. To you, I'll always look normal.'

Vikki was prepared to dispute that – she found the creature both fascinating and irritating. But politeness was a virtue to be culti-vated. 'Are you hungry?' she asked.

'That depends,' said the cat.

'On what?'

'On whether you're observing whether I'm hungry.'

'I'm observing you *eating*', said Vikki.

'That's different,' said the cat. 'Inferences don't count. As long as you're not actually *observing* my state of hunger, then I could be hungry, and I could be bloated with food and desperately stuffing the last morsel down my throat. Or I could be half of each at the same time.'

Aarrrgggh! Why was everyone in the Mathiverse like this? 'Space Hopper, I need your help. This cat isn't making any sense.'

The Space Hopper wandered over.

'That's because you haven't heard my tale,' the cat said.

'Don't be silly, you *see* a tail, you don't hear it. And I can see your tail perfectly well.'

'I'm a bit sensitive about it,' said the cat.

'Don't worry, Mr Cat – I'm not going to tread on it.'

'My name,' said the cat, 'is Superpaws.'

'That's a funny name.'

'What's *your* name?'

'Vikki.'

'And you say *mine* is funny. Ha! Be warned, my tale is a sad one.'

'No it's not! It's stripy and twirly and really quite beautiful!'

The Space Hopper took Vikki to one side and gently corrected her misapprehension. Then they sat down while the cat related its story. (*And if you'd* called *it a story in the first place, Mr Superpaws, none of this embarrassment would have happened!* But she was too polite to say so.)

'For many years,' the cat began, 'my life was uneventful. Until one fateful day I saw a job advertised in an experimental laboratory. I should have realized. "Cat" and "experimental laboratory" – it's a disturbing juxtaposition. But being a bit short of readies, you understand, I took the plunge and sent in my application. To my delight – well, it was delight to begin with – I secured the position.'

'Which was?' Vikki enquired.

'I had to sit in a box. Now, sitting in a box is something cats are pretty good at. "Easy-peasy", I thought to myself. What they didn't tell me was that I'd be shut up in the box with some kind of gadgetry stuff, and I couldn't get out again until some geezer opened the box. All this was before the Animal Rights Movement, you see. Nowadays it would never be allowed, but back then, nobody cared.

'So, I'm sitting in this box, and I can't get out until this geezer lets me out, and I look around to see what's there – being a cat I can see in the dark, and anyway, there was this lump of stuff that was *glowing*, so I thought, "That's nice, they've left me a nightlight." And there was some kind of glass tube, with nothing in it. Well, it *looked* like nothing – I only found out the real story later. The glass was a bit fragile-looking, and then I noticed this dirty great hammer on a hinge, held up by a length of very thin thread. So I thought, "Someone ought to get rid of that hammer before it falls down and smashes the glass." There was a pair of scissors, opened round the thread, and there were lots of coils and springs and gear-wheels and things running from the handles of the scissors to some incomprehensible gizmo that was pointing at the glowing stuff.

'Since it made no sense at all, I went to sleep, like any normal cat. Next thing I know, the lid comes off, and someone's poking their nose inside. So I lie low, hoping to get a bit more shuteye.

'"Oh, look, it's dead!" says a voice. 'Course, I knew I wasn't – we cats can tell that kind of thing – but I wasn't sayin' nuffin'. "The detector must have registered the decay of a radioactive atom and released the poison gas," says another.

'*Poison gas!* Well, I was ready to leap out of that box like a shot, I can tell you. But then the first geezer says something that pins my ears back. "So his wavefunction collapsed, then?" Look, matey, I'm *proud* of my wavefunction, and I'd never let it collapse even if you paid me huge bundles of dosh to neglect it. I wash my wavefunction every month, whether it needs it or not. Anyway, "Yes," says the second geezer. "He must have been in a superposition of states –

part alive, part dead. Then we opened the box, and observed him – and collapsed his wavefunction to 'dead'."

'Well, that did it. I opened one eye, then the other, and glared at them. And do you know what the first geezer said?'

'No.'

'"Perhaps we should have used stronger poison." Well, *really!*' The cat stopped for a moment to lick its paw and wipe it over one ear. 'Later, I figured it out,' he continued. 'I was a quantum cat, see? Subject to the Principle of Superpawsition. Hence the name, of course. Like a wave, I could interfere with myself, if I wanted to – though I hasten to add that I'm not that way inclined *at all*.

'When the box was shut, the two geezers outside couldn't observe what was happening, so they had to assume that the radioactive atom was in a quantum superposition of the states "decayed" and "not decayed". Which, bearing in mind the detector, hammer, glass vial, and poison gas, indicated to them that *I* was in a quantum superposition of the states "dead" and "not dead". When they opened the box and *observed* my state, however, their actions immediately collapsed my wavefunction. Luckily for me, it plumped for "not dead", and I was able to hoof it before they shut the lid and tried again. But they thought I *was* dead. Too busy observing *me* to notice that the hammer hadn't moved.'

'That's awful,' said Vikki.

'The worst is yet to come,' said the cat. 'It so happened that just as I escaped from the box, their attention was distracted by discovering that the poison vial was still intact, and they didn't actually *observe* me escaping. So all they could assume was that I was in some quantum superposition of the states "escaped" and "not escaped". And I've been wandering through Cat Country ever since, wondering exactly when my wavefunction will collapse – and whether, when it does, I'll find I've been in the box all along, when I *thought* I'd eluded their Evil Clutches.'

❋

'Let's see if I've got this straight,' said the Space Hopper. 'For the purposes of physics, you are not so much a cat as an extraordinarily large system of fundamental particles, all interacting in some incredibly complicated way. Since each individual particle is a quantum wave, it has a quantum wavefunction. Therefore *you* have a quantum wavefunction—'

'It's more that I *am* a quantum wavefunction,' Superpaws interrupted.

'—which is therefore subject to the Principle of Superpawsition ... I mean, Superposition. Your quantum wavefunction, when unobserved, can be – indeed, most likely is – in a superposition of states.'

'That's the gist of it,' said the cat.

'When you are sealed up in your impermeable box, then it is impossible for anyone to observe you, so—'

'Wait a minute,' said Vikki. 'Why can't Superpaws observe *himself*? Isn't he an observer . . . inside the box?'

'I wondered about that myself,' said the cat, 'but what they all say is that because I can't communicate my observation to anyone outside the box, it doesn't count.'

'That seems very peculiar to me—' Vikki began, but the Space Hopper was anxious to continue with his summary.

'—since it's impossible for anyone *else* to observe you while you're inside the box, your wavefunction can remain in a superposition of states.'

'Yes.'

'The relevant states being "alive" and "dead".'

'Yes.'

'Why?' asked Vikki. 'Why couldn't Superpaws's state be a superposition of "hairy" and "hungry"?'

'Dunno,' said the cat. 'To be honest, that's my most probable state – what physicists call the "ground state".'

'Or "covered in purple spots" and "descending from a tall building by parachute", for that matter,' said Vikki, warming to the task.

'Not *quite* as likely,' said the cat. The Space Hopper felt a kind of *itch* at the back of his mind, a vague memory that wouldn't pop into conscious view.

'No, but in the quantum world, anything that's remotely *possible* has to be taken into account, yes?' Vikki persisted.

'Yes,' said the cat, 'that's what worries me.'

'Now, let me ask you about observations,' said Vikki. 'Just what constitutes an observation in quantum theory?'

'It's any interaction between the system being observed and its environment that generates a well-defined *number*,' said the Space Hopper. What *was* that elusive thought?

'So if I count Superpaws's tail and get "one", that's an observation?'

'Yes. If you count Superpaws's tail and get *five*, that's an observation, too. But not a very good one.'

'And what happens when someone makes an observation?'

'The wavefunction collapses to some pure state.'

'What's a pure state?'

'One that can't be described as a superposition of other states. Which, by some mathematical trickery, is the same as one that leads to a numerical answer. So pure states are the *only* ones that can be observed.'

Vikki thought about that. 'And "dead" is a pure state?'

'Yes, because you can observe it.'

'I'm not sure that isn't circular logic,' objected Vikki. 'What number do you get for a dead cat?'

'Zero. Breaths per year.'

'Hmm. I'm not convinced. Is "dead" really a quantum state?'

'*Everything* is really a quantum state.'

'No, you didn't hear the emphasis. Is it really *one* quantum state?'

'Sorry?'

'Couldn't a cat be dead in more than one way? I mean – run over by a bus, eaten by an alligator, squashed by a rampaging hippopotamus—'

'Do you *mind*?' protested the cat. 'I think you *enjoyed* that!'

'Sorry, just listing hypotheticals. How can you tell from the quantum state of a cat that it's dead?'

'I don't know.'

'Alive?'

'Same problem. I'm not sure you can even tell it's a cat.'

'So if "dead" is really lots of possible states, and "alive" is really lots of possible states, what happens when you superpose half of each? You get even more possibilities. For all we know, "covered in purple spots and descending from a tall building by parachute" is 13 per cent dead plus 87 per cent alive if you choose the right "dead" and "alive" states. I mean, suppose it's "only just dead and covered in *lots* of purple spots" and "extremely alive and vibrant and descending from a very tall building by an oversized parachute"? Wouldn't 13 per cent dead plus 87 per cent alive work out as "covered in purple spots and descending from a tall building by parachute"?'

'I have no idea. But your general point is a good one.'

'Superpaws, it's all nonsense, you know. You're a *cat*, not a wavefunction. "Cat" is a classical concept, not a quantum one. I suppose that at any given moment you've *got* a quantum wavefunction . . . no, even that's not really true.'

'Why not?' asked the Space Hopper.

'Because he's interacting with his environment. So you can't split off the part of the quantum wavefunction that's *him*, and the part of the quantum wavefunction that's the environment. For instance, are the molecules in the food that have gone into his stomach part of *him*, or part of his environment?'

'I never thought about that,' said the cat. 'At first they're not part of me, and later they are. The main thing is to get as many of them as I can. But this business about the collapse of the wavefunction: it definitely works, you know, they've done experiments!'

'With a cat?'

'Well, like I told you, they were working on it when I . . . No, with electrons.'

'An electron is a very simple quantum system, Superpaws. A cat isn't. It's *immensely* complicated. So terms like "pure state" and "superposition" aren't terribly clear-cut, are they?'

The Space Hopper finally remembered what had been bugging him. 'Vikki, you're right. Superpaws has a very short decoherence time.'

'Blimey,' said the cat, 'now I'm feeling *really* safe.'

'Superpositions of pure states kind of fuzz out in systems composed of large numbers of particles. Their phases decohere.'

'Deco here, deco there – whatever,' said the cat. 'I can't abide jargon.'

'OK. Er . . . quantum states are usually interpreted as probabilities. If you observe a mixture of pure states, say 13 per cent dead plus 87 per cent alive, that is interpreted as a probability of 13 per cent that you observe a dead state, and 87 per cent that you observe an alive state.'

'Well, at least the odds are on my side,' remarked the cat. 'I'd prefer better ones, though. Those are about the same as Russian roulette.'

'However, the probability is just the *amplitude* of the state – the *size* of the wave that corresponds to it, so to speak. As well as an amplitude, every quantum wavefunction also has a phase.'

'I've been going through a phase,' said the cat. 'Didn't know I *had* one, though.'

'The phase is how far through the cycle of wave-motion the state has got at a given moment,' said the Space Hopper. 'Relative to some specific choice.' He was struggling. 'I can show you the formula if you—'

'You mean, like – the wave goes up and down and up and down, over and over again, and the phase is whether it's up, down, or somewhere in between?'

'Thank you, Vikki, that's exactly what I mean. Though "up" and "down" must be taken metaphorically. Now, the number you get when you observe a state *doesn't depend on the phase*. But the wavefunction you get by superposing states *does depend on the phase*. People used to think you couldn't observe the phase, but now they just think it's extraordinarily difficult.

'Anyway, every quantum system undergoes complicated changes in phases as it interacts with its environment. That's "decoherence". If it's a simple system like an electron, it can maintain its phases in much the same relationship for quite a while, so "superposition" has a well-defined meaning, and it can behave like a quantum particle. But the decoherence time – how long it takes for the phases to get jumbled up – increases very rapidly as soon as the number of particles increases. Superpaws's wavefunction would decohere in a time so short that it doesn't even make sense to speak about it in quantum theory.'

'Wonderful!' said Vikki.

'What good is all that to me?' asked the cat.

'It means, my dear Superpaws, that if you were ever in a state that was a superposition of "dead" and "alive", you would have stayed in that state for such an incredibly tiny fraction of a second that no one could ever have caught you in it. Because you are a large quantum system, interacting with your environment, you don't *behave* like a quantum system at all. You behave like a classical one.'

The cat digested this information. 'But the box stopped me from interacting with my environment.'

'No, there was more than enough environment in the box. The interaction of the radioactive atom with the *detector* made the wavefunction decohere – you weren't even involved at that point.'

'I would have been,' said the cat glumly, 'if the detector had registered the decay of a particle. Still, I see what you're telling me. So I was never in a superpawsition of "dead' and "alive"?'

'Not one that lasted long enough to count.'

'What state *was* I in, then?'

'You were *either* dead, *or* alive,' said the Space Hopper. '*You* would know which – at least if it was "alive". An external observer *wouldn't* know, though – not until they opened the box. But there's nothing mysterious about that! Nearly everything that happens to us is like that. We can't predict *what* it will be, we just have to wait to find out. That's not quantum. It's just ignorance.'

There was a long pause. Then, 'I can live with that,' said Superpaws. 'It's my stock in trade.' And his face lit up with a ∪, almost as broad as the Space Hopper's.

❋

Fourday 19 Noctember 2099 [continued]
Something's been bothering me for a while, Diary my Friend, and I finally managed to put my endpoint on it.

You know that the Mathiverse and the Planiturthian universe are different, yet strangely intertwined. The Mathiverse is a collective mental creation of Planiturthian intelligences – yet the structure and behaviour of the Planiturthian universe is somehow governed by the Mathiverse. So have these bizarre creatures *invented their own universe* out of pure mentality?

I asked the Space Hopper. And he laughed.

After a while, he apologized and said it was a really good question, but he found it amusing because some Planiturthian scientists and philosophers believe just that. They think that unless at least one Planiturthian Mind is observing the universe – to 'collapse its wavefunction' – then it doesn't exist.

Most, though, think this is rubbish. ('Fortunately', he added as an afterthought.) A universe is even more complex than a cat, so its decoherence time must be even shorter. And anyway, how could the brain to house a Planiturthian mind ever have evolved in a nonexistent universe?

Good point, Diary.

What WAS going on, then? I asked him.

He pointed out that Planiturthians don't possess a VUE. They can't *experience* the Mathiverse directly, like I'm doing. But that, he said, is because *they* are real whereas *I* am a Virtual Unreality Construct. I got annoyed, but he says he's one too.

So how *do* Planiturthians experience the Mathiverse, then? Instead of a VUE, they use an IMAGER. Imagination, Mathematics, Analogy, Generalization, Extrapolation, and Recursion.

Take, for instance, their conception of space. They look around and imagine themselves to be on a flat plane with an extra up/down direction. (Planiturth is round, but no matter: it's also BIG.) They turn this into the mathematics of 3D Euclidean space. They use analogies with 2D space, where they can draw pictures, to understand 3D. But – and this is crucial to understanding how their minds work – *they don't stop there*. They generalize to 4D, 5D, nD, ∞D. And they extrapolate concepts from their 3D experiences, so planes extrapolate to hyperplanes, spheres to n-spheres, and so on. Finally (only you'll see it's *not* final at all) they recursively go back to the imagination stage and start all over again. Which is what's led them from a simple 3D Euclidean spatial model to the far more sophisticated and intricate geometry of the quantum universe.

'So it's all in their minds?' I asked the Space Hopper.

'No,' he said. 'Their minds are all in It. Their brains are built from Planiturthian-universe matter, obeying Planiturthian-universe rules. Their minds are processes that go on inside their brains – and many of those processes are internal representations of that external universe. So, not surprisingly, Planiturthian minds construct – by the collective use of IMAGER – a Mathiverse that mimics the effects of those external rules pretty well. They don't always get the rules *right* – for all they know there may not be any ultimate rules at all – but they keep tinkering, and slowly the correspondence between Mathiversian rules and observed reality becomes extraordinarily accurate.'

'So that's all there is to it, then?' I asked him.

'Not quite,' he said. 'There's something very mysterious going on, too. Why is it that Planiturthians live in a universe where IMAGER works, anyway?'

'Why?' I asked him, after a long silence.

'Beats me,' he said.

12

THE PARADOX TWINS

'Grosvenor?'

'Yes, Lee?'

'You really miss her, don't you?'

Grosvenor Square dropped his newsscroll and glared at his wife. 'Who?'

'Vikki.'

Grosvenor went dark grey with repressed anger. 'I'm surprised you can bring yourself to utter that name in this house after what she's done to us!' Jubilee said nothing, but she was clearly on the verge of tears. 'Not even a postcard or a phone call . . . that's what I find really annoying, Lee. I might forgive her running away – she's an adult, when it comes down to it. But not like this.' He shook his vertices in disbelief. 'This just leaves us stuck in emotional limbo. It's so *unfair*!'

'It's not like our Vikki, is it?'

'Not like her at all.' He took a deep breath. 'I'm very worried, Lee. Maybe . . . maybe somebody's stopping her from getting in touch. Maybe she's in some kind of trouble. I – I know I don't talk about it much, dear, but it would just upset everyone. So I keep my feelings to myself.'

'And that's what upsets everyone, Grosvenor. Don't you understand that? You don't need to hide your feelings from *me*. How do you imagine *I* feel?'

'I – I know . . . but even so, I think it's sometimes more upsetting talking about her, when we can't *do* anything about it. I just . . . wish . . . she'd get in touch. It would set my mind at rest to know that somewhere on Flatland she's safe and sound, and that she's put all this three dimensions nonsense behind her.'

❋

Fiveday 20 Noctember 2099
OK, Diary: now get THIS!

You'll remember I told you that the Mathiverse is both a Planiturthian construct and the driving force of the Planiturthian Universe. Yes, I *know* it's mad, but that's Planiturthians for you . . .

Anyway, a consequence of this loopy self-referential nature of Planiturthian civilization is that, uniquely among the inhabitants of the Mathiverse, they keep changing their minds about which Space they are actually *in*.

In his *Romance of Many Dimensions*, my great-great-granddad Albert uses the term 'Spaceland' for the geometry of Planiturth. I mean, here's how his memoirs START:

> *I call our world Flatland, not because we call it so, but to make its nature clearer to you, my happy readers, who are privileged to live in Space.*

And he talks about Spaceland sailors, and Spaceland children, and a number of other things which – thanks to some useful guidance from the Space Hopper – make it clear to me that old Albert managed to confuse Planiturth with a Mathiversian Construct. No surprise, then, to find that Spaceland was the Mathiversian Construct that was believed to be a valid geometry for REAL Planiturthian space in the days when Albert visited what he was TOLD was Spaceland. (Remember, Diary Darling, that for profound reasons of Cosmic Synchronicity, deriving from Narrative Imperative, the enumeration of years in the Planiturthian Universe proceeds in step with that in Flatland, except for a numerical difference of 100, so that our 1999 is their 1899, and our 2100 is their 2000.)

Well, as you have no doubt anticipated, by the time Yours Truly got to visit Planiturth the fickle creatures had changed their minds. No longer did they imagine their world to be an ideal 3D

Euclidean Space. Not a bit of it. It had become a 4D Spacetime. With various bells and whistles which I shall reveal at a later date!! They had come to this momentous conclusion, apparently, because of an Albert of their own . . . But I am getting ahead of my story, as usual. I am *so* impatient, Diary Dear, to tell you the astonishing things I am discovering.

❖

Vikki and the Space Hopper were sitting in a bus.

The Space Hopper had bought them two tickets for a kind of historical package tour of Planiturthian Physics. Actually, it was an omnibus, meaning that it could go anywhere. Not any-where on Planiturth, but *anywhere*. It was a Universal Touring Machine. And in the wild expanses of the Mathiverse there's an awful lot of anywhere to go, but most of it is so bizarre that it's probably best not to. The trouble with package tours, though, is that once you've paid your deposit you don't have much of a say in where you go.

The bus was chugging its laborious way along Continuum Carriageway, a metaspatial bypass that avoided the need to drive through Topologica, which was always a nightmare because nothing ever stayed the same shape. The driver was desperately looking for the exit to Pyramid Park and hoping he hadn't passed it by mistake, when Vikki and the Space Hopper heard the sirens screeching in the distance, far behind them. The driver must have heard them too, because he pulled over to the hard shoulder and killed the bus's motor.

WHEEEEEEEEEEEEEEEEEEEOOOOOooooooooooooooooooooooooo

Whatever it was shot past so quickly that they never caught a glimpse of it.

'What was *that*?' screeched Vikki.

'Dunno,' said the Space Hopper. 'I'll have a word with the driver.' He hopped along to the front of the bus and engaged in animated conversation with the person behind the wheel. After a few minutes, he hopped back again. 'Um. Let me see if I can summarize . . . you've heard of the *Fire* Brigade?'

'Of course,' said Vikki. Every city in Flatland had its own Fire Brigade. 'They ride round in fire engines and put out fires. Try to, anyway.'

'That was the Light Brigade.'

'They . . . ride round in light engines and . . . put out lights?'

'Mmm . . . sort of,' said the Space Hopper. 'They'd put out the light if they could catch it, definitely – but they've never succeeded. They *chase* light. But it's a wild-goose chase, because in this Space-time they have no chance of succeeding. Of course that doesn't stop them – it's their *job*, you see. And they're very conscientious, the Light Brigade.'

'What a shame. Why can't they catch the light?'

'Because it's faster than them.'

'I think,' said Vikki, concentrating hard, 'that's just another way of saying they can't catch it.'

'I guess. The real point is, it's faster than *anything* – except itself. It's the fastest thing there is. Didn't you notice all those round signs along the roadside that say ©?'

'I thought they were copyright notices.'

'No, c is the speed of light, 300,000 kilometres per second. Those © signs tell us the universal speed limit in this part of the Mathiverse – the Relativistic Spacetime Continuum.'

Vikki thought about this. 'I didn't realize light had a speed. When you switch on a lamp, you don't see the light seeping across the room towards you.'

'Vikki, even if it was doing that – *what would you see it with*?'

'Light – oh. You only see it when the light arrives, of course. Sorry.'

'There's more to it than that,' said the Space Hopper. 'You don't *hear* the words other people are speaking making their way across the room towards your ears, either. For the same reason. But sound takes a perceptible time to travel from one place to another. That's what makes echoes work – you hear your own words bouncing back to you *with a time delay*. Caused, of course, by the time it takes the sound to get to whatever it bounces off and come back to your ear. With me so far?'

'Yes. But why aren't we aware of echoes in a room?'

'In a *big* room we do. Even in a small room, echoes give the sound its character. But mostly we don't notice because the time it takes sound to cross a room is a tiny fraction of a second.

'Light is similar – but it's a *lot* faster. You see a flash of lightning almost the instant it happens, but the thunder takes time to reach you, and you're aware of a delay. About three seconds per kilometre.'

'I always wondered why that happened.'

'As far as lightning goes, light *could* be instantaneous. Infinitely fast. But it's not. Planiturthians found ways to measure it – astronomical ones, to begin with – and they found that it travels at the aforementioned 300,000 kilometres per second. Our old friend Alberteinstein – yes, the People who realized that light can behave like a particle – used that one simple fact as the basis of an entire theory of Spacetime. He called his theory "Relativity".'

'Because it said that everything was relative?'

'Pretty much the exact opposite! The main thing to remember about Relativity,' said the Space Hopper, 'is that it's an extraordinarily silly name.'

'Then why use it?'

'Historical accident,' said the Space Hopper. 'The Planiturthians are stuck with it. The whole point of Relativity is *not* that "everything is relative" but that one particular thing – the speed of light – is unexpectedly *absolute*. Here, take this gun.' A small pistol had materialized beside them.

'*Gun?*' Vikki squealed. 'What would I do with a gun?'

'It's all right, it's a potato gun. Point it forwards and fire it.'

'But I might hit the driver—'

'No, aim at that big sign beside the road, the one that says TIREDNESS CAN KILL. Oh, and you'd better load it first.' The Space Hopper passed her a potato. She looked baffled. 'Just put it in the chamber there. Like I said, it's a potato gun. It fires potatoes. Whole ones.'

Vikki had got used to strange requests from the Space Hopper, so she loaded the gun with a medium-sized King Edward and took steady aim, just past the driver's left ear. She began to *squeeze* the trigger . . .

'Wait! Hold it! First, a question for you. You're travelling in this bus at 50 kph. A stationary gun fires a potato at 500 kph. How fast will this potato travel?'

'Um . . . Well, it gets a 50 kph boost from the bus, so I guess you add the speeds up, like Running Turtle would have done. That makes 550 kph.'

The Space Hopper pulled a remote velocimeter from the voluminous folds of metaspace. 'We can measure the speed with this. Right, fire away, and we'll see.'

The gun went off with a bang. The driver ducked as a potato-shaped hole appeared in the windscreen next to his head, and the bus wobbled all over the metaspatial road. The driver turned and glared at them, then turned back again quickly before he hit a seven-dimensional truck.

'Sorry,' said the Space Hopper. 'Physics experiment.' The driver muttered something unintelligible and probably obscene. The Space Hopper consulted the remote velocimeter. 'Well, it's 549.999999999 something. Good enough for government work.' He handed Vikki a torch. 'Now, let's try it again with light.'

'Light?'

'Light travels at approximately 1,080,000,000 kph (300,000 kps). But the bus is moving at 50 kph. So at what speed does the light hit the sign? Not *that* sign, we've passed it. The one coming up next.'

Vikki thought about this. 'I guess the speeds add up, like they did for the potato. So that ought to give a speed of 1,080,000,050 kph.'

'OK, let's try it. Ready . . . aim . . . *switch*!'

A pool of light illuminated the sign, before the bus chugged past.

'Too quick for me to tell,' said Vikki.

'Too quick for anyone. But the remote velocimeter knows – it's extremely accurate. And it says the speed was 1,080,000,000 kph.'

'What happened to the extra 50?'

'Not there. Extraordinary, isn't it? If you fire light from a moving vehicle, the light travels at exactly the same speed as if the vehicle wasn't moving at all.'

'That's mad. Surely relative velocities don't—'

'In Spaceland geometry, no. In Relativistic geometry, yes. And to make it worse, even though our bus is moving, the speed we measure for light passing along the bus is exactly the same as the speed that would be measured by a stationary observer.'

'Are you sure?'

'Let's ask one.' The Space Hopper leaned out of the window and shouted to a motorist trying to change a flat torus. 'Oi, mate! What speed do you measure for light?'

The motorist made a rude gesture.

'Picked the wrong observer, I think,' said the Space Hopper, unabashed. 'Ah, here's a policeman. I'll ask him. Driver – slow down! Stop for a moment, there's a good chap! Pardon me, Officer, but what speed do you measure for light?'

'1,080,000,000 kph,' said the policeman. 'It's the lawful speed limit, sir – you must have seen the signs. *Nothing* goes faster than 1,080,000,000 kph. At least, if it does, it'll have me to reckon with. *And* a speeding ticket.'

Vikki still felt that there was a difficulty. 'Look, Hopper, I know I'm probably being unimaginative, but you can't limit the speed of light just by passing a speeding law. The only law that can limit the speed of light is a law of physics. And physics says that relative speeds add up.'

The Space Hopper shook his horns. 'Ah. Physics prior to Albert-einstein said that, certainly. But not after. You can do very sophisti-cated experiments, with highly accurate equipment, and *you get the same answer* – as a People called Michelsonandmorley discovered between 1881 and 1894, Planiturthian time. He was trying to detect the motion of Planiturth relative to the "aether", an all-pervading fluid that was thought to transmit all electromagnetic radiation, light included. If Spaceland physics were correct, that motion should show up as a difference in the apparent speed of light when Planiturth was at opposite points of its orbit, moving in opposite directions. But Michelsonandmorley couldn't find any difference in the speed at all, even with very sensitive equipment.'

'All that proves is that Planiturth must carry the aether along with it when it moves in its orbit,' Vikki objected.

That had never occurred to the Space Hopper, and for a moment it threw him. 'That's quite a cute theory, Vikki. But it's wrong, because . . .' he searched desperately for a counter-argument '. . . you'd expect to see funny effects in the light from distant stars if the aether was swirling around like that. Michelsonand-morley concluded that either there wasn't an aether at all, or Planiturth *wasn't* moving relative to it – which he didn't think was credible – or that there was something pretty weird about light.'

*

The bus resumed its journey, and the Space Hopper continued with his explanation. 'In 1905 Alberteinstein turned Michelsonandmorley's observation into a theory – Special Relativity, it was called – to the effect that there *is* something pretty weird about light. And he pointed out that this meant there had to be something pretty weird about space, too. Well actually he wasn't the first to do that, but he was the first to understand the Big Picture behind it all.'

'How can space be weird?'

'Let me adjust your VUE to exaggerate the effect I'm talking about. It will slow light down to a modest running pace. Now, you sit on that seat, and watch me hopping past you. See if you notice anything different about me.' The Space Hopper bounced past, very slowly.

'Not a thing. You look perfectly normal to me.' Vikki coughed and corrected herself. 'As normal as you ever do, that is.'

'Good. That's what I *should* look like. But now I'll speed up.'

Again the Space Hopper bounced past her, getting some aggrieved looks from the other passengers.

'You look – Space Hopper, you look *thinner*.'

'That's right. And so do you. Not *thinner*, though: you're a line and your thickness is zero anyway. Shorter. But when you say I look "thinner", what you really mean is that my width looks shorter, yes?'

'Yes.' Vikki curled her tip round to look along her length. 'But I'm the same length as usual.'

'To *you*, yes. To me, too – while I'm sitting here and not moving. But if I move fast enough, you look shrunken to me.'

'But—'

'I know, you don't look shrunken to you. That's because you're not moving relative to yourself. But you *are* moving relative to me, so to me you look shorter.'

'But . . . wait. If I'm moving relative to you, then you're moving relative to me. So to me, *you* look shorter.'

'Correct! It's perfectly symmetric! When we are in relative motion, I look shorter to you, and you look shorter to me. Whereas we each look our normal length to ourselves. Isn't that amazing?'

'Astonishing. I don't believe it.'

'It's a necessary consequence of light having an absolute speed.

Light from different parts of a moving object reach you at different times, having travelled different distances. Combined with an absolute speed for light, that makes the moving object seem to *contract* in the direction of its motion. Alberteinstein realized that this contraction was a *real* physical effect. A lot of other Planiturthians, like Hendriklorentz and Henripoincaré, were working on the same idea, but they kind of saw it as a mathematical fiction. Not so old Alberteinstein. He was made of sterner stuff!

'And it doesn't end there,' continued the Space Hopper. 'Time has to slow down when you move quickly, too.'

'Time usually seems to speed up when you move quickly, in my experience.'

'Ah, that's psychological time. I mean time as measured by a clock.'

'Oh. But why does time—'

'I'll bounce past you again, but this time I'll shine a torch. Still with artificially slow light, OK? I'll give you a stick and a clock, and you can measure the speed of the light from my torch. And I'll carry a stick exactly the same as yours, and a clock exactly like yours, and I'll measure the speed of light too. First, I want you to be sure that your measuring instruments and mine are identical.'

Vikki put the two sticks side by side – they were exactly the same length. She watched the clocks ticking for a few minutes – they kept identical time. 'Yes, they're the same.'

'Good. Now, as well as measuring the speed of the light from my torch, I want you to keep an eye on my stick. Can do?'

'Sure. And I can chew gum at the same time, too. I'll do my best, Hopper.'

'Right. Let's go for it!'

The Space Hopper hopped past her, and suddenly switched on his torch. Vikki held up her stick and timed the light as it crawled along the stick's length. A quick mental calculation supplied the speed: 300,000 kps. In VUE-foreshortened kilometres, naturally.

She couldn't help noticing that the Space Hopper's stick had shrunk quite a lot, as she'd seen before. It looked about half the length of hers. So he'd see the light travel the length of the stick in half the time she'd measured for *her* stick. So he'd have to measure—

'300,000 kps,' said the Space Hopper.

'No,' protested Vikki, 'you ought to get 600,000 kps. I was watching, and the light travelled along your stick a lot faster than it did along mine. Because your stick had shrunk.'

The Space Hopper shook his horns in mild irritation. 'I've never heard quite so many misconceptions in one statement!' he complained. 'To begin with, you already *know* that you and I are going to measure the *same* speed for light. So why do you think I was going to get 600,000 kps?' The infectious ∪ lit up his face. '2*c* or not 2*c*, *that* is the question!' he declaimed theatrically. 'And the answer is . . . not 2*c*, but *c*. Then, you say my stick has shrunk. I assure you that from my point of view it hasn't. It's entirely normal. To me, *your* stick has shrunk.'

'Oh. Right. So how come—'

'Think about how we observe each other's *clocks*. According to my clock, light takes the same time to traverse my stick as it does to traverse *your* stick according to *your* clock. We get the same speed, OK? But you observe my stick as being shorter – so what do you deduce about your observations of my clock?'

'Um . . . Oh. Your clock must be slowing down by just the right amount to compensate for the shrinkage of your stick. The light covers a shorter distance, but the clock measures the time as being longer, so the two changes cancel out.'

'As *you* observe my clock and stick, that's a correct description. In other words, from your observational viewpoint, not only do objects contract along the direction in which they are moving, but time also expands by the same amount. If the length halves, the time doubles. That's a consequence of the speed of light being *the same* whether you observe it or I do. Speeds intertwine distance and time: if one changes, so must the other.'

'I guess that makes sense.'

'Yes. Now, it also turns out that an object's mass increases with its velocity, becoming infinite at the speed of light, too – but let's not go into that now. What makes less sense – but is also true in Relativity – is that I don't notice anything strange happening to my stick or my clock – even though you do. Instead, I get the impression that it's *your* stick and clock that are doing funny things. Because, you see, it's just as accurate to say that you're moving relative to me as it is to say that I'm moving relative to you.'

'That's crazy!'

'Planiturthian physics *is* crazy. But that's because the Planiturthian *universe* is crazy. Don't blame the physicists!' The Space Hopper paused. 'Well, not for that, at any rate.' He blinked. 'But you're right, it does seem paradoxical. And, by a remarkable coincidence, the bus is approaching our destination at just the right narrative moment. I want you to meet two acquaintances of mine. The Paradox Twins.'

❋

'But – they're *different!*' said Vikki, unable to stop herself. 'You told me they were twins! Oh! I'm sorry! That wasn't very polite of me, was it?'

'Wasn't it?' one of the Space Hopper's acquaintances asked the other.

'No, it wasn't,' said the other.

'But the explanation—' began one.

'Is very—' the other added.

'Simple. We are—'

'—twins.'

'He is—'

'—Twindledumb. And I am '

'No, *I* am—'

'Have it your own way. *He* is Twindledumber.'

What extraordinarily curious people, Vikki thought. 'Being twins would explain why you're the *same*—' she began. 'But not why you're—'

'But we're *not* the same', Twindledumb pointed out.

'No, *he's* a lot older than—'

'—him.'

'Don't be ridiculous,' said Vikki, 'if you're twins, you must be very nearly the same age as each other.'

'That's the paradox—' the Space Hopper began, but the twins interrupted.

'Do we—'

'—*look* the—'

'—same age?'

'Well, no,' she admitted. 'That's what I was saying right at the start! Twindledumb looks *much* older than Twindledumber.' Then she greyed with embarrassment again. 'Oh! I'm so sorry! I didn't mean to . . . you look *very* distinguish—'

Twindledumb inclined his head of sparse, greying hair to reveal a big bald spot. Twindledumber inclined *his* head of thick, dark hair. 'We're not offended,' they both said at once. 'Yet . . .' they added.

'How . . . how can you be twins, when one of you is much older than the other?' Twindledumb scratched his ear. 'It's a long story—' he began.

'No, it's a short story', contradicted Twindledumber.

'It was to you! To *me*, it was a long one. That's the point!'

Vikki intervened to halt the bickering. 'Surely it has to be either a long story or a short one. It can't be both.'

'Oh, but it can,' said Twindledumb, 'it all depends on who's telling it.'

'No, it all depends on who's *observing* it.'

'Same difference, other way round, yes?'

'No! *Different* difference.'

Once more Vikki tried to calm them down. 'Twindledumb: you said that to you it was a long story. Tell me the story, then – but keep it short. Space Hopper and I haven't got all day, I'm afraid.'

'Tell a long story but keep it short . . . I'll try. About forty years ago, Twindledumber and I were exactly the same age. In fact, we both looked like he does now. But then he went off in a spaceship to a distant star, and he didn't come back until a few weeks ago. That's it. Short enough for you?'

'Admirably concise.'

'It's a pity you don't have time to hear about my onions. I started them from seed, you see, the first year my brother left, and they started to produce *beautiful* little green shoots, and then—'

'Very interesting I'm sure,' said Vikki hurriedly. 'Now, Twindledumber: you said your story was short. So tell it to me. Take your time, no need to rush.'

'Well,' Twindledumber, began, 'it all began when a mutual friend *happened* to remark – it was over dinner, as I recall, munchroom pudding with a salt-cellary glaze – and ...' He droned on, and everyone except Vikki fell asleep ... Three hours later, Twindledumber finally reached the point where he climbed into his spaceship and set off for the distant star. 'The ship was fast – *very* fast. Ninety-nine point nine nine nine nine nine nine nine nine nine nine nine nine per cent of the speed of light, the manufacturers claimed, and I'm pretty sure it did at least Ninety-nine point nine nine nine nine nine nine nine nine nine nine nine eight per cent. Anyway, it took me out to the star, we whizzed round the back of it, and its gravitational pull slingshotted us straight back the way we'd come ... and before I knew it, I was home again.

'To find that *he* ...' Twindledumber pointed at his brother '. . . had gone prematurely old.'

'Prematurely? *Prematurely?* Forty years I waited for you to get back! Of course I was old!'

'But I was only gone for a couple of days!' The twins glared at each other, and then they both laughed; a little sadly, Vikki felt.

'He's right,' said Twindledumb.

'*He's* right, too,' said Twindledumber.

'We're *both* right,' they said together.

'Relativistic time dilation, Vikki,' said the Space Hopper. 'Because Twindledumber was moving so fast, for *him* time slowed to a crawl. So the whole journey only took just two days. But for Twindledumb, stuck at home and not going anywhere, forty years passed.'

Vikki nodded. Then a thought struck her. 'But ... just now, when *I* measured *your* clock as running slow, *you* measured *mine* as running slow too! "It's symmetric", you said.'

'I did. And it was.'

'So why isn't *this* symmetric, too? Twindledumb sees Twindledumber's clock as going slower, so to him Twindledumber hardly ages at all, but poor Twindledumb ages forty years. But, by the same token, Twindledumber observes Twindledumb moving very fast relative to *him*, so to him Twindledumb hardly ages at all, but poor Twindledumber ages forty years. Symmetric, see?'

The Space Hopper frowned. 'The difficulty is, Vikki, that after the round trip is over, they're both back in the same place, not moving. They can't *each* be a lot older than the other.'

'Oh. Sorry, never thought of that. But surely that means Relativity is rubbish?'

'Don't be embarrassed. And it's not. What you're missing is a technical point – an important one, as the stories of the Paradox Twins illustrate, but a subtle one. What I said about the speed of light being the same however fast you're moving, but lengths contracting and time expanding – that's true, but only if your speed is uniform. If you *accelerate*, it all gets more complicated. Acceleration is *not* a relative quantity in Alberteinstein's theory. Like I said, "Relativity" is a silly name. "Inertial frames" is the jargon for "what you observe when moving at a constant speed". Even the speed of light ceases to be constant for an accelerating observer. And the source of asymmetry between the twins is that Twindledumber went off in a spaceship, and he accelerated quite fast to get up to lightspeed, and then he accelerated again when rounding the star, and finally he decelerated to avoid smashing into his brother at lightspeed when he arrived home again. Whereas Twindledumb stayed in an inertial frame – no acceleration. So it's *not* symmetric, and that's why Twindledumb has aged forty years while Twindledumber has aged only two days.'

*

Fourday 19 Noctember 2099
Dear Diary

It's not easy getting the hang of Relativity. There are *so* many pitfalls, you need a clear head. Which, frankly, I lack at the moment.

For instance, there's the paradox of the near-lightspeed train. Suppose that a train is being driven along a railway track at close to lightspeed, and there are small gaps between lengths of the track. Then the driver observes the gaps as moving at near-lightspeed, so they *shrink*, and to him they appear even smaller than they would have been when he was (they were?) stationary. So he expects just the tiniest of bumps as the train passes over each gap.

On the other hand, to a 'stationary' observer beside a gap, the TRAIN is moving at near-lightspeed, so *it* shrinks – so much so that it ought to fall into the gap between the rails!

How do you resolve *that* contradiction, Diary?

You don't know, do you? The answer, as in all of these apparent paradoxes of Relativity, is to remember that relativistic geometry is mathematically self-consistent. Any apparent problems must result from its interpretation. So you use the maths to work out what really happens. In this case, the train *does* 'fall into' the gap – but it's travelling so *fast* that it doesn't fall very *far*! So, even as viewed by a stationary observer beside the gap, all that happens is a very tiny bump.

Which is what the driver experiences, too.

So, if you want to think sensibly about relativity, Diary Dear, then you have to go the whole hogsagon. A mixture of nonrelativistic and relativistic thinking is inevitably fatal.

13

THE DOMAIN OF THE HAWK KING

'They were *such* a sad pair,' said Vikki. 'I'd hate to wait forty years for my brother to return from a voyage, only to discover he'd hardly aged at all compared with me.'

'It's even sadder. You see, Twindledumb could have gone to the star with his brother, but he decided not to.'

'Why?'

'Said he couldn't spare the time.'

There was a long silence.

'Was that . . . a joke?' Vikki asked, finally.

'I wish it had been. It shows how important it can be to understand your universe as it is, and not just as you imagine it to be.'

'I suppose. Still, Twindledumb could always make an interstellar voyage himself, and get their ages back in synch.'

'I'm not sure the spaceship still exists. But there's another way that Relativity could help the twins overcome their paradoxical temporal displacement.'

Vikki waited for him to continue, but he didn't. So eventually she asked, 'What?'

'What what?'

'What *way*. To help the twins.'

'Oh, sorry, my mind was wandering. Time travel.'

'You mean – going into the future or the past?'

'We *all* travel into the future – at one year per year. The past . . . well, that's trickier. But perhaps not impossible. Relativity doesn't just change our perceptions of space, time, and matter. It also affects our view of *causality*.'

'Which is?'

'The link between cause and effect. If you want to understand that, we need to visit Minkowski Space. Now, because of the commercial exploitation of Intellectual Property rights . . . look, it's tricky to explain, but basically somebody *bought* Minkowski Space, along with several other spaces that you really ought to visit. They've been franchised out for the tourist trade, so I'll need to pull a few strings to get us in there without paying. I'll just make a call on my mobile.'

The conversation was lengthy, laced with words that Vikki didn't understand, and mostly consisted of the Space Hopper reminding whoever was on the other end of past favours granted and future favours to come. Occasionally the Space Hopper flashed her his trademark ∪, as if to indicate that the negotiations were succeeding, and once he actually *winked* at her.

'OK, we're in – but only if we can get there in a hurry. Let me reset your VUE, and we can head straight for—'

'—Minny Space. And there she *is*! Hi, babe! Long time no see!'

'Don't you try your alien charms on me, Hopper. If you wanna be my Hopper, *you* have got to *give*, baby. Who's the geom?'

'What's a geom?' asked Vikki.

'Slang for "geometric entity",' said the Space Hopper. 'As a Flatland line, you're an archetypal geom. Don't be offended – it's just Minny's way. She does it to maintain street cred.'

Vikki decided not to ask what street cred was. Life was too short to sort out *everything* you didn't understand. 'Minny?'

'Minny Space. Short for Minkowski Space, you see . . . She's one of the Space Girls. And if I'm not mistaken, here come the others! Victoria: meet Curvy Space, Bendy Space, Pushy Space, and Squarey Space.'

Suddenly Vikki was surrounded by strangely clad – well, that wasn't exactly the word, but it would have to do – Spaces. Rather brash, fast-talking spaces, who used a lot of street slang and for some reason kept breaking into song-and-dance routines. They seemed very confident, very self-aware, and – to be frank – they were a considerable pain in the endpoint.

When they discovered that Vikki was a girl, though, they immediately tried to make her feel at home. And, apparently, to empower her – an operation for which they were an endless fount of novel ideas. 'Yo, Vikki, what you Flatty girls need is *Line Power!*'

'I've heard of a power line,' said Vikki. 'Would that do?'

'No, that's *quite* different!' pouted Pushy Space.

'The Lines of Flatland should assert their power!' asserted Squarey Space.

'Stop giving in to the Polygons!' Curvy Space added. 'Right now! Thank you very much!'

'Above all, get yourself a Good Manager!' advised Bendy Space.

'Exploit your assets!' Minny Space clarified.

'Kick some assets!' shouted Curvy Space, and the others all laughed.

This all sounded like fun, and Vikki would have tried it if she'd had the foggiest idea what any of them were talking about. Female emancipation, of some kind, by the sound of it. 'We're working on it', she told them. 'At least, *I* am. I don't think my mum is. But I kind of suspect she secretly approves. It takes a while . . . I'm not sure I really know—'

'What part of "know" don't you understand, girly?'

'Minny,' the Space Hopper interjected, 'could you oblige and introduce Vikki to modern notions of causality?'

'Yeah, sure. OK, Vikki – pay attention and ignore the grinning idiot who brought you here. In relativistic spacetime, everything depends heavily upon which "frame of reference" an observer uses. Moving and static observers see the same events in different ways. Now, in full-blooded Minkowski spacetime, space is 3D; but I'm Minny Space, and that's not just a nickname like the Space Hopper told you, it's because I'm a miniature version. My spatial coordinate is one-dimensional.

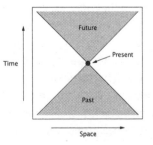

'Now, as a particle moves through spacetime, it traces out a curve, its *world-line*. If its velocity is constant, its world-line is straight. The slope of the world-line depends on the particle's speed. Particles that move very slowly cover a small amount of space in a lot of time, so their world-lines are close to the vertical; particles that move very fast cover a lot of space in very little time, so their world-lines are nearly horizontal. Got it?'

'Sure have.'

'In between, at an angle of 45 degrees, are the world-lines of particles that cover a given amount of space in the same amount of time – measured in the right units. Those units are chosen to correspond with each other through the medium of the speed of light – say years for time units and light-years for space units. Tell me, Vikki, what covers one light-year of space in one year of time?'

Vikki knew that one. 'Light.'

'Right on, babe, and I choose my words with care. So world-lines sloping at 45 degrees correspond to light rays, or anything else that can move at the same speed as light.'

'My head is starting to ache.'

'You ain't seen nothin' yet! Now, Relativity won't let anything move faster than light. There's a maths reason: if things could move faster than light their lengths would become imaginary, and so would their masses and the local passage of time. So the world-line of a real particle can never slope more than 45 degrees away from the vertical. Such a world-line is called a *timelike curve*. The extreme opposite is a curve in Minny Space that *always* slopes more than 45 degrees away from the vertical. That's called a *spacelike curve*, and no part of it can coincide with the world-line of a particle.

'Any event in space-time has associated with it a *light cone*, formed by the two 45 degree diagonal lines that pass through it. It's called a cone because when space has two dimensions, the corresponding surface really is a (double) cone. The forward region contains the *future* of the event – all the points in spacetime that it could possibly influence. The backward region is its *past* – all the events that could possibly have influenced *it*. Everything else is forbidden territory, elsewheres and elsewhens that have no possible causal connections with the chosen event.

'A timelike curve always moves from its past into its future. Spacelike curves are quite different: no point on them lies in the past or future of any other point.

'In ordinary space, the distance between two points tells you how far apart they are. In Special Relativity there's something kinda similar, and it's called the *interval* between spacetime events. Along the 45 degree lines the interval is zero, so those lines are called *null curves*. The interval tells you how time seems to pass for a moving observer.'

'Yes, the Space Hopper told me about that,' said Vikki. 'It's time dilation, isn't it? The faster an object moves, the slower time appears to pass for an observer in a frame that moves with it.'

'Yes. If you could travel *at* the speed of light, time would be frozen. No time passes on a photon.'

'So light is frozen time?'

'I suppose you could put it like that.'

⁂

The Space Hopper was rabbiting on about time travel again.

'But I thought there were paradoxes associated with time travel,' said Vikki. 'For instance, suppose I could go back and warn ancestor Albert that his messing about with the Third Dimension would land him in the pokey! Then he might never have written *Flatland* . . . but then I wouldn't have known about him, so I *wouldn't* have gone back and warned him . . . so he would have written the book and *then* – well, you see what I'm getting at!'

'I certainly do,' said the Space Hopper. 'A concise statement of the Great-great-grandfather Paradox. But we Space Hoppers generally find that it's best to find out what the universe is capable of by trying it out, rather than *ruling* it out because of philosophical paradoxes. The paradoxes have a habit of taking care of themselves, you know. Anyway, we generally find we have more fun that way. Before I can tell you about time travel, though, you have to understand how gravity fits into a relativistic picture of the universe.'

'What does gravity have to do with time travel?'

'Everything. Though I admit it's not obvious. You see, Alberteinstein invented another theory, called General Relativity, which was a combination of Newtonian gravitation and Special Relativity. You know what Isaacnewton said about gravity?'

'No, I've not studied Planiturthian history in that much detail, Hopper!'

'He said it was a force that moves particles away from the perfect straight lines they would otherwise follow. He worked out a law for how the gravitational force exerted by any particle of matter varies with distance.'

'OK, I remember that.'

'Alberteinstein wasn't keen on forces. He preferred to think *geometrically*. The paths that particles follow, in the absence of any forces such as gravity, are called *geodesics*. They are shortest paths – they minimize the total distance between their endpoints. In flat Minkowski spacetime – Minny Space and her full-blown extension to 3D space plus 1D time – the analogous relativistic paths minimize the interval instead.' Vikki had difficulty imagining anything more full blown than Minny Space. 'The problem is to add in effects of gravity consistently. Alberteinstein incorporated gravity not as an extra force, but as a distortion of the structure of spacetime, which changes the value of the interval. This variable interval between nearby events is called the *metric* of spacetime. The usual image is to say that spacetime becomes "curved".'

'Curved round what?'

'That's why Curvy Space is here. She can show you.'

*

'It's not curved round anything, girly. It's just intrinsically distorted compared with flat spacetime. You might as well ask "flat along what?" about ordinary Euclidean space, it's just as sensible – or silly – a question. The curvature is interpreted physically as the force of gravity, and it causes light cones to deform.'

'How can space be curved?' asked Vikki.

'I'm surprised a Flatlander who's seen the Mathiverse can ask that,' said Curvy Space. 'You used to think space had to be flat. Now you know better!'

'Yes, but that was 2D space, and it's easy to imagine a curved surface. But a curved solid?'

'Platterland was curved,' said the Space Hopper, 'but when we were on it, it didn't look *bent*.'

'You mean the disc had a curved edge?'

'No, not the edge – the whole *space* was curved. That's what made the geometry so weird. Platterland has constant negative curvature. A sphere has constant positive curvature. And a plane, like Flatland, has zero curvature. Different curvatures, different geometries. You can get curvature in 3D, too.'

'How?'

'You're suffering from too heavy a Spaceland diet, girly,' said Curvy Space. 'Tell me, what would a curved 2D universe look like *from inside?*'

'Bent?'

'Not at all! Flat. Because light would follow the surface, see? It would go along the geodesics – the shortest paths *that lie in the surface.*'

'Then how could you tell it wasn't flat?'

'Because images would distort as light rounded the curves', said the Space Hopper. 'Distances wouldn't match up to the model of a Euclidean plane. Which is why the shortest paths, the geodesics, in Hyperbolica looked – from an outside VUEpoint – like circles.' She still looked uncertain, so he cast around for another example. 'Remember the squarrel? As soon as you see a five-sided squarrel with all angles 90 degrees, you *know* you're in a negatively curved space. And the same goes for curved 3D space, or curved 4D space-time.'

'Yes, but . . . what would the space be curved *around?*'

The Space Hopper grunted, and Vikki suddenly found herself falling into Squarey Space.

⁕

'Don't ask "curved around what", baby. Ask "*flat* around what"!'

'That makes no sense at all.'

'Yes it does, kid. Look at me – I'm flat.'

'You *look* flat. But Curvy Space just told me that doesn't mean anything.'

'Believe me, take my measurements, I'm as flat as a pancake in a steamroller rodeo. But I'm a torus.'

'Well, I'm Libra, but I don't actually believe in that sort of—'

'No, no. A topological doughnut. And just watch it, OK?'

'I wasn't going to say a word about what kind of nut you—'

'I said, watch it! Know why they call me Squarey Space?'

'No.'

'Because ultimately I'm a flat square.'

'But you said you're a torus, and that's all curves.'

'Ah. A torus embedded in 3D is curved. An unembedded one, just being its own space without any outside assistance, can be flat.'

'How?'

'Take a look over there – no, a bit further to your left. What do you see?'

'Er . . . wow! It looks like *me*!'

'It is you. And beyond that?'

'An even tinier me. And another, and another . . . fading into the distance. The light rays are bending round like a projective lion.'

'The light rays are bending *straight* like a projective lion, babe. In certain directions, you see yourself. That's because opposite edges of my underlying square *wrap round* and glue together, seamlessly. You don't need to bend me to make them join – you just have to declare that they do. Or, if you prefer, you can tile an infinite plane with copies of that square, and insist that whatever happens in one copy, happens in all of them. It's the same thing.

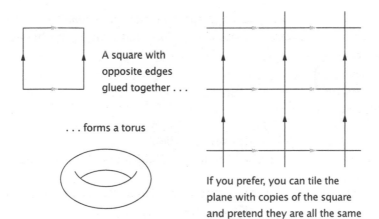

A square with opposite edges glued together . . .

. . . forms a torus

If you prefer, you can tile the plane with copies of the square and pretend they are all the same

'So, you see, I'm flat, and yet I have closed geodesics. Which don't bend *around* anything, because there *isn't* anything else anyway. Intrinsically, a space can be bounded, have no edges, and yet be flat. Compared to that, curved 3D space is a piece of cake. Just squeeze its metric here and there.'

*

With a PLOP! Vikki found herself back in metaspace. 'So now you know,' said Squarey Space.

'And when the Planiturthians made *very* careful measurements,' Pushy Space butted in, 'they discovered that their universe is curved.'

'How did they discover that?'

'Look for the rainbow in every storm, kid. Bent light, you dig? Curved space leads to "gravitational lensing", where light gets bent by heavy objects. You can see it happening during an eclipse of the Sun. And quasars – powerful, distant kinds of superstar – produce multiple images in telescopes because their light is lensed by a galaxy that is in the way.'

'It's easier to visualize,' the Space Hopper said helpfully, 'if you think of a spacelike section of 3D spacetime – 2D space, 1D time – near a star. It forms a curved surface that bends downwards to create a valley, and the star sits inside. Light follows geodesics across the surface and gets "pulled down" into the hole because that path provides a short cut. Just like the circular arcs – to our eyes – that form geodesics in Hyperbolica. Particles moving in spacetime at sub-lightspeed behave in the same way. If you look down from above you see that the particles no longer follow straight lines, but are "pulled towards" the star, which is where the Newtonian picture of a gravitational force comes from.

'Far from the star,' the Space Hopper continued, 'this spacetime is very close to Minkowski spacetime – the gravitational effect falls off rapidly and soon becomes negligible. Spacetimes that look like Minkowski spacetime at large distances are said to be *asymptotically flat*. Remember that term: it's important for making time machines.' He was back to those again. 'Most of our own universe is asymptotically flat, because massive bodies such as stars are scattered very thinly.'

Vikki digested this information. 'So we could give spacetime any form we wanted? That sounds a bit *too* flexible.'

'No. When you're setting up a spacetime, you can't just bend things any way you like. The metric must obey the *Einstein equations*, which relate the motion of freely moving particles to the degree of distortion away from "flat" Minkowski spacetime.'

'You mean,' said Vikki, 'that there's a connection between the distribution of masses within a spacetime and the structure of the spacetime itself? As if matter . . . creates and moulds its own space and time?'

'Exactly.'

Fiveday 20 Noctember 2099
OK, Diary: finally, the Space Hopper explained how to interpret the phrase 'time machine' within the framework of General Relativity.

Here's the gen. A time machine lets a particle or object return to its own past, so its world-line, a timelike curve, must close into a loop. A time machine is just a *closed timelike curve*. So instead of asking, 'Is time travel possible?' we ask, 'Can closed timelike curves exist?'.

So, can they?

Not in Minny Space. There, forward and backward light cones – the future and past of an event – never intersect. But they can intersect in other types of spacetime. The simplest is Minny Space rolled up into a cylinder. Then the time coordinate becomes cyclic, but the spacetime is still flat.

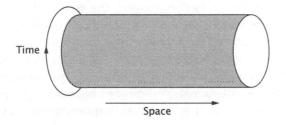

In such a spacetime, history repeats itself, over and over again. Sort of, anyway. *Spacetime* repeats – but what happens to history depends upon whether you think free will might be in operation. It's a tricky question, and one that Einstein's equations don't really address. They just govern the overall coarse structure of spacetime.

I told you that this cylindrical spacetime is flat, Diary Dearest, though I admit it doesn't look that way. It's rather like Squarey Space, but with time thrown in, so you have to be careful. Although a cylindrical spacetime *looks* curved, actually the corresponding spacetime is *not* curved – not in the gravitational sense. When you roll up a sheet of paper into a cylinder, it doesn't *distort*. You can flatten it out again and the paper isn't folded or wrinkled. A creature that was confined purely to the surface wouldn't notice that it had been bent, because distances *on* the surface wouldn't have changed. In short, the metric – a local property of spacetime structure *near* a given event – doesn't change. What changes is the global geometry of spacetime, its overall topology.

✴

'Rolling up Minny Space,' said the Space Hopper, 'is an example of a powerful topological trick for building new Spacetimes out of old ones: *cut-and-paste*. If you can cut pieces out of known Spacetimes, and glue them together without distorting their metrics, then the result is also a possible Spacetime.'

'You're speaking metaphorically, of course.'

'Well, until recently I'd have agreed with you. But now the Hawk King's moved into the spacetime construction business.'

'The Hawk King?'

'A very, *very* impressive being. I'm planning an audience with him, if we can swing it. When it comes to spacetime heavy engineering – and I really do mean *heavy* – the Hawk King is in a class of his own. But I'm getting ahead of myself.'

'Well, you said you were interested in time travel.'

The Space Hopper laughed politely. 'I say "distorting the metric" rather than "bending", for exactly the reason that I claim rolled-up Minny Space is *not* curved. I'm talking about intrinsic curvature, as experienced by a creature that lives in the spacetime, not about apparent curvature as seen in some external representation. Apparent bending of this type is harmless – it doesn't actually change the metric. Now, the rolled-up version of Minny Space is a very simple way to prove that Spacetimes that obey the Einstein equations *can* possess closed timelike curves – and thus that time travel is not inconsistent with currently known physics. But that doesn't imply that time travel is *possible*.'

'I see that. There's a distinction between what's mathematically possible and what's physically feasible.'

'Very good, Vikki. A spacetime is mathematically possible if it obeys the Einstein equations. It's physically feasible if it can exist, or could be created, as part of a specified universe. Which is where the heavy engineering comes in. Unfortunately for time travel in the Planiturthian universe, there's no reason to suppose that rolled-up Minkowski spacetime is physically feasible: certainly it would be hard to refashion the Planiturthian universe in that form if it didn't already have cyclic time. The search for Spacetimes that have closed timelike curves *and* have plausible physics is a search for more plausible topologies. There are many mathematically possible topologies, but you can't get to all of them from a given starting point. But you can get to some remarkably interesting ones, based on black holes.'

'Are those like topological holes?'

'Only very loosely speaking, Vikki. You know that in classical Newtonian mechanics there's no limit to the speed of a moving object, so particles can escape from an attracting mass, however strong its gravitational field, by moving faster than the appropriate escape velocity. In 1783 the Planiturthian astronomer Johnmichell realized that when this idea is combined with a finite velocity for light, it implies that really heavy objects can't emit light at all – because the speed of light is lower than the escape velocity. The light travels too slowly to be able to get away, you understand?'

'Sure. That's easy.'

'In 1796 another astronomer, Pierresimondelaplace, put the same idea in a book of his called *Exposition of the System of the World*. And both Planiturthian astronomers imagined that the universe might be littered with huge bodies, bigger than stars, but totally dark.'

'Wild!'

'You said it. They were both a century ahead of their time. In 1915 Karlschwarzschild asked whether the same kind of thing could happen with relativistic gravitation. He solved the Einstein equations for the gravitational field around a heavy sphere in a vacuum. His solution behaved very strangely at a critical distance from the centre of the sphere, now called the *Schwarzschild radius*. When it was first discovered, People thought this strange behaviour just meant that space and time lost their identity in Schwarzschild's solution, and became meaningless. A mathematical artefact, yes? With no physical implications at all. But then some bright spark asked what would happen to a star so dense that it lies completely inside its own Schwarzschild radius.'

'And what *would* happen, Hopper?'

'It would collapse under its own gravitational attraction! In fact, a whole portion of spacetime around that star would collapse to form a region from which no matter, not even light, could escape. In 1967 Johnarchibaldwheeler called such a region a *black hole*, and the name stuck.'

Black hole

'Does a black hole stay the same for ever, or does it change?'

'It changes. First the star shrinks symmetrically until it hits the Schwarzschild radius, after which it continues to shrink more rapidly until, after a finite time, all the mass has collapsed to a single point, the *singularity*. From outside, all you can detect is the *event horizon* at the Schwarzschild radius, which separates the region from which light can escape from the region that's forever unobservable from outside. Inside the event horizon lurks the black hole.

'If you were to watch the collapse from outside, you'd see the star start to shrink towards the Schwarzschild radius, but you'd never see it get there. As it shrinks, its speed of collapse as seen from outside approaches the speed of light, and relativistic time dilation means that the entire collapse takes infinitely long when seen by an outside observer. However, the collapse time experienced by an observer on the surface of the star would be finite. Once inside a black hole, the roles of space and time are reversed. Just as time inexorably increases in the outside world, so space inexorably decreases inside a black hole.

'That's where the scope for engineering comes in,' said the Space Hopper. 'The Hawk King has developed a whole battery of techniques, from quantum foam enlargement to improbability calculus. Now, the spacetime topology of a black hole is asymptotically flat – its "mouth" opens out and becomes flat at large distances. So a black hole can be cut-and-pasted into the spacetime of any universe that has reasonably large asymptotically flat regions – such as the Planiturthian one. This makes black hole topology physically plausible in such a universe. The scenario of gravitational collapse makes it even more plausible: if you want to build a black hole, you just have to start with a big enough concentration of matter, like a neutron star or the centre of a galaxy. That's what I meant by heavy engineering. The technology of 3001 will be able to *build* black holes. With matter processors – modified neutron stars with gravitational traps and heavy-duty laser-compressors.

'However, a black hole isn't enough, because a static black hole doesn't have closed timelike curves. However, Einstein's equations are time-reversible: to every solution of the equations there corresponds another that is just the same, except that time runs backwards. The time-reversal of a black hole is a *white hole*. An ordinary event horizon is a barrier from which no particle can escape. A time-reversed event horizon is one into which no particle can fall, but from which particles may from time to time be emitted. So, seen from the outside, a white hole would appear as the sudden explosion of a star's-worth of matter, coming from a time-reversed event horizon.'

'Why should the singularity inside a white hole suddenly decide to spew forth a star, having remained unchanged since the dawn of time?' protested Vikki.

'Good point. It makes causal sense for an initial concentration of matter to collapse, if it's dense enough, thereby forming a black hole; but the reverse seems to violate causality. It doesn't, of course – but the cause would have to lie outside our own universe, beyond the white hole's event horizon, so we wouldn't see it coming. Let's just agree that white holes are a mathematical possibility, and notice that they're also asymptotically flat when they open out enough. So if you knew how to make one, you could glue it neatly into your own universe. The Hawk King has just developed an effective method for doing that, based on the uncertainty principle. He uses a Heisenberg amplifier to make the position of matter so uncertain that it may well be outside the normal universe altogether. Not only that, he can also glue a black hole and a white hole together. He cuts them along their event horizons with a cosmotome and sews the edges together with exotic – that is, negative-energy – matter.'

'And what does that give?'

'A wormhole. A sort of tube. Matter can pass through the tube in one direction only: into the black hole and out of the white hole. It's a kind of matter valve. And the passage through the valve is achieved by following a timelike curve, because material particles really can traverse it.

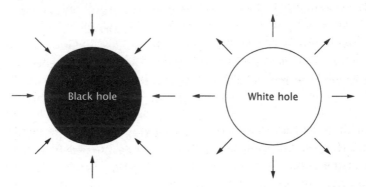

'Now comes the clever bit. Because the topology of spacetime is asymptotically flat at both ends of the tube, both ends can be glued into any asymptotically flat region of any spacetime. You could glue one end into the Planiturthian universe, and the other end into somebody else's; or you could glue both ends into the Planiturthian universe – *anywhere you like*, except near a concentration of matter. Now you've got a – guess.'

'A spacetube?'

'No: a *wormhole*. The Hawk King makes the best wormholes in the universe. They're called wormholes because they look like the holes a maggot bores in an apple. Only here the apple is – well, not so much spacetime as everything that's *not* spacetime.

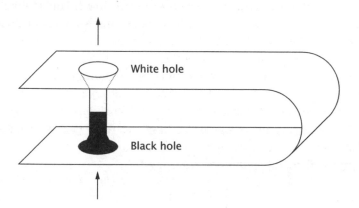

'The next important thing is this: the distance *through* the wormhole is very short, though the distance between the two openings, across normal spacetime, can be as big as you like.'

'I see,' said Vikki. 'A wormhole is a short cut through the universe.'

'Right,' said the Space Hopper.

'But that's *matter transmission*, not time travel.'

'So far, yes,' said the Space Hopper. 'But there's more.'

*

'It ought to be easy to use the VUE to explore a wormhole,' said the Space Hopper. 'Unfortunately, it's not. Most parts of the Mathiverse are in the Public Domain, because mathematicians never understand how important their ideas are until long after they've told everyone about them. Anyway, according to metaspatial law, mathematicians aren't allowed to patent mathematics because it consists of *ideas*. Anyone *else* can patent mathematics, as long as they don't admit that that's what it is, but mathematicians can't because – being mathematicians – they *know* it's mathematics, and are bound by their logical training to say so.

'The Hawk King has acquired a vast commercial empire (so I

suppose he ought to be called the Hawk Emperor, but somehow that doesn't sound right) by securing a monopoly on Time Travel mathematics. In principle he also controls the Mathiverse's supply of magnetic monopoles, so he has a Monopole Monopoly – but since no one has found a monopole yet, that's a bit hypothetical. Since all rights to time machinery are controlled by the Hawk King, we will have to request an audience with His Majesty and petition him for temporal access.'

'How do we do that?' asked Vikki.

'We VUEtravel to where he lives, and approach the appropriate officials.'

'Where does His Majesty live, then?'

'In the Domain of the Hawk King. It's right next to the Public Domain, separated by a domain boundary, so a couple of Space Hops will get us there in no time at all . . .'

*

'Passport? What do you mean, passport?'

'No one enters the Domain of the Hawk King without a passport,' said the official from His Majesty's Customer Extortionists.

'But we haven't got—' Vikki began.

'What *sort* of passport?' asked the Space Hopper. 'Would I be right in thinking that it's made of paper?'

'Of course.'

'Strong paper?'

'Indeed.'

'With lots of fancy engraving on it?'

'Definitely on the right track.'

'And it sort of . . . *folds*?'

'Yup, sure sounds like a passport to me,' said the official.

'Would that be a big piece of paper, or a small one?'

'Oh . . . big. Yes, definitely. Big.'

'How big?'

'How big have you got?'

'How big will secure us an immediate audience with the Hawk King?'

'Oooooooh . . . about five times as big as your run-of-the-mill passport.'

'Would *this* be suitable?' There was a rustling as paper changed hands.

'Definitely. Your documents are completely in order, Mr . . . er . . . Bankofspaceland. And your good lady Ms Travellerscheque too, I'm pleased to say. Let me just call up His Majesty's schedule . . . Right. You have a five-minute audience at 3.50 this afternoon. Just give your ticket to the official at the door.'

'But we don't have a—' Vikki began.

'Vikki, the ticket is without doubt a document *just like a passport*.'

'Uh – oh, right, Space Hopper. I see.'

※

The Hawk King's audience room was vast. He sat on a splendid throne at the far end. It took them *for ever* to make their way towards him.

'This is where a time machine would really come in useful,' the Space Hopper whispered to Vikki.

'Yes. Or a wormhole. I could do with a short cut.'

'I'd be careful using that sort of metaphor in the Hawk King's presence,' cautioned the Space Hopper. 'He has a habit of taking things literally.'

'Ulp.'

Eventually they arrived at the foot of the throne. The Hawk King's piercing eyes dissected their souls.

'You do realize,' he said, 'that people used to think time travel was a theoretical impossibility, a contradiction in terms?'

Obviously he had overheard their whispered conversation. Hawks reputedly have astonishing eyesight – perhaps his hearing was just as acute. Or perhaps the audience room was equipped with sensitive microphones.

'Of course, now we know better,' the monarch continued. 'You are thinking of exploring one of my wormholes?'

'Uh – my companion did *mention* a wormhole, Your Majesty.'

'You cannot afford the price, you realize.'

'We were hoping that wouldn't be necessary, Your Majesty,' said the Space Hopper.

'Is there a connection between wormholes and time machines, Your Majesty?' Vikki asked in a squeaky voice.

'Of course. It was the Paradox Twins that suggested the idea to me originally – you've met them? Yes, I see you have. Never mind, you'll get over it. They experienced a time *discrepancy* – but it led into the future, not the past. However, in conjunction with a worm hole – that time discrepancy can be turned into a closed timelike curve.'

'Uh – how, Your Majesty?'

'Fix the white end of the wormhole, and tow the black one away – or better still, zigzag it back and forth – as close to lightspeed as you can get.

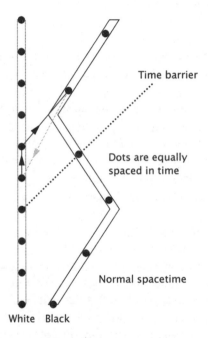

Time barrier

Dots are equally spaced in time

Normal spacetime

White   Black

'The white end of the wormhole remains static, and time there passes at its normal rate. The black end zigzags to and fro at just less than the speed of light. So time dilation comes into play, and time passes more slowly for an observer moving with that end.'

'Ah!' said the Space Hopper. 'I see, Your Majesty. A brilliant insight!'

'Um—' Vikki began.

'Why, Vikki – all you have to do is think about world-lines that join the two wormholes through normal space, so that the times experienced by observers at each end are the same', said the Space Hopper. 'At first, those lines have a slope of less than 45 degrees, so they're not timelike, and it's impossible for material particles to travel along them. But as the black end of the wormhole zigzags back and forth, at some moment that line achieves a 45-degree slope. And once this "time barrier" is crossed, you can travel from the white end of the wormhole to the black one *through normal space* – following a time-like curve. And once you've arrived there, you can return *through* the wormhole, again along a timelike curve. Because the wormhole forms a short cut you can do that in a very short time, effectively travelling instantly from the black end to the white end. And now you're in the same place as your starting point, but in the *past*!'

'Indeed,' said the Hawk King. 'You have travelled back in time. And the actual distance you travel through ordinary space can be quite small – it depends on how far the black end of the worm-hole moves on each leg of its zigzag path. In space of more than one dimension it can spiral rather than zigzag, which corresponds to making the black end follow a circular orbit at close to light-speed.'

'Wonderful, Your Majesty,' said the Space Hopper. 'Vikki, you could do that by creating a binary pair of black holes, rotating rapidly round a common centre of gravity!'

Vikki gave the matter thorough consideration. *Somebody* might be able to do that. Not her. 'Would I be right in thinking that the longer you wait before you start, the further back in time you can go?'

'Yes,' said the Space Hopper, 'but there's a nasty snag. You can never travel back past the time barrier, and that occurs some time *after* you build the wormholes! So there's no hope of going back to the time of the Planiturthian dinosaurs, or the time of the Universal Colour Bill in Flatland.'

'Unless someone found a very old, naturally occurring worm-hole,' the Hawk King pointed out.

'Is that what you've done, Your Majesty?'

'That, my dear young Line, is a commercial secret. And the time allocated for your audience has almost run out, so I strongly suggest that you present your petition immediately.'

Royal hints should not go unheeded. 'We should like to experi-ence time travel', said the Space Hopper.

'Into the past,' Vikki added quickly, just in case there was a misunderstanding.

'Ah. And do you have a reason for this wish?'

Vikki racked her brains . . . why *did* they want to try time travel? 'To see if we can help the Paradox Twins, Your Majesty.'

The Hawk King rose and spread his magnificent feathers. Vikki and the Space Hopper tried hard not to cower. 'That is a worthy motive,' the King remarked. 'I have decided to grant your request. My aides will deal with the details on your way out. You are dismissed.'

14

DOWN THE WORMHOLE

Sevenday 22 Noctember 2099
Thus, Dear Diary, began the most curious adventure that I have yet experienced during my Misguided Tour of the Mathiverse! The King's aides took us into a special room, full of strange, arcane machinery. And in the middle of that room, hovering unsupported, was—

*

'—a *red* hole?' said Vikki, disappointed. It was like a big blood-red bubble, and it *sparkled*. 'I thought they were black.'

'A common misconception – or perhaps I should say "misperception",' said the Master of the Royal Wormhole. Vikki had taken an instant dislike to him: the Hawk King was majestic and awe-inspiring, whereas the Master of the Royal Wormhole was an arrogant snob. She wasn't sure they ought to trust him. But the Space Hopper seemed unconcerned. 'The term "black hole" refers to the manner in which light is sucked into the singularity. However, thanks to relativistic time dilation, the light emitted by anything that is falling into a black hole actually appears red.'

'Oh.'

'For example, the bunch of roses that you see sinking slowly towards the event horizon – the surface of what appears to be a bubble – actually crossed the event horizon several weeks ago, and by now has emerged into a previous century. What we see is the light that the roses emitted, which has spent the intervening time struggling painfully away from the black hole's clutches. And struggling light shifts towards the red end of the spectrum. Not only that, but every black hole is surrounded by a complete record of everything that ever fell into it. But unless the object fell in recently, the image is extremely squashed and redshifted, and mixed up with all the images of all the other objects. And the longer ago an object fell in, the closer it had to get to the event horizon for its image still to be visible. Still, it's an intriguing thought, is it not?'

'So ... er ... how do we *use* the wormhole?' asked the Space Hopper.

'Easy. You fall into it.'

'How do we do—'

'The problem, young lady, is to *stop* yourself falling into it. You see that white line marked on the floor?'

'Yes.'

'Step a micrometre beyond that and the Black Hole will suck you in. Guaranteed.'

'Oh.'

'But the gravity will shred you like cheese in a grater.'

'Space Hopper, I think I've changed my mind—'

'Unless you wear protective suits of exotic matter.'

'Ah. That's different.'

'Which are available for a small – um – *documentary* exchange.'

More rustling. Weird suits that didn't quite seem to be *present* were brought, and the two travellers climbed into them. After a perfunctory safety check they were led towards the fateful white line.

The tip of one of the Space Hopper's horns crossed the line. Suddenly his shape was drawn out into a long, thin tube. His body elongated, then flattened – then shrunk as if all his insides had been sucked away along an unseen dimension. He became a dwindling speck of redshifted light.

Vikki took a deep breath, and followed him in.

※

Wunday 23 Noctember 2099

Diary: it was the second most *HORRIBLE* experience of my LIFE!!!!

What was the FIRST most horrible?

I'm coming to that.

*

'We're trapped!' said the Space Hopper.

They were circling the black hole's singularity, held away by the forces generated by the suits' exotic matter. They should have been swept past it towards the white hole exit from the wormhole.

But there was no exit.

'It was just an ordinary black hole all along,' complained the Space Hopper. 'There never was a way out. The Master of the Royal Wormhole was playing games with us. Very nasty games. I imagine he pocketed the cost of the white hole construction instead of getting it built. And now we're stuck. I'm sorry – I should have realized he wasn't to be trusted.'

'I didn't like him,' said Vikki, 'and I should have said so. But can't we use the VUE to get out?'

'It doesn't work in here. Exotic matter interferes with its conceptical actuvailers.'

'Then we're *trapped*!'

'I already said that.'

'I know – and it's still true! Is there a way out?'

'Does it look like there's a way out?'

'No, but there *must* be! We could *die* in here!'

The Space Hopper gave her a mournful look. 'I'm afraid that's exactly what we will do', he said. 'No food, no drink – and no way out. And I don't think there's any kind of "and with one bound our heroine was free" trick that can save us.'

There was a long silence.

'We're stuck, then,' said Vikki disconsolately.

'You certainly are,' said Vikki.

Vikki thought the voice was familiar, and looked up. To see – Vikki.

'Hold it. You're me!'

'No, *I'm* me. You're you. But you're close. We're both us.'

There was a second Space Hopper too.

'Where have you two come from?'

'No time to explain – you'll find out soon enough. We've brought a portable white hole with us. You can use it to get out.'

With one portable white hole, our heroine was free . . . 'That's *orthog*! You're coming too, of course.'

'No, we can't. It won't work if we do that.'

'What won't work?'

'Causality won't work. Don't try to think about it *now* – there's plenty of time for that later. Just jump into the event horizon of the white hole. Oh, and take it out with you.'

'We can do that?'

'Yes, it's a special model. It shuts itself down automatically after you've gone through, and only opens up when you need it.'

'Then what?'

'You will be contacted,' said the second Space Hopper mysteriously.

❋

'Whew!' said the Space Hopper. 'That was a narrow squeak.'

'It certainly was,' said Vikki. 'And also,' she added after a few moments' thought, 'completely mad.'

'Mad?'

'Hopper, *we rescued ourselves.* But to do that, we had to have escaped, and we couldn't because there was no way out!'

'Mmm. But obviously we did escape . . . or else . . .' He stopped. 'I dunno. You're right, it's mad.'

'So now?'

'We hang around and wait. "You will be contacted", so my alter ego told us. So I imagine we—'

'Hi there!' said the Space Hopper. Two Space Hoppers stared at each other. So did two Vikkis. 'Now listen very carefully, I shall say this only—'

'I think you've got some explaining to do. Anyway, how did you two get out of the black hole?'

'Hmm. You're making a rather *big* assumption there. But you're right, we did. We used the time machine, of course.'

'What time machine?'

'This one. Which, by the way, *you* are going to need, so I'll give it to you now. Oh, and keep the portable white hole, you'll need that shortly too.'

Slowly, an *idea* was forming in Vikki's mind. Now that they were out of the black hole, and were in possession of a time machine and an automatically deploying portable white hole . . .

'Hopper! They were *us*!'

'But they said they weren't.'

'Not exactly. They were a second set of us – from the future. Our *own* future. They were a slightly older version of us!'

'That's right,' said the slightly older version of Vikki, 'and do you see what you've got to do?'

'Most of it,' said Vikki. 'But how do we—'

The slightly older version of Vikki told her.

❖

Knowing where the black hole was kept, this time round, and having full use of the VUE, it was easy to sneak into the Hawk King's Wormhole Room unnoticed. They had travelled back in time, using the time machine they'd just given themselves, to a moment a few minutes after their first disastrous descent into the black hole.

Now they were going to do it again – but this time they were forewarned, and therefore forearmed. With a time machine and a white hole.

Once inside, they went through a now-familiar routine.

'We're stuck, then,' the original Vikki was saying disconsolately.

'You certainly are,' said Vikki – who was now the slightly older version of herself.

The original Vikki thought the voice was familiar, and looked up. To see – Vikki.

'Hold it. You're me!'

'No, *I'm* me. You're you. But you're close. We're both us.'

The original Vikki saw there was a second Space Hopper too.

'Where have you two come from?'

'No time to explain – you'll find out soon enough. We've brought a portable white hole with us. You can use it to get out.'

With one portable white hole, our heroine was free . . . 'That's *orthog*! You're coming too, of course.'

'No, we can't. It won't work if we do that.'

'What won't work?'

'Causality won't work. Don't try to think about it *now* – there's plenty of time for that later. Just jump into the event horizon of the white hole. Oh, and take it out with you.'

'We can do that?'

'Yes, it's a special model. It shuts itself down automatically after you've gone through, and only opens up when you need it.'

'Then what?'

'You will be contacted,' said the Space Hopper mysteriously.

＊

Vikki (slightly older version) and the Space Hopper (slightly older version) watched their younger versions depart, taking the portable white hole with them.

'So how do *we* get out?' asked the Space Hopper. '*They've* got the white hole, so now *we're* stuck here. Do we wait for a *third* version of us to rescue us?'

'Not at all. You're forgetting, *we've* got the time machine.'

'So?'

'All black holes eventually lose their energy by Hawk King radiation, and evaporate.'

Vikki's brain screeched to a halt. 'No, hold it, wait. I thought a black hole gobbles up everything near it.'

'Oops. That's true for a purely relativistic black hole, but not – as the Hawk King discovered – for a quantum one. When quantum effects are taken into account, black holes turn out to be *hot*.'

'Hot? Why should something that nothing can escape from be hot? How does the heat escape, then?'

'It escapes because in quantum physics a vacuum isn't empty.'

'I thought that's what "vacuum" meant.'

'It did, long ago,' said the Space Hopper, 'but not any more. On the smallest of scales, a quantum vacuum is a seething foam of particles and virtual particles, being created in pairs from nothing, coexisting for a split second, and then annihilating each other – or something else. A quantum vacuum is only empty on average. Now, suppose that a particle pair comes into being just outside the event horizon of a black hole. What happens?'

'They both get gobbled up?'

'No. *One* gets gobbled up, but the law of conservation of momentum implies that the other one has to go in the opposite direction, so it escapes. Hawk King radiation is the result of all those escaping particles. So black holes are hot. Over time, they lose more and more heat by radiation, cool down, and eventually evaporate.'

'How much time does it take?' Vikki asked. It affected their current predicament.

'Very quick for atomic-scale black holes, enormously long for bigger ones,' replied the Space Hopper. 'This one will take for ever to evaporate.' He sighed.

'We've *got* for ever,' said Vikki, in a flash of inspiration. 'We have a time machine.' The Space Hopper perked up again. Some careful crosstime planning was in order . . .

And so they fast-forwarded several zillion years, until the black hole evaporated around them and they were floating freely in metaspace. Then they fast-backwarded several zillion years – though not *quite* as many as they had fast-forwarded . . . and again they experienced a familiar conversation from the other side . . .

'So now?'

'We hang around and wait. "You will be contacted", so my alter ego told us. So I imagine we—'

'Hi there!' said the Space Hopper. Two Space Hoppers stared at each other. So did two Vikkis. 'Now listen very carefully, I shall say this only—'

'I think you've got some explaining to do. Anyway, how did you two get out of the black hole?'

'Hmm. You're making a rather *big* assumption there,' said the slightly older version of Vikki. 'But you're right, we did. We used the time machine, of course.'

'What time machine?'

'This one. Which, by the way, *you* are going to need, so I'll give it to you now. Oh, and keep the white hole, you'll need that shortly too.'

Slowly, an *idea* was forming in the mind of the slightly younger version of Vikki. Now that they were out of the black hole, and were in possession of a time machine and an automatically deploying portable White Hole . . .

'Hopper! They were *us*!'

'But they said they weren't.'

'Not exactly. They were a second set of us – from the future. Our *own* future. They were a slightly older version of us!'

'That's right,' said the slightly older version of Vikki, 'and do you see what you've got to do?'

'Most of it,' said the slightly younger version of Vikki. 'But how do we—'

The slightly older version of Vikki told her.

※

'And that's that,' said the Space Hopper.

'Wha— but they've just gone back in time to go into the black hole, and—'

'No, they're earlier versions of us, and we've already been through all that. Think about it: we're out of the black hole, we've done all the time travelling and handing over of technology that was needed to *get* us out—'

'But *where did that technology come from?*'

'The white hole and the time machine? We gave it to us.'

'But—'

'You asked the wrong question. *Where did that technology go to?* We haven't got it now, have we?'

'No.'

'So that's all right. The Mathiverse hasn't gained anything it didn't have before.'

'But it's mad,' said Vikki. 'The causality doesn't work.'

'On the contrary,' said the Space Hopper. 'The causality is the one thing that *does* work! You're just not thinking about it the right way.'

'I don't know how else to think about it!' Vikki wailed.

'Use a Feynman diagram, of course', said the Space Hopper.

'What's that when it's at home?'

'Richardfeynman was a Planiturthian who was doodling pictures of world-lines of particles moving through space and time, when he suddenly realized that antiparticles moving forwards in time could be viewed as ordinary particles moving *backwards* in time.

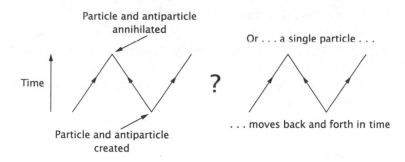

Particle and antiparticle annihilated

Time

Or . . . a single particle . . .

?

. . . moves back and forth in time

Particle and antiparticle created

And then he noticed that there was just one line in his picture, whizzing back and forth through time, and suddenly a really revolutionary idea popped into his head. 'Why are all electrons identical?'

'Dunno.'

'Because they're all the *same* electron! It just keeps shuttling up and down in time, and each new incarnation turns it into what *seems* like a different electron.'

'Cunning.'

'Very. And possibly wrong – nobody knows for sure. But the point is that by drawing a picture of the world-lines, you can sort out the subjective sequence of events from the objective one, and check that the causality works.' And the Space Hopper quickly used the VUE to sketch a Feynman diagram of their adventures down the Black Hole.

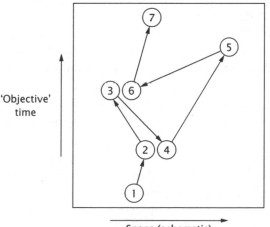

'Objective' time

Space (schematic)

'OK,' said the Space Hopper. 'The Mathiverse's "objective" time runs vertically up the picture. The horizontal space direction is just there to separate out the main events. And our *subjective* time is shown by the arrows.

'Let me run through what happened. We started at (1), in the Hawk King's Palace. Then we got trapped inside a black hole that we'd been told was a wormhole – that's (2). And while we were there, another we came back from the future using a time machine – that's the path from (3) to (4) – and dropped ourselves back into the black hole to rescue ourselves. We also brought a white hole to create an exit. Where did we get it, and the time machine? That's another story – I'll come back to it once we've sorted out the main timeline.

'Anyway, from (2) we used the white hole to get ourselves to (3), back into ordinary space. We left the time machine with the "other" Vikki and Space Hopper inside the black hole and proceeded into the future in the normal way. Then we went from (3) to (4) – I've already told you that bit. After that we used the time machine to go zillions of years into the future, to (5), where the black hole evaporated and we were free of its event horizon. We promptly used the time machine *again* to go slightly fewer zillions of years into the past, to (6). At that point we met our former selves (3) coming the other way – in time, that is – and gave them the hardware they needed to go back to (4). Then we continued from (6) towards the distant future (7), using the normal method of waiting for time to pass of its own accord.'

Vikki ran her eyes over the Feynman diagram, checking each event. It all seemed to fit. But . . . 'I'm still puzzled,' she said.

'Do you see that the passage of subjective time, for us, just moved from (1) to (2) to (3) to (4) to (5) to (6), and now we're heading towards (7)? It's just a single linear chain of experience – for us. Subjectively.'

'*Yeeesss* . . .'

'And each event has the right versions of us, and the right equipment?'

'*Yeeesss* . . .'

'Then I don't see what your problem is.'

'Space Hopper, where did the time machine come from? Where did the white hole come from?'

'Where have they gone? That's what you ought to be asking.'

'I don't know! We're *out*, and we don't have them any more . . . but I can't quite see how the trick worked.'

'Actually, the question is not *where* did they come from, but *when*. Trace the temporal movement of the white hole.'

'Um. We picked it up at (2), carried it to (3), took it back in time to (4) – oh! And then we handed it over to our former selves at (2) again!'

'That's right. The portable white hole is going – was going? Will go? Will have being gone? – round and round a closed timelike curve. A time loop. Its past runs into its future: it has always been in the time loop and it always will be. And what about the time machine?'

'We were first given that – in our own subjective sequence of events – at (3). We took it back to (4), used it to get to (5) without tottering off this mortal coil, used it again to get us back to (6) – and then handed it back to ourselves at (4). The *time machine* is going round a time loop too!'

'Yes. But a different one from the loop that the white hole is in.'

'Right. And because they're in time loops, but we're in an ordinary open-ended chain, we emerge from the whole process without any fancy technology that we couldn't possibly possess.'

'Precisely. All of which goes to show—'

'—that causality is totally *weird* when you've got a time machine. Even if it disappears up its own – er – closed timelike curve.'

'It's only weird *to us*. As far as the Mathiverse is concerned, it all makes perfectly good sense. It seems weird *globally* – viewed as a whole. But each piece of it is entirely reasonable and logical. It's *easy* to explain where the time machine and the white hole come from. They've always been stuck in their time loops, and always will be. The hard thing to explain, Vikki, is where *we* come from. Because that seems to need an infinitely long chain of causality. Like you said, *our* timelines are open-ended.'

That reminded Vikki of something. 'Yes, maybe . . . but Space

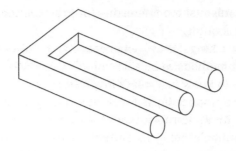

Hopper,' she said, 'do you recall that funny picture that Space-landers sometimes use to baffle themselves with?' She fiddled with her VUE, and a line drawing of a solid object appeared:

'Yes, I remember. The object looks OK, but it can't actually exist.'

'My point exactly. Now, what do you mean by "look OK"? You mean that each piece is entirely reasonable and logical. And when you say "can't actually exist", you're saying that—'

'It seems weird globally.'

'So maybe the kind of twisted causality that we think we've just experienced can't *really* happen in a relativistic spacetime,' said Vikki. 'We're missing a global law of nature that could rule it out.'

'Such as?'

'Such as having to avoid the Great-great-grandfather Paradox.'

The Space Hopper gave this due consideration. 'You could be right,' he said, 'though there are other ways to get round the Great-great-grandfather Paradox. But if you *are* right, how come we got out of the black hole?'

Vikki had no answer to that.

＊

Thanks to the logic, or illogic, of causality in closed timelike curves, Vikki and the Space Hopper were once more free to roam the Mathiverse. But their plan to use a time machine to help the Paradox Twins had to be abandoned, for they dared not return to the Domain of the Hawk King. The twins would just have to pursue a career of hiring themselves out to writers of physics texts.

Despite their narrow brush with death, however, Vikki still wanted to understand more about wormholes and time travel. The whole topic was just too interesting for her experiences to put her off thinking about it.

'The Hawk King's heavy engineers must have some amazing construction methods to be able to *build* wormholes to order,' she said. 'I'd like to know just what's involved in that.'

The Space Hopper jiggled his antennae. 'Well, we can't return to the Hawk King's territory, that's for sure. So we won't be able to *watch* a wormhole being made. But there's another part of the Mathiverse where people think about that kind of problem but don't actually *make* anything to put their thoughts into action. I suppose we could go there if you want.'

'If it's not too much trouble.'

'No more than usual. Anyway, I haven't met up with the Charming Construction Entity for a while. Be nice to find out what he's up to these days.'

'That's a very curious name.'

'It was a mistranslation. He was originally known as Civil Engineer. When he emigrated to his current part of the Mathiverse, he didn't speak the language very well, so he used a dictionary to translate. Unfortunately he chose the wrong meaning for "civil", and a rather roundabout phrase for "engineer".'

'Why didn't he go back to the right translation when he found out?'

'Marketing. His customers were mostly romantics who were uneasy about technology. They found the mistranslated name less threatening.'

The Charming Construction Entity can best be described as a land octopus. It had four stubby legs and eight long, flexible tentacles. If it had ever got round to building any of its designs, the tentacles would have come in useful, but even at the theory and design level they gave it a major advantage over its competitors. When Vikki and the Space Hopper arrived in its metaspatial office, it was building a model of a spinning black hole with two of its tentacles, answering the phone with a third, drawing two separate blueprints with two more, photocopying a letter with the sixth, signing contracts with a seventh, and stirring its tea with the tip of the eighth.

When the Charming Construction Entity saw it had visitors, it dropped all these activities and slumped into a comfortable arm-chair. With eight arm-rests, forming an octagon. Vikki looked wistfully at the phone, but she knew that there was no metaspatial connection to Flatland's rudimentary telephone system.

'I'm not surprised you had trouble with the Hawk King's wormhole,' said the Charming Construction Entity. 'They're unstable things at the best of times. I spend most of my time trying to find improvements.'

'How does he build his wormholes, anyway?' Vikki asked.

'It's not easy. There are several serious technical obstacles. The worst one is the question of whether users can really get through the wormhole. It's not so hard to build the wormhole and move its ends around. That's just a matter of creating intense gravitational fields, which is the Hawk King's forte. The main problem is what you might call the "catflap effect". With the earliest designs, when you traversed the wormhole it would shut on your tail.'

'Why not go through faster?'

'It turned out that, to get through without getting your tail trapped, you'd need to travel faster than light, so that was no good.'

'How does that come about?'

The Charming Construction Entity grubbed around among its papers and tossed one across to her. 'Take a look at the spacetime geometry in this Penrose map.'

'Named after a Planiturthinan named Rogerpenrose,' the Space Hopper added helpfully. 'Not because it's in rows and drawn with a pen.'

Vikki ignored him and stared at the cabalistic scrawls. 'I don't know how to read this.'

'Then I'll tell you', said the Charming Construction Entity. 'You know that when you draw a map of a curved space – a sphere, say – on a flat sheet of paper, you have to distort the coordinates.'

'Sure. Planiturthians suffer from that problem because they live on a sphere. They have to compromise, by drawing curved lines of longitude, say. They can choose to preserve some features – lines of latitude, or directions, or areas. But not all of them.'

'That,' said the Space Hopper, 'happens because curvature is an invariant – you cannot change it. A plane has zero curvature, whereas a sphere has positive curvature. That *proves* you can't preserve all features of a spherical surface in a planar map.'

'Thank you for that,' said the Charming Construction Entity. 'It's the same for spacetimes. The Penrose map of a spacetime also distorts the coordinates – but in a way that doesn't change light cones. They still run at 45 degree angles. Now, Vikki, this is a Penrose map of a wormhole. Any timelike path that starts at the wormhole entrance, such as the wiggly line shown, must run into the future singularity. There's no way to get across to the exit without going outside the 45 degree angle limit – without exceeding the speed of light.'

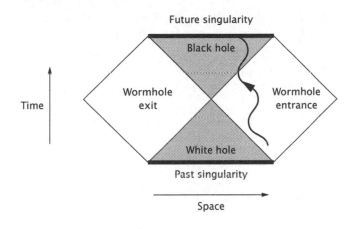

Threeday 25 Noctember 2099

This wormhole stuff is a gripping tale. But I'm feeling rather upset right now, Diary Dearest.

You see, I've just realized: back in Flatland, today is Crisp Moose Day. Traditionally, a time when all families get together to celebrate over a special seasonal meal. And this year it's extra-special, because 2099 is the last year of the century!

Now here's a minor curiosity. You know that the Flatland

calendar and the Planiturthian one coincidentally move in step, except that ours adds 100 to theirs? Well, this isn't *quite* true. The Space Hopper tells me that in the Planiturthian calendar, new centuries *end* with years numbered 00 and start with years numbered 01. Whereas on Flatland new centuries *end* with years numbered 99 and start with years numbered 00. However, it turns out that most Planiturthians don't know how their own calendar works, so most of them celebrate new centuries one year too early. You can understand why: our system is much less confusing and far more logical.

Sorry, Diary. I've been rabbiting on about the numerology of new centuries in an effort to forget how miserable I'm feeling today. It was all right until I became aware of the date. The rest of my family will be sitting round the big table waiting for Mum to finish crisping the Moose . . . and it will all be spoilt because I'm not there, and they'll be worrying about what's happening to me . . . and I haven't even sent them a crisp moose card!

Now *there's* an idea . . .

Flatland telephones may be incompatible with metaspace, but Flatland *cards*?

I'll ask the Space Hopper whether something can be done.

✦

The smell of crisping moose filled the old pentagonal house. Les and Berkeley were charging round like mad things and playing with their new toys; cards from friends, relatives, and acquaintances had been collected in one corner; and the natural logs in the hearth were burning brightly. But the toys just reminded Grosvenor of Vikki's childhood, the cards reminded him that she hadn't sent one, and the fire reminded him of how he had burned Albert's book – an act that he still was convinced had played some part in Vikki's dramatic disappearance.

No doubt Lee was feeling much the same. It was putting a real damper on the proceedings, and the boys would soon notice. He needed something to cheer himself up. So he decided to pour himself and Lee a couple of drinks.

He always kept the drinks cabinet locked, ever since Lester had got hold of a bottle of torquila and been found asleep in the washing basket wearing next door's dustbin lid. He got out the key and opened the cabinet . . .

There was an envelope inside. Addressed to him and Jubilee.

His vertices tingling, he picked it up and took it through to the kitchen, unopened. His wife was busy checking whether the moose was crisp enough yet.

'Lee, have you been putting things in the drinks cabinet?'

'No, dear – what kind of things, dear?'

'An envelope. This one.'

'Nothing to do with me, dear.'

'Well, it's got your name on it.'

Jubilee put down the moose-strainer and came over to take a look. 'It's got *your* name on it too, dear. And it's – Grosvenor, that's *Vikki's* writing!'

'Yes, I wondered about that. It's certainly very similar . . .'

'Why don't you just open it and find out?'

'I'm . . . Lee, I'm scared of being disappointed.'

Jubilee took the envelope from him and ripped it open. 'Don't be silly. Look, it's a card.' She opened the card, which read: 'Wishing you a Very Crisp Moose'. There was also a note – a very long note, by the look of it.

She unreeled the paper, and they began to read.

*

Vikki felt a lot better once the Space Hopper had agreed that she could use the VUE to deposit a Crisp Moose card in the plane of Flatland. It had been his idea to put it somewhere that only Lee or Grosvenor would have access to: that fact alone would support the story that she had insisted on including. She had thought of the drinks cabinet – on Crisp Moose Day, her dad was bound to open it.

To take her mind off what might happen when her father read it, Vikki was badgering the Charming Construction Entity for more details about time machines. 'How does the Hawk King's wormhole work, then?'

'Maybe it doesn't. Maybe it's all marketing propaganda. You didn't actually pass *through* a wormhole, did you?'

'True. But surely customers would catch on if the things never worked.'

'Possibly. But you met the Hawk King. Would they dare say so in public? However, I think that he does have working wormholes. His methods are commercial secrets, of course, so I can't be sure, but I've done a lot of calculations and I think I've figured out how the trick works. I reckon he must be threading his wormholes with exotic matter.'

'That sounds . . . well, exotic. What is it?'

'It's an unorthodox form of matter that exerts enormous negative pressure, like a stretched spring.'

'Antimatter?'

'No, that's different,' the Space Hopper interjected. 'When matter meets antimatter they annihilate in a blaze of energy. Exotic matter just pushes instead of pulling.'

'Antigravity, then.'

'Well . . . technically, no. Sort of, though.'

'Anyway, exotic matter is the most obvious way to hold the catflap open so it doesn't trap your tail. But there's a more old-fashioned method that cuts out the need for exotic matter altogether. And because it doesn't involve *building* a wormhole, there's no time-barrier effect. You can go back to any time you want. Depending on what nature has up her sleeve.'

'I don't follow you,' said Vikki.

'I'm talking about using a naturally occurring time machine. A *rotating* black hole, formed when a rotating star collapses gravitationally. The Schwarzschild solution of Einstein's equations – you know about that?'

'Yes, the Space Hopper told me.'

'Well, that corresponds to a *static* black hole, formed by the collapse of a nonrotating star. In 1962, a Planiturthian called Roykerr solved the Einstein equations for a rotating Black Hole, now known as a *Kerr black hole*.'

'The Planiturthians know about two other kinds of black hole,' the Space Hopper said. 'There's the Reissnernordström black hole, which is static but has electric charge, and the Kerrnewman black hole, which rotates and has electric charge. It is almost a miracle that an explicit formula for the solution exists – and it was definitely a miracle that Roykerr was able to find it. It's extremely complicated and not *at all* obvious.'

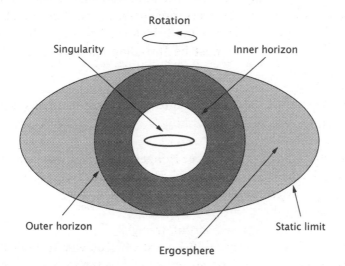

'But it has spectacular consequences,' said the Space Hopper. 'One is that there is no longer a point singularity inside the black hole. Instead, there is a circular ring singularity, in the plane of rotation. The Charming Construction Entity's Penrose map shows that any matter entering a static black hole has to fall into the singularity – but in a rotating one, it need not. It can either travel above the equatorial plane, or pass through the ring.'

'Yes, and a rotating black hole's event horizon also becomes more complex. In fact, it splits into two. Signals or matter that penetrate the *outer horizon* can't get back out again; signals or matter emitted by the singularity itself can't travel past the *inner horizon*. Further out still, but tangent to the outer horizon at the poles, is the *static limit*. Outside this, particles can move at will. Inside it, they have to rotate in the same direction as the black hole, although they can still escape by moving radially.'

'Yes, yes!' said the Space Hopper, getting all excited. He loved this kind of complication. 'And between the static limit and the outer horizon is the *ergosphere*. If you fire a projectile into the ergosphere, and split it into two pieces, one being captured by the black hole and one escaping, then you can extract some of the black hole's rotational energy.'

'The most spectacular consequence of all,' said the Charming Construction Entity, 'is the Penrose map of a Kerr black hole.' He rummaged around and tossed over another map.

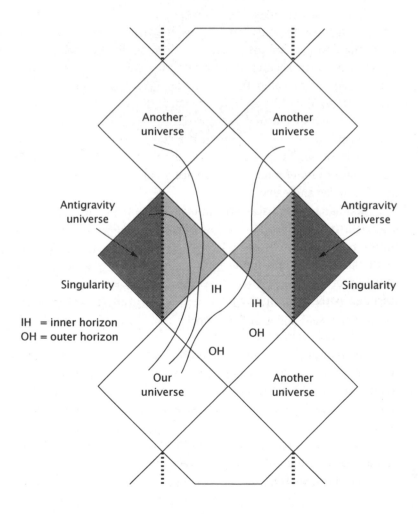

'The white diamonds represent asymptotically flat regions of spacetime – one in the Planiturthian universe, say, and several others that might also be in that universe, but could be in totally different ones. I've drawn the singularity with broken lines, because it's possible to pass through it.'

'How?'

'By diving right through the ring, Vikki.'

'And now comes the fun bit,' the Space Hopper butted in. Beyond the—'

'No, I want to tell this bit. Beyond the singularities lie antigravity universes in which distances are negative and matter repels other matter. In those regions, any body made from normal matter will be flung away from the singularity to infinite distances. Now, Vikki, I've drawn several legal trajectories – ones that stay below lightspeed – as curved paths. As you can see, they lead through the wormhole to any of its alternative exits.'

'The most spectacular feature of all,' said the Space Hopper, attempting to reclaim his part in the conversation, 'is that this is only part of what's going on. The complete diagram repeats the same pattern indefinitely, so there are an infinite number of possible entrances and exits!'

Vikki had to admit she was impressed. But what was all this *for*?

'Well, if you used a rotating black hole instead of a wormhole, and towed its entrances and exits around at nearly lightspeed with the Hawk King's matter-processing equipment, you'd get a much more practical time machine – one that you could get through without running into the singularity or getting your tail trapped.'

'It all looks very complicated.'

'Oh,' said the Charming Construction Entity, deflated by her lack of enthusiasm. 'Well, if you don't fancy trying to control Kerr black holes, you could settle for a much simpler kind of singularity: *cosmic string*. That gives a static spacetime.' And he dug out yet another map.

'Let me run through the details for you. The best way to visualize cosmic string is to use two dimensions of space—'

'Like Minny Space?'

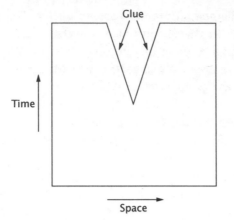

'Oh, you've met the Space Girls? Congratulations on your survival skills. Yes, just like Minny Space, but with some parts snipped out. You have to cut out a wedge-shaped sector and glue the edges together.'

'Like Squarey Space? You don't mean real glue, do you? Squarey was a square whose edges were "glued" together. Conceptually.'

'That's exactly right. But in this case you can actually do the gluing if you insist on it. And it may help you visualize the result. If you make a model out of paper, and really do cut out wedges and glue their edges together, you end up with a pointed cone. But you're right: mathematically you can just identify the corresponding edges without doing any bending or using any actual glue.'

'Wow! Coney Space.'

'Funny you should say that,' the Charming Construction Entity said. 'I hear that one of the Space Girls is leaving and there could be a place for a new member . . . but let's not get distracted. The time coordinate works just as it does in Minkowski spacetime – and to get the right shape for light cones you really should just identify the edges and not make actual cones, OK? Now, throw in a third space coordinate and repeat the same construction on every perpendicular cross-section, and you'll get a fully fledged cosmic string. It behaves like a line mass – nonzero mass concentrated on a line. To make a model of one of those, you can thread lots of identical cones on a length of – well, string. Each cone is a spacelike section of the actual spacetime.'

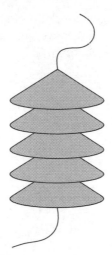

'So what does that do for you?'

'Something very subtle and interesting. A cosmic string has a mass, which is proportional to the angle of the sector that you cut out. But it doesn't *behave* like an ordinary mass. Everywhere except at the tips of the cones, spacetime is locally flat – just like Minkowski spacetime. The apparent curvature of a real cone is "harmless" – yes, Vikki, just as Squarey Space wasn't really curved even though she was a torus. In a cosmic string there is some genuine curvature – which in relativistic gravitation is equated to mass – but what it does is create *global* changes in the spacetime topology. These global changes affect the large-scale structure of geodesics – particle paths. But not the small-scale local structure. If you were standing next to a massive cosmic string, you wouldn't feel any gravitational attraction.'

'Then how would you know it was there?'

'By looking for global effects – things happening over greater distances', said the Charming Construction Entity. 'For instance, matter or light that goes past a cosmic string is gravitationally lensed.'

'Oh, I know about that. The mass bends light. But how can it do that, if the light doesn't "feel" the gravity?'

'The bending is caused by the global form of the spacetime, not by a loss of local flatness. Geodesics on a paper cone correspond to straight lines on the flat paper, but when you bend the paper to make a cone, those lines get "bent" too – in the sense that what were originally parallel lines can converge. Let me draw you some geodesics, and you'll see what I mean.'

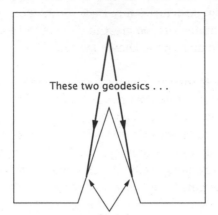

These two geodesics . . .

. . . meet **here** because
the edges of the cut are glued together

'For time travel purposes,' the Charming Construction Entity continued, 'a cosmic string is much like a wormhole because the mathematical glue lets you "jump across" the sector of Minkowski spacetime that you've cut out. Way back in 1991 a Planiturthian named Richardgott exploited this analogy to design a time machine. He showed that the spacetime formed by two cosmic strings that are whizzing past each other at nearly lightspeed contains closed timelike curves.'

'Fair enough, but could you actually make a time machine that worked that way?' asked Vikki.

'A shrewd question.'

'Yes, she's learning,' the Space Hopper said with pride.

'Well . . . in 1992 by the Planiturthian calendar, Seancarroll, Edwardfarhi, and Alanguth proved that there isn't enough available energy in the Planiturthian universe to *build* a Gott time machine', the Charming Construction Entity answered. 'More precisely, that universe never contains enough matter to provide such energy from the decay products of stationary particles.'

'Oh. Pity!'

'Though if the Planiturthians could develop a sufficiently powerful new energy source ... but I'm afraid that's not in the works yet. However, I recall that surveys of the distribution of galaxies in their universe has revealed that they clump on vast scales, forming structures hundreds of millions of light-years long. This clumpiness is too great to have been caused by gravitational attraction among the known matter.'

'So?'

'One theory is that the clumps were seeded by naturally occurring cosmic strings,' said the Charming Construction Entity. 'Not by gravitational attraction, of course, because there isn't any, but by unexpected convergence of geodesics. If so, those cosmic strings ought still to be around. So maybe, just maybe ...'

'The Planiturthians really could build themselves a cosmic string time machine,' the Space Hopper finished for him, 'which would be nice.'

'But what about the Great-great-grandfather Paradox?' asked Vikki.

'Ah, that. Yes.' The Charming Construction Entity always found such objections tiresome. 'If you can *make* a time machine, then presumably the paradoxes will iron themselves out.'

Vikki didn't find this entirely convincing. 'Maybe they won't, though. Maybe when you build a time machine the logic of your universe unravels and it comes to pieces. Or maybe history becomes something that can be changed, and you get huge Time Wars as people range up and down history trying to alter it to suit their own wishes.'

'Could be,' said the Space Hopper. 'On the other hand, every time you change history, you might get switched to a different timeline in an alternative universe. So you'd think history had been changed, when actually the original timeline was still present, elsewhere in the Mathiverse. No paradoxes, then.'

'That sounds suspiciously like a cop-out to me,' said Vikki.

'Not at all,' said the Space Hopper. 'It's one way to make sense of quantum indeterminacy.' And before she could protest, the VUE once more took control of her senses.

*

'It's like this,' said the Space Hopper. 'Despite what everyone seems to think, quantum superpositions don't tell you anything very interesting about cats. But they could be important for time travel, by resolving the Great-great-grandfather Paradox.'

Vikki wished he hadn't reminded her of Albert. Visions of Crisp Moose Day filled her head, and for a moment she felt dizzy. To distract herself, she asked, 'How could they do that?'

The VUEfield shimmered ... Flatland was below them. If anything, that made her feel even worse, but she struggled against a rising tide of emotion. The Space Hopper, who wasn't exactly tactful at the best of times, didn't notice.

'Is that—?'

'Your ancestor Albert? Only in VUE simulation. So don't be upset by anything that happens, OK? Promise?'

'Promise,' Vikki snivelled. 'Oh, look, he's in prison, poor thing – you can see the dots over the window. And he's writing something. Is it *Flatland*?'

'The very same. Now, let's run time back to before he was imprisoned. When the Sphere was about to visit him. That's what started it all.'

'Oh, there he is in his house. And – I can see the Sphere rising up towards the plane of Flatland!'

'Yes. What would you do to stop Ancestor Albert encountering the Sphere?'

'I'd ... I'd turn up just before and find some excuse to get him out of the way.'

'And that's just what you *are* doing. Look, he's got up and gone to the door.'

'Yes, but – he's stayed behind as well! And both versions of him are semitransparent!'

'Yes. His universe has split into a quantum superposition of two different versions. In one, you managed to distract him; in the other, you didn't. From now on, both universes will follow distinct paths.'

They could hear the conversation in Universe-1, faintly. The time-travelling Vikki was pretending to be collecting money on behalf of a charity. The Sphere materialized in Albert's room – but the room was empty. Puzzled, the Sphere pottered around for a bit, and then disappeared again.

In Universe-2, the Sphere materialized in Albert's room, confronted Albert – and at that moment his eventual imprisonment became inevitable.

'OK,' said the Space Hopper, 'Universe-2 is the one in which Albert went to prison, and therefore it's the universe that you were in when you used the time machine to go back to distract him. Universe-1 is what happens instead, once you *have* distracted him. Let's fast-forward to the moment when you climbed into the time machine. Got it. Here you are, in Universe-2 . . . you get into the time machine, go back, still in Universe-2 . . . until eventually you're back before the time when Universes 1 and 2 split. Now, in Universe-1 you *do* manage to distract him . . . which means that in *that* version of the universe there was no need for you to go back in a time machine to stop him encountering the Sphere. Because he never did anyway, right?'

'Right.'

'So do we see you get into a time machine in Universe-1?'

'No. Only in Universe-2.'

'Exactly! And when you come back from time travelling, you remain in Universe-2 because that's where you came from. And Universe-2 is the one where he did go to prison and you did need to go back and try to distract him. So it's all consistent. More generally, if the universe splits into alternatives every time some decision could or could not be made, then time travel would just switch you between alternatives, maybe creating new ones in the process or changing their probabilities. But there wouldn't be any time travel paradoxes.'

Vikki thought about this, and spotted what seemed to be a major flaw. 'I thought you kept saying that real cats don't superimpose. How come real *universes* do?'

'Ah. They don't: they become alternatives. The people in them perceive one or the other, never both. But in terms of quantum theory, the physics makes more sense if you pretend that both possibilities coexist. It's a way to represent quantum uncertainty and make it mathematically respectable. Planiturthians call it the "many worlds" interpretation of quantum theory.'

'Is the Planiturthian universe *really* a branching network of alternative possibilities, then?' asked Vikki.

'That's certainly a consistent interpretation of the mathematics,' said the Space Hopper. 'The question is, does every consistent interpretation of physicists' mathematics represent reality?' There was a long silence.

'Well, does it?'

'You'll have to work out your own VUEs about that.'

15

WHAT SHAPE IS THE UNIVERSE?

Another day, another trip through the Mathiverse. The sphere of Planiturth hovered before them – dazzling ultramarine, smeared with white, patched with greens and browns.

'How anyone could ever have doubted that the Planiturthian universe is based on geometry is beyond me,' said the Space Hopper. 'Just look at the thing they're *living* on!'

'I guess they were too close to it to understand what it was,' suggested Vikki.

'You're learning, aren't you?' said the Space Hopper, impressed.

'Not to go by appearances?'

'Exactly. You've put your tip right on it. Yes, it often helps to take a step back and see the whole more clearly, as well as to take a really close-up look at all the nuts and bolts . . . Speaking of which, we've had a very close-up look indeed at the small-scale structure of the quantum world, but we haven't yet—'

The jewelled topaz sphere receded as if snatched away. Its diminutive, pockmarked satellite sped past them, vanishing to a speck. The entire Planiturthian solar system turned into a child's toy and disappeared against the velvet backdrop of stars.

The stars radiated away as if the universe were contracting to a point.

The speckled dust of pinpoint lights merged, acquired form – a whirlpool of fuzzy light. The sedately twirling spiral arms of the Home Galaxy.

This was just the beginning. Now the whole process repeated on a galactic level. The heavens were filled with luminous skeins, cosmic cobwebs millions of light-years across, now shrunk to the size of a paper doily.

'What's happening?' asked Vikki, breathless at the sheer *pace* of the motion.

'We're taking a step back. Looking at the cosmos *as a whole*.'

'And what do we expect to see?'

'The shape of the universe. And its origins.'

Now the contraction had ceased. The Planiturthian universe hung before them, a dark smudge visible only because metaspace has no existence at all and therefore cannot be any particular colour, not even black. The smudge was fuzzy, inchoate, and impossible to see all at once.

The Space Hopper sighed, and a message wrote itself across the formless smudge of the Planiturthian universe:

OUT-OF-INFORMATION-ERROR

'As I thought,' said the Space Hopper. 'The VUE can only show what it's programmed to. It shows Virtual Unrealities, not Realities. It doesn't know what shape the Planiturthian universe should be, so it can't show us any detail. But there's one thing it *does* know. Look at the smudge – what's it doing?'

'I think . . . it's getting bigger! Yes, it is! Or are we getting closer to it?'

'No, it's getting closer to us. It's *expanding*. I don't mean that the stars are moving away from one another through space – I mean that *space* is moving away from itself. Growing of its own accord.'

'Obviously somebody decided that the Planiturthian universe needed more space,' said Vikki, 'but how do you know it's expanding if you don't know what shape it is?'

The Space Hopper's grin was a big ∪ as the smudge swelled and enveloped them.

＊

They orbited a pale blue galaxy.

'Oh! It's *beautiful!*' cried Vikki, entranced.

'Well, I chose this one because it's particularly pretty,' said the Space Hopper. 'And it's out near the edge of the universe. But the main thing I want you to remember is its colour.'

'Blue,' said Vikki. 'A wonderful, delicate, heartbreaking blue.'

'It's a very special blue,' said the Space Hopper. 'This is the only monochromatic galaxy in the universe. Meaning that the light that it emits is *all of one wavelength*. It's been like that since it first appeared, and it's always been the only one. Remember that. Because now we're going to travel to the centre of the universe and look back at this galaxy.'

Space surged past them, too fast for the eye to follow; then it stopped.

'Turn around, look back the way we came, and use the VUE's zoom facility to locate that pale blue galaxy,' the Space Hopper instructed her. 'Set the VUE for monochromatic light; then you won't be distracted by billions of other galaxies.'

Vikki searched, using higher and higher magnification, but she couldn't see the blue galaxy. In fact, in all the universe the VUE could detect only one monochromatic galaxy. But that one was red.

'I've found a red one,' she told the Space Hopper.

'Not blue?'

'No. But didn't you say the blue one was the only monochromatic galaxy in the universe?'

'I did. And I was right.'

'Then where did this red one come from? And where's the blue one gone?'

'You tell me!'

❋

Fiveday 27 Noctember 2099

The Space Hopper is *such* a tiresome creature! Try as I might, I couldn't puzzle it out. 'Follow the logic,' he told me. But I couldn't see any logic to follow. All I could see, Diary my Sweet, was a red galaxy when I was expecting a blue one.

'You mean this red thing *is* the blue one?' I eventually asked him. 'It's changed colour?'

'That's a very interesting question,' he replied, in that irritatingly smug way he has.

Eventually I figured it out. Since the blue galaxy was the only monochromatic one in the universe – *and* the only one there had ever been, which turns out to be important – and I was LOOKING at a monochromatic galaxy, it had to be the blue one.

The fact that it was red didn't change that conclusion, you appreciate.

So . . . it must have *changed colour*, right?

Sort of.

My first thought was that, seeing as the blue galaxy was at the edge of the universe, and we were in the middle, then it had to be an awfully long way away. And since light can cover only 300,000 kilometres in a second, the light that was reaching us must have started out billions of years ago.

So, of course, the blue galaxy had actually been red, *then*.

Not at all.

'Blue from the day it was born,' the Space Hopper insisted. So I sat down and thought very hard. According to the Space Hopper, that galaxy was blue when the light left it. So the light must have changed along the way!

Nope.

Nothing had happened to the light. Not *as such*.

Then I remembered the Light Brigade. You'll recall that when they first overtook our Universal Touring Machine, when we were cruising along Continuum Carriageway, the siren made a noise like this:

WHEEEEEEEEEEEEEEEEEEEEOOOOOooooooooooooooooooooo

Now, it may not have been obvious at the time, but the EEEE part was a *higher pitch* than the OOOO part. This, the Space Hopper had told me, was caused by the Doppler effect. (Really, Diary, the next bit ought to be done relativistically, but the calculations are messy and the answer is qualitatively – though not quantitatively – the same.) Because the Light Engine was moving, it was catching up with the sound waves its siren was emitting in the forward direction, so anyone listening to them received *more* waves per second than they would have done if the Engine had been stationary. Higher frequency, right? And that pushed the pitch UP. When the Light Engine had overtaken us, it was getting away from the sound waves its siren was emitting in the back-ward direction, so anyone listening to them received *fewer* waves per second than they would have done if the Engine had been stationary. Lower frequency, you see. And that pushed the pitch DOWN. So the sound started out as an EEEE and ended up as an OOOO, when really it had been an in-between IIII all along.

But this was the *Light* Brigade, right? It had a flashing blue light on top too, didn't it? As they do. BUT – and I regret I hadn't spotted this at the time, or I would have told you – as it sped away from us, that light looked RED. It only looked blue when the Light Engine was catching up with us.

Now, all you need to complete the puzzle, Diary, is the information that red light has a lower frequency than blue light.

Yes, that's right. Diary, you are a veritable GENIUS. The Light Engine's light had undergone the Doppler effect too. So whenever you see something that ought to be blue, but looks red, it must be moving *away* from you.

Let me rephrase that. My adventures with the Space Hopper have honed my critical faculties – which is to say that I'm not impressed by oxagondung any more. It's not really the *colour* of a moving object that changes. What happens is that all the *frequencies* of the light that emanates from it have to shift a bit. Now, even if the blue light shifts down into the red part of the spectrum, the object may still *look* blue, because the ultraviolet has also shifted down into the blue part of the spectrum. If it's *emitting* any ultraviolet, of course.

And that's why it was so important that the blue galaxy was monochromatic. If *it* looked red, then the frequency really must have shifted – so it had to be moving. Away from the centre.

You can look at lots of galaxies, and although none of the others are monochromatic, you can use 'spectral lines' to tell whether the frequency has shifted. And what you find is this: they're *all* moving away from you! Which means they are also all moving away from one another. It's as if they're dots on a balloon and someone is blowing the balloon up. Except that this is a balloon with a 3D skin.

And that means—

Not true

Some, Andromeda included, are moving towards us.

'—That the universe is expanding,' the Space Hopper agreed. 'And since we're pretty sure that all of the space that exists contains much the same proportion of galaxies, the only way that can happen is if space itself is expanding.'

Vikki gave this information careful consideration. 'Well, Hopper, I'm not sure that's really a surprise. Most creatures get bigger as they grow up. So presumably it's telling us that the universe is some kind of gigantic organism.'

'Wha—?' The Space Hopper was outraged.

'Only thing is, *what does it eat*? Maybe it eats *time*. It gobbles up the past, and that's what causes everything to move into the future!'

'Vikki, that's the silliest theory I've heard in a . . . well, maybe not . . . it might just *possibly* be—'

'Hopper, it was a joke.'

'Many a good theory starts as a joke. Most end that way, too. But I think I ought to warn you that what you've just said is highly unorthodox and there's no serious evidence for it.'

'I told you, it was a joke.'

'*You* say it's a joke. Others may take it more seriously. You realize, it might even be *right*?'

'Hopper, calm down. You were telling me why the Planiturthians think space is expanding. So tell me this: if it's not because the universe is growing up, why *does* it expand?'

'Let's find out,' said the Space Hopper.

*

Vikki waited, but nothing much was happening. The nearby stars seemed to flicker a lot, but that was all.

'Hopper, is the VUE working?

'I don't see why not. We'll soon see. It's supposed to be running the universe backwards in time. To see where it came from.'

'Well, I can't see— *Hold it, that star just evaporated!* Look, it's turned into a cloud of gas!'

'Hydrogen and helium,' said the Space Hopper. 'Most of the matter in the universe used to be hydrogen and helium – the stars made the rest in their nuclear furnaces. When the universe runs backwards, all the heavier elements decompose back into hydrogen and helium. In fact, if I'm not mistaken . . .' he fiddled with the VUE and zoomed in on some of the nearby atoms '. . . yes, the mix is pretty close to one part helium, three parts hydrogen, as I expected. Now, let's see where *they* came from.'

'The helium is the big guys?'

'Yes, a helium atom contains two protons (the yellow blobs), two neutrons (green), and two electrons (pink), whereas a hydrogen atom is just one proton and one electron. And a proton is really a neutron with a different mix of quarks . . .'

'The atoms are breaking up! It's all going green!'

'That's right. We're back into the Era of Free Neutrons.'

'What's driving all this change?' Vikki asked.

'Well, in forward time the universe is expanding. So in backward time?'

'It has to be . . . contracting.' That made sense.

'Yes. And as it contracts, there's less and less space to hold the same amount of energy – so everything heats up.'

Vikki gasped. 'You're right! I can feel it!'

'I'm afraid some of the heat is seeping through the VUE's simulation boundaries. Don't worry, it will only get comfortably warm – I hope,' the Space Hopper added.

'What's the temperature now, then?'

'Ooohhh . . . no more than a billion degrees.'

Ulp! '*I hope you know what you're doing!* And space is contracting, you said? Shouldn't we get out before there isn't enough room for us to fit inside?'

'We're only "in" in Virtual Unreality,' said the Space Hopper, unruffled. 'We can exit the simulation before the universe gets *too* cramped. Or too hot. But we have to adopt an internal VUEpoint to see what's happening.'

They watched. Vikki imagined she could *feel* the universe shrinking around her. It was like painting yourself into a corner, except that the paint was nonspace.

'Now it's all going pink, Hopper, why's that?'

'The quarks have reassorted themselves into electrons. The temperature's risen to about two billion degrees, now, Vikki. And when it gets to three billion—'

FIZZZZZZZZZZZZZZZZZZ!!!!!

'—a lot of vacuum will pull apart into electrons and anti-electrons. A billion times as many as there were just now.'

'I see. In backward time, they're unannihilating each other. And that means *we have only thirteen seconds left.*'

'Until what?'

'Until the End of the Universe! Rather, the Start of the Universe VUEd in backward time. I think it might be a good idea to slow down the VUE's clock.'

Backward seconds ticked away . . . backwardly. And, to their perceptions, more slowly.

'It's all gone sort of . . . *transparent.*'

'That's the neutrinos decoupling from the rest of matter. The temperature must be up to about ten billion degrees now. One second to go!'

'Nothing much going on at all, now, so far as I can tell. Are you *sure* the VUE is working? I think something's broken—'

'No, the temperature's up to thirty billion degrees, that's all – too hot for any atomic nuclei to stay together. It's just independent particles now. That's why we can't see much going on any more.'

'What's that wispy stuff, then?'

'Time. The VUE has decided to show us time as if it's something material. Watch the wisps shrink! A tenth of a second to go.'

FIZZZZZZZZZZZZZZZZZZ!!!!!

'Ah. The unannihilation of the hadrons,' said the Space Hopper, as if he'd been expecting this. 'Yes. The heavy particles, like protons and neutrons and antiprotons and antineutrons, have multiplied a billionfold, just like the electrons did.'

'Whatever there was, there's a lot more of it now,' said Vikki, 'but crammed into a much smaller space.'

'More vacuum converted into particles and antiparticles, I'm afraid. It'll soon run out altogether.'

'What will?'

'The supply of vacuum.'

'Oh. I thought vacuum was nothing, anyway. How can nothing run out?'

'It's empty space, and the *space* is running out. Anyway, a quantum vacuum isn't really empty: it's a seething torrent of particles and antiparticles winking into existence and back out again, I've told you that. Look, the time-wisps are shrinking – time is *literally* running out, there's only a hundredth of a second left. I'll slow the clock some more or we'll miss it. Oh, and we're up to a hundred billion degrees, by the way, and that means we ought to—'

GLOMP

'—get out sharpish.'

Vikki was getting better at adapting to sudden shifts of VUEpoint, and the dizziness lasted only an instant. 'Is *that* the Planiturthian universe, Hopper?'

'Yes.'

'That soggy thing like a deflating football?'

'Yes. But a very hot football. Three hundred billion degrees and rising. And in a thousandth of a second . . . see how tiny the time-wisps have become? . . . it will—'

FLOOmp

'—disappear.'

They stared at empty metaspace. No particles, no vacuum, no temperature . . . and no time-wisps.

'That,' declared the Space Hopper proudly, 'is known as the *Big Bang*!'

'More of a Big Flop,' said Vikki. 'What an anticlimax!'

'That's because we saw how it looked *backwards*,' the Space Hopper pointed out. 'It's like reading a story starting from the end and working back to the beginning. Of *course* it's an anticlimax. But in forward time, it's like a sudden humongous explosion! Space, time, and matter all coming into being from absolutely nothing.'

'Why did you show me it backwards, then?'

'Because that's how the Planiturthians figured out what must have happened. Take an expanding universe and track it back in time, and you can see it must collapse. And that raises the temperature, and then all the matter comes to bits, and that leads to everything we've just seen. Tell the story in the right time-direction, and you have the story of the origins of the Planiturthian universe.'

It all sounded exceedingly far-fetched, even so. 'Is the expansion – the redshift – the only evidence for the Big Bang?'

'No, there are other things that corroborate it. You can even detect the Bang's echoes. No, I don't mean sound – "Bang" is a metaphor, and so is "echo". But electromagnetic radiation has been bouncing around the universe for twelve to fifteen billion years, ever since the Big Bang went off, and that radiation has been detected – and it looks right.'

'What *caused* it?'

'Sorry?'

'What caused the Big Bang?'

'There wasn't a cause. Couldn't be.'

'But – what happened *before* the Big Bang?'

'Vikki, there wasn't a "before"! Look at where the universe was in metaspace. What do you see?'

'Nothing. Just . . . metaspace.'

'Which is a Mathiversian fiction and doesn't really exist. Do you see any *space*?'

'No.'

'Does that bother you?'

'No. Space appears when the universe blows up.'

'Do you see any *matter*?'

'No.'

'Does *that* bother you?'

'No. Matter appears when the universe blows up, too.'

'Do you see any *time*? Any time-wisps hanging around out there?'

'No. They vanished along with the soggy football.'

'Does *that*—'

'You're telling me that *time* arises when the universe blows up?'

'Exactly. Without time, there can't be a "before". Since causes occur before their effects, there couldn't have been a cause, either.'

'But—'

'Of course, maybe there really is some sort of . . . extrinsic paraspace and paratime . . . and the Big Bang *did* have a cause,' the Space Hopper mollified her. 'Some Peoples think so. They even think that universes might bud off black hole babies that can *evolve*. So you never know. That's what makes physics such fun.'

*

Sixday 28th Noctember, 2099
Dear Diary,

The Space Hopper got so carried away showing me the ORIGIN of the Planiturthian universe that he completely forgot what we started talking about, namely, its SHAPE!

Until I reminded him.

Well, it turns out that the Planiturthians don't actually *know* what shape their own universe is! I told him that proves how ignorant they are, but he said that working out the shape of a universe *from the inside* is pretty tricky, especially if you can't go and visit places. All you can do is look in various directions, and see whatever you can see. Which may not be everything you'd *like* to see.

I said that we Flatlanders *know* that our world is a plane. He said we're right – as it happens – but that if we weren't, we might find it very difficult to discover we were wrong.

You know something? He's right, dammit. I hadn't thought about it before, but the problem is, we only ever see a limited part of our world. If it *looks* like part of a plane, we assume the whole world IS a plane. But for all we know, it might be the surface of a very big sphere, or a flat torus, or a hyperbolic plane, or a finite hyperbolic surface, or some kind of awful super-teapot with seventeen holes . . .

Basically, it's like trying to work out the geography of some distant country without ever being able to go there.

Except: you're allowed to *look*. And that opens up some fascinating possibilities.

Let me tell you what would happen if Flatland wasn't really a plane, but a flat torus. Remember Squarey Space? A flat torus is a square whose edges 'wrap round' and join seamlessly. The way Planiturthians always draw tori makes them LOOK curvy, but that's because they embed them in 3D space. If you don't bother about this, the tori can be flat. Which, you'll recall, just means that the angles of a triangle add up to 180 degrees, and so on. It doesn't mean you could *iron* them.

The easy way to think of a flat torus is to tile the plane with infinitely many copies of a square, and insist that whatever things you find in one copy, you will find it in exactly the same place in

ALL copies. Now, if Flatland were a SMALL flat torus, then you could look in certain directions and *see yourself in the distance.* You'd immediately know you weren't on a plane, yes?

But what, Diary Dear, if you're on a *very big* flat torus – so big that light hasn't had time to go all the way across it? Well, you're then in much the situation that the Planiturthians are in right now.

The simplest possibility for the *spatial* shape of the Planiturthian universe is a 3-sphere, like the one in my nightmare, a few weeks ago (when I started painting a ball and got myself trapped *inside* the paint!). That fits the simplest Big Bang mathematics – space is a sort of 3D balloon that blew up very big. But there are other possibilities, depending on what the shape was right at the beginning and exactly how it grew. In the simplest of these, space is curved, but the curvature is the same everywhere – a nice, symmetric condition that fits rather nicely with the symmetry of natural laws. Of course that symmetry *could* be broken, but the easiest assumption is that it's *not*, OK? Well, that assumption leads to three possibilities: positive curvature, zero curvature, and negative curvature.

The 3-sphere has positive curvature, but so do other things – in particular various shapes that *tile* a 3-sphere, with suitable 'wrap-around' rules for going across edges. Do that with half a sphere, by the way, and you get the confounded Projective Plain – again. There's a 3D flat torus – a *cube* with opposite faces wrapped round – and that has zero curvature. And in the negative curvature department there's 3D hyperbolic space, plus whatever you can extract from it by using a shape that tiles it. With wrap-around rules as well, of course, or else your universe would have an edge – and that's bad because the laws of nature would be different at a genuine edge: you wouldn't be able to *go beyond it*, and that's contrary to symmetry, you see.

Anyhow, in any of these finite universes with wrap-around rules, you're in much the same situation as a Flatlander in a flat torus. If the universe were so small that light could cross it very quickly, then in principle you could look in various directions and see yourself. By mapping all the copies of yourself that you could see, you could work out whether the universe had positive, negative, or zero curvature, and what shape it was.

But in a *BIG* universe . . . well, let me show you how it goes on the flat torus. The region of space that's visible from a given point forms a circular disc, and as time passes that disc grows. When it grows to roughly the same size as the whole universe, it starts to OVERLAP ITSELF. At that point – and not before, Diary Dear, because of the speed of light, I'm sure you can see that – it becomes possible to observe the same object in more than one direction. Any object in the overlap will do, but the others won't, of course. The first objects you can see that way will be sitting at the points where the boundary of that disc overlaps itself.

As time passes . . .

. . . the region of space visible from a given point grows . . .

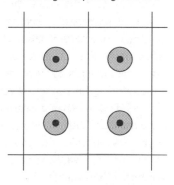

. . . until it touches itself . . .

. . . and then overlaps itself

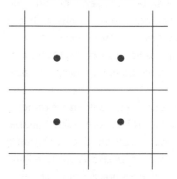

From then on, some regions of space can be seen in several different directions

Now, the Planiturthians start with a few advantages. They reckon they know roughly how old their universe is, and roughly how big (because they know how fast it expanded from the Big Bang). And they've calculated that their light sphere, if it exists, ought to have started to overlap itself by now.

So the Planiturthians are planning to hunt the overlap down. Since their space is 3D, the disc has to be replaced by a solid 3D ball. So the places where it first overlaps itself form big circles in the sky . . .

Why circles? Because, Diary Dear, a sphere intersects another sphere in a circle. Even if the 'other' sphere is just a different bit of the first sphere that's been wrapped around and overlaps!

To return to my story: the pattern of those circles – if you can find them – will tell you what shape your tile is, and that will tell you what shape your *universe* is.

The only problem is that what the Planiturthians see repeated many times over on those special circles is either empty space (not much use, Diary of Mine, since *all* regions of empty space look identical) or randomly scattered stars. And the rest of the sky is ALSO randomly scattered stars, *and* the Planiturthians have no idea where to look for those circles. So picking out the right circles from the random speckling of the night sky is next to impossible. The best they can do is trial and error – mostly error. Pick some circle – which may or may not be the right one – and record the positions of its stars. Then search the sky for other circles whose stars seem to match it unusually well. There's an awful lot of circles to try. But the Planiturthians are nothing if not persistent, and their answer to that is to build faster computers and just crunch circles until they find a match.

Or not.

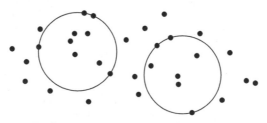

Do the stars on these two circles match up?

Intelligent it isn't. Except that there doesn't seem to be a cleverer way to go about it.

You know, I think that when I get back to Flatland I'll try to find out what shape *that* really is.

Bother, now I've reminded myself. I'm homesick, Diary. The Mathiverse is tremendous fun, and the Space Hopper is a competent, if sometimes irritating, guide – despite being utterly weird. But in the early hours of the morning, when I find myself awake and can't get back to sleep, I miss my home and my family more than I dare admit.

And I *hope* they're missing me, and I'm worried that they may very well be doing just that. And I'm even more worried that they're not.

I hope they found the Crisp Moose card I sent them.

16

NO-BRANES AND P-BRANES

As usual, the opportunity to bring up the topic of a return home never arose. The Space Hopper was far too enthusiastic about whatever bit of the Mathiverse he wanted to show off next, and Vikki was too kind-hearted to disappoint the poor creature. And its ∪ was kind of cute, in a ghastly sort of way.

They were discussing the state of Planiturthian physics – the nature of space, time, and matter.

'Of course, the Planiturthians weren't content to leave it at that,' the Space Hopper observed. 'And you can see why.'

'I don't see why at all,' said Vikki. 'The Planiturthians had worked their way towards one amazingly effective and accurate theory of the large-scale structure of space, time, and matter – and a different, even more amazingly effective and accurate theory of the small-scale structure of space, time, and matter. So between them, those two theories covered everything.'

The Space Hopper's ∪ widened. 'Actually, that's the one thing they didn't cover.'

'What?'

'Everything!'

'You mean – they didn't cover the medium scale?'

'No, I mean they didn't cover *everything*. Not all in one go. What the Planiturthians wanted was a Theory of Everything. *One* theory. Not two. One set of laws to explain the large scale and the small.'

'I must be missing something here,' said Vikki, deeply perplexed. 'Why can't they have one theory with two options? *These* laws for the large scale, but *those* laws for the small scale. Like groceries – one price for a small order, but a different price for a big one. I don't see the problem.'

'Well . . . I guess they just felt that kind of conditional law wasn't elegant enough.'

'Oh,' said Vikki. 'They wanted it *elegant*, too? Why not just stick to something that worked?'

The Space Hopper bobbed uncomfortably. 'Because it didn't, not entirely. I know, it sounds all right in theory: one set of laws for the large scale, a universe-sized law; another set of laws for the small scale, a subatomic-sized law. And never the twain shall meet. But then came the Big Bang, as you already know. And in the Big Bang—'

'What ends up as a universe-sized object starts out as a subatomic-sized one! And it grows continuously from small to large . . . so there's no obvious place to swap the laws.'

'Correct. And in some respects it was even worse than that. You see, the large-scale laws had implications for the small scale, even after the Big Bang was long past. That's because the large-scale laws indicated that there was a "force of gravity" that acted on the small scale. Between any two particles.'

'I thought General Relativity explained the force of gravity away by reinterpreting it as the curvature of spacetime.'

'Yes, but that really works only on the universe-sized scale. It doesn't fully explain why the solar system behaves as if each body attracted all the others. Sure, you can come close . . . but what would really sort everything out would be a gravitational particle. A graviton. Just as a photon is a particle of light, so a graviton should be a particle of gravity.'

'Hold it. Gravity is a force. Light isn't.'

'On the face of it, that's true. But it's not that simple. And there are other types of particle for which the analogy works better.'

'Oh.'

'And just as the large-scale laws had implications for the small scale, so the small-scale laws had implications for the large scale. They meant that in a sense the large-scale universe didn't really exist at all. Because the mathematics of General Relativity assumes that the universe is an infinitely divisible spacetime continuum, whereas the quantum theory says that space, time, and matter can be subdivided only so far before they become indivisible. You can subdivide them a long way, I grant, but not for ever.'

'That's something of a hair-splitting argument.'

'Hair-not-splitting, really. But you're right, it wouldn't have mattered so much if the Planiturthians hadn't been so set on finding a Final Theory that unified the whole shebang in one fell swoop. Wrapped up the entire ball-game, all at—'

'Hopper, I think you're overdoing it. I get the picture. Anyway, why would anyone want to do that?'

'Well, the Planiturthians had all sorts of rational reasons, but when it comes down to it, I think it was because Planiturthian science had grown from a monotheistic religion. Most of their science was the product of a culture whose religious beliefs attributed their entire universe to a single act of creation by a single deity. Whether or not the scientists themselves were religious, this cultural trait led them to seek a single explanation for *everything*. The search for One Final Theory is psychologically very close to the search for One True God – though the Planiturthian scientists wouldn't have agreed with that view at all. They didn't like religious explanations. None the less, they adopted a very fundamentalist attitude – they used that word a lot, "fundamental". They seemed to think that their mathematical equations – if they ever found them – would be How the Universe Really Works. Which is a breathtaking piece of arrogance, coming from a bunch of creatures that have experienced only one tiny planet, and then only for a short period of time and on a small range of scales.

'But maybe that's being unfair. A lot of them understood that their hoped-for theory would be fundamental only in a metaphorical sense – that *in principle* it might be possible to base most of their other theories on it. What they expected to be done in practice was much less ambitious. And I think some of them even realized that what they would get would be a description of how the universe seems to work, not the actual rules by which it runs. Because – well, because there might not be any such rules. A *rule* is a very Peoplish concept, and even more so a *law*. Those are methods Peoples use to run their own society. So it seems to me that they had a mental picture of their universe that was modelled on their own social interactions. The amazing thing is that it worked pretty well.'

∗

Sevenday 29 Noctember 2099
We're getting into very difficult intellectual territory here, Diary Dear, and not just philosophically. This stuff is right out on the frontiers of the Mathiverse, where new concepts are still popping into existence ... and the physics is pretty hairy too. So I'm going to make some notes for you.

The most important item of background information, the one that sets the problem up, so to speak, is that the Planiturthian universe seems to be governed by exactly four different kinds of force. What's a force? Something that lets matter affect other matter. How does it work? Forces are produced by *fields*, which in turn are associated with bits of matter, and other bits of matter respond to those fields. For instance, a magnet is surrounded by a magnetic field, and any matter that responds to magnetism is affected by whatever magnetic field it finds itself in.

Got that? Good.

What are the four forces? Here goes:

- *Gravity.* This is a very weak force – it takes the entire mass of Planiturth to generate enough gravity to hold Planiturthians on the ground, and even then they can jump to roughly their own height (with training, effort, and skill). In compensation, though, gravity is a long-range force – it acts over extraordinarily large distances. Right across the universe, in fact – it's what holds their universe together.

- *Electromagnetism.* Originally the Planiturthians viewed this as two different things: magnetism, which made needles point north and lined up iron filings in patterns; and electricity, which gave them shocks when it built up on metal objects, and powered their lights and televisions. Both magnetism and electricity have fields associated with them, which you can measure with the right instruments. After the work of Jamesclerkmaxwell, who invented a single mathematical framework for both the magnetic and electric fields, the Planiturthians recognized that they'd merely been seeing two different aspects of the same thing. Electromagnets can turn electricity into magnetism, and dynamos can turn magnetism into electricity. This was the first *unification* of apparently distinct physical fields and the associated forces. Electromagnetism is intrinsically stronger than gravity, but it comes in two kinds – positive and negative. Because those tend to cancel out, the dominant large-scale force in the universe is gravity, not electromagnetism. This is why General Relativity works pretty well on cosmological scales.

- *Strong nuclear force.* You don't come across this directly in everyday life, Diary! However, without it there wouldn't BE any everyday life, because it's what keeps protons and neutrons together in the atomic nucleus. No strong nuclear force, no nuclei; no nuclei, no atoms; no atoms, no molecules; no molecules, no anything. The strong nuclear force really *is* strong, which is why nuclei are so hard to break up, but it acts only at short range – about a quadrillionth of a metre.

  More accurately, the strong nuclear force acts between quarks, which are the fundamental (that word again!) constituents of protons and neutrons. Quarks are complicated beasties, and, as you know, a proton or a neutron contains a bunch of them . . . so the strong nuclear force is a rather messy thing to work with.

- *Weak nuclear force.* A lot of particles – the technical terms is 'leptons' – don't 'feel' the strong nuclear force at all. But they do feel the weak nuclear force, surprising as this may sound. Basically, some particles are 'immune' to the strong nuclear force – the Force isn't *with* them, OK? The weak nuclear force is a lot weaker than the strong nuclear force (surprised?) and has about a hundredth of its range.

OK, Diary Dear: now you have the *ingredients*. The problem is to make sense of it all!

That's hard.

＊

'I still don't fully follow this business of fields and forces,' said Vikki in a troubled tone. 'It seems to mean that in some mysterious way a particle can affect another, possibly quite distant, particle, without anything passing between them.'

'In a classical picture, *and* in a relativistic one, that's true, and it's not just a philosophical difficulty. It's one reason why Planiturthian physicists found it necessary to try to marry gravitation and quantum theory. In a quantum picture – well, let's take a look.'

The VUEfield zoomed in on their surroundings, homing in on a fuzzy pink ball. 'Look, an electron!' said the Space Hopper. 'Listen closely, and you'll hear it singing.'

'Electrons don't sing!'

'VUE-enhanced electrons do. For heaven's sake, Vikki, we *spoke* to the Charge on the Electron not long ago. Don't balk at a bit of harmless singing! At least they're not dancing too, like the Space Girls did. Turn up the volume, and you'll hear it.'

Vikki did as she was bid, and sure enough, a high-pitched voice was singing a curious, repetitive little song:

'I can't *get* no / more mo*men*tum / got fixed *en*ergy / can't in*vent* 'em . . .'

'What's all *that* about?'

'It's singing about conservation laws. Which is nice.'

'No, I mean, how come it's singing at all?'

'It's how the VUE represents a quantum field. Electrons don't really sing—'

'That's a relief!'

'—they hum.'

The singing went on for several minutes, and then a second, lower-pitched voice started to join in, in a weird descant:

'. . . *take* you down / 'cos I'm *go*ing to / Yang-Mills *Gauge* Fields / Nothing *is* real . . .'

A second pink ball came into VUE, closing in on the first one. 'This should be interesting,' said the Space Hopper.

'They're on a collision course!' cried Vikki.

'Maybe. They'll come close, certainly.'

As the two particles approached each other, their songs became strangely intermingled, and odd snatches of other songs began to intrude:

'I can't *get* down / 'cos I *really really want* / got nothing ...'

'... *take* you no more / fixed *energy* Fields / did it *my* way / *is* real ...'

'They're interacting,' said the Space Hopper.

'Sounds more like *over*acting,' Vikki commented. 'They're going to *hit*— Hey! What's that?' But as the Space Hopper started to answer, Vikki interrupted: 'Hey – they *bounced!*'

'Ho-o-o-*on*ky / -tonk *lep*tons! / Gimme, gimme, *gim*me / the honky-quark-gluon-*plas*ma ...'

'You ain't nuthin' but a hadron / nucleifyin' all the time / You ain't ...'

'And their songs have changed.'

'Yes,' confirmed the Space Hopper. 'The collision has altered their quantum states – energy, momentum ... *could* have been a change in charge, too, but not this time.'

'Why?'

'You noticed something when they came close to colliding, didn't you?'

'Yes, it was a sort of red squiggle.'

'That was a photon. They exchanged it.'

'Why?'

'Well, in the quantum world, energy and momentum and charge and suchlike are all quantized – they come in whole-number multiples of tiny, irreducible amounts. When particles interact, their quantum fields affect each other, creating forces between them, and the result is to *change* their energy, momentum, charge, whatever. That's how the electrons bounced. *But*, for the reasons I've just given, those changes come in whole-number chunks. A tiny whole-number bit of momentum, say, gets transferred from one electron to the other. Something has to *carry* that chunk of momentum – take it away from one and give it to the other. While the momentum is in transit between the two electrons, it in effect forms – or more properly, can be represented as – a tiny particle of its own. In this case, a photon.

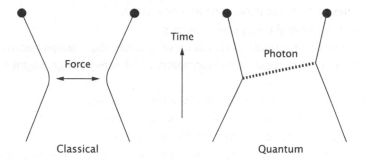

Force ⟷

Time ↑

Photon

Classical   Quantum

'*All* quantum force interactions are carried by particles in this kind of way', the Space Hopper went on. 'Electromagnetic forces are carried by photons, strong nuclear forces by eight different gluons, and weak nuclear forces by the W^+ boson, the W^- boson, and the Z boson.'

Vikki mused on these remarks. 'I thought I saw a purple squiggle passing from one electron to the other, as well as a red one. Was that a gluon or a doubleyouplusboson or something?'

'A something,' said the Space Hopper. 'That was the infamous graviton, and you were extremely fortunate to see it. The graviton is the carrier particle for the force of gravity – assuming that any such particle exists, which for narrative purposes the VUE just did. Any unification of Relativity and quantum theory has to bring the gravitational force into line with the other three – so, in particular, it has to introduce a particle to carry the gravitational force.'

The Space Hopper warmed to his theme. 'But that's not so easy. The scheme that works for the other three forces – known as the Standard Model – is pretty complicated. You can't bring in a new particle without upsetting all the delicate logical implications of the mathematics behind the Standard Model. The newcomer has to be introduced with care, forethought, and the very best taste. Otherwise all it will do is disrupt the logical harmony of the Standard Model, with disastrous consequences.

'And one of the main features of the Standard Model – one that pretty much qualifies it as a Geometry in the Felixkleinian sense – is symmetry.'

※

Well, now we're getting to the heart of the matter, Diary Dear. What drives the whole enterprise is a curious kind of symmetry of the Standard Model of fundamental particles and forces. I've told you already that the deep nature of a Geometry – that is, of a Space or a Spacetime – is best captured by its symmetries. If you're a mathematician, the symmetries characterize the geometry; if you're a physicist, they tell you what the possible laws of nature are – because the laws have to be *invariant* under the symmetries, OK? The laws must respect the symmetry, and not bash it about.

The most obvious symmetries of the Planiturthian universe are those of Space and Time. Every region of space behaves, in principle, like any other; ditto for instants of time. I don't mean that every bit of space looks the same as every other – you might have an atom of carbon at one point of space and vacuum at another. But in principle it could have been the other way round: there aren't regions of space that *must* have carbon atoms in them, or *can't*.

Those symmetries imply that the laws of nature must be the same at all places and at all times. But they don't give much more of a clue as to what those laws ought to be. A more interesting restriction comes from *time-reversal*. If you run the universe backwards in time, it obeys the same laws that it did in forward time. That symmetry is more puzzling – especially since the Planiturthian universe seems to run in just ONE time direction. But again, the point is not that some particular realization of the universe possesses time-reversal symmetry; just that whichever behaviour you encounter, it could equally well have run backwards in time without the *LAWS* changing.

However, there are other, less obvious symmetries on the quantum level. For instance, you can 'reflect' an electron – not in an ordinary spatial mirror, but in a 'charge mirror'. By which I mean you can change its charge from negative to positive. When you do that, the electron becomes a different particle: a POSITRON. However, the laws that govern positrons are just like those that govern electrons, provided you 'reflect' all charges.

Well, nearly. I lied, OK?

In fact, there are slight differences: the charge-reflection symmetry is 'broken' in the actual Planiturthian universe. Some particle interactions involving positrons look slightly different from the corresponding interactions involving electrons. An attractive explanation for this breaking of symmetry is that at the time of the Big Bang, the nascent universe possessed exact charge-reflection symmetry, but then – as the universe expanded – that symmetry became broken. This idea has another advantage: it suggests that at the time of the Big Bang, ALL four forces of nature were unified into a single force. All the different carrier particles for those forces were in effect the same kind of particle – and the differences we now see arose when that original symmetry broke.

So this setup provides a scheme for unifying all the forces of nature – a plausible route to a Theory of Everything. All you have to do is set up a really symmetric version of physics, appropriate to the time of the Big Bang, and then break the symmetry in the right way.

Not easy. But symmetry, Diary Dear, is the key.

*

'It's like politics,' said the Space Hopper. 'All a question of spin.'

'Spin?'

'In certain respects, quantum particles behave *as if* they are spinning around some axis. Like a top.'

'You mean, if we used the VUE to look closely at an electron—'

'Let's do that and find out. But I warn you, what we'll see is really too classical an image. The spin of a quantum particle isn't really *movement*. At least, if it is, it's not movement in *space*. Think of it as some kind of intrinsic excitation – a "state of mind", if you wish. But, for now, let's program the VUE to realize spin as . . . spin.'

No sooner said than acted upon: a fuzzy red ball rotated gently before their eyes. The VUE caused a thin blue line, the axis of rotation, to become visible, and decorated it with an arrow to indicate the direction of rotation.

'That's a photon,' said the Space Hopper. 'Its spin is 1 quantum unit. Now this guy over *here* . . .' he gestured towards a fuzzy brown ball '. . . is an electron, with spin ½. Which, by the way, is the minimum size that quantum spin can be. Except zero, of course.'

'Shouldn't the minimal unit be spin 1?' Vikki objected.

'Well,' said the Space Hopper, 'spin ½ is more traditional.'

'What's tradition got to do with it?'

'When there are Planiturthians around, lots. And there are . . . other reasons. For that choice of units.'

'Such as?'

'Particles with whole-number spins, like the photon, behave just like classical spinning particles in one important respect: what happens to their spins when you twirl their axes in space. Keep a close eye on that photon, and I'll show you.'

Vikki aligned herself with the photon's axis, so that the blue arrow showing the direction of spin ran clockwise. The Space Hopper grabbed the axis of the photon and began to move it. 'Hard work, this, it's like trying to turn a gyroscope,' he muttered. 'All that angular momentum – wears a chap out.' Slowly, the photon's axis turned; the photon continued spinning, without visible interruption or change. After a lot of shoving and swearing, the photon's axis had turned through a complete circle. The arrow continued to point clockwise, a fact that the Space Hopper pointed out with considerable excitement.

'Don't be so over-dramatic, Hopper!' protested Vikki. 'That's exactly what you'd expect!'

'Ah, but this is the quantum world, where the wise person expects the unexpected. Let's try it with an electron – which has spin ½ – instead.'

Vikki lined herself up with the particle's axis, as before, and again the blue arrow showing the direction of spin ran clockwise. The Space Hopper moved the axis in a circle, still complaining under his breath. After a lot of shoving, the electron's axis had turned through a complete circle.

The arrow now pointed anticlockwise.

'But – that's mad,' said Vikki.

'Welcome to the quantum world.'

'You must have turned it through 180 degrees by mistake.'

'No, it was a full circle, 360 degrees, I guarantee. How far must I turn the axis to get the direction of spin back to clockwise, Vikki?'

'Well – if a 360-degree turn of the axis in space reverses the spin, I suppose that a second 360-degree turn of the axis in space would reverse it again. That means that after a 720-degree turn of the axis in space, the direction of spin should come back to where it was.'

They tried it.

It worked.

'This is very puzzling,' said Vikki.

'It illustrates one of the ways in which quantum spin is *not* rotation about a spatial axis,' said the Space Hopper. 'That behaviour is a consequence of the mathematics of quantum spin. And it means that quantum particles come in two very different kinds. They're called *bosons* and *fermions*. Bosons have whole-number spin – an even number of basic spin units of ½ – but fermions have an odd number of basic spin units of ½. The photon, with spin 1 – two units of ½ – is a boson. The electron, with spin ½, is a fermion. And if the much-sought graviton, the "missing link" between quantum theory and Relativity, exists, it should have spin 2 – making it a boson – and (as it happens) mass 0.

'Anyway, bosons behave like classical particles when their spin axis is rotated. Fermions don't. There are all sorts of other differences, too.'

Vikki leaned back to digest all this. 'It's complicated, Space Hopper.'

'Sure is. I'm skimming the surface of a detailed – and sophisticated – piece of geometry, OK? Don't expect to get it all, I haven't *told* you it all. The big point here is that there are these two very different kinds of particle, with different kinds of spin, as unlike each other as odd and even.'

'Got that.'

'So of course, Planiturthian physicists got used to thinking of them as completely different things.'

'Fair enough.'

'Until one day they discovered that bosons and fermions could be viewed as two different aspects of the same thing. There was a symmetry of the universe – or, at least, of a mathematical scheme to represent the universe – that could turn bosons into fermions, and vice versa. They called this *supersymmetry*. It implied that associated with every particle there should be a corresponding superparticle – and if the particle is a boson, then its superparticle is a fermion, and vice versa. It was a huge surprise.'

'I'll bet,' said Vikki. 'But how can a symmetry of the universe change an even number of spin units into an odd number? Won't that change the laws?'

'Oddly enough, no – one reason why this was an exciting discovery. It's because of the way quantum spin works.'

'So the VUE ought to be able to start with a photon, apply a supersymmetry, and give us an electron?'

'It's not as easy as that. There's no reason why the superparticle corresponding to a known particle has to be another *known* particle. In fact, the superparticle corresponding to a photon isn't – it's believed to be a hypothetical particle called a "photino". Let me show you how supersymmetry turns a photon into a photino.'

Vikki watched as the Space Hopper captured a fuzzy red photon and lined it up for a supersymmetry transformation. 'Here we go!' he yelled. The fuzzy ball promptly turned brown, and the Space Hopper beamed with pride.

'Um,' said Vikki, in a bored voice, 'was that it?'

'What? Not impressed by my marvellous – oh, you weren't using the full power of the VUE! Vikki, you really must pay attention to *everything* that the VUE can show you. Let's try it again, but first – activate *this* VUE-extension, OK?'

The Space Hopper recaptured the errant photino. 'I'll turn it back into a photon. Tell me what you see as I'm doing that.'

'Well, it starts out as a brown ball – no, wait, hold it. It's not a ball and it's not brown. What have you done now?'

'I've set the VUE to show you the hidden dimensions of super-space.'

'Oh. Well, it *is* a ball, but it's a much higher-dimensional ball, and it's all sorts of colours. But there's a sort of brown stripe—'

'That's the photino state,' said the Space Hopper helpfully.

'—and another red stripe—'

'The photon state.'

'—but they're not really stripes, they're fuzzy balls of lower dimension . . . sort of, it's hard to describe in words.'

'Count the dimensions of spacetime that are present in the image, Vikki.'

'Uh – one, two, three, four, five – *five*?'

'Keep going.'

'Er – five, six, seven, eight. *Eight*?'

'Yes. Four dimensions of spacetime, and four more, called superspace. According to the theory of supersymmetry, every particle in ordinary 4D spacetime carries along with it a kind of attached ghost in a second, nonphysical 4D space – its super-partner. Well, really I should say that superspace is a *physical* but not a *spatial* 4D space, I guess. Tell me, now: which component is the brown stripe in?'

'Um – ordinary space.'

'That's right. So we're seeing a photino in ordinary space, but there's also a lot of attached ghostly gadgetry that we don't normally observe, which extends into four further dimensions – inside which there is what?'

'A red stripe. A ghost photon? In superspace, not real space?'

'Exactly. Now, all we have to do is *rotate* the whole picture so that real space and superspace get swapped – see, in 8D it makes perfect sense – and once we've done that, what do we get?'

'A red photon in real space and a brown photino in superspace. The ghost has become real and the real one has turned into a ghost!'

'Elegantly put,' said the Space Hopper. 'And *that* is super-symmetry.'

*

Twoday 31 Noctember 2099
Deep stuff, Diary Dear. The untamed frontiers of the Mathiverse are looming before me. And back home (sniff) it's New Year's Eve. Everyone will still be eating the leftovers from Crisp Moose Day, and waiting to welcome in a new year and a new century . . .

I'm getting maudlin. Back to the untamed frontiers.

Ingredients: four forces of nature. Three unified by advances in quantum theory; the fourth – good old gravity, still holding out.

Needed: a new particle, the graviton, to carry that force. Spin 2, mass 0: impossible in conventional quantum theory.

Implication: reformulate quantum theory AND Relativity. And you can't do it with point particles.

Required structure: hierarchies of particles, each with its own peculiar properties, somehow all part of one unified picture.

Hint: *SUPERSYMMETRY.* There's a new kind of extended space out there, superspace. Particles spill over into that, as well as into ordinary space.

So what, Diary Darling, do you think we are missing? What would tie the whole picture together?

That's right.

String.

＊

'Superstring, actually,' said the Space Hopper. 'If you want to bring gravity into the scheme of things, you can't keep the Standard Model exactly as it is. You have to be prepared to modify it a little. Hah! I say "a little", but that "little" includes a complete rethink of the structure of spacetime. Not just a supersymmetric add-on. Something more significant than that.'

It seemed to Vikki that this was going Over The Top. 'Why does spacetime have to change, Hopper?'

'Because when you try to quantize gravity, it turns out that particles can't actually *remain* particles. That just doesn't work – pointlike objects just don't fit all the requirements. So they have to be replaced by something else.'

'What?'

'Like I said: superstrings.'

'Yes, I know that's what you said, but it made no sense then and it doesn't make any more now!'

The Space Hopper gave the criticism due consideration. 'Very well,' he said. 'A particle is a point – or, at least, it looks like a point, with no internal structure. It's a pointlike object, yes?'

'Sure.'

'Moving up in dimensions, you could replace a pointlike particle by a curve – a string. Come to think of it, Vikki, *you're* a string. Like all Flatland women. Geometrically, you're a line segment.'

'Do quantum strings have two ends, like I do?'

'Some do.'

A constant worry of Flatland women surfaced. 'Do you think my endpoints make my bum look flat?'

'I'm not a good judge of Flatland womanhood,' the Space Hopper said tactfully. 'But it seems to me that – er – *quantitatively* speaking, you have the exact correct number of endpoints. One at each end, which is ideal.'

Vikki decided to be flattered. 'That's very kind of you. So what happens to quantum strings without ends?'

'They loop round and form a closed loop. A topological circle.'

'Ah.'

'That's most of them, actually.'

'Tidier that way. Otherwise the ends would flap around.'

'They can, in some string theories. Anyway, curves are intrinsically one-dimensional. The next step up from curves leads to two-dimensional surfaces – membranes. Perhaps with exotic topologies, like Moobius, or the Projective Plain, or a doughnut.'

'Don't remind me about Moobius! That *cow*!'

'Well, she *was* a cow,' the Space Hopper pointed out.

'That doesn't justify her behaving like one!'

'Beyond membranes,' the Space Hopper said, diplomatically changing the subject, 'are three-dimensional analogues of surfaces, which the Planiturthian physicists insist on calling 3-branes. And then come 4-branes, 5-branes and so on. They also insist on using the symbol p for an arbitrary number of dimensions, rather than the customary N . . . and I think I know why. Guess what you get in dimension p?'

'Oh no! p-branes?'

'Absolutely.'

'So a surface is a 2-brane?'

'Yes.'

'And a string is a 1-brane?'

'Naturally.'

'Which makes an ordinary particle, with dimension zero, into a no-brane?'

'I had a feeling that's where you were headed', said the Space Hopper.

*

'You said "*super*strings",' Vikki remembered. 'You've only explained strings.'

'Well, you remember that particles – no-branes in your terminology – are accompanied by ghost extensions into superspace?'

'Yes. You mean superstrings are strings that extend into super-space as well as ordinary space?'

'Correct. It's quantum string, it can do that.'

'Quantum things can do anything you want, it seems to me. Where do you find these superstrings? At a superstationers?'

'In yet another extension of ordinary space, Vikki. Good job I updated the VUE's HyperZoom facility. Let me just check it's been installed ... good. Follow me!' And down they went, into the smallest scales of the Planiturthian universe – into a world where an electron was too huge to contemplate, where its component quarks glistened like tiny jewelled specks.

'Right now we're at the limits of the VUE's *spatial* resolution,' said the Space Hopper. 'Down at the Planck length, where quantum effects make space so fuzzy that it's not even clear that space really exists at all.'

'It's frothy,' said Vikki, 'not fuzzy.'

'That's quantum foam – particles springing into and out of exis-tence, creating space and time along with themselves. Try some, it's quite tasty.'

'No thanks!'

'Go on. It's a bit like chicken.'

'I'm not hungry.'

'Suit yourself. See those bright specks?'

'Yes. They're quarks, aren't they?'

'Among other things, yes. What do they look like on this scale?'

'Dots. Points. No-branes'

'Yes. And yet, those points have to support all sorts of quantum states. Spin, charge ... would there be *room* for such diversity on a no-brane?'

That thought hadn't occurred to Vikki before. 'In what sense?' she asked, cagily.

'All will shortly become clear. I'll use the HyperZoom to improve the resolution in any other dimensions that may be around—'

'Like superspace?'

'Yes, but there might be others – there's more to a particle than its spin, you know. Ah, yes ... coming into focus now ... Look at that!'

'It's – hey, that quark's not a point at all! It's a tiny loop!'

'Yes.'

'And . . . isn't it *vibrating*?'

'A little bit, maybe. This one's in its ground state, lowest energy. But if I give it a—'

TWANGGGGGGGG!

'—then something really interesting happens. Zoom out for a moment, and you'll see.'

'Oh. It's changed colour!'

'Yes. That's the VUE's way of showing us that it's actually become a *different particle* altogether. A much more massive relative of a standard quark, as it happens. Doesn't have a name. Anyway, the main thing here is that anything from a 1-brane up can vibrate in all sorts of different ways, whereas a no-brane can't. That means that a 1-brane or a 2-brane or a 3-brane or a zillion-brane can easily support all sorts of different quantum states. Whereas for your traditional point particle the states are just some kind of unexplained add-on.

'So here's the idea. On really small scales, spacetime isn't 4D at all. What looks like a tiny point in 4D spacetime is really something else – some kind of *p*-braned topological hypersurface in a higher-dimensional space.'

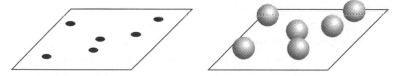

Every point in spacetime . . .   . . . is really a multidimensional hypersurface

'How many? Dimensions, I mean? Equal to *p*?'

'No, could be bigger. For a while 7D and 22D were hot favourites, making the revised spacetime come to 11D or 26D. Right now, though, the consensus is settling on 6D for the extra dimensions – a total of 10D altogether.'

'Spacetime is really ten-dimensional?'

'That's what every well-informed Planiturthian thinks right now.'

'You mean there's a choice?'

The Space Hopper laughed. 'Oh, yes! A huge choice. The range of n-dimensional spaces is inexhaustible! The problem, Vikki dear, is cutting that number down enough to be able to fix the exact one. Not just the value of n – the number of dimensions – but the topological shape of the corresponding space.'

'Put that way, I see the difficulty. So how *do* they sort out all those possibilities?'

'Still working on it. But they're making progress. Turned out that the original 11D model – supergravity, it was called – had a fatal flaw. It couldn't encompass the broken symmetry of the weak nuclear force. A People called Edwitten pointed that out in 1984, by their calendar. The way to deal with that was to reduce the dimensionality to 10D.

'Now, when you do quantum theoretic calculations, as often as not you get stupid answers.'

'No I don't.'

'Why not?'

'I don't do quantum theoretic calculations at all.'

'Ah. When *anyone* who does quantum theoretic calculations *does* do quantum theoretic calculations, as often as not they get stupid answers.'

'Easy to make mistakes?'

'No, even when they get the calculations right, they still get stupid answers. Infinity, usually.'

'That's bad?'

'It's nonsense. When a physical theory gives you infinity as an answer, it's always a sign of trouble. The real universe doesn't have infinities.'

'Hang on, Hopper – we went to infinity in the Projective Plain.'

'Yes, but that wasn't a real universe, OK?'

'Only an idealization, that's true.'

'And in a sense Infinityville wasn't a real infinity, either. But you're distracting me. There is a way to get round these quantum infinities, and it's called renormalization. Doesn't matter exactly what it is – just take my word that it's not an easy trick to pull off. So most potential superstring theories don't work because they're not renormalizable. It turned out that for a 10D superstring theory to be renormalizable it has to be one of five competing possibilities.

These are known by their symmetries. One is called SO(32), another is $E_8 \times E_8$, and they both have an extra 16 dimensions of 'internal' states, as well as the 10D of the string itself. See? 26D in all. And the other three are known as Type I, Type IIA, and Type IIB.'

'Imaginative terminology.'

'Very. The fascinating thing – a strong hint that such theories could unify gravity and quantum theory, the physicists' Holy Grail – was that they all predicted the occurrence of a particle with spin 2 and mass 0. In quantum theory *by itself*, that would have been an embarrassment because no such particles are known. But—'

'The graviton, if it exists, has to be a particle with spin 2 and mass 0!' yelled Vikki, caught up in the excitement.

'Precisely. String theory seemed to be telling physicists that if they wanted an effective theory of quantum particles, then gravity would be a necessary consequence. *All* consistent string theories include gravitons.'

'It would have been more satisfactory if only some had,' said Vikki. 'To help pick the right one.'

'True. But it didn't work out that way ... and it may not be necessary. You see, that People named Edwitten has recently discovered that all five superstring theories fit into a bigger 11D picture, known as *M*-theory.' The Space Hopper noticed Vikki hopping up and down. 'Yes, Vikki, I agree – that's a very imaginative name too, isn't it? But back to my story. There are five different ways to shrink away one of the 11 dimensions of *M*-theory, and they lead to those five 10D superstring theories. So all five com- peting theories are actually part of the same Big Picture. Maybe it's the Big Picture that really matters.'

He paused. 'There's only one problem with all this stuff', he said. 'Which is a pity, because it's *so* beautiful.'

'What's the problem with it?'

'It may not be true,' said the Space Hopper sadly.

❋

'There's no experimental evidence, you see,' he explained. 'Hard to come by – desperately hard to come by. For that matter, the calculations are so difficult that there aren't many theoretical *predictions*, either. So there's precious little to experiment *on*.'

'But couldn't the Planiturthians *tell* if they really lived in a 10D universe?'

'Couldn't the Flatlanders tell that their 2D world was really just part of 3D Spaceland?'

'Touché. Even so, surely there are experiments that would reveal a whole six extra dimensions? For that matter, why didn't they notice them ages ago?'

'Because, Vikki, they didn't have a HyperZoom. Think about a sheet of paper. What's its dimensionality?'

'Two.'

'Really?'

'Oh. In Flatland, yes. In Spaceland, say, it would really be 3D, but very thin along the third dimension.'

'Quite. And the Planiturthian universe *looks* like a 4D spacetime, but in Superstring Territory it is really 10D, but very thin along the fifth, sixth, seventh, eighth, ninth, and tenth dimensions.'

'So thin that the Planiturthians didn't notice?'

'So thin, Vikki, that the Planiturthians *can't* notice. The structure is below the Planck length – the smallest size their instruments can detect.'

'That's a pity. Convenient for the theorists, though.'

'Suspiciously so. But there might be other ways to find out whether they're right. Indirect ones. For instance, in *M*-theory there is a class of branes called Dirichlet branes, because they look rather like a surface discovered long before by a People named Peter-dirichlet. They turn out to be black branes – branes from which light can't escape. You can even interpret a superstring with ends as a superstring that forms a closed loop, part of which is covered by a black brane. And by doing that, you can reformulate black holes in terms of intersecting black branes wrapped round inside a 7D space.'

'And what good does all that do?' asked Vikki.

'It makes very accurate predictions about evaporating black holes. But that kind of evidence is just circumstantial. So right now, all anyone can really do is point to the elegance of the theory, and the beautiful way in which it unifies Relativity and quantum theory.'

'Which makes it right?'

'Not at all. Lots of physicists don't like that approach. They say that beauty could be totally irrelevant. And there are lots of other possibilities in the Mathiverse that don't roll up the extra dimensions of spacetime into very tiny shapes, and there are all sorts of other reasons why the Planiturthians wouldn't notice *them*, either . . . Beauty can be a trap, Vikki.

'Anyway, *everything* in the Mathiverse is beautiful, if you get used to it.' The Space Hopper's ∪ faded momentarily, then renewed itself in a dazzling display of teeth. 'None the less, the idea that the extra dimensions are curled up really tightly, so you can observe them only on the extraordinarily small scale of the Planck length, is still the most appealing explanation of why Planiturthians don't observe ten dimensions.' He paused. For once, the bouncy creature seemed at a loss for words. 'Um – you know something?'

'What?'

'Back in Flatland, Vikki, it's the eve of a new century. Your tour of the Mathiverse has reached its climax. You've learned as much as I can teach you and as much as your brain can digest at one sitting . . . I . . . I think it's time I took you home. Don't you?'

Vikki's centroid leaped. *Oh, yes . . . But.* 'I'll miss you, Hopper! But you're right. It's time I returned to my family. Um.'

'Yes?'

Vikki wanted to ask one last question, to make sure she'd understood the essence of the Planiturthian universe. 'You're saying that when the extra dimensions of spacetime get so thin that they're only *one* Planck length across, they become undetectable?'

'That's right.'

'So the only features of the universe that Planiturthians can observe are those that are . . . as thick as *two* short Plancks?'

'You have it exactly,' declared the Space Hopper.

17

FLATTERLAND

The whatever-it-is that moves narrative through the realms of metaspace did whatever-it-does. Victoria Line was going home. Never again, though, would she imagine that just because Flatland *looked* like a plane, it must therefore *be* a plane. In this, her thinking went beyond eccentric Planiturthians who were convinced that because their world looked flat, therefore it *was* flat; it even went beyond the modern Planiturthians who were convinced that because their world looked three-dimensional, therefore it *was* three-dimensional. However, there was still some way to go before she could compete with those Planiturthians who were convinced that they had no idea what kind of space or spacetime they lived in, but were enjoying the challenge of finding out.

'It would be wonderful,' she mused wistfully, 'to return to Flatland and discover it has hidden dimensions that no one had ever suspected. Even if they're rolled up so tiny that nobody can see them. But I don't suppose that will ever happen.'

'I wouldn't be so sure,' said the Space Hopper. 'Look, we're getting near Flatland now.' He waggled his horns thoughtfully. 'I've got an idea. Instead of dropping you straight back into your home territory, why don't we heave to somewhere nearby and see what it looks like from there?'

'Nearby?'

'In the quasi-metric of metaspace. *Conceptually* nearby. Don't worry what that means – come to think of it, I have no idea what it means, I just know how to *do* it. Oh, and switch on the HyperZoom extension.'

'Why?'

'I've just got this feeling that . . . well, we may come across some surprises.'

The glowing plane of Flatland loomed closer. They could tell, because suddenly it was possible to pick out details – first, the great polygonal oceans, then the zigzag edges of huge forests, which quickly resolved into leafy fractal structures with circular cores.

The Space Hopper muttered to himself and made some adjustments to the VUE. The forest slid away and was replaced by a maze of houses and streets.

They zoomed ever closer.

'The Palace of the Prefect!' Vikki yelled, as she saw a complex of shapes that she recognized. 'And – look! *There's my house!*'

The Space Hopper made some further fine adjustments, and the familiar pentagonal house grew until it was all they could see. Vikki hadn't seen it from this angle, of course – except for a split second when she was first whisked away from her own world, and she hadn't been in the mood to appreciate the fine points at that stage – but she'd got so used to the effect of the VUE that she had little trouble recognizing the layout of the rooms.

Grosvenor and the boys were sitting by the fire; Jubilee was bustling about in the kitchen. Vikki felt a deep-seated twinge of guilt. Her mother always threw herself into the housework when something was troubling her – and Vikki knew very well what that was. Their daughter had gone off mysteriously, without leaving a trace, and (despite the very best of intentions, Vikki told herself) had been too preoccupied with herself to get in touch . . .

She was so busy feeling guilty that it took her quite a long time to notice that there was something very strange about her mother. There was a clear, solid line segment, bustling about in the plane of Flatland . . . but *above* it, pointing along another direction entirely, was a ghostly pentagonal shape. Her mother's lineal features were one of its edges: the rest pointed *out of Flatland altogether.*

Vikki stared at the ghostly apparition, and then at the Space Hopper. 'You *knew* about this,' she said. 'What, exactly, is going on here?'

'Shadow matter,' said the Space Hopper. 'Flatlanders think that their males are two-dimensional polygons, but their females are "only" one-dimensional lines. Quite why they place such importance on apparent dimensionality, beats me – but social hierarchies are usually absurd. However, what neither the males nor the females realize is that Flatland is supersymmetric. It's one of the most basic social symmetries – male/female duality. As different as even and odd, bosons and fermions. But there is a social *super* symmetry, unnoticed until now. Flatland females extend into a third dimension – not *the* third dimension in a Spaceland sense, just a dimension that's different from the ordinary two spatial dimensions of Flatland. Along that dimension, matter has different properties – reflected in the difference in mental outlook between Flatland males and Flatland females. The shadow world and the ordinary world of Flatland meet along lines – not just one line, but *all* lines . . . one reason why the Spaceland model is inadequate. Female consciousness has evolved to recognize the ordinary world, but not the shadow world. But the female *subconscious* has always known about the shadow world.'

Vikki stared at him. 'And you say *all* Flatland females have this extension into the shadow world?'

'Yes.'

'Even – even *me*?' Her voice had gone all squeaky at the impli-cations.

'Of course. You're a Flatland female, right?'

'What – what shape am I really?'

The Space Hopper fiddled with the VUE. 'Mmm, must be a setting for a shadow-matter mirror somewhere . . . not that it's something I often *use*, you see . . . not much call for it most of the time. Where did I put the manual? Oh, yes, tucked away inside the tenth dimension, here it is! Right, see for yourself.'

A ghostly image appeared in front of her VUE-enhanced senses. It was—

'An *octagon*?'

'Very much so. I don't know what your father would think, from that hidebound position of his in which the number of sides deter-mines social position. Your mother is a pentagon – one step higher than him. And you are *much* higher in the social hierarchy.'

Vikki thought about this. 'Not really. The males determine what counts. They'd just say that shadow dimensions don't count.'

The Space Hopper bobbed in agreement. 'Indeed they would. So?'

'So? So what?'

'Exactly.'

'Sorry?'

'So: *what are you going to do about it?*'

Vikki's mind was whirling. Obviously it wouldn't do any good to explain any of this to the men. They'd just declare her insane, and she'd get the modern equivalent of what had happened to poor old Albert.

But – she could tell the *women*.

The only problem was, *how*?

And it was then that the idea came to her.

＊

Threeday 1 Angulary 2100

Well, Diary Dear – that was quite a homecoming! I suppose it was a bit of a shock when I suddenly materialized in the living room! Bang on the stroke of midnight at the century's end! Talk about high drama . . .

I don't think I can write down my feelings. Or anybody else's. Some things just don't translate into print.

I chose the dramatic entrance because – well, because I'm *like* that, but mostly because it was the best way to make my story sound credible.

Because Grosvenor and the boys were there, it wasn't possible for Mum and me to have a woman-to-woman talk about important things like the Shadow World . . .

Silly name. Makes it sound unreal. So I've come up with a better one.

Flatterland.

Now, I know what you'll say, Diary my ever-present critic, because you're a pedantic little so-and-so: since Flatland is a plane, which is about as flat as you can get, how can anything be *flatter*? But that's not my meaning. As the Space Hopper said, technically speaking, Flatterland *is* flat – something to do with zero geodesic curvature and other technobabble. But even so, that doesn't make it *flatter*. Obviously.

But flatness isn't the only place where this is a problem. Take 'wetter'. Look: either you're wet or you're not. The *extent* to which you are wet may be lesser or greater, but not your actual state of wetness or dryness.

My dictionary says that you add '-er' to a word to indicate the *comparative*: one interpretation is that X-er is 'like X, only more so'. And that's what Flatterland is. Like Flatland, only more so. The 'more so' is what the Space Hopper called the Shadow World.

So, my idea has a name. In effect, I have a Brand. And in today's market-oriented world, branding opens many doors.

Not, however, the door of distribution. Or dissemination, since what I have to sell is a concept, a Philosophy, a Big Idea. An idea that, given time to take root, will empower all Flatland women. Like the Space Girls said I should. And replace Flatland by Flatterland in *everyone*'s minds – even our shadow-blind males.

Distribution, that's my problem . . .

I can't just wander out on to the streets preaching the Gospel of Flatterland. It would be poor old Albert all over again, in spades. But – this is the age of electronic communications. Which the young understand much better than their elders, and use much more. And the youth of Flatland will be my shock-troops . . .

Ah, now you see it too, Diary.

All it needs is a smattering of HyperDot Mark-up Language and an Anonymous InterLine Link. Then, I'm in business!

*

Jubilee stared at the screen of Vikki's computer. She couldn't understand why her daughter had been so insistent that she should learn how to use the InterLine.

Vikki had gone out, leaving her mother with a scroll of detailed instructions about which buttons to press and so forth. Jubilee had started tentatively, but now she was feeling distinctly proud of herself, for she had successfully gone on-Line and was even now surfing a variety of sites that her daughter had suggested.

An advertisement caught her eye.

WOMEN'S TALK CHAT-POINT.

She looked again at the scroll. Yes, Vikki had listed this as a really interesting site. Suggested she tell Grosvenor all about it. Well, she'd tried to raise the matter, but her husband didn't really seem interested in such things.

She positioned the cursor and clicked.

What she had learned to call an 'interval' opened up. Within were several subintervals – COSMETICS was one, and DRESSES another. There were headings for SHOPPING and SLIMMING and HOW TO MAKE YOUR POLYGON NOTICE YOU and HOW TO DUMP YOUR POLYGON AND BE YOUR OWN LINE, and lots more. About two-thirds of the way down the list was an item on Vikki's scroll: GLOBAL GOSSIP.

Click.

Whatever Jubilee had been expecting, it wasn't what she got. The next screen flashed a brief message: IS THE POLYGON IN YOUR LIFE IN THE HOUSE?

She typed 'NO'.

The screen went blank for a second, while the computer downloaded something called a SQUIF file, and then—

FLATTERLAND, the heading said, in big, antique lettering. Then, in smaller type: *Supersymmetric Sister! The shadow world of gender equality awaits. Superiority, even. If you want to raise your station in Life, click here and be empowered.*

For some reason, the thought of being empowered appealed to Jubilee – even though she wasn't quite sure what it meant. She hesitated, then—

Click.

And a new universe opened.

18

THE TENTH DIMENSION

Seen from space . . .

But it *was* a space. Well, a spacetime. Start again.

Seen from a ten-dimensional supermanifold, it was a strange world, with the austere beauty of a page from Einstein. In fact, it *was* a page from Einstein, geometry made flesh. A sprawling, humming world of three-dimensional shapes stacked together along one-dimensional time: women, men, infants, toddlers, adolescents . . . People, of their own kind. They lived Peoplish lives, ate Peoplish food, drank Peoplish drinks, made Peoplish love, bore Peoplish children, and died (Peoplishly) in a 3+1-dimensional universe, and never thought it the least bit curious. Their relativistic spacetime continuum was all they could see, all they could hear, all they could feel. To them, it was all there was.

As long as nothing disturbed that perception, it was *true.*

But times (and spaces) were changing in Spacetimeland . . .

INDEX